DREAM MAKERS, DREAM BREAKERS

DREAM MAKERS, DREAM BREAKERS

The World of Justice Thurgood Marshall

CARL T. ROWAN

LITTLE, BROWN AND COMPANY
BOSTON TORONTO LONDON NEW YORK

First Paperback Edition

Library of Congress Cataloging-in-Publication Data

Rowan, Carl Thomas.
    Dream makers, dream breakers: the world of Justice Thurgood
Marshall / Carl T. Rowan.
        p.   cm.
    Includes bibliographical references and index.
    ISBN 0-316-75979-1
    1. Afro-Americans — Civil rights.   2. Civil rights movements —
United States — History — 20th century.   3. Marshall, Thurgood, 1908–.
4. Judges — United States—Biography.   5. Afro-American judges—
Biography.   6. United States.   Supreme Court — Biography.
I. Title
E185.615.R65   1993
323.1'196073'0922 — dc20   92-29892

10 9 8 7 6 5 4 3 2 1

MV-NY

*Published simultaneously in Canada
by Little, Brown & Company (Canada) Limited*

Printed in the United States of America

To my grandchildren,
Lisa Jones and Gwendolyn, Elizabeth, and David Rowan.
May they pursue unbreakable dreams of justice with the bravery
and conviction that glorified the life of Thurgood Marshall.

CONTENTS

PREFACE

AS A SEVEN-YEAR-OLD second grader at the Bernard School in McMinnville, Tennessee, I went to the compulsory assemblies where every few days we would sing this spiritual:

> Go down, Moses,
> Way down in Egypt land,
> Tell old Pharaoh,
> Let my people go.

I'd barely heard of Moses in my Methodist Sunday School, and had no idea who Pharaoh was. But I got the sense that I was singing for the release of some people from bondage — black people, I supposed.

I later would learn that that spiritual referred to the Children of Israel but was universal in intent. It was a cry of liberation to be sung by all peoples in all times who were under the tyranny of some conqueror, some monarch, some slave master.

In high school I came to understand that centuries earlier some dreamers in England and other parts of Europe determined that their people could "go," so they fled the "Old World" for the "New World" of America, nursing visions of a society in which a common man counted for as much as a king. They dreamed of a land in which the state's tax collectors could not seize property or impose prison terms at their whim. But the search was for much more than representation with taxation. The dreams were far bigger than had been the thoughts of Sir Thomas More when he said, "Would that our workers might have glass in their windows and eat meat once a week."

In urging war to fight off the oppressions of a relentless King George III, Patrick Henry said in 1775: "Is life so dear or peace so sweet as to be purchased at the price of chains and slavery? Forbid it, Almighty God. I know not what course others may take, but as for me, give me liberty or give me death!"

Because the yearning to be free is as old as man, there are no new words in which to express it. Patrick Henry was simply improvising on the words of Aeschylus, written almost five hundred years before the birth of Christ: "Death is better, a milder fate than tyranny."

America's pioneers believed that they could do what no freedom-lovers had done before: put in words some binding limitations on the powers of government, and set broad parameters for personal liberty. So those determined to frame a Constitution more protective of human freedom than Magna Carta called a convention in Philadelphia. Patrick Henry declined to attend because he "smelt a rat." Henry underestimated the passion for freedom that some men took to Philadelphia. He saw it when Pennsylvania tried to ratify the agreed-upon Constitution in 1787. Some Pennsylvanians objected to the lack of a bill of rights guaranteeing free speech, a free press, the right to bear arms, in the approved document. They insisted on undergirding their dreams with a written document that protected the humblest citizen against the overweening powers of the state.

Two objectors were carried physically from their homes to the assembly hall to achieve a quorum, enabling Pennsylvania to ratify the Constitution by a vote of 46 to 23. But objectors in Pennsylvania and other states persevered and won approval two and one half years later of the ten amendments we know as the Bill of Rights.

But the framers and those who forged adoption of the Bill of Rights never mentioned slaves, clearly never assumed that they were spreading liberty to black people. It would be 130 years before black Americans would cry out for liberty with the same life-risking passion as Aeschylus and Patrick Henry and declare that the Constitution protected them, too.

The Aeschylus of our time has been Thurgood Marshall.

To try to write a book about "the world of Justice Thurgood Marshall" is tantamount to trying to write the social, legal, economic, political, and moral history of this nation over most of the twentieth century. That is because Marshall's life encompasses the violent years of the great black migration out of the postbellum South; the years of frightening powers wielded by the Ku Klux Klan and later the White Citizens Councils; the years of the Great Depression and of economic recovery forged by Franklin D. Roosevelt and a world war; a postwar black revolution in both the courtrooms and the streets of America; and a counterrevolution led by politicians who were and are determined to break every dream of liberty that Marshall and black Americans ever embraced.

Throughout six decades, Marshall has been a demanding spirit of freedom, a sort of ghost inside Jim Crow schools, and on buses and trains, in theaters and restaurants where African-Americans once were insulted with impunity. Marshall's legal visage patrolled voting booths of South Carolina and Texas and thousands of precincts in between. Presidents of all-white universities quaked at rumors that Marshall was visiting their state.

As a Supreme Court justice, Marshall was controversial, to put it gently. But readers of this book will want to decide when, and how far, he ever wandered away from these words of James Madison in Federalist Paper No. 51:

> *Justice is the end of government. It is the end of civil society. It ever has been and ever will be pursued until it be obtained, or until liberty be lost in the pursuit. In a society under the forms of which the stronger faction can readily unite and oppress the weaker, anarchy may as truly be said to reign as in a state of nature, where the weaker individual is not secured against the violence of the stronger. . . .*

Carl T. Rowan
Washington, D.C.
August 11, 1992

ACKNOWLEDGMENTS

THIS BOOK is not an authorized biography. It is in fact more than the life story of one of the great human beings of our time. This is a chronicle of more than half a century of this nation's struggles and conflicts over race and human rights, over the relationships of the privileged and the poor to their government. It illuminates Marshall's life with stories of his most important — or obdurate — friends and foes.

Though "unauthorized," this book is not a hostile assault on Justice Marshall. I must, in full disclosure, tell you the reader that I have had a friendship of almost forty years with this extraordinary man. He spent hours in interviews with me when I did two prize-winning television specials — one on the Constitution and America's search for justice, the other on "Thurgood Marshall the Man." I am grateful to Justice Marshall for these and other interviews, and for his authorizing his law clerk, Crystal Nix, to provide to me promptly the facts that I requested about Justice Marshall's majority opinions and his dissents.

In these chapters you will read many dialogues and quotations that may be twenty, even forty, years old. I have reconstructed them from transcripts of tape-recorded interviews, newspaper and magazine articles that I have written, and from notes that have yellowed with time. I have had my memory refreshed by a participant in some conversations.

Where I have used quotes and written the drama of situations where I was not present, I have relied on interviews with, and the memories of, at least one of the actual participants — and in most cases two to five of those involved. The integrity and reputations of the people upon whom I rely makes it possible for me to vouch for the integrity of my reports of court cases and events that were crucial to the life of Justice Marshall.

I am profoundly indebted to the people who had long associations with Justice Marshall who granted me interviews, of great length or short, which have enabled me to reconstruct events and discussions with authority. Among them are retired Supreme Court justice William J. Brennan, Jr.; retired chief judge of the U.S. Court of Appeals for the District of Columbia Spottswood Robinson III; Alice Stovall, Marshall's secretary for most of the years when he was chief counsel of the NAACP; the late Wiley Branton, who worked with Marshall on the Little Rock school desegregation cases; Kenneth Clark, the noted psychologist who used dolls to bolster the contention that school segregation stigmatized black children; Ada Lois Sipuel Fisher, a brave guinea pig in the desegregation of the University of Oklahoma; Autherine Lucy, another brave woman, who was rescued from the mobs at the University of Alabama by Marshall; Governor George Wallace, the Alabama defender of segregation who now says he regrets his role; Dr. George L. Cross, who was president of the University of Oklahoma during the struggle over desegregation; Jack Valenti, a top aide to President Lyndon B. Johnson, who watched the drama of getting Marshall onto the Supreme Court. Over the years I have had invaluable discussions with retired chief justice Warren Burger and former Howard University president James Nabrit, who have illuminated portions of Marshall's life.

Many of the remarkable family photographs in this book were loaned to me graciously by Justice Marshall's wife, Cissy. Yet, this is an arms-length report in which Marshall himself may learn, or be reminded, of some extraordinary moments in his life. That is because Julius Chambers, chief counsel of the NAACP Legal Defense Fund, granted me unprecedented access to the closed records of the "Inc. Fund" that are in the Library of Congress. I express my thanks to Mr. Chambers and my special gratitude to James Williams, publicity director of the national office of the NAACP; to Dr. Debra Newman Ham, the remarkably knowledgeable Joseph Sullivan, and the other truly dedicated employees of the Manuscript Division of the Library of Congress. They gave me invaluable assistance. I am also grateful for the help of David Pride and Clare Kushman at the Supreme Court Historical Society.

In addition to the photographs provided by Mrs. Marshall, this book contains exclusive photographs from the Johnson Publishing Company, publisher of *Ebony* and *Jet* magazines. I thank publisher John H. Johnson for permitting me to share these historic photographs with those who read this book. I thank Washington photographer Ken Heinen for the marvelous portrait of Justice Marshall that graces the cover of this book.

There is no one to whom I am more indebted than my brilliantly perceptive, sometimes agonizingly demanding editor at Little, Brown — Fredrica Friedman. She helped to make my autobiography, *Breaking Barriers,* a national bestseller. She worked zealously to make Justice Marshall's life story a document of passion and zest that will elevate the thinking and the lives of millions of people. I also thank her associates at Little, Brown.

Access to closed Library of Congress files, or to any public library, would have profited me little had I not had a skilled and dedicated research team of Jeanne Bowers, Kristine Bock, David Mazie, and Barbara Jones. Ms. Bock, who is a third-year law student at Georgetown University and was my full-time administrative assistant, gave laudable devotion to the production of this manuscript — including producing a special friend, Pat McDevitt, a computer expert who bailed me out of trouble on a few occasions.

Most of all, I thank my wife, Vivien, for suffering two more years in which she lost her breakfast nook, her dining room, the den, the guest bedroom, and more to ever-mushrooming piles of books, documents, newspaper and magazine clippings, photographs, and other research materials. I will give back to her, with the first copy of this book, her home, pristine and full of joy.

DREAM MAKERS, DREAM BREAKERS

CHAPTER ONE

CHANGING "THE AMERICAN WAY OF LIFE"

HE SAT THERE like a giant, brooding American Buddha on this morning of June 29, 1991. His half-rimmed glasses fit tightly over an expansive nose and sat on fat cheeks that merged into a couple of ample chins. There was a hearing aid in his left ear, and many eyes were focused on the cane that he had used as he limped in, and on the white hose that supported legs that had grown weary of carrying his 250 pounds for so many years.

His purple striped tie hung loosely from an unbuttoned shirt collar, saying that he cared more about comfort than a reputation for sartorial elegance.

His eyes of fading fury seemed as tired as his legs.

The silky, straight locks atop his head were almost solidly white, his ruddy cheeks Indian red, characteristics that had provoked one Mississippi editor to lash out at him as "that damned mulatto" who was bent on destroying "the Southern way of life."

"What's wrong with you?" asked one of the mob of reporters, some of whom had come with a sense of great national loss, others with the joy of celebrating the departure of a man whose views they had long despised.

"What's *wrong* with me? I'm old, and coming apart!" was the reply.

The testy voice that occasionally screeched toward a high C was that of an American legend. Thurgood Marshall was announcing his retirement as a justice of the United States Supreme Court after twenty-four years as one of the most powerful men in America.

Questioning this eighty-two-year-old man was a group of report-ers who knew Marshall primarily as the first black American ever to sit on the nation's highest tribunal — one of nine jurists whose schol-arship, wisdom, integrity, and political persuasions affected in some way the lives of every person in America. The reporters also knew Marshall primarily as the black civil rights lawyer who won the *Brown v. Board of Education* 1954 case in which the Supreme Court declared that racial segregation in the public schools violated the U.S. Con-stitution. Every reporter there knew that, with that legal triumph, Marshall had opened up two generations of litigation, political warfare, and even street violence over the proper place of black chil-dren in schools, and of black people in general in the myriad aspects of American life. But few of the reporters at Marshall's retirement press conference knew or understood the man, or the magnificence of his early achievements. Few even recalled his telling the Supreme Court in 1953 that "candor requires recognition that the plain pur-pose and effect of segregated education is to perpetuate an inferior status for Negroes which is America's sorry heritage from slavery."

One writer at this retirement scene would say "good riddance" and add angrily that "the Supreme Court of the late 1960s was quick to accept Justice Marshall's strident judicial philosophy and New Deal Liberalism." Few newsmen could recall that the late conserva-tive columnist David Lawrence had written in turbulent 1969 that "Justice Marshall has performed a public service in speaking out on the subject of how racial friction is intensified by militants and in pointing to the prerequisite of harmony in any community — the recognition of one's own responsibility, irrespective of race, to be a law abiding citizen."

Few understood how Marshall continued to revere "the law" de-spite almost losing his life to lawbreakers.

Not many of the "young" reporters knew how Marshall had es-caped being lynched along the Duck River in Columbia, Tennessee, after he prevented the railroading to prison of blacks after riots in that city. They didn't know how Marshall had fought racism in Lou-isiana despite the fact that a powerful political leader had put out a "contract" for the destruction of this "burr-headed nigger." Feigning fearlessness, Marshall told Louisiana newsmen, "I ain't burr-headed."

Those reporters saying farewell to "Mr. Civil Rights" did not un-derstand what Marshall's life as the most renowned civil rights law-yer and as a Supreme Court justice had meant to white people. Marshall had earned hero status among millions of white women through his earthy but uncompromising support of a woman's constitutional right to an abortion. He had said that he didn't even need a doctor's opinion — that it was up to a free woman alone to decide whether and when she would have a baby.

No American jurist has ever argued more forcefully than Marshall for the right of poor people accused of crimes to have a competent lawyer. Many millions of white families, as well as others, have benefited from Marshall's crusade to deliver justice in the courtroom to the most vulnerable people in America.

Thurgood Marshall changed this country's criminal justice system profoundly. But he did not begin to change this nation only after he became a member of the Supreme Court. His first "revolutionary" act, in 1934, was of revenge against the University of Maryland, which had refused him the right to study in its law school.

There is no easy or simple place to begin a story of this man's life, but I think the defining days began in 1951 when he went to South Carolina with an incredible brigade of black and white legal and social experts to challenge racism in South Carolina schools, indeed to assault the whole system of racial injustice in this country.

Only those old enough to know how virulent racism was in America in 1951 will understand before reading further the drama of Marshall's intrepid journey into the social and moral shadows of Fort Sumter, into the bowels of a viciously postbellum South, to begin his crusade to change a nation.

On May 24, 1951, Spottswood Robinson III, a Richmond, Virginia, lawyer, got a telephone call from Marshall, by then the celebrated forty-three-year-old special counsel of the National Association for the Advancement of Colored People.

"Where the hell are you, Spot?" Marshall asked in agitation.

"At the other end of the number you just dialed," answered Robinson.

"Well, goddamn," said Marshall, "I was counting on you to go to Charleston with us to argue the *Briggs* school segregation case. We need you. I'm scared as hell we're gonna lose this fucking case."

Robinson and Marshall were very close, probably, as Robinson puts it, "because both of us were almost impossible to get along with." Marshall had hired Robinson in 1947, at $4,600 a year, to represent the NAACP in Virginia and "go from county to county and file the required cases to clean up the problems of discrimination in educational facilities." Robinson had done so well at finding plaintiffs, filing lawsuits, shaking up the forces that controlled education, that on November 17, 1949, Marshall had written to Robinson: "Some of our branches are hell-bent on getting cases started concerning elementary and high school education, and you have worked out a technique which has the best possible chance of winning. Now, we must have that procedure written down in understandable English by you."

So on that May day of 1951 Robinson felt genuinely needed, even though his compensation from an impoverished civil rights organization did not reflect it. The promised pay was pitiable, the lateness of payment scandalous. At one point, Robinson had written to Marshall, just prior to a Marshall visit to Richmond, saying, "Please bring check with you. Can't pay any more bills until I get it." The dunning and begging had become routine.

Robinson tolerated it because he had learned that Marshall also was just a step ahead of his creditors, or even in worse financial shape. He knew that for all this civil rights hero's urban flair, Thurgood was a nervous Nellie who was always semiparalyzed by fear that he was about to lose a case.

"Thurgood put on a facade of being supercool," Robinson recalls, "but he was roiling inside. He was a you-do-it-your-way guy as long as your way was his way. But when trouble came he could explode, in vile curse words, making it clear that he was the architect, the coach, and that everything had to be built his way." Since they were peas of a pod, Robinson had no trouble with Marshall's lapses into authoritarianism.

"Thurgood, the goddamn train comes through Richmond," Robinson said. "I don't need to come to New York to get on it."

Robinson, a wiry, pale yellow "black" man who could have passed for white in a Virginia that was all mixed up racially by the miscegenations of Thomas Jefferson and other white slave owners, in fact never thought of missing that train to Charleston, where he would listen to and perhaps participate in the most important legal case of his life.

A black man named Harry Briggs had, at Columbia, South Carolina, lawyer Harold Boulware's and Marshall's "delicate" urging, filed a lawsuit against R. W. Elliott, the chairman of the board of the public schools in South Carolina's district 22, contending that forcing black children to attend schools where they were separated from white children by state mandate was a violation of the U.S. Constitution. No lawyer in America besides Marshall could have been more interested in this case than Robinson, who was making a similar legal assault on the Jim Crow* public schools of Prince Edward County and other communities in Virginia.

But Robinson was ill with a respiratory infection. He was sicker than anyone other than his wife, Marian, knew. He had no idea that Marshall also was sick, simply ground into chronic misery by dozens of trips from one corner of America to another to fight the myriad manifestations of racism. Robinson thought of Marshall as a "suicidal crusader," but of himself as more rational and careful. This was an exercise in self-delusion.

"Why the hell does Thurgood need *you?*" Marian had asked as she watched Spottswood pack his bags. "You're going to South Carolina, where you have no way to protect yourself from getting shot in the back. You and Thurgood could be murdered. You're just gonna antagonize these white bigots till one of 'em kills you."

"No, honey," Robinson responded. "I can't argue a case while looking to see who might shoot me in the back. But Thurgood says he needs me. If he needs me, I'm going. If I get killed, I get killed. But I gotta be on that train to Charleston."

When the locomotive dragged a long string of cars into Richmond, having picked up a large contingent at Union Station in Washington, Marshall greeted Robinson warmly, even as the Virginian saw behind "Mr. Civil Rights" the most impressive collection of civil rights advocates he had ever dreamed might exist. Robinson recognized some of the key black lawyers, but not even half the assortment of Negroes, and almost none of the surprising number of whites, most of whom he had never heard of. A group of black and white men and women were murmuring in erudite terms about the Constitution, the Fourteenth Amendment, the *Dred Scott* decision (in which the Supreme Court said ex-slaves were not citizens), the 1896 *Plessy v. Ferguson* ruling that the post–Civil War Amendments required that on trains and in other public accommodations black people were entitled only to separate but *equal* facilities. This remarkably integrated NAACP team was in little bunches, talking about the troubling political situation in America, the legal and social ramifications of their mission.

Every member of this NAACP team knew that those days of May and June would be watershed moments in American race relations. The organization had launched an assault on "the Southern way of

---

* "Jim Crow" describes a practice or policy of segregation or discrimination against Negroes in public places, public vehicles, employment, schools, etc. The term derives from a song sung by Thomas Rice in a mid-1800s Negro minstrel show.

life," which meant keeping black people as close to slavery as possible. Marshall had chosen to fight a defining battle not far from the place where the first salvos were fired in the Civil War. This was a calculated gamble.

As the train left the Cradle of the Confederacy, to hurtle through the night to the Palmetto state, Robinson realized that for this case Thurgood had produced a scene of "race mixin' " in transportation that the South had never known. Robinson himself had begun the precedent-setting case of *Irene V. Morgan v. The Commonwealth of Virginia* that permitted this. Blacks now had parlor-car seats, drank in the dining car, shared the Pullman cars with whites.

One team member tried to ease the tension, escaping from discussions of law by telling risqué jokes: "His mama told him to take the hardest thing he had and put it where his bride peed, so he put his bowling ball in the toilet stool!"

Hah, hah, hah!

Robinson, a straitlaced summa cum laude graduate of the Howard University Law School, was at first dismayed to hear a black voice say, "How're we gonna win this fucking case when the chief judge is opposed to niggers voting?"

"Let me ponder that dilemma over another Jack Daniels," was the reply from someone in the semidark club car.

Robinson let the vulgarities slip by, focusing on the fact that Marshall, he, and the other lawyers and witnesses would appear before a three-judge federal panel. Presiding would be John J. Parker of North Carolina, chief judge of the Fourth Circuit Court of Appeals. In 1930, President Herbert Hoover had chosen Parker for a seat on the U.S. Supreme Court. But Parker had asserted publicly that he opposed giving Negroes the right to vote. Parker had been rejected by the Senate, the first nominee in fifty-six years to be denied confirmation to the high tribunal. This was why Marshall was so nervous about *Briggs v. Elliott,* the case they were about to argue, and why his fellow passengers were engaged in such angry pretrial vituperations against Parker.

The other members of the panel were John Bell Timmerman, judge of the Western District of South Carolina, a known segregationist from a bitterly racist town, Batesburg, and J. Waties Waring of the Eastern District, who had shocked and infuriated his fellow socialites in Charleston by outlawing the "white primary" system in which blacks were denied the vote and any influence in the totally dominant Democratic party.

*   *   *

A groggy contingent of NAACP people got off that train in Charleston on a typical May morning. It was hot and absurdly humid. Boulware, the incredibly brave local lawyer who had represented, coached, shepherded, and financed the black children and parents who had sued Elliott, was at the train station. So was Briggs, whose name must forever have a place of honor in black history. Also at the station was a small band of black parents, teachers, farmers, redcaps, ordinary people, all wanting to show their respect for and adoration of Marshall.

Women who scrubbed white people's floors for a pittance were there, fanning themselves with one hand while lifting their gingham dresses off their moist bodies with the other. Black men who believed that the hotter it got, the more layers of clothes you should put on, were wearing thick wool.

Robinson was thrilled by the outcries of affection for Marshall. He saw a tall, crayon-brown farmer in mud-splattered overalls and brogans sealed against water by dried cow dung and horse droppings embrace Marshall and buss him on the cheek. This was especially impressive because in black America in 1951 "real men" did not kiss other men.

The redcaps were piling up a mountain of luggage brought by the NAACP team. As Robinson watched the pile grow higher and higher, he heard a desperate cry:

"Don't let the train leave. I forgot my dolls!"

He watched a lean, short black man rush back onto the train and then emerge with a black doll under one arm, a white doll under the other.

Robinson turned to Marshall and asked, "Thurgood, who's the nut toting those goddamned dolls?"

"That's Mr. Stigma," Marshall said with a subdued chuckle.

"Mister who?"

"Kenneth Clark, a remarkable psychologist from the City College of New York. He's gonna use those dolls to win this case."

"You're shitting me."

"Spot," Marshall continued, very serious now, "if we're going to win this goddamned case here, and if we're ever going to get 'separate but equal' outlawed by the Supreme Court, we've got to prove 'stigmatic injury.' "

"Stigmatic what?"

Marshall laughed, then explained: "No state offers clearer proof than South Carolina that separate school facilities and opportunities never have been, are not now, and never will be equal. The race that controls the money will always favor its own kids. So we'll never win shit arguing for 'separate but equal.' "

Marshall said Clark and some other noted psychologists, psychiatrists, educators, were going to help prove that wherever black children were subjected to the stigma of state-imposed segregation, they were injured egregiously, damaged in heart and mind for the rest of their lives.

"Our challenge is to convince Judge Parker and others on this panel, and eventually the Supreme Court, that stigmatic injury is real, it's cruel, and it's forbidden by the Constitution," Marshall added.

The NAACP had crossed a legal Rubicon. It had made a decision, fateful for it, black Americans, and the nation as a whole, that it had to deliver a frontal legal assault on the fundamental issue of whether the U.S. Constitution permitted state-sanctioned separation of the races.

Marshall, Robinson, and others on the NAACP team knew that they were on a seeming mission impossible. Racial attitudes among South Carolina's whites appeared not to have changed one whit from those of 1861, when that state's Senator James Henry Hammond said:

> In all social systems there must be a class to do the menial duties, to perform the drudgery of life. That is, a class requiring but a low order of intellect and but little skill. Its requisites are vigor, docility, fidelity. Such a class you must have, or you would not have that other class which leads progress, civilization, and refinement. It constitutes the very mudsill of society and of political government. . . . Fortunately for the South, she has found a race adapted to that purpose at her hand. A race inferior to her own, but eminently qualified in temper, in vigor, in docility, in capacity to stand the climate, to answer all her purposes. We use them for our purpose, and we call them slaves.

Marshall, Robinson, Clark, were going all out for integrated schools, an issue that had long divided the NAACP and black Americans in general. Blacks were arguing in NAACP chapters and conventions much of what W. Rhett Donaldson of Greenwood, South Carolina, had written to the *Charleston News and Courier:*

> It is true that we have evils in segregation but in order for any race to progress there must be certain unnecessary evils. Segregation as we have known it has been a greater help to the Southern

Negro than a hindrance. . . . The Negro will always be a problem to the white man and to his own race. He must learn to live
harmoniously with his own race before wanting to mingle into
other races.

Here was evidence of the extent to which slavery and white mas-
ters had brainwashed the Negro. The NAACP leaders, state and
national, and the board of directors had fought over this issue for
years. But just prior to dispatching Marshall and his team to Charleston, the decision had been made by the board, Executive Secretary
Walter White, and his deputy, Roy Wilkins, in favor of a broad attack
on Jim Crow in all its forms. The NAACP explained its decision in
a *Crisis* magazine article.

The organization acknowledged the fears of many black people
that attacking Jim Crow would anger whites, provoking them to fire
black employees, including teachers and administrators. It noted
warnings that the South would never accept school integration, and
that a legal assault might produce only a more circumscribing Supreme Court endorsement of racial segregation. Then the NAACP
said:

> What have we to lose? Nothing! The law says conclusively that
> Negroes are entitled to equal facilities. And it appears that the
> standards of equality which the courts will apply will be more rigid
> than ever. If the Association now refrains from its attack on seg-
> regation per se, basing its cases on the right to equal facilities, all
> we can reasonably expect are decisions applying the *Plessy v. Fer-*
> *guson* formula with stricter emphasis on the equality aspect of the
> separate-but-equal doctrine.
>
> Since this is the worst we can expect in a court decision, re-
> gardless of the legal policy pursued, there is little logic in the con-
> tention that a frontal attack jeopardizes the Negro's fight for better
> educational opportunities.
>
> The stakes are high, but the hazards are relatively fewer than
> they were ten years ago.

Robinson would learn within hours that most of the people on his
train, and the expert witnesses coming to Charleston by car, plane,
other trains, were committed to Marshall's scheme to use claims of
"stigmatic injury" to get the Supreme Court to overrule an 1896
declaration in *Plessy v. Ferguson* that racial segregation was legally
permissible if equal facilities were provided to those marked for isolation. But it was a dark little secret that the larger NAACP team

put together by Marshall was harshly divided on the merits of this "stigmatic injury" approach to the Supreme Court.

And what a team! Robert L. Carter, Marshall's deputy, would become a distinguished federal judge in New York; Spottswood Robinson's destiny included years as chief judge of the U.S. Court of Appeals for the District of Columbia; among the "of counsel" team members, a young lawyer named William T. Coleman, Jr., would serve as Secretary of Transportation in the administration of President Gerald Ford; Constance Baker Motley was bound for glory as a powerful and universally respected federal judge; James M. Nabrit, Jr., would serve as president of Howard University and on the U.S. delegation to the United Nations.

Coleman had opposed relying on the dolls and the doctrine of "stigmatic injury." He had clerked for Justice Felix Frankfurter, whom he regarded as a "strict constructionist," a curmudgeon who would laugh Clark, his dolls, the other sociologists and psychiatrists, out of the Supreme Court building. Clark became his friend, but lawyer Coleman never accepted the strategy proffered by psychologist Clark.

But Marshall's deputy, Carter, was an unwavering supporter of Clark. In fact, he personally arranged for David Krech, associate professor of psychology at the University of Southern California; Helen Trager, a lecturer and curriculum consultant at Vassar College; Harold J. McNally, an assistant professor at Teacher's College at Columbia University; Ellis Knox, a professor of education at Howard University, and others to testify as with one voice that when an agency of government says to a black child, "We, by constitution and statute, declare that you may not attend the same school as white children," that black child is demeaned, insulted, rendered unable to learn at a normal rate, and the damage done to the heart and mind of that stigmatized child is often permanent. Marshall had decided that Frankfurter could reject the dolls or not, but that the NAACP would base its case upon stigmatic injury, on a dolls test that indicated that young children were acutely aware that the people who ruled their communities, their schools, were saying that black children were inferior, that they were potential social and sexual contaminants and had to be treated accordingly. Marshall believed that all but brazenly racist judges would see how Jim Crow damaged black children.

Alongside the train that May morning in South Carolina, Boulware winked at Marshall and Robinson and tilted his head slightly toward uniformed white policemen who watched sullenly. These cops clearly viewed Marshall and his interracial entourage as the newest invasion of northern carpetbaggers. A few white people in plainclothes were, in Robinson's view, part of South Carolina's police-state apparatus.

But neither Marshall, Robinson, Boulware, nor anyone else in the NAACP party had come under any illusions that they would be welcome in South Carolina. They had read the May 21 editorial in the *Charleston News and Courier* saying:

> Law or no law, no matter what decisions federal courts shall hand down, in South Carolina there will not be "integration" of the white and Negro races in schools.
> Talk about integration of the races in public schools in South Carolina is jargon, the nonsense of the weak-minded.

Marshall and his colleagues were acutely aware that Governor James F. Byrnes had said, with the backing of South Carolina's General Assembly, that if the courts banned racial segregation in South Carolina schools, the state would abandon the public school system.

In the courtroom that Monday morning in May, representing district 22, were Robert McC. Figg, Jr., of Charleston, and S. E. Rogers of Summerton, the heart of district 22. South Carolina's attorney general T. C. Callison was in the courtroom, as was the attorney general of Virginia, a sort of scout preparing for the NAACP's assault on Jim Crow schools in that state.

The NAACP had worked for months to build up factual evidence of the inequality of the black schools in Clarendon County, particularly in district 22, compared with the white schools. Figg and other South Carolina officials knew this, so they dropped what they thought would be an early bombshell when Figg told the court that the Clarendon County trustees conceded that inequalities existed between white and Negro schools. But he said that the state legislature had passed a sales tax that would raise $75 million with which to remedy the inequities. What the state and the county wanted, he said, was time in which to produce a system that was racially separate but genuinely equal.

Marshall told the court that he would accept the admission of inequality, but he insisted on putting on the record the details of the injustices. He then proceeded to get South Carolina officials to confirm that in the previous year Clarendon County had spent $395,329 to educate 276 white children, as against $282,960 for 808 black children. Marshall got an admission that in district 22 the three

Negro schools with 808 pupils had 12 teachers, while the two all-white schools with 276 students also had 12 teachers.

Kenneth Clark then testified that he had conducted tests in district 22 schools in previous days and had seen that the black children had been harmed in their personality makeup. He said that it was clear to him that these black children were enduring injuries that would continue as long as the system of racial segregation existed.

On May 28, at 10 A.M., Carter began the questioning:

Q.: Mr. Clark, would you kindly state your occupation?

CLARK: I'm assistant professor of psychology at the New York City College, and associate director of the North Side School for Child Development in New York City.

Clark then told the entranced judges how he had determined the existence of personality damage. His testimony, in layman's terms, was that he showed black children two dolls, identical except for skin colors of black and white, and asked the child which doll he or she liked best; which was the "nice" doll and which the "bad" one. The children were asked, "Which doll is like you?"

Black children knew from brief life experiences that being a white doll had many advantages. It was the "nice" doll.

Q.: Have you reached any conclusion as to the effect of racial discrimination on the personality development of the Negro child?

CLARK: Discrimination, prejudice, and segregation have definitely detrimental effects on the personality development of the Negro child. The essence of this detrimental effect is a confusion in the child's concept of his own self esteem — basic feelings of inferiority, conflict, confusion in his self-image, resentment, hostility towards himself, hostility toward whites, intensification sometimes of a desire to resolve his basic conflict by sometimes escaping or withdrawing.

I found that, of the children between the ages of six and nine whom I tested, which were a total of sixteen in number, that ten of those children chose the white doll as their preference: the doll which they liked best. Ten of them also considered the white doll a "nice" doll. And, I think you have to keep in mind that those two dolls are absolutely identical in every respect except skin color. Eleven of these sixteen children chose the brown doll as the doll which looked "bad." This is consistent with previous results which we have obtained testing over three hundred children, and we interpret it to mean that the Negro child accepts as early as six, seven, or eight the negative stereotypes about his own group.

These children in Clarendon County, like other human beings who are subjected to an obviously inferior status in the society in which they live, have been definitely harmed in the development of their personalities; that the signs of instability in their personalities are clear, and I think that every psychologist would accept and interpret these signs as such.

The three judges appeared bemused when Clark argued that the segregation of a black minority by a white majority also damaged white children. He said feelings of guilt and confusion arose which were detrimental to the personalities of white youngsters.

The entire nation was watching this legal struggle, but nowhere was it watched as intensely as by the white people of South Carolina. Segregationists there felt under siege. They wanted the sympathy of white people everywhere. Marshall would get a sense of the paranoia, the desperation, of some whites when he read the newspaper after the first trial day.

He picked up the *News and Courier* early and saw an editorial headlined "THE SOUTH ON TRIAL" that said:

A good and perhaps a convincing statement can be made that public schools for Negroes in South Carolina are not equal in facilities to public schools for whites. Millions of dollars are being spent by the state to make them equal in the near future.

But the NAACP wants more than equality. It wants to force whites to mingle with Negroes, and it wants to force Negroes to mingle with whites. It wants the Supreme Court of the United States to rule that it is unconstitutional not to have such mingling.

The case will go automatically to the Supreme Court, and may be docketed for the fall term. In a sense, not only the school system but the people of the South, and of many places outside the South, are on trial. The decision may rank in importance with the Dred Scott decision of 1857.

The following morning, May 29, Chief Judge Parker asked what kind of decree the defense suggested that the court hand down. Figg said that what he was requesting was time to "correct the situation in district 22." "I'm not much impressed with that suggestion," Parker said. "You're coming into court and admitting that facilities are not equal. It is not up to the court to wet-nurse the schools." Faces brightened on the NAACP team: here was a hint that Parker might rule against "separate but equal."

When the court recessed for lunch, Marshall sat alone, going over in his own mind the major points that Figg and Rogers had made, determined that he would be ready when the court resumed at 2:30 P.M.

Marshall was to speak under a handicap. Because the NAACP could not afford to pay witnesses, Clark or anyone else, to travel to South Carolina, taking time away from their jobs to testify, his legal team was at the mercy of those who promised they would show up on time. But Marshall was still waiting for two expert witnesses when he was chided by Judge Parker, who said, "Our Supreme Court once said that the best thing a man can do, when he has a case in court, is to attend to it. Both sides ought to have given this case more attention."

Marshall was wounded, knowing how many hours of attention he had given this most important case of his life. He said, "If Your Honor please, these witnesses are — it is just almost impossible to get them. They are all coming on a volunteer basis, and they have commitments." Parker's gaze made it clear that he was not impressed by this excuse.

Marshall put this rebuke in the back of his mind. He knew that in his closing statement the challenge was to lay out an argument that would be persuasive, if not to this three-judge panel, then certainly to the U.S. Supreme Court. He knew that he would have to counter an emotional statement Figg had made about what blacks wielding sudden power had done to whites during the Reconstruction period.

"May it please the court," Marshall said, as he assailed Figg's speech, "I see no relevancy whatsoever." Then he went into the heart of his argument. Marshall was careful not to come across as the slick black lawyer from the big city of New York. He outdid Figg in humility, showing deference to the three judges but never walking away from the legal and intellectual context of what he was trying to put across.

Considerable argument has been made as to the great progress that has been made, especially in South Carolina, toward educating Negro pupils. It has been greatly emphasized, but I think we should recognize that that point is directed to the question as to whether or not this court will issue a decree giving them time to equalize the physical facilities. Yet in their own argument they admit that they have operated these Negro schools in South Carolina over a period of eighty years, and after a period of eighty years the best that they can possibly show to the court in good faith, or to demonstrate the good faith of South Carolina, is that as of today the Negro schools are forty million dollars behind the white schools.

The only question in this case, since both sides agree, I assume at this stage, that the plaintiffs in this case are entitled to equal school facilities. . . . The only dispute is as to what we mean by "equal." The mere fact that there are two equal physical buildings does not mean there is equality as intended by the Fourteenth Amendment.

So we take the position that equality means all of the education that is offered by the state.

The argument of Mr. Figg certainly does not stand in the face of scientific studies, and Mr. Clark's testimony of the plaintiffs in this case and the other Negroes was that there were roadblocks built as a result of segregation in that county which made it impossible for those children to absorb education like the white children would normally do, and that it was a lasting injury, not a temporary one, but a lasting injury. That testimony stands unchallenged.

Injecting Negroes here and there is not the issue in this case. The force involved in this case is by the State of South Carolina. They forced Negroes out of one set of schools into another set. The only thing the Fourteenth Amendment says is that the state shall not do it; this state shall not put upon one group of people anything that is not put upon another group.

Marshall went to bed that night thinking that he had done a very good job. But he was reminded anew of the depth of opposition to him and the NAACP when he picked up the *News and Courier* and saw another editorial saying: "Since it is a reality that white South Carolinians will not voluntarily send their children to mixed schools, and since courts cannot force white South Carolinians to send their children to such schools, it is difficult to see what, except confusion, the National Association for the Advancement of Colored People hopes to achieve in the Clarendon suit."

The following day, the *Charleston Evening Post* weighed in with this comment: "If the NAACP should win its case before the Supreme Court, the negro people of South Carolina will be the losers."

Back in New York, Marshall found that there wasn't enough bourbon in the city to calm his nerves as he awaited the decision of this federal panel. It didn't help that he was getting daily from Boulware copies of editorials in the white press of South Carolina. Marshall read one of June 6 in the *News and Courier* that was so vicious that he said to himself, "If those judges have been poisoned by even a teaspoonful of this thinking, we don't have a chance."

That editorial was entitled: " 'Segregation' to Civilization." It said:

> The Southern Negroes have been generously treated since they were brought to North America out of savagery — and SLAVERY — in Africa.
>
> In the last 5,000 years the one bloc, the one large group of Africans who have made substantial advances in civilization, in literacy, in industry and business, have been and are the Africans brought to the Southern states and "segregated."

Fifteen days later, on June 21, Marshall got the bad news from Boulware. Parker and Timmerman had voted against the black plaintiffs on every issue at stake. Parker had cited *Plessy v. Ferguson*, which said Louisiana could impose segregation in railroad trains under conditions of "separate but equal," as well as the 1927 case of *Gong Lum v. Rice*, in which former President William Howard Taft spoke for a unanimous Supreme Court in declaring that state legislatures had the power to force Chinese students to go to schools set up for nonwhites.

Parker and Timmerman completely rejected Clark's dolls and the testimony of other sociologists, psychiatrists, and educators.

"There is testimony," Parker wrote, "that mixed schools will give better education. . . . There is testimony, on the other hand, that mixed schools will result in racial friction and tension. . . . The federal courts would be going far outside their constitutional function were they to attempt to prescribe educational policies for states in such matters, however desirable such policies might be in the opinion of some sociologists or educators. . . .

"We conclude, therefore, that if equal facilities are offered, segregation of the races in the public schools as prescribed by the Constitution and laws of South Carolina is not of itself violative of the Fourteenth Amendment."

Marshall at first could find only the scant consolation of a dissent in which Judge Waring said:

> The whole discussion of race and ancestry has been intermingled with sophistry and prejudice. What possible definition can be found for the so-called white race, Negro race or other races? Who is to decide and what is the test? For years, there was talk of blood and taint of blood. Science tells us that there are but four kinds of

blood: A, B, AB and O and these are found in Europeans, Asiatics, Africans, Americans and others. And so we need not further consider the irresponsible and baseless references to preservation of "Caucasian blood." So then, what test are we going to use in opening our school doors and labeling them "white" or "Negro"? The law of South Carolina considers a person of one-eighth African ancestry to be a Negro. Why this proportion? Why not one-sixteenth?

I am of the opinion that all of the legal guideposts, expert testimony, common sense and reason point unerringly to the conclusion that the system of segregation in education adopted and practiced in the State of South Carolina must go and must go now.

Segregation is per se inequality.

The more Marshall and his colleagues rehashed *Briggs*, the more importance they saw in Waring's words, which carried extra impact because they came from the scion of five generations of Charleston aristocracy. More important, Waring had ripped the covers off a charade in which the segregators pretended that state-imposed Jim Crow had nothing to do with master-slave relationships, or a claim of God-given superiority of white people compared with those of African descent. Waring talked openly about "Caucasian blood" and "Negro blood," attacking the "sophistry" of Governor Byrnes and others who claimed that the state's classifications by race were just "no-harm, no-malice" administrative measures. If this white Charlestonian found Jim Crow to be a farce of hatred, what federal judges in the North would openly defend segregation?

Marshall began to take heart in the hope that the members of the Supreme Court would be as loath to embrace the doctrine of black blood "tainting" white school children as Waring had been. After all, there presumably was no one on the Supreme Court as committed to keeping the Negro "in his place" as Judges Parker and Timmerman were, and had been all their adult lives.

The *News and Courier* was ecstatic: "In upholding the rights of the states to local self-government, the majority opinion of a three-judge federal court has upheld the basic principle of American democracy. . . . Judge Waring's dissent in effect is a sociological treatise on race doctrines. The majority opinion is a legal pronouncement with much wider significance. . . . It is difficult to see how [this] wise ruling can be upset on appeal."

Marshall would recall that day of wrenching defeat in 1951 by saying to me more than three decades later:

"When I got that telephone call from Boulware I felt as though

Max Schmeling [the German boxer] had hit me in the solar plexus. I had no reason to expect Parker and Timmerman to vote for me, but I was still disappointed. I held to a naive belief that in the face of the evidence we presented about the damage of segregation to black children, any decent white judge would say, 'You're right.' But I didn't know then, and most Americans don't know now, how irrational and destructive the forces of racial bigotry were then and are today. The idea that blacks were not just inferior, but a contaminant, was ingrained beyond my understanding. We just never had a chance in that Charleston courtroom, because the whole judicial system was dominated by a mean public opinion that was fostered by the editorial writers.

"I started out believing that we would win because the free press would side with us. But when Boulware called me, and I read that editorial in that Charleston paper, all I could think was that the fuckin' press had lynched some black schoolchildren. I slammed that *News and Courier* editorial on the floor and stomped on it, and I talked to it and said, 'It ain't over yet, baby!'

"It took me a long time to realize that all white people were not bigoted brutes — that even in South Carolina we had found an incredibly important ally, Judge Waring, who symbolized better times and better courtrooms to come.

"As the pain in my heart and my contempt for Parker and Timmerman subsided, I knew that the challenge to me and the NAACP team was to find more Warings and get them dedicated to our cause of racial justice. The *Briggs* case taught me that we [in the NAACP] were bound to face confrontations in and out of the courtroom that would be far more traumatic, even violent, than that 1951 setback; so we had to fine-tune our legal strategy if we hoped to use the Constitution peacefully to wipe out Jim Crow."

Throughout this courtroom drama an unpublicized human tragedy was taking place. Harry Briggs, thirty-nine, and his thirty-four-year-old wife, Eliza, were sitting in that federal courtroom in brave pride, admiring the skill of Marshall's arguments, smiling over the way Summerton's lawyer Rogers was scrambling as he tried to figure out which tack Marshall was about to take.

The three federal judges, the other courtroom spectators, had no idea that the Briggses had come to that hearing under terrible stress. Clarendon County's white leaders had demanded that this black couple withdraw their petition challenging "separate but equal." The Briggses had refused to do so. As they feared, when they returned to the little town of Summerton, Harry Briggs was fired from his job pumping gas at a filling station. The White Citizens Council later stopped all deliveries of food, drinks, laundry, almost everything, to a motel that was resisting the Council's demand that Eliza Briggs be fired. The motel caved in under the boycott and let Mrs. Briggs go.

Harry Briggs, who had never finished high school, tried farming. No one would give him credit. The white-owned cotton gins refused to process his bales of produce. Briggs moved to Florida to take a forty-dollar-a-week job. Mrs. Briggs, who had a tenth-grade education, spent four years of economic desperation in Clarendon County, trying to raise five children on the money her husband could send from Florida. Then she went to Florida for a year, but at the begging of their children, she returned to the Clarendon County home. But Harry Briggs spent twenty years in exile in Florida and New York before returning to the land of his bravest struggle. He is now buried in Clarendon County.

Mrs. Briggs, now seventy-five and widowed, has become one of the most respected people in a still-defiant community. I sat with her recently in her modest home, listening to her recount the myriad reprisals and retaliations that white segregationists imposed upon her family.

"I'm still proud that Harry stood up for justice," she said. "I just lie awake some nights thinking how we suffered and regretting that my children never gained a good education from our fight. Not one of them ever got a college education."

Asked what she would do if Thurgood Marshall walked into her house and asked her to sign another petition requesting that the courts wipe out the remaining racism in Summerton's public schools, she said: "I'd sign it — I'd do it all over again."

Only that generation of northern Americans who served on ships that pulled into the Charleston Navy Yard during World War II, as I did, or who served at Army bases in the Deep South, can read these pages and understand the violence with which Jim Crow was defended by whites in the 1940s and 1950s. They can understand the perils of Marshall's legal crusade. Blacks who had been born in and lived in the South, as I had, realized as no white person ever would the dangers that faced a dedicated forty-three-year-old lawyer who, armed only with a piece of paper called "the Constitution," would indeed challenge lawmen tied to lynch mobs and become a towering figure in America's system of criminal justice.

CHAPTER TWO

THE MAKING OF A MAN

W HAT TURNS a man born into ordinary circumstances into a great, brave, uncompromising leader? Thousands of prophets and poets have written that adversity is the key. Ecclesiasticus (2:5) wrote 180 years before the birth of Christ that "gold is tried in the fire, and acceptable men in the furnace of adversity." My mother quoted someone whose name I don't remember in telling me that "God leads men into deep waters, not to drown them, but to cleanse them."

Well, God knows that Thurgood Marshall had his face-offs with adversity. But there have been millions of young males in this century who have known more hardships and personal tragedies in a year than Marshall faced in the entire first two decades of his life. So no proverb or bromide gives us the answer. Perhaps we must accept the reality that there is no clichéd answer to the question of how Marshall rose from shabby beginnings and a somewhat less than "honorable" boyhood in Baltimore to become a monumental force for justice.

That is like asking how John Brown turned up at Harpers Ferry; why Sherman wound up in Atlanta, or Dwight Eisenhower at Normandy; or why Martin Luther King wrote from a Birmingham jail. It is like asking how a polio victim, Franklin D. Roosevelt, came to lead America out of the Great Depression, or how his socialite wife, Eleanor, became the spirit of hope to millions of emotionally and physically wounded people of a suffering society. We can never know why an era of economic, political, or social tribulation can produce a Hitler, a Mussolini, a Hirohito in some countries, a Winston Churchill or Charles de Gaulle in others.

Some of Marshall's relatives had a "divine" explanation for his rise to fame. When Thoroughgood Marshall was delivered by a midwife across from a Baltimore slaughter pen on July 2, 1908, some felt a premonition (or so they said half a century later) that a great man had been born. But there was nothing about this poor African-American baby or the environment into which he was delivered to suggest that he was anything special. Nothing in Marshall's life as baby, child, or teenager could have given anyone credible reason to believe that he would grow up to strike terror in the hearts and minds of governors, attorneys general, judges, and jurors in South Carolina or any other state. In fact, the year of Thoroughgood's birth to Norma and William Marshall was not an auspicious one for the arrival of any black person in any city in America. Marshall was born in the midst of one of the greatest periods of violence and propaganda against black people since the end of slavery and the Reconstruction era.

In 1906, terrible rioting had erupted in Atlanta — this despite the fact that Booker T. Washington, the preferred "black leader" of the white establishment, had caved in to the economic fears of white people and agreed to restrict black aspirations to vocational fields. A young, fair-skinned, blue-eyed "Negro" named Walter White almost saw his family murdered in this Atlanta riot.

But worse was to come, primarily because of the organized agitation of fearmongers about the rush to northern cities by blacks fleeing peonage, semislavery, wretched destitution, in the cotton fields and peanut patches of the Deep South, but also trying to escape the humiliations and degradations of cities such as Baltimore and Birmingham.

The spirit of racial violence was exploding everywhere in 1906. In Manhattan, bigots as well as those denying any touch of racial prejudice flocked to a play called *The Clansman*. This was a piece of demagoguery written by a Tarheel preacher, the Reverend Thomas Dixon, Jr., who warned, "The beginning of Negro equality is . . . the beginning of the end of this nation's life."

The Clansman was the precursor of the "Willie Horton" presidential campaign of 1988, because it focused on fears of black men raping white women. Dixon's incendiary play would show up in less than a decade as a movie, *Birth of a Nation*, whose scenes of black lust, rape, and rage would befoul the sensibilities of an entire nation. Meanwhile, *The Clansman* was a sensation in New York in 1906 because many thousands of New Yorkers were alarmed that the city's black population had increased more than 50 percent, from 42,816 to 65,894, in the decade preceding the turn of the century.

In 1907, the year that Thurgood Marshall was conceived, the situation of blacks in America would worsen. In the South, blacks were systematically disfranchised; some states and communities made it unlawful to teach them to read and write; northern cities seeing their first blacks in any number passed ordinances to segregate them — in schools, jobs, public accommodations, or anyplace else lawmakers could think of.

This anti-Negro wave of emotion in the North was caused by a dismaying alliance of southern racists and the most influential media in the North. In 1907, the *Saturday Evening Post* carried an article by Harris Dickson, who quoted Mississippi Governor James K. Vardaman on what should be done to or about America's Negroes:

> The Negro should never have been trusted with the ballot. He is different from the white man. He is congenitally unqualified to exercise the most responsible duty of citizenship. He is physically, mentally, morally, racially and eternally the white man's inferior. There is nothing in the history of his race, nothing in his individual character, nothing in his achievements of the past nor his promise for the future which entitles him to stand side by side with the white man at the ballot-box. . . .
>
> We must repeal and modify the Fourteenth Amendment to the Constitution of the United States. Then we shall be able in our legislation to recognize the Negro's racial peculiarities, and make laws to fit them.

Who could have imagined a black kid born into this cauldron of conflict surviving, let alone leaving South Carolina forty-three years later a loser before Parker and Timmerman, a winner before Waring, and certain that he would win before the Supreme Court, the nation, and the world? In 1908 Marshall's parents surely didn't figure that he could ever be a winner when they saw a stronger white response of violence against any Negro who dared to challenge white supremacy.

Just a month after Thoroughgood's birth, the nation was shaken by ghastly rioting in Springfield, Illinois, where a white woman's false cry of rape by a black man led to two lynchings, many other black deaths, the driving of thousands of black immigrants from the city, and great destruction of property. Because the riot was in the place of Abraham Lincoln's birth, and because it was led, abetted, approved, by the "best" white people in Springfield, the entire nation watched in either satisfaction or anguished embarrassment.

Among those watching in outrage was William English Walling, a native Southerner, who wrote for the *Independent* a gripping account of the atrocities committed against blacks in Springfield. He said: "Either the spirit of the abolitionists, of Lincoln and of [black slavery foe Elijah] Lovejoy must be revived and we must come to treat the Negro on a plane of absolute political and social equality, or Vardaman and [South Carolina's Senator Ben "Pitchfork"] Tillman will soon have transferred the race war to the North."

Walling had spent time in Russia, where his Jewish wife had been imprisoned for her work in behalf of the revolutionists, and was profoundly influenced by her assertion that Negroes were treated with greater inhumanity in the United States than were Jews in the Soviet Union.

Walling's article seared the heart of a young white woman, Mary White Ovington, who had done social work among blacks in the South and at the time was living in a tenement for Negroes in a black New York neighborhood, trying to glean the truth about what happened to the children of former slaves who came to New York thinking it was "the promised land."

Ovington wrote Walling, asking that he meet with her and Dr. Henry Moskowitz, who had an influential job in the office of New York's Mayor John Purroy Mitchell. These three white people, described by Ovington as "a southerner, a Jew, and the child of an abolitionist," met and decided that on Lincoln's birthday, February 12, 1909, they would make a national "call" for concerned people to attend a conference on "the Negro question."

The three knew that without media help their plan to promote racial justice was dead. They called upon Oswald Garrison Villard, president of the New York Evening Post Company and grandson of the most famous of slavery foes, William Lloyd Garrison. Oswald Villard pledged heart, mind, and resources to the endeavor.

How terrible, revealing, dismaying, that the political and economic power of twelve million black Americans was so low in 1909 that they were impotent, yet an all-white band of four people could take steps that would profoundly change the future of black people in America.

For despite their numbers, black Americans had no political clout in 1909 because most of them lacked the right to vote. Blacks had no economic power, so they could not influence the nation's leaders with campaign contributions. Blacks had no roles in the major media of America — only a friend or two at places such as the *New York Evening Post*. No profiles of courage about who moved black people toward freedom and America toward greatness must ever exclude the names of Walling, Ovington, Moskowitz, and especially Villard. This publisher put the economic stability of his newspaper and his personal reputation at risk by writing the call to a national meeting on the centennial of Lincoln's birth and by ensuring that the call was widely publicized in his newspaper and in such other media as he could influence.

Villard's contemporaries said that his call to the conscience of America was no less important than Lincoln's Emancipation Proclamation. It gave life to an organization in which Thurgood Marshall could later work, at a time when civil rights for black people were not on the minds or consciences of many Americans. Villard wrote bravely:

> If Mr. Lincoln could revisit this country in the flesh, he would be disheartened and discouraged. He would learn that on January 1, 1909, Georgia had rounded out a new confederacy by disfranchising the Negro, after the manner of all the other Southern States. He would learn that the Supreme Court of the United States, supposedly a bulwark of American liberties, had refused every opportunity to pass squarely upon this disfranchisement of millions, by laws avowedly discriminatory and openly enforced in such manner that the white men may vote and black men be without a vote in their government.
>
> In many states Lincoln would find justice enforced, if at all, by judges elected by one element in a community to pass upon the liberties and lives of another. He would see the black men and women, for whose freedom a hundred thousand soldiers gave their lives, set apart in trains, in which they pay first-class fares for third-class service, and segregated in railway stations and in places of entertainment; he would observe that State after State declines to do its elementary duty in preparing the Negro through education for the best exercise of citizenship.
>
> Added to this, the spread of lawless attacks upon the Negro, North, South, and West — even in the Springfield made famous by Lincoln — often accompanied by revolting brutalities, sparing neither sex nor age nor youth, could but shock the author of the sentiment that "government of the people, by the people, for the people; should [*sic*] not perish from the earth."
>
> Hence we call upon all the believers in democracy to join in a national conference for the discussion of present evils, the voicing of protests, and the renewal of the struggle for civil and political liberty.

When Villard spoke, some remarkably powerful people listened . . . and responded. His call was signed by Jane Addams of Hull

House in Chicago; Professor John Dewey of New York; Dr. W. E. B. Du Bois of Atlanta; William Lloyd Garrison of Boston; Bishop Alex Walters, New York; Rabbi Stephen B. Wise, New York; Lincoln Steffens of Boston, and of course, Moskowitz, Ovington, and Walling.

But the call faced many problems. Most of the people of conscience allied with it had little money. There were too few blacks involved. Ovington would write of the first gathering, at Cooper Union on May 30, 1909, that "the white people in attendance . . . engaged in religious, social and educational work, for the first time met the Negro, who demands, not a pittance, but his full rights in the commonwealth."

At that 1909 meeting, the National Association for the Advancement of Colored People was born. But by 1910 the black intellectual and "militant" Du Bois knew that a white-dominated NAACP could not long endure. It had to be merged with the Niagara Movement, formed in 1905 by blacks who demanded:

- Freedom of speech and criticism
- An unfettered and unsubsidized press
- Manhood suffrage [*note, no "womanhood"*]
- The abolition of all caste distinctions based simply on race and color
- The recognition of the principle of human brotherhood as a practical present creed
- The recognition of the highest and best training as the monopoly of no class or race
- A belief in the dignity of labor

Du Bois and others in the Niagara Movement had little or no influence on the White House or any other powerful segments of white America, so they quickly joined the white crusaders, Ovington, Villard, and others, in the creation of a multiracial force for black justice.

This construction of a civil rights organization to ensure black equality could not endure. It was too white, too Jewish, too little black, and most of all too impecunious, even with the letterheads of famous white people who were giving a pittance of dollars to the causes the NAACP was created to fight.

Even as they were creating the NAACP, the man who would become "Mr. NAACP" had become part of the great migration that so roiled the white people of so many northern cities. Marshall's parents left Baltimore for New York City in late 1908, never suspecting that *The Clansman* and diatribes by Dixon, Vardaman, and others would guarantee them a chilly reception. Only after five disillusioning years, in 1913, did they give up and move back to Baltimore, to live in the home of Thurgood's uncle Fearless Williams, his mother's brother.

Stories of lynchings had pained Norma and William Marshall all their adult lives — 235 mob killings in 1892, 200 in 1893, a mere 63 in 1907, the year Thurgood was conceived. Neither the Marshalls nor any other black couple could ever become inured to the headlines and stories they had to read every week:

LYNCHED FOR THEFT OF A COW
[headline out of Crescent, Louisiana]

10,000 VIEW BODY OF LYNCHED COLORED MAN ON SUNDAY

SUNDAY SCHOOL CHILDREN ARE AMONG SUNDAY THRONGS
THAT GAZE AT HALF-NAKED BODY OF VICTIM
BRUTALLY MURDERED BY WHITE MOB IN MARYLAND

Those headlines were in the Marshalls' hometown paper, the *Baltimore Sun*. In 1908 the number of lynchings rose to one hundred, mostly of blacks accused of murder, but some because of "disappointment at a Colored entertainment," "offensive language," and "insulting a white woman."

In 1911, newspapers reported that in Livermore, Kentucky, a Negro charged with the murder of a white man had been taken to the "opera house" and tied to part of the stage. Admission was charged for those wanting to see the lynching, the money to go to the family of the white victim. Fatcats purchasing an opera seat were allowed to bring revolvers and fire into the swinging body of the black man until all bullets were dispensed. Those able to buy only a gallery seat got just one shot at the lynch victim.

Charles Flint Kellogg, in his history of the NAACP, detailed a grisly series of lynchings. Five black people, two of them women, were lynched in Gainesville, Florida, after a black man quarreled with a white man over a pig.

Lynchings put an indelible scar upon the souls of black men and women, indeed upon the psyches of all black children who could read and write. When he was ten, Marshall read a story from Vicksburg, Mississippi, saying that six white men had tarred and feathered two Negro women who had refused to do household work. The white men were charged with disorderly conduct.

At age eleven, Marshall read the following Associated Press dispatch from Hillsboro, Texas:

Bragg Williams, negro, under death sentence for the murder of Mrs. Geo. Wells and her child at Itasca, was taken from the Hill county jail here at noon today by a mob and burned at the stake.

The crowd was orderly and there was little excitement. . . .

Between 300 and 400 persons, including dozens of women, looked on as the negro burned.

The body was entirely consumed in about forty minutes, after which the crowd quietly dispersed.

In retrospect, it seems that the most tragic aspect of this period was the cowardice of government, of political intellectuals such as Woodrow Wilson who refused to speak out against the mobs. On October 16, 1912, the politically ambitious Wilson wrote to Bishop Alexander Walters of New York City to say that he could not attend an NAACP meeting, adding:

It would afford me pleasure to be present, because there are certain things I want to say. I hope that it seems superfluous to those who know me, but to those who do not know me perhaps it is now necessary for me to assure my Colored fellow citizens of my earnest wish to see justice done them in every matter, and not mere grudging justice, but justice executed with liberality and cordial good feeling. Every guarantee of our law, every principle of our constitution, commands this, and our sympathies should also make it easy.

The Colored people of the United States have made extraordinary progress towards self-support and usefulness, and ought to be encouraged in every possible and proper way. My sympathy with them is of long standing and I want to assure them through you that should I become President of the United States, they may count upon me for absolute fair dealing and for everything by which I could assist in advancing the interests of their race in the United States.

Villard and his *New York Post* gave support to Wilson's candidacy for governor of New Jersey, and then for the presidency, even though Villard was warned that Wilson would be a disappointment. It wasn't long after Wilson assumed the presidency that he was declaring racial segregation to be "in the interests of the Colored people." In 1917, after terrible anti-Negro riots in many cities, especially East St. Louis, some fifteen thousand blacks protested in the streets of New York City. Then an NAACP delegation went to Washington, headed by the great writer James Weldon Johnson, author of the

"Negro national anthem" and soon to become the first black chief executive of the NAACP.

Wilson wouldn't receive the group, so he ordered an aide to listen to Johnson say:

> We come . . . praying that the President may find it in his heart to speak some public word that will give hope and courage to our people. . . .
> In the last thirty-one years 2,867 colored men and women have been lynched by mobs without trial. Less than half a dozen persons out of the tens of thousands involved have received any punishment whatsoever for these crimes, and not a single one has been punished for murder. . . . In the latest atrocity at East St. Louis nearly a hundred innocent, hardworking citizens were done to death in broad daylight for seeking to earn an honest living.

Johnson's appeal did not stir Wilson, so the racial outrages continued.

In 1918 and 1919, when Thurgood was at an especially impressionable age, he saw that even as black soldiers were just coming home from fighting in World War I, the lynching of blacks reached what was probably its bloodiest, most grotesque peak in America. There was a five-day orgy of lynchings in Lowndes and Brooks counties of Georgia, with eight Negroes murdered. Mary White Ovington would shock an NAACP board meeting by describing what happened after the lynching of what she swore was an innocent man, Haynes Turner:

> His wife, Mary, after her husband's death, mourned and loudly proclaimed his innocence. For this she was slowly burned to death, watched by a crowd of men and women. She was pregnant, and as she burned, the infant fell to the ground and was trampled under a white man's heel.

Lynchings were so commonplace, so brutal, so embarrassing to the nation, that they became the focus of almost all NAACP activity. They also aroused cries in the Congress and the media for legal and other steps to curb such lawlessness. The *Charlotte Observer* called lynch mobs "The Curse of the South," asserting boldly: "The white man is in danger of letting his relations with the Negro brutalize him; already those relations have caused him to replace his ancestor's profound reverence for law with almost incredible lawlessness." The South was now bitterly divided over lynching, but not yet over a belief in the need to segregate black people.

The *Jacksonville* [Florida] *Times-Union* said: "In the South, ever since the emancipation of the Negroes, there have been occasional instances of summary punishment meted out to men of the colored race who perhaps inherited the savagery of their ancestors and defied all laws. Assaults upon women — white — and black — have been responsible for 90 per cent of the violent deaths of Negro men at the hands of mobs in [the] South — and the other 10 per cent includes cowardly attacks upon the aged and the helpless, old men and small children murdered by brutal Negroes, have been avenged by their neighbors."

This editorial was a searing insult to blacks at the NAACP such as James Weldon Johnson. They decided that even though they had failed before to get President Wilson to take a stand against racial segregation, perhaps another appeal would get him to speak out against mob violence. It might be a ghoulish "blessing," NAACP leaders thought, that whites suspected of being enemy aliens or sympathizers with Germany's Kaiser Wilhelm were also being lynched. Wilson just might speak out in behalf of white victims of mobs.

On July 26, 1918, without ever referring to the lynching of any Negro — without ever using the word Negro — Wilson spoke to the nation:

> No man who loves America, no man who really cares for her fame and honor and character, or who is truly loyal to her institutions, can justify mob action. We are at this very moment fighting lawless passion. Germany has outlawed herself among the nations because she has disregarded the sacred obligations of law and has made lynchers of her armies. Lynchers emulate her disgraceful example. I, for my part, am anxious to see every community in America rise above that level, with pride and a fixed resolution which no man or set of men can afford to despise.

Mobs apparently don't listen to presidential speeches; sixty-four people were lynched in the United States in 1918.

Amid this milieu, Marshall could sense his mother's anger and fear, his father's sense of outrage and helplessness, even when they said nothing to him about the lynch stories that black people would spread by word of mouth. William Marshall did not want his sons growing up feeling helpless. That is why he began to instill in Thurgood a will to fight, with his fists, his voice, his mind. "If any white boy calls you a nigger, you got to fight him," he told Thurgood, who had now legally shortened his name from Thoroughgood.

So this younger son became an example of the racial hostilities created by politicians, judges, and mob leaders permeating all of society and turning friendly children against one another. Marshall related to me with obvious sadness the fact that he resented his white neighbors going to a school to which he was denied admittance. White kids would pass his house, his all-black school, on their way to and from the "white" school. Black resentments and white assumptions of superiority made fistfights the rule of existence. Eventually, school officials changed the going-home times for the two schools so black and white youngsters would not have to confront each other.

Thurgood was lucky that he never became the target of a mob after he pounced on some white child, because in those days a young black could get lynched, as a boy was in Bryson, Georgia, for allegedly stealing 75 cents from two white boys. In this climate, no white person who was considered "a nigger lover" was safe, either.

In August 1919, in Austin, Texas, the first of state actions to destroy the NAACP — actions that Marshall later would have to fight off — began when the Texas attorney general subpoenaed the branch president to bring all NAACP books and records into court. John R. Shillady, who would be the last white chief executive of the NAACP, rushed to Austin to try to protect the names of the NAACP members, many of them whites, who were suddenly vulnerable to economic reprisals, or worse.

Shillady found that even a white man working against Jim Crow was in grave peril in Austin. The morning after Shillady left the office of the attorney general, he was attacked by whites and beaten unconscious. Shillady was damaged gravely, physically and mentally, and was afraid to go back to Austin for a trial of those accused of brutalizing him. He resigned as the NAACP secretary with a grim assertion that he saw "no probability of overcoming, within a reasonable period, the forces opposed to Negro equality."

James Weldon Johnson replaced Shillady, beginning a profound transformation of the leadership of the NAACP. What emerged was a powerful partnership of black and Jewish leaders, a fact that racist politicians tried to exploit in the 1950s and 1960s by declaring that the Jewish influence was proof that the NAACP was part of a "communist plot" to "mongrelize" and overthrow America. Johnson's accession to leadership was in fact evidence that educated black people could, with the support of other Americans, begin to set their own goals and priorities and attempt to manage their own destinies.

That it took the brutal beating of a white man in Austin to give blacks a greater voice in the NAACP was itself an ironic commentary on the state of American race relations at the end of World War I.

CHAPTER THREE

THE EARLY YEARS

Do NOT THINK that by this time Thurgood Marshall was saddling up a white horse, ready to ride off to the rescue of the black people of America. During the worst of the lynchings and riots of the early twentieth century, Marshall was in grade school, goofing off, driving his mother crazy, showing no signs whatsoever that he was destined for a leadership role in combating the racism and the atrocities that seared the minds of his older relatives. Thurgood was manifesting irresponsibility in ways his mother could not understand — perhaps because she had no idea of the extent to which her boy was influenced by her and her husband's talk about lynchings and the overall terrible plight of black people.

Let me emphasize here that Thurgood was not born into poverty as it is understood today by blacks, Hispanics, and others of the American underclass. His was a two-parent family, something 15.9 million of America's children, or 25 percent, did not know in 1990, in an era of births out of wedlock, divorce, separation, and the mindless killings of black males by black males. Even when compared with his black peers at the turn of the century, Marshall was relatively privileged, despite the five years of tribulation when his family was part of the great black migration. Marshall's mother, Norma, was educated, a teacher for more than a quarter century and proud of it, despite the fact that she was working for pay far below what Maryland bestowed upon white teachers. His father, William Canfield, was a man of class and dedication whose pride kept him from being destroyed by his resentment of having to work as a Pullman car porter, or as a steward at a country club that barred blacks and

Jews. In his spare time, Thurgood's father would hang out around courtrooms, then come home and challenge disputatiously any member of the family to argue against his view of whatever case was at issue.

Thurgood was sheltered by grandparents, especially his paternal grandmother, Mrs. Annie Marshall, who taught him that if you have guts "you can beat city hall." Thurgood recalls that when the electric company in Baltimore tried to put up a pole on the sidewalk outside Grandma Annie's grocery store, she perched on a kitchen chair over the spot where the pole was to go, daring the workers to touch her. Every day she sat there, arguing that she had paid for the sidewalk, and no damn body had the right to stick an electric pole in the middle of it. The electric company finally gave up.

Marshall had uncles and others in an extended black family — something that has almost vanished in America. The importance of this is evident in the fact that long before "black pride" in an "African heritage" became popular, Marshall was regaling anyone who would listen with stories of his African forebears. This is how Marshall explained his "roots" to me:

"Some of the snooty members of my family went for years pretending that my great-grandfather had belonged to a very cultured tribe in Sierra Leone, on the West Coast of Africa. But we all knew that he really came from the toughest part of the Congo. A big-game-hunting family had picked up my great-grandfather on one of their safaris into the Congo and brought him back to the Eastern Shore of Maryland — only to find that this black man didn't cotton to the idea of slavery. He expressed his objections so rebelliously that one day the slavemaster said to him:

" 'Look: I brought you here, so I guess I can't shoot you, which is what you deserve. I can't in good conscience sell anyone as vicious as you to another slaveholder. So I'm gonna set you free on one condition: You get the hell out of this county and never set foot here again.' "

So, as Marshall told it, he had gotten the spirit to war against America's system of semislavery in his genes.

There is documentation that Thurgood came from a fighting clan. The *Baltimore Sun* of August 6, 1875, reported that his maternal grandfather, Isaac O. B. Williams, had risen in a mass meeting to protest police brutality in the killing of a Negro.

But Thurgood was such a hellion as a kid, and even through elementary and high school, that his uncle Fearless began to call him a bum.

As a child, Marshall suffered from a hernia problem serious enough to cause the doctor to tell his mother — within Thurgood's hearing — to "see that he doesn't do any crying." Thurgood exploited his "sickness" ruthlessly, starting to cry whenever he wanted to take something from his three-years-older brother, William Aubrey, or when he wanted something his parents could not afford. He told me that he cried once too often, provoking his mother to bandage him tightly around his hernia and then beat the stuffing out of him.

Marshall said, with a measure of pride, that that beating stopped the crying but not his penchant for exploiting every seeming advantage he had. He figured that in elementary and high school there was no need to study, or become a Thurgoodie-two-shoes, when his mother was a teacher and none of her peers was ever likely to flunk him, or any principal to expel him. Marshall recalled without apparent remorse what he did to an assistant principal who thought he could discipline him and the five other students in a teenage gang that Marshall was running. One of the three girls in the gang was assigned to go see the offending official and, at a synchronized time on her watch, jump on the lap of the assistant principal as her five buddies burst into the office to catch the official in a sophomoric version of flagrante delicto. This high school foray into extortion worked marvelously, according to Marshall.

The principal at the high school figured that Marshall was too big and strong to whip, even though corporal punishment was permitted in those days. So Mr. Lee came up with a special kind of torture for a big, ne'er-do-well kid. He would banish Marshall to the furnace room, give him a copy of the U.S. Constitution, and tell him to memorize it. "If you don't think that's terrible, just you try memorizing the Constitution sometime," Marshall once said to me with belly-shaking laughter. Terrible, but fortuitous, because it gave Marshall his first knowledge and understanding of a document that would become central to his life.

Thurgood didn't go to jail for his extortion caper, but he was soon arrested and locked up for an incident in which he was not at fault. While in high school he got a job delivering hats that were custom-made for the richest people in the area, including Mrs. Woodrow Wilson — hats selling for exorbitant prices of $75 to $150. About 5 P.M. one day Marshall tried to squeeze onto the trolley while carrying four boxed hats. Suddenly he was pushed by a white man. "Nigger," the shover said, "you just stepped in front of a white woman. Don't ever do that again!"

Marshall had been commanded by his father "to lay some knuckles on any white man who called me a nigger," but recalls that pure instinct also told him to fight. He says he was "beating this guy up pretty good" when the police arrived and arrested him. Marshall made one telephone call, to his Jewish employer, whom he remembers as Mr. Mortimer Schoen, who rushed to the jail to post $50 and get young Thurgood out. As they left the jail, Thurgood said:

"I'm really sorry that I busted up four of your hats in that fight."

"Was it worth it?" Schoen asked.

"Sure as hell was," said Thurgood, recalling more than sixty years later that the man never asked him to pay for the hats or to repay him the $50 spent to free him from jail.

"There were some good white people around, even then," says the reminiscing Marshall.

The job delivering hats was not the only evidence that Marshall was something more than a brat. He had taken his first job at age seven as an errand boy at Hale's Grocery Store in Baltimore. He also worked later with his father on railroads as a porter, and as a waiter at the "exclusive" Gibson Island Country Club on Chesapeake Bay. It was the work ethic, and especially seeing what his father had to do to make a living, that surely built up the spirit of militancy in this gangly, high-spirited young man.

I think I understood for the first time in my life the term "stream of consciousness" when I sat down in a suite in Washington's Capitol Hilton Hotel to just talk, to let Marshall reminisce, about his childhood, his formative years, his life as one of the most famous lawyers in American history.

"This is the suite in which President Truman used to hold his poker games," I said. That triggered an important memory for Marshall.

"You know, I once was desperate to get a stay of an execution from Chief Justice [Fred M.] Vinson. It seemed like forever, but I finally got someone who would tell me that he was in this suite, playing poker with President Truman. So I called here and got the stay."

Marshall added, "They have a Supreme Court poker game, I understand, but they don't invite me."

I knew that I was about to talk with a man who bore a thousand scars of racism, of social rejection, of people determined to think of him as just "the Negro justice." I felt that Marshall knew that he could outlive Methuselah and triumph in a thousand legal joustings, but most of his white contemporaries would still wish to think of him as less than their intellectual — and especially social — equal.

As we settled down in that suite and Marshall began to talk, I became mesmerized by Marshall's candid discussions of his father, his mother, his other relatives, and the forces that shaped their lives. It was clear that he had spent his life regretting the fact that while his mother was a schoolteacher, his father never graduated from high school. Listen to Thurgood:

"The high school notified my grandfather that my father had misbehaved. My grandfather went to the high school, took my father out into the hall, and whipped him in the presence of all the other students. Pop was so embarrassed he never went back to school.

"My father was castrated mentally and emotionally by the bigots who controlled employment and almost all other aspects of life in and around Baltimore. But he and my uncles tried to look out for me — but by exposing me to a destructive world of special privilege. One uncle was the waiter, handyman, everything, on the private railroad car of Diamond Jim Brady. I remember one time I was sitting on the back of Mr. Brady's car, watching him smoke a big black cigar. I was puffing away on my little chocolate cigar. You'll never guess what Diamond Jim and I were talking about: 'Wonder what the poor folks are doing.'

"I told my mother, and with a slap she tamed me down.

"But, God, how my parents sacrificed! During those terrible years in New York we lived in a dingy tenement at a hundred and fortieth Street and Lenox Avenue in Harlem. I later learned that often my father would take a walk and come home furious over signs that said, 'This part of a hundred and thirty-fifth Street guaranteed against Negro invasion.' "

We were nearing lunchtime. "Where's the liquor?" the justice asked.

"I've got gin or Jack Daniel's," I said.

With a wave of disdain, he said: "Gin will make you spin. No Jack Daniel's. I don't drink sour mash. A former member of the Court introduced me to Wild Turkey. I drink it because it has some bite."

I ordered that some Wild Turkey be brought to the suite as Marshall continued to talk about his parents and their influence upon him.

"Once, when my brother and I were both in college, we wanted to go to the Lincoln-Howard University football game on Thanksgiving Day, but we had no money. My parents said they didn't have a dollar to send us. It looked like the two of us would be the only ones stuck in the dorm. But the morning of the game my father telephoned to say that he had sent money by Western Union to get us to the game. I later learned that he had said to our mother, 'Norma, we didn't quite tell the boys the truth. We do have twenty dollars that we've saved for Thanksgiving food. I think I'll "invest" it.' 'Go right ahead,' she said, so he went to a gambling joint and shot craps and got three hundred dollars out of that twenty. When needed, Pop was always there.

"But aside from the sparse financial help they gave, they provided something more precious — a lesson about the pervasiveness of racism, and that Negroes had to have some independence from white people. My father was very sensitive about the tiniest of nuances of racism. He never said, 'That's very white of you.' He said, 'How very black of you,' when a white person said something condescending and stupid. He'd never say, 'There's a nigger in the woodpile.' He'd say, 'There's a white cracker in the woodpile.'

"My mother could drive just as hard as he did. She didn't believe in physical fighting, but if you called her a 'negress' you'd have to fight her. Anyone she really hated she'd call a 'slitch.' Man or woman, anyone racially offensive was a 'slitch,' which was a cross between a slut and a bitch. I once told her, 'Mama, when you go for it, you really go for it.' "

Marshall was aware of the economic troubles of a relatively poor black family trying to get two sons through college. He knew that as a country club steward his father got a trifling salary and had to depend on tips that were often far from bountiful. Marshall explained the economic plight to me this way:

"My daddy earned so little that Mama had to work as a teacher. But she was getting a dollar a day. It was awful. Still, to offer a decent life to us, they bought a house, which they couldn't afford. I listened to my parents whisper about their economic desperation, and I finally said, 'Mama, sell the house.'

"She said stubbornly that she was determined that my brother and I inherit it — a house at the time worth about $4,000. I said, 'Mama, if you died this morning we'd sell the damned house this afternoon.' So she sold it.

"And my father, I mean he told you to stand up for your rights, and no matter what the situation he stood up for his. That's why he lost so many jobs. Most of the time he'd lose 'em, or leave 'em, because he was blond and blue-eyed, and every now and then he'd hear someone say 'nigger,' and there would be an argument, or a fight, and he'd get fired, or leave out of pride.

"He worked like a dog. First, on the railroad as a waiter. He worked the New York Central, and the Pennsylvania and the Atlantic Coastline, and the last job was on the Baltimore and Ohio.

"He also served as a butler, and I don't remember all the families he worked for, but I do remember that he worked for Judge Symington, the father of Stu Symington [who would become senator from Missouri]. He was the judge's head butler.

"One night Mrs. Symington heard a lot of rattling at her front door, where my father and Judge Symington were as drunk as they could be, clamoring to get in. Mrs. Symington saw my father first and jumped all over him, saying, 'You ought to be ashamed of yourself,' and on and on. At the first opening my father said, 'Yes, Mrs. Symington. But if you think I'm in bad shape, you better take a look at the guy I'm carrying.' "

People would whisper that Marshall's father was a drunk, but Marshall recalls that none dared to say it in his presence. He remembers that perhaps once a week, more likely once a month, his frustrated father would "tie one on" and simply come home and go straight to bed. "Poor damn fella," Marshall murmured to himself.

"Well, one butler job he quit," Marshall went on, "was when he was working for a widow woman, very wealthy. One night after dinner for a lot of white people, who were sitting around drinking coffee and brandy, she decided to show off her little poodle, Nanky.

" 'Nanky,' she said, 'show the people which you would rather be, a nigger or dead.'

"The dog lay on its back with four feet up as if to say it would rather be dead. Pop walked right out the door and never went back."

I sat in that old "Truman suite" listening to Justice Marshall and was forced to think about the reasons that America's prisons today are crammed by young black men, Hispanics, the poor, the uneducated, and so many who were jobless at the time of their arrest. The judicial system that Marshall tried so desperately to reform still makes no allowances for human nature, for the acts of desperation of people seeking to survive economically, or even of those who want to enjoy some of the luxuries of life that they see being consumed by others. I shall never forget the answer Justice Marshall gave me when I asked where he got the name Thurgood. He responded:

"Got it from my grandfather. He had two names, and he collected money on both of them. I don't mind mentioning it, because the statute of limitations is long gone. He was in one of those wars after the Civil War — the Cuba business with Teddy Roosevelt, I think. So he was entitled to some veterans' benefit checks, and my grandmother collected checks under both names until she died. Two checks for the same man."

But that bit of illegality had nothing to do with the justice-to-be changing his name from that of an illegal double-dipping grandfather.

"I didn't like having to spell 'Thoroughgood,' so in about the second or third grade I got my mama to change it."

I was not sure whether Marshall suddenly decided that he was telling too much about his parents and grandparents, but it was interesting that he changed the subject drastically:

"This is a funny kinda suite. It's homey. If it's Truman's suite, that's enough for me. Boy, I loved that man. The best thing I loved about him was, when I went to Israel to lay the cornerstone of a building honoring him, I asked the top Israeli why he picked me. He said, 'Hell, I didn't pick you. We gave President Truman a list of six people, and he rejected them all. He said he wanted to be represented by someone who stood up for civil rights when it wasn't fashionable, when it was hard to do so — someone like Thurgood Marshall. So Truman picked you.'

"Boy, that Truman was something!"

Then, inexplicably, Marshall drifted back to memories of his early years, and I could again relate his beginnings to the social trauma of America near the turn of this century. Remember, now, that Marshall was in a two-parent family, both working, both giving educational help and overall guidance. They lacked wealth but were not on welfare. An aunt ran a grocery store. His parents, aunts, and uncles were religious, holding places of prestige in Baltimore churches. The double-check grandparents notwithstanding, young Thurgood's marvelously extended family stood for law and order and social responsibility.

But suddenly Marshall was telling a story of a fatherly adventure and influence that could have made Thurgood just another crime statistic, and certainly no one about whom anyone might write a book six decades later. Thurgood speaks again:

"I used to work for a bootlegger on Sundays. His name was 'Smoothie' — that's all I remember. In my late teens, my father used to take me to Smoothie's operation on an island just outside Baltimore. We'd take a motor launch, climb onto a pier, and face a bunch of guys with machine guns and rifles. Boy, was I impressed!

"The first thing I noticed was the number of rich guys who came to the island to gamble. It was incredible to watch. No IOU's, just cash. The gamblers had their molls nearby playing blackjack, and often I'd hear one of these women shout, 'Daddio, I'm broke again.' And one of the guys would say, 'Bitch, don't you ever save any money?' Then he'd turn to me and say, 'Take this over to her.' And I'd look and see that I had five or six thousand dollars in my hand. I'd rush the money over to his moll.

"Every Sunday night Smoothie would close the operation by asking a guy named Warren to bring a box of decks of cards. They'd shuffle a deck and the gamblers would bet five thousand dollars on a cut of the cards — all cash at risk."

I asked Thurgood if the island never got raided, or if the bootleggers were paying off Maryland officials.

"With all the machine guns out there, who was gonna raid 'em? They were paying off somebody. They took one bottle of genuine whiskey and turned it into twenty-four bottles of bootleg stuff, which they took right into Baltimore and sold it."

I asked Thurgood if he and his father had "totin' privileges," a term applied to the practice of many white employers of letting black workers take canned goods or other merchandise home in lieu of cash. Marshall emphasized that he and his father never took home any of the abominable cut bootleg booze, but that they were allowed to take home one bottle of the "good booze."

I asked Thurgood if this adventure into criminality had influenced Uncle Fearless to call him a bum. Marshall said Uncle Fearless never knew of this bootlegging adventure that lasted for about a year. "Nobody knew but Pop and me," Marshall said. "We were scared to tell anybody."

Booze. How many emotionally castrated black men, like Marshall's father, have tried to drown their sense of humiliation in alcohol? I knew that this was such a hard subject for any proud man of great achievement to talk about, but I had to ask Justice Marshall:

"Did your mother drink at all?" Again, he was remarkably honest in his remembrances:

"She was about a one-drink-a-day person. But I'd get her drunk every Mother's Day because she was a sucker for sweet drinks, and I'd just put a lot of Cointreau and stuff in her glass, real thick. On Mother's Day they drink it. My mother was a lot like a friend of mine, a girl in New York, who would drink any kind or amount of alcohol if it was in a Coca-Cola. She never liked liquor, she liked the damned Coke."

Suddenly, Justice Marshall was telling me a story that influenced his life that had nothing to do with booze. It was about a more toxic substance, called racism, and how it killed his brother. He spoke of William Aubrey:

"He went to Lincoln and graduated in 'twenty-six. Then he went to the Howard University Medical School, and he interned at Providence Hospital in Baltimore. He was in private practice for a couple of years . . . and then the TB showed up. He had one lung removed, and he survived. After five years they said he was completely cured.

"Strange thing about doctors and nurses who get cured of TB. They stayed in TB work. Aubrey went to schools in New England, the South, the West Coast, to study all that stuff about the chest. I think he was one of the first members of the College of Chest Surgeons in Delaware.

"He wound up running a TB sanitarium, but not getting credit for it. He never was made the top man. He started out as an assistant, and ended up as the assistant, and might have had twenty white people promoted over him. I used to tell him to fight about it, but he was not a fighter. He was a nice peaceful guy, bless him. But the last thing they did . . . they put a guy over him who not only was not a doctor, but who knew nothing about medicine. The officials insisted that he clear everything with this guy. He told 'em he wasn't gonna do it. They said, 'Do it or go.'

"One morning he called me, and I told him to tell them to go to hell. I said, 'Why not go out [into private practice] and make yourself some money, boy?' He said that would be giving up on all the poor people in the sanitarium who needed him. He hung up and just sat grieving about it.

"His wife went to the market, and when she came back he was dead. From his heart. His heart just gave out."

When Marshall graduated from high school — thanks to his teachers' compassionate concern for his mother — he could not go to the University of Maryland because Negroes were not admitted. He did not want to go to all-black Morgan State because he then regarded it as an abominable excuse for a college, far below its current high status. He chose to go to a small private school for blacks, Lincoln University in Oxford, Pennsylvania.

The costs of tuition, room, and board at Lincoln totaled more than $300 a year, which his family could not afford, so Marshall worked at many campus jobs. The first was in the school bakery, where he and others kneaded bread and cooked pies and cakes for 360 people. Marshall described with relish how he appropriated a loaf of hot bread every night, slitting the top and filling it with a pound of "confiscated" fresh butter. "God, what heavenly eating," he recalled. He had lost no appetite from his knowledge that he and the other bread kneaders worked without shirts, sweating profusely in the incredibly hot bakery. "They didn't need to put salt in the bread; the sweat took care of that," he said. The college would wait a day to serve the bread to the students on the assumption that "the fresher it is, the more they will eat."

Marshall was no less irresponsible during his undergraduate college days than he had been as a high school senior. He was suspended, or on the verge of being thrown out of Lincoln, every year. He was accused of being involved in drunken celebrations after football games, of hazing underclassmen viciously, of leading a strike for better food.

His classmates told me that on the nights before crucial exams, when most students were cramming, Marshall would stay up all night with whoever was foolish enough to join him, playing pinochle or poker. Marshall felt that if he could get a passable grade of three without studying, "Why bust my ass to get a one," which was tops.

His peers remember that the only thing to which Marshall gave his full devotion was chasing women and getting them to join him in guzzling alcohol, and, hopefully, sex. They told me that Marshall was engaged nine times before he first married.

"At *least* nine times," Justice Marshall confessed to me. "At one point I had six fraternity rings out at the same time."

This man, who was the embodiment of "tall, dark, and handsome" at six feet two, with rippling muscles and the skin color of a Cherokee Indian, was adored by the young ladies. As he neared retirement from the Supreme Court, I asked him: "So it's a fact that you spent your college years chasing women and drinking booze?"

Marshall looked at me as if he thought me nuts and said:

"What else is good?"

Marshall's parents had hoped that he would become a dentist and live a more prosperous life than they had known. But his pre-med efforts at Lincoln ran afoul of a professor, H. F. Grimm. This white man (all the professors at Lincoln were white, and Marshall got knocked around by his parents when he revealed he had stupidly stood against a campus uprising of blacks demanding some Negro teachers) taught anthropology and a hygiene course in which Thurgood got into real trouble. Marshall told me:

"He was teaching about sexual intercourse and that sort of thing, and I didn't agree with some of the stuff he was saying. Like he said that you only have intercourse with a woman in order to have a baby. Now he had a simply beautiful wife, and they'd been married for some twenty years, but they had only three children. So I asked him if in all those years he'd screwed his wife only three times. He gave me hell, and then he flunked me. And I had to give up any notion of becoming a dentist. At times I think I'm sorry . . . that I could have made a lot more money as a dentist. Then I tell myself I'm glad. Hell, my hands are too big to put in somebody's mouth. "But Grimm. He flunked me. But he was a great teacher. He was just one of those 'way out' people, like today's 'born again Christians.' I remember being at a White House luncheon where a woman started talking to me about this 'born again' stuff. I said, 'Madam, please. I cannot be born again.' She asked why, and I said, 'My mother's dead, so how am I gonna be born again?' And boy did she get mad. Really mad!"

Many black men of Marshall's era found a sense of manhood that no white oppressor could erase in their chasings and conquests of women. Yet every black "stud" went hunting with a sense that *he* really wanted to be conquered. By the right woman.

The hunt took Marshall and a couple of buddies to a Baptist church in Philadelphia that by reputation was attended by the most beautiful women. At this church Marshall met a young woman named Vivien Burey, a student at the University of Pennsylvania who had grown up in Steelton, Pennsylvania. Asked what about Vivien attracted him to her in ways that other women had not, Marshall told me that he used the same judging system as Robert Weaver, the man who became the first black cabinet officer in U.S. history:

"First you look at a gal's ankles, and if they are attractive, you look at her legs, and then you get right up to her butt, and to her breasts, and if all that's all right, you look at her face. So 'Buster' [Vivien Burey] came through. She had everything. She wasn't beautiful. No way all that beautiful. But she was put together nicely — black hair, black eyes, and *very nice.* She got along with me."

Marshall fell in love with Buster and suggested they get married, provoking her parents to bring her to Baltimore to meet the swashbuckling Thurgood and his parents. Things were going beautifully until the would-be groom's uncle Fearless called Buster aside and said to her what he later would say to her parents:

"I've seen that you are a fine young lady. You ought to beware of Thurgood. He always was a bum, he *is* a bum, and he always will be a bum!"

I once asked Marshall if Uncle Fearless was just joking, and he said, "Hell no! He meant every word."

"Why?"

"Because of my reputation. Hell, when Uncle Fearless died he didn't leave me a penny. He bequeathed $36,000 to Catholic Charities."

Buster saw something better, more promising, in this "bum" than Uncle Fearless did, making it clear to her parents that she wanted to marry Thurgood. When they asked her to wait until she graduated from college, she negotiated a compromise that they would wait until *Thurgood* graduated — and then she and Marshall violated their verbal contract and got married in 1929, in his senior year.

When Thurgood graduated from Lincoln University in 1930 — incredibly with "honors" despite his poker and pinochle playing at exam time — he was a far different man from the one who had gotten drunk, disrupted all sorts of campus activities, insulted professors, and almost gotten himself thrown out as "hopeless." His young bride, Buster, would party and drink with him, but always had the guts to tell him, "You've had enough!" She had calmed his glands so that he didn't need "the hunt" and could redirect his brain toward conquests of information. She told him again and again that he could become someone important, he could make a difference, if he so willed.

Marshall and Buster discussed the realities of being a black college graduate. In those days, the only jobs of prestige that payed good money to blacks were as doctors, dentists, and lawyers because, even as now, there was a shortage of them. There was some prestige in teaching or preaching, but no real money. Buster and Thurgood agreed that, with dentistry lost as an option, he would have to become a lawyer.

Both his state of poverty and the inconvenience of travel outside Maryland told Thurgood that he should study law at the University of Maryland at College Park. When Marshall applied for admission, President R. A. Pearson had an aide write to Marshall to tell him, in effect, to drop dead. Maryland and all the professional schools of all southern state universities rejected black applicants. Some offered the palliative of saying, "But we'll pay the difference between our tuition and the cost of your going to a northern school that accepts Negroes." The Maryland law school offered Marshall nothing. In fact, Thurgood's application provoked Pearson later to draw up a form letter to be given to black applicants:

Under the general laws of this State the University maintains the Princess Anne Academy as a separate institution of higher learning for the education of Negroes. In order to insure equality of opportunity for all citizens of this state, the 1933 Legislature passed Chapter 234, creating partial scholarships at Morgan College [in Baltimore] or institutions outside of the State for Negro students who may desire to take professional courses or other work not given at the Princess Anne Academy.

This infuriated Thurgood. He had endured the anger of seeing his white playmates go off to elementary and high schools that he was barred from attending. He had seen the state pay his teacher mother the wages of a charwoman, compared to what it paid white teachers. He had seen his father castrated psychologically by being relegated to menial jobs. Now Pearson was messing with his future. This insult by his state university reinforced Buster's occasional lectures that there was more to life than drinking booze and having sex. The University of Maryland had imposed a humiliation that Marshall would never forget.

Thurgood and Buster told his parents that he wanted to attend the Howard University Law School in the District of Columbia, but that they couldn't afford it. "You're going," his mother said. "I'll pawn my engagement and wedding rings to help you." She did. And never got them back.

You begin to learn something about the lost brainpower, the waste of talent, the failure to tap minority leadership potential, when you listen to Marshall tell of his metamorphosis at Howard. There he fell under the influence of the dean, Charles H. Houston, a black man already distinguished by his record at Amherst and at the Harvard Law School. Marshall spoke to me reverently of his mentor:

"Charlie Houston was one of the greatest lawyers I've ever been privileged to know. He was a perfectionist of the first order. I have seen him writing a brief and spending the whole day looking for one word — just the right word. The nearest to him would be Bill Hastie [professor and later a federal judge], who also was a perfectionist.

"I never was and never will be a perfectionist. All I've ever been interested in was getting the job done as well as I could, without trying to be perfect. But Charlie was dedicated, and he insisted that we all be dedicated. I don't know of anything in the legal history that concerns the rights of Negroes that Charlie Houston did not have an effect on.

"We called Houston 'cement drawers' and 'iron shoes' because he banged our heads with his belief in dedication. He set up a flat rule that any professor could take five points off your finals score without giving a reason. So you tried to please. Houston instilled in you the idea that the state, the school, the professors were giving you something for nothing, and that you had to *give something back.* A lot of people have forgotten Charlie, but I ain't about to forget him."

Marshall and his wife had all the financial troubles their parents had predicted when they broke their pledge not to get married before finishing their education. The years in law school were financial misery, alleviated only by the couple's excitement over the personal interest Dean Houston had taken in Thurgood. Just before Marshall's graduation from law school in 1933, Dean Roscoe Pound of the Harvard Law School offered him a fellowship that would have given him and Buster living expenses for a year and allowed him to earn a doctor of jurisprudence degree.

But Houston had set a fire burning in Marshall's belly, a rage to go out into the legal profession immediately and reverse the myriad injustices of Maryland and America. This neophyte lawyer had some personal scores to settle. "Stupid, stupid," Marshall says of himself and his decision to reject Dean Pound's offer.

"So I turned it down, went into private practice, and my first year I lost between three and four thousand dollars," Marshall recalled. "Shows how smart I am. I would have had three or four thousand in my pocket, and I ended up with nothing."

Marshall recalls those private practice days as "a scuffle, that's all. I'd bring lunch for two one day, and my secretary, Little Bits [Lucille Ward], would bring lunch for two the other day. The phone company would call up and say that they were going to disconnect my phone. I would bluff and say, 'You gonna disconnect *my* phone? Do you realize I'm a lawyer? You mess with my phone and I'll sue you until *you* pay *me.* . . . As a matter of fact, you call me one more time and I'm going to rip this phone off the wall and throw it out the goddamn window.' And they'd say, 'It's all right, Mr. Marshall, it's all right.' "

It was Marshall's good fortune to get a telephone call one day from John Murphy, who helped to run the *Afro-American* newspapers, black-owned publications that were in their financial heyday. Marshall figures that even in the 1930s, John Murphy was pulling in $120,000–$180,000 a year. Thurgood was asked to come to see Murphy, who, it turned out, wanted him to take over legal matters that had been in the hands of Warren McClinton, a lawyer with whom Marshall had once worked. Marshall told Murphy that it would be unethical for him to take on McClinton's cases. Murphy said that Thurgood should simply call McClinton, who told Marshall: "It's all right. Murphy can hire you, but I know it will be temporary. You'll fuck it all up and he'll come back to me."

So Marshall took over the settling of some real estate problems that Murphy had and got them straightened out promptly. He called Murphy and said, "Everything's okey-doke."

Murphy said, "Great, send me a bill." Marshall turned to Little Bits and instructed her to send a bill for a certain amount. Then he paused and said, "That's just too much. It doesn't make sense to demand that kind of money and lose a client." So he gave Miss Ward another figure, then hesitated, saying, "That's so small that it may give the impression that I don't know what I'm doing, so I'm going to live or die with the bigger bill."

"Send that by messenger," Marshall instructed.

"You can't do that. It will look like you're hungry," Little Bits said.

"Well, goddamit, I *am* hungry!" said Marshall, whose lean, almost bony frame confirmed it.

"No!" said Little Bits, so the bill went by regular mail.

The next day a messenger delivered the check with a handwritten note from Murphy saying, "Nice going. Get going on the other stuff."

Marshall chuckled as he waved the check and said, "Little Bits, call up and tell a few friends to come up to the house, 'cause we're gonna have some lunch, dinner, and everything else at one time."

Marshall still chuckled half a century later as he told me that he "took the check and cashed it as fast as hell, and went by and got a steak about *that* thick, and a bottle of liquor. I took all that and went to the house and Buster cooked it all up real good, and we just drank and ate and laughed ourselves silly. At that time I was telling myself that practicing law was a glorious way to make a living. Trouble was, when that meal was over, I fell back into the realization that I didn't have any other clients like John Murphy."

It was his inability to make a living as a private-practice lawyer in these toughest years of the Great Depression that pushed Marshall into his fateful alliance with the NAACP. Houston, who had gone to New York as chief counsel of the NAACP, knew that Marshall, like all but a few blacks, was in financial distress, so he encouraged the Baltimore branch of the NAACP to hire his favorite student, knowing that this would enable him to throw a bit of work to Thurgood.

The restricted files of the NAACP Legal Defense Fund, to which I was granted access, are loaded with funny and sometimes moving stories of the struggles of Marshall, Houston, and the NAACP to survive financially in the 1930s.

At one point, Houston sent Marshall a check for $50, causing Marshall to write back:

Dear Charlie:

Received the check. You cannot imagine how much I needed it or appreciated it. I have had a terrible month and everything has been in a jam. However, I think I can make out all right now.

On another occasion Houston wrote to Walter White:

The Association sent Thurgood Marshall a $35 advance for travel expenses to St. Louis Conference. Marshall did not go to the conference. . . . He still has the $35. . . . Write a letter to Marshall [and ask that] he please refund the $35.

But Marshall was less concerned about returning money than in settling a score with the University of Maryland law school. On September 21, 1934, Marshall wrote Houston asking, "What is the proposed action on the University of Maryland? . . . The only thing I say is that something should be done and a suit should be filed."

Thurgood was not ahead of his law school dean and mentor. Houston had decided months before that the future of black people in the Jim Crow states would remain bleak as long as they could not attend the colleges, universities, and professional institutions that they supported with their sweat and their tax dollars. Houston and NAACP lawyers in Texas and Oklahoma, Arkansas and Alabama, were working feverishly on a strategy for knocking down legally the bars of racial exclusion in institutions of higher learning.

Marshall, still scarred by Pearson's insult, wasn't waiting for any "game plan" from New York. He wanted to go after Maryland immediately. His proud former dean, Houston, sent him $100 of NAACP money and said, "Go, man, go!"

CHAPTER FOUR

REVENGE—THEN A NATIONAL CRUSADE

SERVING as the lawyer for the Baltimore chapter of the NAACP at age twenty-six exposed Marshall to some bizarre new faces of bigotry in that city. He thought nothing could top the humiliation he had experienced when he rushed to a streetcar to go home, knowing that he could not enter a bathroom in downtown Baltimore, only to soil his trousers on his front stoop. He would hear stories as a lawyer that made him shake his head in disbelief, and sometimes weep, over the cruelties that were imposed upon human beings in the name of racial purity. It made his blood boil that there were so many areas in Maryland where there was only one high school, for whites, with black teenagers left bereft of any meaningful opportunity for learning. He began to draft lawsuits to remedy that situation.

But nothing preoccupied young Marshall to the point that he muted his anger toward the University of Maryland law school.

"The sonsabitches turned away the guy who finished number one at a better law school — Howard," Marshall said at many social occasions, when his memory and anger had been refurbished by a cocktail or two.

In 1934, Marshall became aware that a black Baltimorean, Harold Arthur Seaborne, had applied to enter the University of Maryland law school, only to have President Pearson reject him, in writing, in a way that made it clear that Seaborne was eligible in every respect — except for his "Negro blood." Marshall was striving hard to earn a few more bucks by representing the NAACP in the Baltimore area. So he began the first of his legal crusades by looking for a student he could recommend to Houston as the candidate for a lawsuit against the University of Maryland. His mentor warned him to be careful that he did not open himself to a charge of barratry — of a lawyer instigating lawsuits.

Soon Marshall rejoiced that he could write Houston that he had his candidate: a young graduate of Amherst College (Houston's alma mater), the grandson of the late bishop of the African Methodist Episcopal Church, Abraham Gaines, named Donald Murray.

Under Marshall's guidance, Murray sent a registered letter to Pearson asking for admission to the law school. He enclosed a $2 money order to defray the cost of the president's reply. On March 8, 1935, Pearson sent the money order back with a letter saying:

> May I bring to your attention the exceptional facilities open to you for the study of Law in Howard University in Washington. . . . It's rated Class "A." It is fully approved by the American Bar Association and it is a member of the Association of American Law Schools. . . . The cost of attending the Howard University School of Law is only about $135 per year. This is considerably less than is paid in the Day School for Law in the University of Maryland — approximately $203 per year.

That letter was a salted dagger, plunged into an emotional wound that Marshall had carried for years. He rushed to prepare documents asking the Baltimore City Court to issue a writ of mandamus (a court's *command* that a certain thing be done) requiring the University to admit Murray to law school in September. The lawsuit was filed on April 20, provoking extraordinary media attention.

This case, tried on June 18, 1935, before Judge Eugene O'Dunne, was a classic that set the pattern for the wave of civil rights litigation that was to come. Marshall got, pretrial, an admission from Maryland's registrar, W. M. Hillegeist, that the university had not admitted a single Negro since it was placed under state supervision in 1920. Brash young black lawyer Marshall went *personally* to Pearson's office, demanding to read the minutes of the meeting of the board of regents in which it was decided that Murray would not be admitted. In the midst of heavy publicity, Pearson let Thurgood read the minutes.

Houston came to Maryland at the trial's beginning to take charge, an indication that he knew a historic case when he saw one. He allowed his protégé, Marshall, to introduce Murray to the court, and to establish his residential and academic qualifications for admission to Maryland. Then the older "perfessor," Houston, put on a clinic, with Marshall and another attorney, William I. Gosnell, watching in admiration.

"If Your Honor please," Houston said, "since Dr. Pearson is an adverse party and also, very obviously, from the letters here, a hostile witness . . . I ask the privilege of proceeding with leading questions."

"All right, go ahead," said Judge O'Dunne.

Houston first pried out of Pearson an admission that the Princess Anne Academy, the separate-for-Negroes "Easton branch" of the university, was really an unaccredited junior college whose faculty contained only one person with an earned college degree. The reality of separate but *unequal* was firmly established.

"In your extension department, are Negro students admitted to extension work?" Houston asked.

"We admit no Negroes to our extension work," Pearson replied.

Houston then elicited an admission that in the state of Maryland the University of Maryland's law school was the only one accredited by the American Bar Association.

Marshall watched with pleasure mixed with anger as Houston cited the 1930 U.S. census showing that the population of the state of Maryland included Caucasians, Negroes, Mexicans, American Indians, Chinese, Japanese, Filipinos, and others. Houston then got Pearson to admit that, without a fuss or special deliberations by the board of regents, the University would admit Mexicans, Chinese, Japanese — all racial groups in the state except for Negroes. With biting sarcasm, Houston got Pearson to concede that he would admit a Mexican from Mexico City, but no Negro citizen, however big a taxpayer the Negro might be.

Houston then forced President Pearson to read to the court the minutes of the board of regents in which Murray's application was discussed.

Judge O'Dunne watched almost with a scowl as Pearson read from minutes about "Application from Negro to enter the School of Law," concluding with the notation "It was the unanimous decision of the Board that the application of Mr. Murray . . . be denied."

It took only minutes for O'Dunne to make up his mind. At 5:05 P.M. on June 18, Houston sent a telegram to Walter White at NAACP headquarters in New York:

MANDAMUS GRANTED TODAY ADMITTING MURRAY TO LAW SCHOOL
UNIVERSITY MARYLAND

Marshall, Murray, Houston, Gosnell, and others celebrated with gusto their first great triumph in the then-nascent struggle to deliver equality of educational opportunity to the children of former slaves. But Marshall, Houston, White, and others at the NAACP would soon learn what remains a truism in 1993: *Where a minority is involved, no rights are ever permanent, no victory securely won.*

On June 25 Judge O'Dunne made the court's command official, decreeing that Murray had to be admitted to the law school on September 25. The judge made it clear that no appeal by the university or the state attorney general was to keep Murray out of the classroom on opening day of the law school.

Still, the university appealed, asking the Court of Appeals to hear the case before July 1, 1935, hoping to avoid admitting Murray. The Court of Appeals declined, saying it would hear the case in its October term, meaning that Murray would be in law school when the appeal was argued.

Meanwhile, Marshall and the old pros in NAACP headquarters in New York realized that the *Murray* case was the start of something big. *Time* magazine, the *New York Herald-Tribune,* and the *New York Times* had written about the great legal breakthrough in Baltimore. White and Houston wanted to be sure that members of the NAACP branches understood why they had committed so much in terms of time and resources getting one black man into the Maryland law school. On September 4, 1935, they sent a long message to each branch, the heart of which said:

> The Murray case is not an attempt to obtain higher education for a selected few; it cuts much deeper than that. The denial to Negroes of the higher branches of education reflects an attitude and determination on the part of the whites to exclude Negroes from that preparation which would give them a chance to compete on equal terms with whites in the struggle for existence in America. The inferior training condemns the Negro generally to a subordinate position and perpetuates his inferiority.

Marshall and Houston already had their eyes on other states, especially Virginia and Missouri, hoping to open the doors to professional school for thousands of black people. But August of that grim Depression year of 1935 brought these militant black lawyers down to the reality that the war over Murray and the university was far from won.

By August of 1935 Pearson was out as president of the university, and H. Curley Byrd was acting president. Byrd took the gambit of trying to sway the Court of Appeals with the argument that many white parents would feel that their daughters were in sexual peril if a Negro were admitted, that these parents were threatening to withdraw their daughters, which would damage the university grievously.

Byrd approved a petition to the Court of Appeals stating that some five hundred of the university's students were females, and that since Judge O'Dunne's order to admit Murray, other Negroes had applied for admission to the law school, the school of pharmacy, and even the undergraduate college. The petition said Byrd had received a letter from a white man, George M. Quirk of Washington, D.C., saying that he had three daughters enrolled at Maryland and that he wished to remove them if a Negro were admitted.

Marshall sent a sarcastic note to Houston saying, "We ought to point out that the racists pay blacks to go study in Northern states. Let's see how many white Maryland girls are on Northern campuses with blacks, and whether this has put them in sexual peril."

No such courtroom argument was necessary, however, because the Court of Appeals flatly rejected the Byrd gambit. It said it absolutely would not advance its hearing, meaning that Murray was going to the law school.

Well, maybe!

Byrd's resort to sexual scare tactics was nothing compared with the bombshell that Murray dropped on Marshall. On September 17, just eight days before Murray was to enroll, Marshall sent this telegram to Houston:

> MURRAY CANNOT RAISE MONEY BAD SUMMER FOR WORK FAMILY
> CANNOT RAISE IT HAVE BEEN TRYING TO RAISE MONEY IN CITY BUT
> WITHOUT SUCCESS COULD NOT GET A LOAN EVERYTHING LOOKS
> BAD SISTER IS TEACHING AND COULD PAY BACK THE LOAN
> THURGOOD

The dumbfounded Houston exclaimed, "After all our fucking work, that sonofabitch can't enroll?"

On September 19 Houston sent Walter White this memo:

> A letter from Thurgood Marshall [states] that we will have to advance $160 as a loan [to Donald Murray]. I regret sincerely even the temporary expenditure of this money but we must get Murray in the University; otherwise our case will become moot and you can see what that would do to our plans and program.

Here was a situation that spoke pathetically about the inability of poor people to get justice in America. Marshall did not have $5 of spare money, let alone $160. Nor did Houston, White, or the nation's oldest civil rights organization, the NAACP. So it became necessary for those involved to do some fast wheeling and dealing to get Murray registered.

Walter White sent an urgent telegram and letter of September 19 to the famous lawyer and fighter for racial justice, Morris Ernst, who was vacationing on Nantucket Island. Ernst was a trustee of something called the Garland Fund, which had given modest support to some NAACP efforts. White didn't want University of Maryland lawyers to know that the Garland Fund was financing Murray's admission. He proposed that the $160 be "laundered" through Carl Murphy, publisher of the *Afro-American* newspapers, who was intensely interested in breaking the color barrier at Maryland. Houston instructed Marshall to deliver the Garland Fund check to Murphy, who would then "loan" $160 to the Murray family, with precise legal papers drawn up as to how and when they would repay it.

Ernst and Murphy delivered, and on September 24 Marshall wired Houston:

MURRAY REGISTERED FEES PAID NOTE TO MURPHY PICTURES TAKEN OUTSIDE BUILDING DEAN HOWELL COOPERATIVE SUGGESTED THAT MURRAY SIT IN SEPARATE SEAT THIS OBJECTED TO, AND FOR FIRST FEW DAYS BEFORE SEATS ARE ASSIGNED HE WILL SIT ANY PLACE WILL ATTEMPT TO GET STUDENTS ASSIGNED BESIDE MURRAY WHO HAVE NO PREJUDICE

The editor of Murphy's *Afro-American* sent a reporter to the campus to do a feature story. The reporter claimed he couldn't find any students who welcomed Murray's admission. He said they all vowed to get the black guy out by getting teachers to flunk him, or through whatever means they could find.

Marshall and Houston did not just convince Judge O'Dunne to mandate Murray's admission to the university. They didn't just beg and conspire to get $160 for the first half of his year's tuition and fees. They wet-nursed Murray into an understanding of the importance of his not flunking out, of his putting study ahead of personal appearances. They provided him with a dollar or two of "spending change" from time to time. In 1935 the civil rights movement was a very personal labor of love — and, for Marshall, of sweet revenge.

But revenge was not saccharine when there was a chance that the Court of Appeals would reverse O'Dunne and tell Murray to get out and go to Howard or some other all-black law school. Lawyers awaiting decisions in such cases not only keep fingers in the wind, but they look for every occasion, ethical or not, to get advance indications as to whether they will be winners or losers. On December 6 Marshall wrote Houston:

> Dear Charlie:
> I just attended a luncheon of the Junior Bar Association. Judge [Morris A.] Soper was one of the speakers. He requested me to tell you that he was seated beside Judge Bond of the Court of Appeals at a dinner, and that Judge Bond was very much impressed with your argument of the Murray case, however, he made no intimation of the probabilities of the case. I am taking the liberty of sending Judge Soper a copy of our brief.
> No news on the Murray case.
>
>   Thurgood

Judge Soper had in fact intimated to Marshall the truth about the leanings of Chief Judge Carroll T. Bond and the seven other members of the Court of Appeals — all of them white, of course. On January 15, 1936, Marshall was able to fire off a telegram to Walter White declaring MURRAY CASE DECIDED OUR FAVOR.

Bond spoke for a unanimous court in holding that the law school was discriminating illegally against black residents and that as the only accredited law school available, it had to admit blacks. But the door was left open for creation of a real law school for blacks.

Houston, Marshall, and Murray had for the first time made white judges acknowledge that "separate but equal" was a grotesque fiction. Their joy over the Court of Appeals victory, however, was muted by their personal knowledge that they believed that the U.S. Constitution entitled them to a lot more than Judge Bond had given them — that is, a clear-cut outlawing of Jim Crow.

But how to get it? West Virginia, Missouri, Maryland, Virginia, Oklahoma, and Kentucky had rushed to pass laws giving blacks scholarships if they would just be "nice" and seek graduate or professional study in a northern university. In several Jim Crow states there were murmurings in legislatures about appropriating money to set up medical, law, and other schools "just for Negroes."

With a lot of financial and emotional help from Marshall and Houston, Murray was doing well, and seemed on his way to graduating with his law degree. But in 1937 Curley Byrd was asking Maryland's attorney general Herbert R. O'Conor if he could legally oust Murray and another black law student, given the fact that the state legislature had recently provided out-of-state scholarships for Negroes seeking law educations. O'Conor's ruling to Byrd was that the legislative act was "not retroactive."

Murray graduated in June 1938. On the sixth of that month he wrote Walter White: "I have been aware during my three years in Law School of the responsibility which rested upon me — as you succinctly put it in your letter of encouragement early in my course — of developing within the minds of the students and faculty 'a new concept of the Negro.' As I told Thurgood, I feel that in some small way I have."

Marshall and Houston wanted to move on, to fight bigger wars in the field of education. They learned, however, that Byrd was a don't-give-up racist of unmitigated gall. In September 1939, four years after Judge O'Dunne ordered the admission of Murray, William H. Murphy, the nephew of *Afro-American* publisher Carl Murphy and a graduate of Oberlin College, applied for admission to the law school at Maryland. Byrd invited William Murphy in personally to lecture him on why it would be "better for race relations if you went to the Howard University law school."

Carl Murphy appealed to Marshall, who by this time was chief counsel of the NAACP. When the NAACP threatened legal action, Byrd acquiesced in the admission of the third black student in the law school. Hoping to expose and humiliate Byrd, White sent a telegram to the *Baltimore Sun:*

SUNPAPERS WILL BE INTERESTED IN REGISTRATION WEDNESDAY UNIVERSITY LAW SCHOOL OF WILLIAM H. MURPHY. MURPHY, AIDED BY NAACP THREATENED INSTITUTE COURT ACTION SIMILAR TO MURRAY CASE BUT PRESIDENT CURLEY BYRD ON SATURDAY TELEPHONED CARL MURPHY THAT APPLICANT WOULD BE ADMITTED.

Marshall knew that William H. Murphy was admitted because Curley Byrd was under duress, not just from the NAACP and the *Afro-American,* but from the state's most powerful newspaper, the *Baltimore Sun.* It was clearer to Marshall than ever that he would not live long enough to see any right he won for black people totally secured. Like freedom in general, for all people in all times, there would always be someone, or some force, trying to erase liberty, blur justice, restore one race or one bad man to power. Marshall knew that he would have to watch Curley Byrd as long as he was president at Maryland, but that he could not let Byrd divert him from carrying out legal challenges to bigotry in education in other states.

CHAPTER FIVE

WARFARE AMONG NAACP BLACKS

WHEN MARSHALL made his first official connection with the NAACP in 1934, he had no way of knowing that the organization was in peril because of conflict among blacks. Neither Marshall nor the white liberals who at the time still controlled the organization could have dreamed how many crises would be brought on because black people could not rise above ideological disputes and power grabs and get their act of freedom together. A withering internal war plus tax law pressures incited by racists would lead to a destructive schism between the "regular" NAACP leaders and the legal staff, which soon became a separate "Legal Defense Fund." An ugly, emotional conflict would eventually arise over racial intermarriage.

But no conflict between NAACP blacks was more basic, because it kept coming back in various mutations, than the struggle that began in 1934 over whether the NAACP should fight for total integration, or should accept some compromises within the concept of "separate but equal." Marshall would eventually become embroiled in this war over NAACP policy, but in 1934 it was a pit-bull battle between Walter White, the light-skinned, blue-eyed Georgia "Negro" who had succeeded James Weldon Johnson as secretary, and W. E. B. Du Bois, the black intellectual who had been a founder of the NAACP, and the only editor of its voice, the *Crisis* magazine.

I found in the Library of Congress's restricted files of the NAACP Legal Defense Fund a record of that personal war that is tawdry, laughable, pathetic, and in all dimensions instructive as to why it has taken so long for black people to get out from under the heels of white people. Those records shattered my ideas about who and what Du Bois was. I'd been taught that he was a black revolutionary, quick to fight the "accommodationist," the historic "Uncle Tom," Booker T. Washington. But in 1934, the record makes clear, Du Bois was the egotistical accommodationist, willing to tolerate Jim Crow to protect the jobs of some blacks, while White was the one crying "desegregation or die." Simmering rancor over this issue had caused Du Bois to go back to Atlanta University in 1934, editing the *Crisis* in his way, at a geographical and ideological distance from NAACP headquarters in New York.

In the January issue of 1934 Du Bois wrote an editorial suggesting that it might be wise for blacks to accommodate some measure of racial segregation. When White saw it he almost lapsed into apoplexy. He alerted Du Bois to his indignation and then sat down to write an uncompromising assault on segregation in any and every form — which he expected would be published in the *Crisis.*

Du Bois thought himself untouchable by the NAACP "minions" who had come in the wake of his work as a founder, but he was smart enough to protect his flanks. He telephoned John S. Brown, Jr., a prominent and powerful NAACP supporter in New York City, and told him that the new and less than secure secretary, White, was out to get him. Brown quickly got eight other influential NAACP supporters to lend their names to the following letter to *Afro-American* publisher Carl Murphy:

> We beg to advise you of a condition, popularly rumored to have arisen within the N.A.A.C.P. and The Crisis, which we feel constrained to call to your attention. If the sort of thing alleged is permitted to be carried out, it may or will result in the loss of Dr. W. E. B. Du Bois to the Association and the magazine.
>
> It is hardly necessary for us to remind you that both of these instruments of redress, the Association and The Crisis, are the children of Dr. Du Bois' brain and earlier efforts. Everybody in the country recognizes this fact. Dr. Du Bois' name, due partly to this fact, is indelibly associated in the minds of the colored people all over this broad land with the two organizations. They would as soon think of the United States without its Mississippi River as they would think of the two organizations without Dr. Du Bois.
>
> Therefore, any severance, implied or real, of Dr. Du Bois from this work will be looked upon as a great calamity to the organizations and to the people they are designed to protect, defend, and

advance. Unless, however, something is done and done promptly, this catastrophe will take place. Already currents are moving, steps are being taken, impossible situations are being created, which will surely make this catastrophe a certainty.

Murphy had no idea what the dispute was about. He replied: "I have confidence in the members of the board that they recognize the worth of Dr. Du Bois, and that they will do nothing to injure him or the Association." In the meantime, Du Bois' backdoor campaign caused Ruby Darrow, wife of the great Chicago lawyer Clarence Darrow, to write White, Senator Arthur Capper of Kansas, and others to inquire as to who was trying to oust Du Bois.

White gave them all a nonanswer, saying only that the NAACP was allowing Du Bois to edit and control the *Crisis* from Atlanta, and paying him $1,200 a year to do so. In fact, White was going to the mat with the man who considered himself a black icon. He sent a telegram to Du Bois asserting that racists were using his editorial in the *Crisis* to justify denying twenty black families admission to a West Virginia Homestead Subsistence Colony — this, White said, after he had gotten Mrs. Franklin D. Roosevelt to insist that the colony not be segregated. He also insisted that his statement opposing segregation be printed in the February issue of the *Crisis*.

White, *the chief executive* of the NAACP, was stunned to receive the following response from Du Bois:

My Dear Mr. White:

I have your article on segregation. I will not publish it. You may in the March number of THE CRISIS express your idea of the attitude of the N.A.A.C.P. on segregation but you have no more right than I have to speak for the Association, and your statement that the Association has never budged on segregation is false. If and when the Association makes an official pronouncement as to its position on segregation, a thing which it has never yet done, THE CRISIS will, of course, print it and give it the utmost prominence. But you are not the Board of Directors and you have no business to speak for them.

Very sincerely yours,
W. E. B. Du Bois

White knew that, more than a decade after James Weldon Johnson became the NAACP's first black secretary, the organization could not function effectively without the support of its chairman, Joel E. Spingarn, his brother, Arthur, and the other nationally respected, absolutely dedicated white people who were on the board of directors.

But White felt, as is often the case in corporations and associations, that directors are there merely to rubber-stamp the decisions of the chief executive. White was a hater of government-imposed or black-sanctioned racial segregation. Lawyer Houston would tolerate no compromise on the issue. White felt Du Bois had let his ego, his yearnings for personal power, confuse him with regard to the ultimate aspirations of black people. White had no doubt that he could speak for the NAACP as confidently as a Henry Ford could speak for the Ford Motor Company.

So in that article that Du Bois refused to publish, White committed the NAACP in perpetuity to a war against racial segregation in any form.

Doubly shocking for White — who carried the "burden" of looking "white" — was the "confidential" memorandum that he got from Joel Spingarn.

> You should not make any statement that indicates that you are speaking officially for the N.A.A.C.P., except as to its *past and present status*. The Board may reverse itself on any issue at any time, and cannot be committed by you or anyone else as to its *future programme*. Dr. DuBois is suggesting certain possible future plans, and in regard to these future plans, you should express only "personal" opinions, not "official" opinions. . . .
>
> The Amenia Conference voted in favor of cultural nationalism for the American Negro as the most important thing for the Negro to aim at. This represents the attitude of most of the Negro intelligentsia, or at least of the most advanced groups, and is akin to what certain advanced groups of Jews are aiming at, such as Ludwig Lewison's opposition to all forms of "assimilation" and the Zionists' desire for political separation. Whether one likes it or not, it is a strong contemporary trend, and is in the direction of self-imposed "segregation."
>
> Confidentially, may I advise you to act carefully when dealing with this whole question, as you are at somewhat [of] a disadvantage? I am not suggesting that you hide your opinions in any way, but that you realize that hundreds of Negroes think you are really a white man whose natural desire is to associate with white men. Many have said this to me about you, and all I suggest is that your opposition to segregation must not seem to spring from a desire to associate with white people. This suggestion is made entirely out of friendly regard.

This memorandum set off a tornado in the stomach of White, who became even more troubled when Spingarn wrote him on January 12 saying:

> As to your suggestion that the Board "define anew its position on segregation" and that "we should in no wise change our attitude," this creates a more difficult problem than you appear to think. The Board has never "defined" its attitude on this subject; it has merely authorized certain concrete steps. The word has become a sort of shibboleth, and unthinking people use it indiscriminately; but surely we cannot attack segregation in the abstract without attacking the Negro college, the Negro church, etc. To distinguish merely between voluntary and involuntary segregation is another way in which unintelligent people try to avoid the difficulty, but that raises more problems than it solves.
>
> I disagree with the direction in which Dr. DuBois seems to be tending, but I think he is doing a service in trying to make the real meaning of the problem clearer than it has been, and certainly a hot controversy on the subject will help to keep interest in the N.A.A.C.P. more lively than ever. I should be very glad to see whatever you may suggest as a proper action for the Board, but of course no action of the Board at any given time can prevent a member or officer from agitating further in favor of a future change of policy.

White replied to both the "confidential" memo and the letter on January 15, saying:

> Dear Mr. Spingarn:
>
> To dispose of the least important aspects of the matter first, I am not disturbed by the fact that there are Negroes who think that my opposition to segregation springs "from a desire to associate with white people." If this were true I long since would have stopped living as a Negro and passed as white when I could associate exclusively with white people. As you of course know, I choose my friends and associates, particularly the former, not on the basis of their race but wholly on mutual points of interest.
>
> If the Association's attitude is not one of opposition to segregation, then, I have misinterpreted it for nearly twenty years. I am frankly not interested in the Association unless that is its policy, not only because of the ideals involved but because all my experience has convinced me that whatever the Negro may do in his churches, lodges, or private affairs he must continue to fight for

integration in public matters and against segregation. Were any other course followed by the Association I could not with a clear conscience continue to work in its cause. I do not in any sense put this as an ultimatum but simply as an honest and frank expression of opinion.

Right now we have to accept Jim Crow schools in the South but I do believe that they are an evil and eventually must go. You and I may never live to see it but I am convinced that we must continue to oppose them not only for our own sakes but for the sakes of white people and colored of future generations.

Ever sincerely,
Walter White

White was not alone in this fight. Charlie Houston was an unyielding foe of racial segregation. So was William H. Hastie, one of Marshall's professors and the man who was to blaze the trail for blacks seeking power within the judiciary by becoming the first black federal judge when President Truman named him to the U.S. Court of Appeals for the Third Circuit in 1949. On January 25, Hastie wrote a withering column in a short-lived journal, *New Negro Opinion*, entitled "DuBOIS, Ex-Leader of Negroes." Hastie said:

For fifty years prejudiced white men and abject, boot-licking, gut lacking, knee bending, favor-seeking Negroes have been insulting our intelligence with a tale that goes like this:

Segregation is not an evil. Negroes are better off by themselves. They can get equal treatment, and be happier too, if they live and move and have their being off by themselves — except, of course, as they are needed by the white community to do the heavy and dirty work, and why should we object to being set off by ourselves if we are with our own people, who are just as good as anyone else.

But any Negro who uses this theoretical possibility as a justification for segregation is either dumb, or mentally dishonest, or else he has, like Esau, chosen a mess of pottage.

On page 20 of The Crisis for January, 1934, Editor DuBois indulges in all these old sophistries and half-truths. If you don't believe it, read for yourself. I refused to believe it until my own eyes had convinced me. DuBois, William Edward Burghart, himself — or not himself — making a puny defense of segregation and hair splitting about the difference between segregation and discrimination! Oh, Mr. DuBois! How could you?

It has been a real blow to lose you, Mr. DuBois, and we will not deny that your statement, coming from you, is a powerful weapon in the hands of our enemies.

Oh, Esau!

Marshall recalled this bruising conflict for me:

"I was still a wet-eared lawyer who spent a lot of time worrying about where the next meal was coming from. I didn't really know Du Bois or White. But I know that I read Du Bois' articles in the *Crisis* with astonishment. My heart and soul were devoted to wiping out racial segregation at the University of Maryland, but here was the magazine of the NAACP suggesting a compromise with segregation.

"When you saw that a man of Du Bois' stature was calling for compromise, you became confused. But when I saw what Bill Hastie wrote, my confusion ended. I respected Hastie as much as any man I'd ever known other than my father and Charlie Houston.

"I remember 1934 and Du Bois the way I remember Malcolm X. Their reputations in death became different from what they were in real life."

Actually, Du Bois was on all sides of a debate that would bedevil black Americans for at least the rest of the century. He was manifesting the intellectual schizophrenia that would produce the "black separatists" of the 1960s, and people like journalist Tony Brown, who in the nineties would justify joining the Republican party with an assertion that "integration amounts to nothing more than a tragedy of exaggerated expectations."

The outraged NAACP board, siding with White, tried to wipe away the ambiguities that Du Bois had created by passing a resolution saying:

The National Association for the Advancement of Colored People is opposed both to the principle and the practice of enforced segregation of human beings on the basis of race and color.

Enforced segregation by its very existence carries with it the implication of a superior and inferior group and invariably results in the imposition of a lower status on the group deemed inferior. Thus both principle and practice necessitate unyielding opposition to any and every form of enforced segregation.

The board had tried to send Du Bois a message, even silence him, and, in its May meeting, it approved the following resolution by the new chairman, Dr. Louis T. Wright: "*The Crisis* is the organ of the Association and no salaried officer of the Association shall criticize the policy, work, or officers of the Association in the pages of *The Crisis;* that any such criticism should be brought directly to the Board of Directors and its publication approved or disapproved."

Nonetheless, in the June issue Du Bois took sarcastic note of the board resolution opposing segregation and asked whether the board approved "of the Negro Church or believes in its segregated activities in its 26,000 edifices where most branches of the NAACP meet and raise money to support it."

Still, many members of the board were fearful that if Du Bois resigned, as he threatened to do after the May resolution, the organization would be damaged severely. At the board meeting of June 11, Dr. Wright presented a resolution encouraging Du Bois to reconsider. On June 12, White wrote a bitter letter to Joel Spingarn, saying, "I am thoroughly nauseated at the lack of moral courage on the part of some members of the Board. . . . The results of yesterday's meeting can be construed as nothing more than a moral victory for Dr. Du Bois. . . . When I left the Board meeting yesterday I very definitely had the feeling that with the present constitution of the Board it is no longer possible for me to remain with the Association as its Secretary. . . . My own self-respect will not permit me to do so."

So the board meetings that White said were devoted to "ridiculous and acrimonious discussions" of segregation would have to end. The board would have to choose.

In a June 26, 1934, letter to the board, Du Bois claimed that his freedom of expression had been unfairly curtailed. He asserted that "this organization, which has been great and effective for nearly a quarter of a century, finds itself in a time of crisis and change, without a program, without effective organization, without executive officers, who have either the ability or disposition to guide the NAACP in the right direction.

"These are harsh and arresting charges. I make them deliberately and after long thought. . . .

"I am, therefore insisting upon my resignation, and on July 1st, whether the board acts or does not act, I automatically cease to have any connection whatsoever in any shape or form with the NAACP."

At its July 9 meeting the board accepted "with the deepest regret" the resignation of Du Bois as editor of the *Crisis,* as a member of the board of directors, as director of publications and research, as a member of the board of the Crisis Publishing Company, and as a member of the Spingarn Medal Committee. Du Bois returned to a professorship at Atlanta University.

A happy twenty-six-year-old lawyer in Baltimore, Thurgood

Marshall, felt free to write Houston that it was time to move against other aspects of segregation in education.

Almost everything about Marshall's life before he went to the Howard University Law School indicated that his uncle Fearless was a sterling judge of human behavior. Thurgood was a "bum," and seemed destined forever to be one. If you can figure out why he was that way as a teenager and young man, you can fashion programs to wipe out America's current problems of young people guzzling booze, using drugs, producing babies out of wedlock, drifting into street gangs and criminal behavior that defies explanation. I reiterate that Marshall was not some wretchedly poor latchkey kid growing up with only a mother who was off working all day, as is the plight of millions of kids now. Marshall grew up with two working parents and an extended family of people who earned decent money and knew how to cope in a world where black people had to know "their place."

Thurgood learned his "place" early, when his parents, uncles, grandparents, talked about lynchings. Once, at Lincoln University, a fellow student from the north asked Marshall if he had ever tried to go to a whites-only movie theater in Baltimore.

"No," Marshall said.

"Why not?"

"Hell, you just didn't do it. Shit, you were told in some way every day of your life that you couldn't do it. Say we were cowed, brainwashed, but it never left your mind that you could get your ass killed just trying to go see a goddamned Tarzan movie."

When I heard that story from Marshall I thought, wrongly perhaps, that the trauma of being unable to go to a movie house could not explain his many years of irresponsible behavior. It seemed obvious that having a father who seemed to vacillate between anger and insecurity took an emotional toll. Marshall had learned to gulp booze early — from his father, who exposed him not only to the fast life of the Diamond Jim Bradys, but to the criminal world of violent, big-bucks bootleggers. You sense that some deep secrets are being held back when Marshall talks of the frequency with which his father got drunk, then later drops a floating comment about his mother's relationship to his father: "Maybe she was afraid of him."

We have millions of psychiatrists and psychologists who cannot tell us for sure what the relationship, the strengths and weaknesses, of mothers and fathers have on the children.

It is clear in Thurgood's life, as in that of millions of American kids, that he needed the intervention of an outside force more disciplined and dominant than his family. What is even clearer to me is that Marshall's life gives great glory to teachers who have high standards and who care enough to press and prod youngsters in whom they see great potential. Marshall and the nation owe a grotesque sort of debt to the bigots who wouldn't let Thurgood enroll at the University of Maryland law school. Jim Crow delivered Marshall into the hands of Charles Hamilton Houston, the vice dean at Howard, and Marshall was transported from "bum" to national hero.

Note that title of "vice dean." Racism reigned at Howard as well as at Maryland. Little Howard got most of its financial support from the federal government. Key white members of the Congress didn't want a black man running much of anything, and some had cronies whom they owed a piece of "pork," so they insisted that a white man, Judge Fenton W. Booth, be named the figurehead dean of the law school. Howard's first black president, Mordecai Johnson, joined in this ploy. Houston was wounded to the quick of his heart, but usually dismissed the situation with the comment, "Hell, considering the pennies they're paying me, why should anybody think I'm the dean?"

Marshall thought his mentor was not only the dean, but the essence of black manhood. Houston stood so tall in work ethic and inspiration that neither Marshall nor the few other law students noticed that in terms of brick and mortar, faculty, the library, their law school was a joke by normal American standards. It was located in a three-story former family residence in a block of row houses occupied by black families. There was a walk up to a vestibule where students sat on wooden seats to listen to lectures, the best by Houston and the bigwigs of Washington government that he could lure there. On the second floor was the office in which Houston pounded an ancient typewriter with two fingers, always setting an example of unceasing hard work for his admiring students. They had no hint of the fact that their hard-driving dean had contracted tuberculosis while serving as a GI in France in World War I. Houston always seemed vibrant and impassioned in the chase for justice as he tried to expose his students to everything relating to the law that might give them an advantage.

Marshall took a seemingly macabre delight in telling me, in detail, about the time Houston took his class to observe an autopsy. The coroner warned all students to hold onto something. Marshall, the macho man, scoffed. Then the coroner "slit the guy's belly and rolled it down like a window shade" and the first student who fainted, falling hard to the floor, was Thurgood Marshall.

Houston got to Marshall in ways that no member of his family, or Buster, ever had, or could.

"I never worked hard until I got to the Howard Law School and met Charlie Houston," Marshall told me. "I saw this man's dedication, his vision, his willingness to sacrifice, and I told myself, 'You either shape up or ship out.' When you are being challenged by a great human being, you know that you can't ship out."

So Houston rescued Marshall and launched him into a career as one of the greatest lawyers in American history.

The estrangement of Du Bois and the organization that he helped to found lasted for ten years, leaving Marshall, Houston, and the NAACP leadership relatively free to proceed, without internal strife, in their efforts to crush the legal underpinnings of Jim Crow.

CHAPTER SIX

A BLACK AGENDA EMERGES

IN 1934, Marshall was so involved in waging war against the University of Maryland, and staying a step ahead of his creditors, that he barely had time to reflect upon the tumultuous war between Du Bois and White over the issue of segregation. But he was immensely pleased when Houston told him that Du Bois had resigned, that a young official named Roy Wilkins was the new editor of the *Crisis,* and that he and Marshall had a green light to go against Jim Crow, not only at Maryland, but at other institutions of higher education and professional training across the land. Even as Marshall was wreaking revenge upon Maryland, he was instructed to write immediately the brief and other papers that Houston might use to challenge the denial of black students at the University of Texas.

These developments of 1934 were fateful for both Marshall and the NAACP. The Association had had seven white men and women as secretary, or top official, from 1909 to December 13, 1920, when James Weldon Johnson became the first black man to assume the post. The board of directors had been dominated by Walling, Villard, Ovington, and the brothers Joel and Arthur Spingarn. In 1932 Walter White had succeeded Johnson, bringing a new level of confrontation to the organization. White looked like a white man, but his heart was "blackened" to its core by a "black gene" or two and by the Klan and other mob violence that he had witnessed as a young man. He, like Marshall, carried the wounds of the humiliation of racial insult and rejection.

Marshall recalls that throughout the fight to open up the University of Maryland he was living from hand to mouth.

"I bought some fancy stationery that made me look like a hugely successful lawyer," he told me, "when I didn't have a damn dollar to pay for it. I would close out one telephone number and open another account when I couldn't pay the bill. Hell, how can you be a big-time lawyer if you don't have a telephone number?

"Then I got the break of my lifetime. Charlie Houston called in 1936 to ask me to come to New York as his deputy, as assistant special counsel of the national NAACP. He said they would pay me twenty-four hundred dollars a year. I whooped and hollered so loud that Buster ran in to see if I was dying.

"When I calmed down I thought about the reasons why Charlie might have called me. I knew that he was sick as hell, and still traveling like a maniac. I knew that the internal strife, like the struggle between White and Du Bois, was driving him crazy. Charlie didn't like internal wars. But I was too naive to think I was rushing into a fool's paradise. Hell, twenty-four hundred dollars a year was a lotta money.

"Buster and I wouldn't have to live with my parents [at 1838 Druid Hill Avenue in Baltimore] anymore. We gathered up our rags and moved to New York, where we rented a little apartment near the Polo Grounds.

"I felt that I suddenly had a real chance to do something to end Jim Crow."

On October 19, 1936, lawyer Sidney R. Redmond of St. Louis, a member of the national board of directors of the NAACP, wrote to Marshall:

"Accept my congratulations upon your appointment to the staff of the N.A.A.C.P. You have a wonderful opportunity and I am sure the race will benefit from your efforts." Marshall, still only twenty-eight, was deeply appreciative. His opportunities to display his extraordinary legal skills had been multiplied beyond calculation.

In his new job Marshall would move relentlessly to expand on two years of work in Baltimore — to try to stop other southern states from doing what Maryland had tried to do: prevent the enrollment of blacks into white institutions by paying part of their tuition at northern institutions. Working with Sidney Redmond, he and Houston came upon a young man they thought would be the ideal Missouri plaintiff — Lloyd L. Gaines. On September 27, 1935, at his own initiative, Gaines had written to Houston:

Because of its reasonable rates as a state institution, and its particular emphasis upon Missouri law, I applied for admission to the Missouri University Law School, August 19, 1935. Instead of granting me admission, however, the University countered by having my attention called to Section 9622 of the 1929 Revised Statutes of Missouri, wherein provisions are made for paying the tuition of Missouri Negroes to graduate schools in any adjacent state.

My scholastic record is a commendable one: finished high school in three years, ranking first in a class of fifty; won a $250, Cash Essay Scholarship, and a $50 Curators Scholarship to Lincoln University, Jefferson City, Missouri; was active in extracurricular activities, including the presidency of my graduating class, and received the Bachelor of Arts degree in history, August 8, 1935, with better than a general average of "B." Subsequently, I see no reason why I should be denied the opportunity of continuing my studies in a school of my choice, especially when that school — Missouri University — is a public institution of the state wherein I live and pay taxes. I am appealing to you in the name of social justice, to back my efforts to receive my rightful consideration. May I rely upon your assistance at such an urgent time of need?

Houston referred the letter to Marshall, urging him to "get going," and wrote Redmond saying that as soon as Thurgood's briefs arrived from Baltimore he hoped to move in behalf of Gaines, preferably by December 15.

Reminiscing, Marshall told me that "when it comes to productivity, there's no substitute for being young, hungry, and angry. In 'thirty-five and 'thirty-six the work piled up on me to get Murray into Maryland and keep him there. I was trying to ensure high school educations for Maryland blacks. I was drafting plans to force Maryland to pay black teachers, my momma included, the same money as it paid white teachers. And I had Houston on my ass demanding a brief for the court efforts to get Gaines into the University of Missouri. All this when there was hardly money to get a damned brief typed. It was frustrating, nerve-racking, but so exciting that I never complained."

It was not until mid-January that he finished the brief for *Lloyd L. Gaines v. S. W. Canada, Registrar, U. of Mo.* On January 24, 1936, a terribly snowy day, Redmond and Houston borrowed a car from Dr. Robert M. Scott of St. Louis and drove two hours and forty-five minutes to Columbia, Missouri, where they petitioned Judge Walter

S. Dinwiddie to issue a writ (akin to the one that Judge O'Dunne had signed in Maryland) that would order the University of Missouri to admit Gaines.

According to a confidential memorandum written by Houston after a three-hour-and-thirty-minute drive back to St. Louis in an intensifying snowstorm, "Judge greatly surprised. . . . Said it would be better to file original action in State Supreme Court in Jefferson City because it would have no publicity, and would be authoritative pronouncement for entire state; that filing petition in Columbia would cause local resentment and make community boil for a while. . . . Judge Dinwiddie said that there would probably be no trouble at U. of Mo. as long as only one or two Negro students were there . . . that if the right sort of boy presented himself the students probably would go out of their way to make it easy for him; but that trouble would begin if 30 or 40 Negroes went there." Dinwiddie had sunk into cowardice.

Marshall fumed upon reading Houston's account and began immediately to write another brief for the filing of another lawsuit in behalf of Gaines. This preparation was prescient, because on March 27, two months after Judge Dinwiddie chickened out, the university's board of curators passed a resolution saying:

> WHEREAS, Lloyd L. Gaines, colored, has applied for admission to the School of Law of the University of Missouri, and
>
> WHEREAS, the people of Missouri, both in the Constitution and in the Statutes of the State, have provided for the separate education of white students and negro students, and have thereby in effect forbidden the attendance of a white student at Lincoln University, or a colored student at the University of Missouri, and
>
> WHEREAS, the Legislature of the State of Missouri, in response to the demands of the citizens of Missouri has established at Jefferson City, Missouri, for Negroes, a modern and efficient school known as Lincoln University, and has invested the Board of Curators of that institution with full power and authority to establish such departments as may be necessary to offer students of that institution opportunities equal to those offered at the University, and have further provided, pending the full development of Lincoln University, for the payment, out of the public treasury, of the tuition, at universities in adjacent states, of colored students desiring to take any course of study not being taught at Lincoln University, and
>
> WHEREAS, it is the opinion of the Board of Curators that any

change in the State system of separate instruction which has been heretofore established, would react to the detriment of both Lincoln University and the University of Missouri,

THEREFORE, BE IT RESOLVED, that the application of said LLOYD L. GAINES be and it hereby is rejected and denied, and that the Registrar and the Committee on Entrance be instructed accordingly.

"Ho, ho, ho!" exclaimed Marshall when he read the resolution of the Missouri board of curators. This lawyer who often sounded like Santa Claus would recall:

"They gave us a legal gift that was bigger than anything we could expect at Christmas. The problem in all these education cases was that the bastards never wanted to fight on the real legal issues. They didn't want a challenge to state actions based solely on race, so they always tried some subterfuge of pretending that blacks were excluded because they had body odor or might put some VD on a toilet seat. They wanted judges to believe that all blacks, however clean, intellectually brilliant, patriotic, or whatever were being kept out of the state university for practical reasons other than racial discrimination.

"God, I couldn't believe it when the curators made it clear in their instructions to registrar Canada that Gaines was being rejected solely because of his race. Hell, the curators saved the NAACP about a hundred thousand dollars, which it didn't have, by that admission."

So Marshall, Houston, Redmond, and a St. Louis lawyer named Henry D. Espy on April 15 filed a new suit claiming that the university violated the Fourteenth Amendment when it excluded "a qualified Negro citizen and resident of the state from the school of law of the University of Missouri, which is maintained by tax money which Negroes help to pay, solely on account of his color."

Lawyers for the university realized the magnitude of the curators' error, so, notwithstanding the boasting about the quality of Lincoln University, set up for blacks only, they told the court that Gaines was not scholastically qualified to enter the white law school because Lincoln, from which he had graduated, was not "accredited." Houston was stunned — but argued that Lincoln was indeed accredited, and a member of the North Central Association of Colleges and Secondary Schools.

University officials were in a panic by this time, because three more blacks had applied for admission — Arnett G. Lindsay for the law school, John Boyd for the graduate school of mathematics, and N. A. Sweets to the School of Journalism.

Judge Dinwiddie, back in the case, to his unhappiness, set arguments for July 10. Houston and Redmond would face six lawyers for the university: two from St. Louis, one from Kansas City, one from Springfield, and two from Columbia, where the university was located. (Marshall was back in Baltimore, in court, protesting the fact that there were eleven high schools for whites in Baltimore County, but none for Negroes.)

The July arguments were dramatic, partly for their content, and partly because of the emotional atmosphere of the courtroom. In his memorandum following the hearing, Houston noted the blacks' concern about the fact that "there had been two lynchings in Columbia," and that that had intimidated blacks who might have come to the courtroom. He was concerned about the way the university's Kansas City lawyer, William S. Hogsett, had pounced upon Gaines.

"Gaines was the first witness," Houston noted. "Redmond carried him through direct examination. Gaines has courage and can't be bluffed, but he is not quick in his mental reactions. He likes to be meticulously exact, and being slow in thought, sometimes under Hogsett's pounding on cross-examination he nearly gave us heart failure. . . . He made a fair but not a good witness."

Marshall knew by this time that the NAACP was picking up powerful allies outside that Missouri courtroom. He had always believed that he had to have the press on his side to win in the long run, no matter what the judges said in the short term.

"I felt great," Marshall told me, "when *Time* magazine, the *New York Times*, the *New York Herald Tribune*, began to write about how we were stirring up a 'revolution' in higher education. Charlie Houston was contagiously excited when he told me that *Time* was going to do a piece explaining the Missouri challenge, and tell the nation that this was only the beginning. Houston would ask *Time* to report that I already was writing briefs demanding an end to Jim Crow in the School of Pharmacy of the University of Tennessee, the medical school of the University of North Carolina, and all kinds of professional schools in Virginia and other states."

Not just Marshall, but Walter White and Roy Wilkins knew the critical importance of media support. They courted the press as assiduously as they did the judges.

On July 27, Dinwiddie ruled in favor of the university, provoking editors at *Time* to barrage NAACP headquarters with questions that White and Wilkins could not answer, such as "Why did the judge do this?" Wilkins warned Redmond that *Time* would carry a story, adding: "You are reaping the benefit of the attention stirred by the Maryland case. People all over the country are watching Missouri. I want to congratulate you because the case is a very tough one and must not be judged by the results at this early state of the fight. This was only a scrimmage." (On August 4, Wilkins would write Redmond: "How do you like *Time*'s characterization of you as 'barking'? Anyway, it was good publicity for you and the association. You know *Time* has a 600,000 circulation weekly.")

But the very next day Gaines threatened to deal a blow to the NAACP. He wrote Houston and Redmond that "pending final action on my application and suit to enter the Missouri University Law School, I have decided to seek a master of Arts in Economics at the University of Michigan." The problem was that Gaines was ready to take money from the state of Missouri to finance his studies at Michigan, which would have undermined the NAACP case against the practice of paying blacks to study "up North." Houston wrote White and Joel Spingarn that the Association had to pay Gaines's tuition at Michigan, even if through another "laundering" deal with Carl Murphy. Gaines wrote "Dear Brother Houston" asking for $150 for tuition for the first year at Michigan, and "a friend" provided it.

But there was bad news ahead. First the Missouri Circuit Court refused to issue a writ of mandamus ordering the university to admit Gaines; on December 9, 1937, the Supreme Court of Missouri affirmed the decisions of Dinwiddie, and then the circuit court. The *Gaines* case seemed to be a loser on a grand scale, especially since it was taking up the time of Houston, Marshall, and others who had compelling cases to deal with across much of the country.

Around this time, Houston sent a letter to all black fraternities, sororities, and college NAACP chapters, saying: "This fight for equality of higher education essentially must be the fight of the young Negro college student and college graduate. The N.A.A.C.P. cannot go out and make students go into court. If the students themselves do not want graduate and professional education enough to make the fight, the N.A.A.C.P. stands tied." And Houston begged for money.

This former Howard University dean who had had such a powerful influence on so many black lawyers-to-be was litigating himself to death — simply destroying his health by rushing from Missouri to Maryland, Texas to Tennessee. The man never lay awake at night worrying about one crucial case; there were always four, or nine, each of almost the same level of importance as the *Gaines* case. By 1938, Houston knew that he could not take the grind any longer, so he tapped Marshall to succeed him as the chief legal officer of a civil rights organization that had won the attention of the world.

I asked Justice Marshall to recollect his feelings when Houston left the NAACP and designated him, at age thirty, to lead a legal and social revolution.

"The first thing I thought about," Marshall said, "was not what it meant to me, but what a loss it was to the NAACP. No organization can afford to lose a dedicated legal giant like Charlie. Then I thought about why Houston was leaving. This man had ignored tuberculosis to give his life to the cause of freedom for Afro-Americans. I looked at his travel schedule from one end of America to the other and saw that it was a killer. Buster asked me how I expected to survive such a travel schedule. I said, 'Shit, I'm sure I can make it till I'm forty.' She didn't think that was much of a damn joke."

The *Gaines* case dragged on, with the NAACP secretly funneling money to its precious plaintiff to keep him in the University of Michigan until a ruling could be secured from the U.S. Supreme Court. The Missouri Supreme Court had upheld the University of Missouri's argument that it had a right to reject Gaines because the colored Lincoln University would eventually establish a law school. Marshall argued that a promise of "separate but equal" was no remedy for what he called a clear violation of Gaines's constitutional rights.

On December 12, 1938, the high tribunal gave Marshall and the NAACP what seemed to be a colossal victory. Speaking for the Court, Chief Justice Charles E. Hughes said:

> Here, petitioner's right was a personal one. It was as an individual that he was entitled to the equal protection of the laws, and the State was bound to furnish him within its borders facilities for legal education substantially equal to those which the State there afforded for persons of the white race, whether or not other negroes sought the same opportunity.
>
> It is argued, however, that the provision for tuition outside the State is a temporary one — that it is intended to operate merely pending the establishment of a law department for negroes at Lincoln University. While in that sense the discrimination may be termed temporary, it may nevertheless continue for an indefinite period by reason of the discretion given to the curators of Lincoln University and the alternative of arranging for tuition in other States, as permitted by the state law as construed by the state court, so long as the curators find it unnecessary and impracticable to provide facilities for the legal instruction of negroes within the State. In that view, we cannot regard the discrimination as excused by what is called its temporary character. . . .

The judgment of the Supreme Court of Missouri is reversed and the case is remanded for further proceedings not inconsistent with this opinion.

Missouri officials pressured the curators at Lincoln to move speedily to set up a law school for blacks, which they did. Marshall, Houston, and others counseled Gaines not to enroll in this school, because they believed that they could prove it was grossly inadequate — just part of a Jim Crow farce. Months of legal sparring rolled by. Houston was now back in Washington as editor of the *Journal of the National Bar Association*, but he stayed involved in the *Gaines* case. On October 10, 1939, he wrote Marshall a letter that included this shocking, mysterious, and ominous paragraph:

> The last communication from Gaines was received in April (so he said) by Frank Wethers, an assistant in the library at Lincoln U. Law School. Wethers could not remember where Gaines was at the time; said Gaines had written him about his frat pin, and he in turn had written to a fellow at Lincoln who had now graduated. The *St. Louis Post-Dispatch* and the *St. Louis Globe-Democrat* are starting to look for Gaines. If we do not find him soon we will have to advise the court, because counsel suavely suggested that if we had no client the cause was moot. Counsel told Taylor and Wethers to help us locate Gaines because they want him too. Better send out word in press release this week that no contact with Gaines since spring, that we have been trying to locate him, that his family does not know where he is, and any one knowing his whereabouts will please contact the N.A.A.C.P. No secret.

The media soon got rumors that Gaines had disappeared. Several newspapers and magazines launched their own search. They got "tips" that he had been seen in Mexico and other places. Some got whispers that Missouri racists had paid him to vanish. Others got rumors that bigots had murdered him.

On May 17, 1940, Neil Dalton, the managing editor of the *Louisville Courier Journal*, wrote to Houston asking for whatever information he had about Gaines. Houston and others at the NAACP appealed urgently to Gaines's family, to NAACP officials and educators all over America, for any information they could provide about Gaines. On July 8, 1940, Houston finally wrote to Dalton:

> In October, 1939, we took depositions in Gaines' case in St. Louis of the Dean and faculty of the Lincoln University School of Law, which the state had just established to keep Gaines out of the

University of Missouri and meet the mandate of the United States Supreme Court. Counsel for the University of Missouri, William S. Hogsett of Kansas City, at the hearing announced he wanted to take Gaines' deposition. We admitted we could not contact Gaines and stated that if we were not able to do so within a reasonable time we would not resist a motion to dismiss the suit.

At that point the Dean announced that his student assistant in the library knew where to reach Gaines. Mr. Hogsett had the student called in and questioned him. The student who had known Gaines in Gaines' college days at Lincoln University in Jefferson City stated he had had a card from Gaines in the Spring of 1939 asking about a fraternity matter. Mr. Hogsett directed the student to produce the card and to give us all possible cooperation in locating Gaines because, he said, the University of Missouri was just as anxious to locate Gaines as we were. The student could remember nothing further. . . .

Rumor has had Gaines working in an institution in Illinois, spending money like a sailor in Vera Cruz, and teaching under a false name in Chase City, Virginia. We have tried to verify these clues but they have all evaporated.

Counsel for the University of Missouri moved in due course to dismiss the Gaines suit for want of prosecution. We did not oppose the motion. Suit was dismissed January 1, 1940, and the case closed.

Marshall sinks into a mixture of pride and regret when he talks about *Gaines.* "This case produced the victory, the legal precedent, that we used to wipe out Jim Crow in Oklahoma, Texas, Louisiana, and other states. In *Gaines* we dragged the federal courts one more step away from 'separate but equal.' We stopped the outrage of a state rejecting its black, taxpaying citizens by paying for them to study in a university in some other state. We stopped the delay of justice by getting the Supreme Court to say that it was not enough to promise black kids that sooner or later they would establish medical, law, and other professional schools 'just for blacks.'

"I remember *Gaines* as one of our greatest victories, but I have never lost the pain of having so many people spend so much time and money on him, only to have him disappear."

Marshall sits in silence for a while, half a century after this celebrated court triumph, and says of Gaines: "The sonofabitch just never ever contacted us again."

CHAPTER SEVEN

TRIPLE MURDER

MARSHALL would have had a cakewalk if he had had to worry only about the *Gaines* case, or the other cases he fought to make higher education available to black Americans. But so many assaults on justice were taking place.

Over forty years of discussions with Marshall, I have rarely seen the lingering anger that became apparent when he talked about the late 1930s and the early 1940s, when America was mobilizing for potential warfare and then was sucked deep into a brutal struggle. Marshall would, half a century later, speak of the policies of Franklin D. Roosevelt, of War Secretary Henry Stimson, and of the leaders of Congress as a racial shame almost equaling the infamy of the racial lynchings that occurred.

"As the *Gaines* case ended," Marshall recalled, "America was mobilizing for what turned out to be a historic war in Europe and the Pacific. Of course, we had no premonition of the Japanese attacking Pearl Harbor, or of great land and sea battles at Normandy or Okinawa, but we knew the nation was at risk. Negro people wanted to reduce that risk. They wanted to work for America in the industrial enterprises that were girding for war. But somebody in Roosevelt's White House, or Stimson's War Department, decreed that Rosie the Riveter could not be dark-skinned. They shut blacks out of the economic preparations for a war that would imperil the very existence of this country. When war came, blacks wanted to fight for America, in the skies, on the seas, on the battlegrounds of European towns and African deserts. But Roosevelt let the generals and admirals say that colored Americans could only serve in Jim Crow units that did the menial chores of cooking, cleaning up, loading dangerous ammunition.

"It was just one utterly stupid manifestation of the grip of racism on this society that Roosevelt and others would tell Afro-Americans that they could defend their country only under circumstances of semislavery and humiliation.

"What really burned my ass was when I learned that as more and more blacks were drafted into the military, more and more found themselves subjected to courts-martial, mostly because they refused to submit meekly to white supremacy regulations."

The status of black people before the law was still abominable. A black man accused of a serious crime, such as murder or rape, was only so lucky if he escaped lynching; he would face white judges and juries that were all too likely to order him executed. Marshall's days at Howard, with Houston, Hastie, and others, had instilled in him a passion for achieving justice under the law. Phrases such as "due process," "right to counsel," "jury of one's peers" really meant something to him. So even as he agonized over *Gaines*, he listened to appeals from the accused in every corner of the land.

Marshall said to me that he realized that "no matter how much education black people got, they would remain semislaves until they got meaningful political power."

"Political power means the untrammeled right to vote," Marshall told me. "There could be no political power in areas where there were 'white primaries,' poll taxes, grandfather clauses, registrars asking outrageous questions, and white people armed to kill, standing in the way of the enfranchisement of Afro-Americans. But I believed that the Constitution was broad enough to deal with this problem."

Marshall said that in those days of terrible challenge to the NAACP he would sit around with colleagues and advisers, sipping bourbon, telling jokes, and launching into a discussion of what "freedom of travel" meant in America.

"I would argue," he recalled, "that freedom of mobility was the key to upward mobility, and that it handicapped Negroes in ways that violated the Constitution if they could travel across state lines only under circumstances of racial segregation, humiliation, and possible physical abuse."

Thurgood despised the ghettoization of America, the bigotry that blocked black people from buying houses or renting apartments wherever they wished. Marshall found it especially galling that a white Anglo-Saxon Protestant could place a "restrictive covenant" in the deed of his house declaring that a buyer or future owner could never transfer that property to a black person, a Jew, an "Asiatic," or anyone other than another WASP. Marshall was sure, in his outrage, that the Constitution did not allow the courts to become parties to the enforcement of such bigoted restrictive covenants, so he launched a campaign against that, too.

Marshall simply believed that every injustice could be redressed under the rules of law — if the NAACP could just muster up enough money and lawyers to go to court against the myriad outrages.

When you look at NAACP records in the Library of Congress and comprehend the written legal work load, the travel itineraries, the speeches and appearances in court, you see that if Houston was working himself to death at age fifty-four, Marshall was on a mission of perhaps earlier self-destruction.

But in the late 1930s and early 1940s he was on a mission of heart, mind, and soul. To lawyers paid well to defend segregation and other forms of official racism, Marshall seemed omnipresent. "That mulatto lawyer," "that fancy New York lawyer," "the nigger lawyer," were terms thrown at Thurgood every time he entered a case. "Ho, ho, ho," he'd bellow as he read the intended insults. Then, on a miserably cold January day in 1940, Marshall answered a call for help that would affect his thinking forever.

In terms of constitutional law, Marshall was still a neophyte when he got a telephone call from Tulsa, Oklahoma. But Marshall already was on his way to becoming a legend in black America because of his victories in the *Murray, Gaines,* and other cases. The word had spread fast in black communities throughout the land that if you saw real trouble, "call Thurgood to the rescue!" Tulsa attorney Amos Hall, a stern fighter for racial justice, was looking for help.

"Thurgood," Hall said, "the bootlegging crackers have set up a black kid and are blaming him for a gruesome triple murder. We need you to help us save the boy's life."

Just about the last thing that Marshall wanted at that time was a cry for help from Oklahoma. He had been sitting in his chilly office at 65 Fifth Avenue in New York City trying to figure out priorities for the use of his meager budget. He was also consumed with a Bridgeport, Connecticut, case in which a socially prominent white woman, Mrs. Eleanor Strubing, had accused her chauffeur, Joseph Spell, of raping her. Marshall, White, Wilkins, and others in the NAACP believed that no rape had occurred, so they had pledged the organization's limited resources to clearing Spell. Why in the world would Amos Hall think that Marshall would give first thoughts to the plight of a semiliterate black ex-convict who was accused of murdering a man, chopping up his wife after shooting her in the stomach, and then burning down the house with the couple and their four-year-old son in it?

Poverty is a relative concept, so some readers will wonder what I mean when I refer often to the NAACP's lack of money. Just follow me through the years:

In 1917, eight years after the NAACP's founding, the organization had a total income of $14,088.79, and its total outlay for salaries was $5,338.48.

By 1919 the Association had grown from 3 branches and 329 members in 1912 to 310 branches and 91,203 members. Of those members 42,588 were in the South and 38,420 in the North, along with others in the West and some foreign and at-large members. Still, its total budget was $61,755.70, less than seventy cents per member. It wasn't just that blacks were impoverished; their white allies were not donating the huge amounts that the segregationists imagined. In 1919 Oswald Villard had given $275, Paul M. Warburg $100, Henry Morgenthau $25, and Jane Addams $5.

In June 1935, when Marshall and Houston were raising the pressure on Jim Crow in colleges, they requisitioned $50 from the national office for Houston and $35 for Marshall to cover their expenses at the NAACP national conference in St. Louis. The stipulation was that "Marshall will come west in Houston's car if Houston's physician permits him to make trip." They never got to the conference, and Marshall was quickly ordered to send back the $35.

In August 1935, Marshall wrote to Houston: "Just received report from National Bar Association that with an allowance of $25 for me to purchase stationery the treasury is again busted with a deficit of $131. Therefore, it seems that I will have to bear expenses of a stenographer, etc., until the next convention. I have purchased a typewriter and Mr. McQuinn is going to let me have a desk from his old office."

On September 9, 1935, upon receiving a bit of money from Houston, Marshall wrote, "I received the check. Thanks. It will keep the wolf away from my door. . . . Colored pupil will apply to the white high school tomorrow morning."

When Houston returned to Washington and Marshall was named to the top legal job in 1938, the NAACP gave Thurgood a $200-a-year pay increase.

"I rushed home proudly to tell Buster about my raise," Marshall recalls. "She just sat in silence for a few seconds, counting on her fingers. Then she said, 'Excuse me, but how much is that a week?' "

By 1949, under pressure from the Treasury Department on the issue of the tax-exempt status of donations, the NAACP and the Legal Defense and Educational Fund (known as "Inc. Fund," or LDF) had become "separate" entities, but there was a bit of collusion in paying salaries. Even though Marshall had won the *Murray* and *Gaines* cases, had knocked out the white primaries, was about to win cases opening up the Universities of Oklahoma and Texas, the NAACP itself was paying him only $1,890. On August 19 Roy Wilkins wrote to Marshall: "Although I do not know where we are going to find the money, I nevertheless ordered some small increase in pay. Your increase amounts to $300 annually, bringing you to $2,190. It is retroactive to January 1, 1949."

Wilkins then wrote to Arthur Spingarn, who headed the legal committee of the Inc. Fund: "Mr. Marshall's total salary has remained, until recent weeks, at $7,700 annually. I authorized during August an increase of $300 for him in his NAACP salary, making his total salary now $8,000.

"My feeling is that this is not a sufficient raise and I recommend that the Inc. Fund Board vote an increase of $500 in his salary from that corporation, raising his total salary to $8,500." Spingarn concurred.

So $8,500 a year was the pay available to the man who was leading the greatest legal movement in America.

Marshall was not surprised or offended. Ten years earlier he had submitted a budget of $2,500 for legal actions to combat discrimination in universities, of $4,000 for lawsuits to equalize the salaries of black and white teachers, and $3,000 for legal action to force southern states to equalize the money spent on transportation, equipment, and other facilities in black and white public schools. And in 1941 Marshall had personally informed branches that so many requests for legal help had been received that "due to limitations of staff and funds" his department had had to "refuse a number of worthy cases."

"Hell, the raise that Wilkins worked out — $800 a year — seemed like half the money in the world to Buster and me," Marshall recalled. "Shit, back in 'thirty-nine I had a nothing expense account and thought it was heaven."

One of those expense accounts was for a trip he took to Anne Arundel County in Maryland, where he was fighting to get fairer pay for black teachers. He turned in an expense account of ten cents for baggage checking, forty-five cents for breakfast, seventy-five cents for lunch, twenty-five cents for a railway porter . . . well, total expenses of $25.11. His written account noted that the NAACP national office had advanced him $25, and thus owed him eleven cents.

Marshall complained ad nauseam in memos and speeches about the failure of black people to give better financial support to the NAACP. He found powerful support on occasion. In August 1941, when he was wrecking his health trying to win equal pay for members of the black Palmetto Teachers Association in South Carolina, the *Charleston Lighthouse & Informer, the* black newspaper in the state, carried a column in which Osceola E. McKaine wrote: "The teachers as a whole are not heroes and have no desire to become heroes. But this does not explain why they are especially afraid to adhere even passively to the NAACP. It was this organization which led and financed the struggle for equal pay for teachers in the South. In South Carolina the NAACP has exactly 1,140 members; there are more than 5,000 Negro teachers in this state. This lack of support, this lack of appreciation, this lack of gratitude is so shameful as to be scandalous."

Marshall would say "amen" a few thousand times, but that did not produce black dollar support that was sufficient to give NAACP lawyers a fighting chance of pursuing successfully all the cases of injustice that black people everywhere in America wanted Marshall to embrace as his priority.

Marshall was in fact pissed with South Carolina. In November 1943 he wrote the Reverend James M. Hinton, chairman of the state conference: "What about the money the South Carolina people were to send up in the Texas Primary case?"

"It was all but impossible to get Negroes in one state to give a shit about what was happening to black people in another state," Marshall recalled for me in 1955. "Hell, even in another city. Our legal efforts were tied to a shoestring because in those days brainwashed Negroes who had a little money couldn't get their fucking act together."

In 1946 Marshall sent a memorandum to Walter White: "If we are to carry out an expanded program of legal action, we will have to raise more money. . . . I think we have always agreed that some method should be devised for the raising of funds in addition to the one-dollar memberships. Experience has shown that we can raise money on criminal cases providing they are properly presented to the people."

It must be noted here that Marshall told me many times that the NAACP lacked the public relations skill to present its cases properly. I demurred. Henry Lee Moon, the Association's public relations director, was a friend of mine, and working his butt off to influence a mostly hostile white press. At one mention of Moon's name, Marshall gave me a stare of incredulity and said,

"If he peed out this hotel window, that, for him, would be news!"

Marshall recalled that in 1946 he was up against lawyers financed by taxpayers, white and black, though without the consent of the latter — lawyers who never had to beg publicly for funds with which to pay for a court transcript, as Marshall had had to do in nation-changing court appeals.

"I felt sick as hell," Marshall told me, "when Bob Carter [his deputy] told me that Walter wanted me to agree that we would pay a lawyer on one of our cases no more than $25 a day plus proven expenses incurred in connection with the court proceedings."

Marshall felt sicker when he read a response to his appeal for money from Joe Simmons of Charleston: "As a lawyer, I think your Mr. Thurgood Marshall is a rank fizzle. With all his mouthings in this state, can he get any of our people as clerks in the post office — or in the custom house?

"And look at the industrials — Coca Cola Company employs Negroes only on hard laborious jobs, that are the dirty ones. No Negro allowed to work in their office. Nothing done for us by Mr. Marshall, but we are asked to give liberally. Ise regusted."

Meanwhile, Marshall was traveling more than fifty thousand miles a year, always begging for a family in some city to give him bed and board. Even if he could have broken the race bar in hotels in the South, the NAACP could not have paid for his room.

The sad state of the offices from which Marshall and the other legal warriors worked in June 1949 is manifested in a Marshall bulletin board memo to the staff saying: "Due to the heat, the office will close at 4:30 P.M. . . . Please initial."

That was the year when the NAACP was so impecunious that Marshall had to give a written reason for a $1.11 telephone call to Washington to inquire about a segregation proposal of the Public Housing Agency.

In 1958, after winning *Brown* and dozens of other cases, Marshall's salary was $15,000 a year. When John F. Kennedy chose him for a federal judgeship, Marshall was earning only $18,000 a year from the NAACP and the Inc. Fund combined. This was evidence that the NAACP was declining as a national force, because in all the wars that matter in America, "money talks." In February 1986 the NAACP's budget was less than $11 million, which was less than penny-ante in an America of political action committees (PACs) and high-powered individual lobbyists, some of whom earned more than all the NAACP staff combined.

A *New York Times* article in 1986 said: "The association's membership continues to fluctuate after reaching a high of 550,000 in the 1970's. According to [NAACP executive director Benjamin] Hooks, membership dropped two years ago when the basic fees were increased from $5 to $10. He said the membership had since increased and now stands at 450,000, but critics say it is closer to 150,000."

Even now the NAACP is impoverished in many ways.

Marshall really admired Amos Hall as a sacrificing, life-risking black lawyer in a state where racial passions were deep and volatile. So he heard out this Oklahoma pioneer, who gave him a dismaying chronology:

December 31, 1939: Mr. and Mrs. Elmer Rogers and their four-year-old son, Elvie Dean, were murdered in their tenant house a short distance northwest of Fort Towson, in Choctaw County, Oklahoma. The murderer poured kerosene on the bodies of the parents and set the house afire. Another son, eight-year-old James Glenn Rogers, escaped the house, carrying his one-year-old brother, Billie Don, with him.

January 2, 1940: Oklahoma governor Leon C. Phillips was informed that a convict at the Sawyer prison camp near Fort Towson had been arrested in connection with the murders. Phillips announced immediately that he was personally entering the case. He said he was concerned that trustys at the prison camp had been going out and getting drunk. The trusty arrested was serving a thirty-year term for murdering his wife, and allegedly was away from the camp and drunk at the time the Rogers were shot, then axed to death.

January 5, 1940: The governor's operatives arrested a twenty-eight-year-old woman as a possible "witness" to the murders.

January 9, 1940: Roy Harmon, Choctaw county sheriff, announced that he would pay a $100 reward from his personal funds for information leading to the arrest of "the two men" who murdered the Rogerses. There was no explanation as to how the sheriff knew at that time that "two men" committed the crime.

January 11, 1940: A twenty-one-year-old Negro named W. D. Lyons was arrested by civilians who allegedly had connections with a bootlegging ring *and* the office of Governor Phillips. Lyons had served two prison terms, one for chicken stealing, and one for burglary, which Hall figured made him an easy scapegoat. Hall told Marshall that Lyons had not been officially charged, had not been carried before a magistrate, and was rumored to be under pressure to confess.

Despite his occupation with the *Spell* case, Marshall had heard enough. "Amos," Marshall said to Hall, "we've got no time and less money, but surely we'll find some way to help you in this murder case."

Hall became disturbed when newspapers of January 12 reported that a confession had been obtained "in the mysterious arson deaths." These stories apparently referred to the convict out of the Sawyer prison camp. From January 11 to January 22, Lyons remained in the custody of the sheriff, the county attorney, and assorted unofficial hangers-on. They turned the inquiry over to Vernon Cheatwood, a "special investigator" from the office of Governor Phillips. Cheatwood told the sheriff and county attorney that he was an expert of many years in securing confessions from people accused of committing crimes. Hall had no idea of what would come out in court about the ways in which Cheatwood got his confessions, but he sensed that "there's something rotten in Denmark." Hall called again and told Marshall that the black maids and yardmen had been listening to their white bosses talk about a huge bootlegging ring that supposedly was controlled out of the office of Governor Phillips, and Hall had become convinced that Elmer Rogers was killed because he had gotten at odds with some of the bootleggers and had threatened to expose them. Hall's theory was that after the triple murder, somebody in the bootlegging ring had said, "Now, let's get us a nigger and convict him."

Weeks went by with no attempt to prosecute Lyons. In April, Roy Wilkins got a telegram from Roscoe Dunjee, the publisher of the *Black Dispatch* in Oklahoma City, asking urgently for $100 with which to hire a lawyer for Lyons. On April 12, Wilkins sent Dunjee a telegram saying: "Have not sent money because we did not have it. However, am mailing Dr. Bullock [the state treasurer of the NAACP] check for $75 today. Best we can do. Sorry."

More months went by without Lyons being brought to trial. On December 11, 1940, Marshall wrote Dunjee, in effect dunning him for the $75 "loan" that Wilkins had advanced to the Oklahoma state conference in April. "I wonder if you would let us know whether or not the loan will be repaid in the near future so that we can use it on our other cases," Marshall said. "We would like to have a full report on this case for our files because we consider it a most important one, and the type of case which deserves the attention of all of us. . . . I am wondering about the possibility of taking some form of legal action to compel the state to either try Lyons or release him."

Marshall got back a letter from Dunjee telling him that it was almost certain that Lyons would go on trial in January 1941, and that Dunjee would like the national office to give Marshall travel expenses so he could come to Hugo, where the trial would be held, and help try the case.

On January 18 Marshall dispatched the following letter to Dunjee:

> If Belden will send me the facts in the case I will prepare a brief for him to use and give all other help possible. We are with you on the case but simply do not have the money now for a trip. I am sure you understand our position. One of these days Negroes will support this organization in sufficient numbers and with sufficient money for us to do a real job. In the meantime, we will have to do the best we can.

The "Belden" to whom Marshall referred was a white lawyer named Stanley Belden from Cushing, Oklahoma. Hall knew that he himself could not handle the case. No white Oklahoma lawyer of any esteem would take it. But Belden was a socialist who was defending Lyons mostly out of personal conviction. He worked hard, compiling a record of the terrible beatings and torture the black man was subjected to in order to get him to confess that he and another black man named Vanzell [*sic*] had murdered the three members of the Rogers family. The other Negro actually arrested was Van Bizzell, thirty-nine, who denied any part in the crime and was released on $5,000 bond on July 10, 1940, and never brought to trial. Belden had talked to the father, mother, and other relatives of Mrs. Rogers, the murdered woman. Her father, C. A. Colclasure, had picked up enough information to convince him that Lyons was being railroaded. He joined the NAACP by way of saying to white Oklahomans that he, too, knew that "there was something rotten in Denmark."

Dunjee went on a begging campaign and got blacks in southeastern Oklahoma to raise $322 for the expense of bringing in Marshall, who went with unusual enthusiasm because the case was fascinating. He could not have imagined that it raised human rights issues that would bedevil him the rest of his life: the arrest of a poor black by citizens who had no warrant; a prisoner held for days without charges, and without being taken before a magistrate; a prisoner denied the right to talk to a lawyer; a prisoner beaten and tortured into a "confession."

When Marshall got word that Lyons's trial would begin in the Choctaw County courthouse on January 27, he hopped a plane to Oklahoma City, where he talked for a couple of hours with Dunjee, who provided him with a bag full of peanuts, boiled eggs, and bologna sandwiches, telling him, "I don't know where the hell you're going to eat down there, so you may find this bag of food comes in handy."

Some of Thurgood Marshall's letters back to Walter White and others on the NAACP staff about his experiences in Hugo are telling:

Dear Walter:
Reached Oklahoma City 8:10 A.M. and caught 12:30 bus for Hugo. Arrived here 6:30 Sunday night. Worked on preparation of the case Sunday night. Started trial yesterday morning.
At least a thousand white and Negro people in Court House. Courtroom jammed. Everyone here to see trial and also to see a certain Negro lawyer — first time in the court — so sayeth the bailiff.
Jury is lousy. State investigator and county prosecutor busy around town stirring up prejudice, etc. No chance of winning here. Will keep record straight for appeal.
Only point we will have in our favor is use of confession secured after force and violence was used.

Marshall later wrote:

The court room is crowded beyond capacity, the building itself is crowded every day. More than a thousand people from all over county. Coming in trucks, wagons, etc. All of the sentiment is good. No evidence of mob spirit. Several white people have complimented us on the type of defense.
Judge Childers announced from the bench that this was a trial involving "two nations," white and black.
White schools have turned out and teachers have brought

classes to the court — both elementary and high schools. Yesterday judge said it was good for the children to be there because it was truly "a gala day." Imagine it — a Negro on trial for his life being called a "gala day." Trial started early Monday morning and has been going on ever since. The State attempted to introduce confessions. We opposed them and asked that jury be excluded while we put on evidence to show that the confessions were secured by force and violence. They beat him all night. Sometime later he was taken up to the County Prosecutor's Office where there were ten or more officers who took turns beating him with blackjacks and what is known as a "Nigger beater" which is a special type of black jack. They went to the place where the murder occurred — where the bodies had been burned and took some of the bones of the dead people, put them in a pan and put them in the defendant's lap (this is admitted by the state). He was told what the bones were including the upper jaw bone and teeth of the dead woman. (including the bones of a dead child — also were in the pan). One of the officers admitted that this would have scared him if he had been Lyons. They beat him all night until two-thirty in the morning then he "confessed." They then took him to the scene of the crime and then to the State Pen at McAlester the same night where he made another "confession."

Marshall's letters and telegrams back to White and others at the NAACP were sarcastic, sometimes humorous, and repetitive. He mentioned several times the carnival atmosphere in and around the courtroom. He told how the judge puffed a cigar, with his feet high on the bench, and then let people know the trial was about to begin when he put blacks on one side of the courtroom and whites on the other. Marshall joked about how the white spectators were saying that "the nigger lawyer from New York ain't done nothing yet," and he then bragged that they got "a lesson in constitutional law" when he cross-examined the white police officers who were accused of beating Lyons.

"We figured they would resent being questioned by a Negro and get angry and this would help us. It worked perfect," Marshall wrote. "They all became angry at the idea of a Negro pushing them into tight corners and making their lies so obvious. Boy, did I like that — and did the Negroes in the Court-room like it."

Marshall wrote that when he arrived in Hugo he had some fear of being attacked by whites. But in the middle of the trial, he said, some white spectators had said to him what the father of the murdered woman had concluded: that there was something fishy about this long-delayed prosecution of Lyons.

The *Lyons* case embodied everything that Marshall had vowed to work against: the ease with which powerful white criminals could frame indigent blacks; the paucity of lawyers who would defend the poor, or minorities; the practice of cops and prosecutors holding powerless people in their custody for long periods without charging them with any crime; the practice of officials, such as the governor's "special investigator" Vernon Cheatwood, of using a "nigger beater" to extract confessions; the denial of a "speedy trial," in this case a delay of more than a year, leaving a fair presumption that the prosecution knew its case was weak; the absence of blacks in the criminal justice system, except as defendants; and the costliness and difficulty of appeals, usually before judges who had never been sensitized regarding the injustices that were rooted deep in the American system of justice.

As Marshall had indicated in his letter to White, there was no way of winning in that courtroom. Forty-five years later, Marshall would shake his head in disbelief as he told of being admonished by Judge Childers to "get on with picking a jury." Marshall recalled it to me in this way: "The first man called up was a potbellied farmer who looked at me as though he'd like to put a noose around *my* neck. I used the first of my peremptory challenges. They brought up a woman who was so meek that I knew the prosecutor would twist her into a knot with a gruesome recounting of the horrors of the New Year's Eve murders. I used again my right to reject a potential juror without explaining why.

"Judge Childers looked at me in obvious disgust, then crooked his finger to beckon me to the bench. I walked up and turned my head to the side, to be sure I heard him.

" 'You ever tried a case in Oklahoma before?' he asked.

" 'No, Your Honor,' I replied.

" 'You know anything about Oklahoma court procedures?'

" 'I thought I did.'

" 'Well, you see that panel of potential jurors? When you exhaust it, that's the only panel you're gonna git. After that we go out into the streets and git pedestrians.'

" 'Who goes into the streets?' I asked.

" 'The sheriff and the prosecutor,' Childers said.

"I tried not to gulp noticeably. I just pointed over to the remaining members of the panel and said, 'I'll take them, Your Honor.' "

Those jurors heard and added to a sad chronology:

January 23, 1940: Lyons had been taken from the Choctaw County jail in Hugo and driven to Antlers, the seat of Pushmataha County, by Deputy Sheriff Floyd Brown and "special officer," meaning civilian, Reasor Cain. Lyons was put in the county jail at Antlers. He still had not been brought before a magistrate, given access to a lawyer, or been formally charged with anything. It was 2 P.M. on that day when Lyons formally signed the "first confession."

That same day, around 6 or 6:30 P.M., Deputy Sheriff Van Raulston and an Antlers barber, Roy Marshall, took Lyons to the state penitentiary at McAlester "for safekeeping." Roy Marshall said he went along because Raulston was too weak, following an automobile accident, to drive.

Lyons was brought before the penitentiary warden, J. F. Dunn, who testified as follows: "I talked to the boy. I knew him before he came up there [to the McAlester prison]. And I asked him had he told the truth about this case, and he said he hadn't. I asked him did he want to tell the truth about this case, and he said he did. Then I told him his rights in the case. I told him what statement he made would be used against him. . . . Then I asked him did he want to make a statement, and he said he did. . . . Then I called in my secretary."

About 9:30 P.M. on January 23, Lyons signed his "second confession."

Warden Dunn produced in court the "confession" in which Lyons admitted that he and Vanzell [*sic*] had murdered the three members of the Rogers family. Remember that the Negro actually arrested, Van Bizzell, denied any part in the crime. Dunn denied speaking with Cheatwood, the governor, or other state officers before talking Lyons into a "second confession." He said he didn't know any of the facts of the murder, yet asked Lyons about the axe that "Vanzell" allegedly had used to chop Mrs. Rogers to death after she had been shot in the stomach. The warden denied having Lyons taken where he could see the electric chair, but admitted telling the poorly educated Negro that he, Dunn, had presided over fourteen electrocutions.

January 25, 1940: A guard at the penitentiary went by Lyons's cell. The trial court admitted his testimony that Lyons made a "third confession" during a conversation with him. (Justice Stanley Reed would later note that "Only [Lyons], police, prosecuting and penitentiary officials were present at any of these interrogations, except that a private citizen [Roy Marshall] who drove the car that brought Lyons to McAlester witnessed the second confession.")

January 27, 1940: Lyons was formally charged before a magistrate. He was still without counsel.

February 4, 1940: Court was given first advice that Lyons had a lawyer.

December 30, 1940: One day short of a year after the murders occurred, Lyons was officially arraigned.

January 31, 1941: Jury found Lyons guilty. He was sentenced to life imprisonment, with a recommendation of mercy.

March 1941: NAACP's *Crisis* magazine said:

"When a white jury in Oklahoma finds a Negro guilty of shooting a white family to death, hacking the bodies to pieces with an axe, and then setting fire to the home and burning the bodies — *and still recommends mercy* — something is rotten in Denmark! . . . while we are talking about the beauties of democracy and the necessity of strengthening our American system by giving justice to all, why not make a contribution to this Lyons case a testimony to our faith in democracy and our determination that it *shall* work?"

Marshall wrote that Negroes in the area were suddenly eager to fight for their rights and told of raising $275 in Idabel. He told the national office it should use the beatings and the police putting the bones of dead people in the defendant's lap as the basis of a national effort to raise at least $10,000.

"I think we are in a perfect position to appeal," Marshall wrote to White. "The Spell [Connecticut rape] case is in the local papers. . . . The NAACP did all right this month. . . . We have been needing a good criminal case and we have it."

White replied, "You certainly did a superb job at Hugo, and you deserve unstinted praise for courage and ability."

Dunjee expressed confidence that Lyons would be freed by a three-judge panel of the Oklahoma Criminal Court of Appeals. Part of his confidence was based on the fact that the presiding judge would be Bert B. Barefoot, a man of American Indian descent whom Dunjee regarded as a personal friend as well as a supporter of racial justice.

Marshall was equally confident that the Choctaw jury's decision would be reversed somewhere along the line because the United States Supreme Court had spoken so clearly about convicting people and taking their lives on the basis of coerced confessions. In preparing a brief for the appeal, Marshall noted that in 1934, in Mississippi, three Negro farm laborers, Ed Brown, Henry Shields, and Yank Ellington, were convicted of murder in DeKalb County. When arrested, Ellington was hanged from a tree in an effort to make him "confess," which he eventually did. The marks of the rope were still on Ellington's neck when he was brought in for trial, and the deputy sheriff admitted that he had had a role in the torture. In 1936, Justice Charles E. Hughes delivered a decision for the Supreme Court reversing the convictions and ordering a new trial. Mr. Hughes said: "The rack and torture chamber may not be substituted for the witness stand. . . . The duty of maintaining the constitutional rights of a person on trial for his life rises above mere rules of procedure, and whenever the court is clearly satisfied that such violations exist, it will refuse to sanction such violations and will apply the corrective."

Marshall also noted that on February 12, 1940, Associate Justice Hugo L. Black had spoken for the Court in reversing the death sentences of four Negroes convicted of murder in Pompano, Florida. After five appeals from their 1933 convictions, Justice Black said: "No higher duty, no more solemn responsibility, rests upon this court, than that of translating into living law and maintaining this constitutional shield deliberately planned and inscribed for the benefit of every human being subject to our Constitution — of whatever race, creed, or persuasion."

Black had delivered as sweeping a judgment against the coercion of confessions as had ever been delivered in an American courtroom.

But Marshall became disturbed that months and months had passed without the Criminal Court of Appeals of Oklahoma taking up the *Lyons* case. On March 27, 1943, Marshall got the following letter from Dunjee:

> I called Judge Barefoot and talked with him about the Lyons case. The Judge said he had been delayed by the current legislature, now in session, but promised he would get on it and complete the decision as soon as possible.
>
> He was very cordial and my general impression is Barefoot is going to render a decision in our favor.
>
> Sincerely yours,
> Roscoe Dunjee, Editor
> BLACK DISPATCH

The chronology continues:

June 4, 1943: The Criminal Court of Appeals of Oklahoma began consideration of Lyons's request for a rehearing.

August 18, 1943: The Criminal Court of Appeals denied Lyons's request. Judge Barefoot affirmed Lyons's conviction in a fifty-page opinion asserting that "a careful consideration of this record clearly reveals that this defendant deliberately murdered Elmer Rogers and his wife in a cruel and brutal manner."

In a dissent, Judge Thomas H. Doyle said: "The law is not designed to be a swift engine of oppression and vengeance, but it was and is designed to try and convict men only after due hearing and a fair trial. . . .

"I do not believe [Lyons] has been tried and convicted in accordance with law, and he did not have that fair and impartial trial which the law guarantees to one charged with crime. . . . The petition for rehearing should be allowed, the judgment of conviction reversed, and the case remanded to the trial court with direction to grant a new trial."

On this same day, Dunjee announced that the *Lyons* case would be appealed to the United States Supreme Court, with the help of Marshall, the NAACP, and the American Civil Liberties Union.

An apologetic Judge Barefoot said to Dunjee, "No need to worry, you'll win on appeal."

Marshall also thought that he would win on appeal. He had a fresh and powerful Supreme Court precedent — a March 1, 1943, decision written by Justice Felix Frankfurter in the case of *McNabb v. U.S.* The Court struck down the convictions of two men who had been arrested in the middle of the night, put in a barren cell for fourteen hours, then "for two days they were subjected to unremitting questioning by numerous officers," Frankfurter wrote, concluding that "a conviction resting on evidence secured through such a flagrant disregard" of the laws "cannot be allowed to stand."

On April 26, 1944, the *Lyons* case was argued before the Supreme Court. The issue was simple but of landmark proportions: Where a defendant is coerced into confessing that he committed a crime, and that first confession is ruled inadmissible, can the state secure a second confession only hours later and argue that the second confession does not violate either the Fourteenth or Fifth Amendments of the Constitution? Marshall, Hall, William H. Hastie, and Leon A. Ransom represented Lyons. Morris Ernst, longtime counsel of the Civil Liberties Union, in an amicus curiae brief, urged reversal of Lyons's conviction. Sam H. Lattimore, assistant attorney general of Oklahoma, with attorney general Randell S. Cobb on the brief, represented the prosecution.

On June 5, 1944, the Supreme Court upheld the conviction of Lyons. Justice Stanley F. Reed delivered the opinion for the Court. To the dismay of many, Justice William O. Douglas concurred. Reed seemed ambivalent, even apologetic: "The Oklahoma Criminal Court of Appeals in the present case decided that the evidence would justify a determination that the effect of a prior coercion was dissipated before the second confession and we agree." However, Reed said: "A coerced confession is offensive to basic standards of justice, not because the victim has a legal grievance against the police, but because declarations procured by torture are not premises from which a civilized forum will infer guilt. The Fourteenth Amendment does not provide review of mere error in jury verdicts, even though the error concerns the voluntary character of a confession. We cannot say that an inference of guilt based in part upon Lyons's McAlester confession is so illogical and unreasonable as to deny [Lyons] a fair trial."

In simple language, the majority said, "Yes, they beat Lyons to get the first confession, but the effects of the abuse had evaporated before he confessed the second time." Justice Frank Murphy said with great passion: "This flagrant abuse by a state of the rights of an American citizen accused of murder ought not be approved. The admission of such a tainted confession does not accord with the Fourteenth Amendment's command that a state shall not convict a defendant on evidence that he was 'compelled to give against himself.' "

Justice Black concurred in Murphy's dissent. Justice Wiley B. Rutledge dissented on his own.

Lyons stayed in prison.

It was this triple-murder case, which Marshall lost so painfully, that transformed an improverished, angry young Baltimore lawyer into a celebrated user of the Constitution. The *Lyons* case taught Marshall that the entire American judicial system was stacked against nonwhites, the weak, and the poor in myriad ways.

"Hell, Lyons wouldn't have had a single sumbitch in the world to try to save him if the NAACP had not waded in," Marshall told me.

The *Lyons* case illustrated to him the ease with which powerful crooks, under cover of government, could railroad to prison a "chicken thief," an impoverished fall guy. It told Marshall that when forces of evil penetrated the judicial system, no lawyer, no defendant, could rely on social relationships with a Judge Barefoot, or any member of a court of appeals or the Supreme Court. They all had their own social and political agendas.

The *Lyons* case drilled into the mind of Marshall the ugly reality that America's system of justice, however praised it was in comparison with those of Germany, Italy, Japan, was still poisoned by brutality, coerced confessions, judges beholden to partisan political debts, the inability of the poor or the unpopular to get good counsel, racially and politically stacked juries, and so much more.

Marshall would forever wish to wipe this Oklahoma and Supreme Court defeat off his résumé of triumph, but when I talked to him half a century later it became clear that *Lyons* had left a gaping wound in his heart. He had tried to heal the hurt at many Christmastimes by mailing $3, $5, or whatever he could scrape up to Lyons, telling the prisoner to "use this to buy some candy, or cigarettes, or whatever you need most."

Marshall said to me recently, softly, sadly: "I *still* think Lyons was innocent."

So did many Oklahomans, white and black. After a quarter century of incarceration, Lyons was pardoned by Governor Henry Bellmon on May 24, 1965. I have not been able to find Lyons or anyone who knows what happened to him after he walked out of the McAlester prison.

CHAPTER EIGHT

═══════════

RACE WARS

MARSHALL had little time to lick his wounds from that failed defense of Lyons. He just had to swallow the Supreme Court decision read by Justice Reed and get on with the other problems that almost overwhelmed him.

"Hell, the civil rights war was still raging on a hundred fronts. I didn't have any time to regurgitate *Lyons.* I knew that you journalists would do that. I had to figure out what the future priorities of the NAACP had to be. I saw that the old-style 'necktie parties' where they lynched Negroes were not so numerous [there were only three mob murders of blacks in 1943, according to the Tuskegee Institute in Alabama, the national authority]. But I knew that that figure misled the White House, the Justice Department, and millions of other Americans, because it did not reflect the depth of racial hatred in America. Shit, they weren't hanging black men from trees much anymore; they were lynching them 'legally' in courtrooms of the sort that Lyons was tried in. The police, with rare exceptions, were anti-Negro, and willing to lie and lie to put any black defendant in prison. The ordinary defendant had no chance of getting a good, competent, caring lawyer. The whole damn court system was stacked against Afro-Americans, other minorities, poor whites — all but the rich who were members of the same clubs as the judges, the fancy lawyers, the newspaper editors.

"In those days I would lie awake some nights worrying that Detroit and other cities that had industries that were critical to the war effort were becoming tinderboxes because whites, from the Roosevelt brain trust to the unions, wanted to keep Negroes out of the war mobilization jobs.

"The tragedy was that Roosevelt didn't have a fucking clue as to the explosive tensions that were building up. I tried to explain it to Attorney General Francis Biddle, but he never could comprehend a damned thing if it related to Negro rights.

"Hell, Walter White, Wilkins, and I once tried to convince Roosevelt, Biddle, Stimson, and others that retaining Jim Crow in the U.S. war effort was 'immoral, inviting God's punishment.' Next thing I saw was war propaganda in which heavyweight champion Joe Louis was saying, 'We'll win, because God is on our side.' "

They struck out with FDR, but convinced Eleanor Roosevelt that every governmental act of racial discrimination would be multiplied a thousand times within a frightened and frustrated population. They argued that mindless members of the Ku Klux Klan and agents of Hitler would create racial strife and weaken the solidarity of the American people. Mrs. Roosevelt believed. She knew that this was not the NAACP crying wolf. The Office of War Information had warned that "all hell will break loose in Detroit" unless public officials dampened the racial hostility. *Life* magazine had used nine pages in its August 1942 edition to say "Detroit Is Dynamite."

The U.S. had not been in the war for a year before the truth of the NAACP appeals was evidenced in racial outbreaks in Los Angeles; Beaumont, Texas; Mobile, Alabama; Newark, New Jersey; El Paso, Texas; Philadelphia; and other places.

Despite all the pressures Eleanor put on him, FDR remained prisoner of his dilemma: he believed that southern segregationists in Congress had ultimate control over his mobilization and war efforts. Thus he dared not heed the appeals of blacks who warned of social peril.

On the morning of June 21, 1943, White and Marshall got a telephone call from Gloster Current, then head of the Detroit NAACP office, in which he reported that "About one o'clock this morning, an altercation at Belle Island occurred. It is rumored that a white sailor stationed at the naval base there started it, and that a Negro baby was thrown into the lake." Meanwhile, the media were reporting a variety of versions of how the violence began, but all reported many deaths and injuries.

White wired President Roosevelt (with a copy to Elmer Davis of the Office of War Information) urging a nationwide address in which the president would order an end to "deliberately provoked attacks which are designed to hamper war production, destroy or weaken morale, and to deny minorities, Negroes in particular, the opportunity to participate in war effort on same basis as other Americans. We are certain that unless you act, these outbreaks will increase in number and violence." The consummate operator, White immediately got press credentials from the *New York Post* and asked for priority in getting an airline flight to Detroit.

The next day, probably more because of an urgent request from the governor of Michigan than because of White's telegram, Roosevelt ordered federal troops into Detroit to quell the worst civil disturbance in America since the end of World War I. By this time twenty-five people were dead — twenty-two Negroes and three whites — and seven hundred people were injured. Detroit's Receiving Hospital was overwhelmed with 422 bleeding or dying patients. United Press said that in one ward "a Negro sat in a chair, his sightless eyes staring at the ceiling. He was dead on admittance and police hurriedly had placed him in the chair until he could be taken to the morgue."

Wilkins sent this angry telegram to Detroit's Mayor Edward Jeffries:

ASSOCIATED PRESS REPORTS TABULATE KILLINGS IN DETROIT RIOT INDICATING VAST MAJORITY OF VICTIMS WERE PUT TO DEATH BY DETROIT POLICE. NOT A SINGLE WHITE PERSON IS RECORDED AS HAVING BEEN SHOT BY POLICE. . . . IMPRESSION POLICE WERE BATTLING NEGROES AND NOT SEEKING TO QUELL RIOT. . . . KILLINGS HAVE SHOCKED NATION AND WARNED 30 MILLION NEGROES EVERYWHERE THAT REGULARLY CONSTITUTED POLICE AUTHORITIES ARE NOT PROTECTORS OF COMMUNITY BUT DEADLY ENEMIES OF THE NEGRO RACE. . . .

This hit Detroit's white leaders — white was all there were then — as an insult no white man would take from a black one.

Detroit had long been a hotbed of racial hatred. Newspapers pointed out that in March 1942, scores of blacks and whites had been injured in disorders when blacks tried to move into the Sojourner Truth Settlement housing project in the wake of a cross burning. And just a month before the Belle Island eruption, twenty thousand whites at the Packard automobile plant had staged an unauthorized walkout after three Negro workers were promoted. This was only one of many organized efforts to keep black migrants off the auto assembly lines and out of other jobs in Detroit.

The War Production Board was alarmed. Joseph D. Keenan, its

vice chairman, said on June 25 that the war effort had lost *a million man hours* as a result of the rioting.

Rabbi Israel Goldstein of Temple B'nai Jeshurun in New York City saw the Detroit violence as a rebirth of the Ku Klux Klan and as "a danger to be reckoned with." He said in a sermon, "If our Federal, State, and municipal authorities address themselves with the same energy to this problem on the home front as they have manifested in the provision of manpower, money, and implements for overseas war needs, our domestic troubles can be solved."

That sermon was still resounding in the synagogue when William E. Dowling, the Wayne County (Detroit) prosecutor, charged that the Negro press and the NAACP were responsible for the rioting. He said that Louis Martin, editor of the *Michigan Chronicle*, was "the principal instigator of dissension." (This is the same black Louis Martin who became a powerful aide to President Kennedy and remains one of the most beloved men in America.) Detroit's Police Commissioner John H. Witherspoon backed Dowling in public, then fired off a letter to White saying that if NAACP officials "would devote as much time to educating the people they represent to respect law and order . . . as they do to charges of alleged improper conduct on the part of police officers . . . the organization would be more helpful than detrimental."

That really lifted the hackles of Marshall, who decided to join White in Detroit. In July they produced their own document on "What Caused THE DETROIT RIOT?" White wrote a long sociological treatise about immigration, the work force, the bad housing situation for blacks, the role of the labor unions, and then offered President Roosevelt a detailed program to cure everything. Marshall was, as usual, blunt:

"In the June riots of this year," he wrote, "the Detroit police ran true to form. The trouble reached riot proportions because the police of Detroit once again enforced the law under an unequal hand. They used 'persuasion' rather than firm action with white rioters while against Negroes they used the ultimate in force: night sticks, revolvers, riot guns, sub-machine guns, and deer guns. As a result 25 of the 34 persons killed were Negroes. Of the 25 Negroes killed, 17 were killed by police. The excuses of the Police Department for the disproportionate number of Negroes killed is that the majority of them were killed while committing felonies, namely, the looting of stores on Hastings Street. It is true that some Negroes were looting stores on Hastings Street. . . . It is equally true that white persons were turning over and burning automobiles on Woodward

Avenue. This is arson. Others were beating Negroes with iron pipes, clubs, and rocks. This is felonious assault. Several Negroes were stabbed. This is assault with intent to murder." This report was surely, in its boldness and uncompromising language, a definition of Thurgood Marshall. Those riots, added to the Lyons defeat, made him fiercely angry at a criminal justice system stacked against minorities, the poor — anyone who lived outside the circles of power and privilege.

"War is hell in every place and time," Marshall told me, "but it was a special hell for people who were forced to fight for freedoms they had never known, for liberties that thousands of them would die without knowing. But I was no war protester, no pretender that I had some great religious or other objection of conscience to fighting. Hell, I had fought white men at the drop of the word 'nigger.' Walter [White] and Roy [Wilkins] worried like hell that I might be drafted, but I didn't. My *draft board* knew where I was more than Buster did. I think the people on my draft board agreed secretly that they didn't need a damned troublemaking lawyer in the military. So I never got drafted. But every day I knew that I was in the army, in heart and spirit, when I got an endless string of telephone calls, telegrams, letters, from colored GIs, or their wives, parents, girlfriends. I got some heart-wrenching stories of bigotry on base and off base, of blacks sentenced to the brig, given dishonorable discharges, or being abused in many ways for racial reasons. Nobody was into that war more than I was."

Fighting a war against Hitler, Naziism, the Holocaust, "Aryan supremacy," and all the inhuman depredations of the Third Reich and the Axis nations should have made any American believe devoutly in the Declaration of Independence, the Bill of Rights, the post–Civil War Amendments. Few Americans wanted to believe in them more than Marshall, even in the wake of his bitter defeat in the *Lyons* case, in the face of other courtroom setbacks, and of mounting evidence that at no level of American life did the behavior of the people match the wartime platitudes.

World War II was oozing bloodily and atomically to a climax in the fateful year of 1945. President Roosevelt had died of a cerebral hemorrhage in Warm Springs, Georgia, in April, the same month in which Italy's Benito Mussolini had been caught while trying to escape to Switzerland, and executed. Two days later Hitler had killed himself, and the flamboyant Nazi propagandist Joseph Goebbels and his wife had poisoned their children and committed suicide. President Truman had ordered the dropping of atomic bombs on Hiroshima, Japan, on August 6, and Nagasaki on August 9. The "war to end all wars" had opened up an era in which Marshall saw vast opportunities for lifting black Americans to legal equality in their homeland. As Spottswood Robinson has said, Marshall worried a lot about the worst things that could happen, yet in some of the most vexing moments he could find reason for optimism.

"I watched the bravery and patriotism of blacks, of the Japanese in World War Two," Marshall said, "and I couldn't believe white Americans would continue to treat them as semislaves. People who died flying fighter planes in an Air Force that didn't welcome them. Japanese boys who fought valiantly even though their parents and other relatives were behind the barbed wire of our concentration camps. I'd have bet a bundle that after that war the white Americans who controlled things would respect the Thirteenth, Fourteenth, and Fifteenth Amendments, and the statutes passed after the Civil War, and that this country would move to place the colored race, in respect to civil rights, upon a level equal to whites."

But Marshall's dreams were crushed by the reality of a society saying to homecoming black GIs, "Niggers, get back in your place." By the end of 1945, Marshall had become a very angry black man.

He saw black people being shoved by the military, the courts, state legislatures, even the White House, into a legal status barely removed from the harsh days of involuntary servitude. In schools, universities, on buses and trains, in the workplace, in restaurants, hotels, and theaters, Marshall saw the stigma of Jim Crow being stamped upon the brows of any American deemed by some "white" person to have enough "African blood" to classify him or her as "a Negro," and thus an object of scorn, to be isolated like a leper.

Marshall was appalled by the docility, the lack of spirit for legal revolt, displayed by the great masses of black people, especially where the education and dreams of their children's future were at stake. On October 24, 1945, he sent this memorandum to Walter White:

> I am more than worried about our inability to get cases started on the equalization of educational opportunities in the South. I have mentioned so many times that this type of case is not only of tremendous importance to our branches, but in addition to this reason, it should be recognized that these are the easiest cases to win.
>
> We have the lawyers ready but we do not have the cases. It

seems to me that we should sit down in a conference of some sort with the staff and see if there is some way to get our branches to work in this field. I think the lawyers have done everything they can do without being guilty of [soliciting] litigations, yet there must be some other way to remedy this situation.

"I thoroughly agree," White wrote back the same day, and called a staff meeting for a week later, where it was agreed that the legal staff would be increased to four full-time lawyers — Marshall, his deputy, Robert L. Carter, Franklin Williams, and Miss Marion Perry — plus a part-time legal clerk, Miss Constance Baker.

Marshall rushed a letter to the Association's eight hundred branches informing them of the new staff potential, and saying:

> To Officers of N.A.A.C.P. Branches:
> The N.A.A.C.P. has established court precedents guaranteeing the right of absolute equality in education in all levels from the highest graduate school to the lowest elementary school. However, we have not been diligent in enforcing these principles in any areas of the country. We do not have a "separate but equal" school system any place in the United States.
> The National Office is ready and willing to cooperate with you in your efforts to equalize educational opportunities.
> Returning veterans are denied the right to attend graduate and professional schools throughout the south. No other education is offered them within their states. This is a flagrant violation of the principle established in the *Gaines* case and it is the duty of the N.A.A.C.P. to see to it that our returning veterans are not denied their constitutional rights.

As Marshall's unease and anger grew, he drafted an article on the issue of "separate but equal" which he submitted to the *New York Age* in December 1945. He wrote:

> On the question of whether or not it is lawful to segregate American citizens solely because of their race or color, most of the courts in the land, including the United States Supreme Court, have unfortunately adopted the fiction of "separate but equal." Under this fiction there has grown up a group of court decisions holding that the equality guaranteed by the Fourteenth Amendment can be given in a segregated system providing equal facilities are maintained. This fiction built up by the courts must at some time be cast aside in favor of the establishment of a policy that segregation is discrimination.

There are at present cases in the Interstate Commerce Commission challenging the application of Jim Crow travel statutes to interstate passengers. There is a similar case now pending in the United States Supreme Court which is the first case clearly raising this point before the United States Supreme Court. There are cases in local federal courts challenging the policy of segregation in Federal Public Housing Projects. There are cases in many state courts challenging the constitutionality of racial restrictive covenants preventing Negroes from owning or occupying certain private homes.

The right not to be discriminated against in registering and voting is paramount. Last year the United States Supreme Court declared illegal the "white primary" prevalent throughout the South. Despite this clearcut decision and despite the fact that Negroes are still denied the right to vote in primary elections in many of the southern states, the United States Department of Justice has refused to prosecute any of these election officials.

Marshall lashed out at Democrats Franklin D. Roosevelt, Alben Barkley of Kentucky, and Harry Truman, accusing them of sabotaging the Fair Employment Practices Commission. Then he wrote of two pending legal cases that held his heartfelt interest.

Dr. Benjamin F. Mays, the long-distinguished president of Morehouse College in Atlanta, had gone to the dining car of a Southern Railway Company train traveling through South Carolina to find that the section curtained off and supposedly reserved for "colored" passengers was occupied by white diners, even though tables were vacant in the main dining car. Mays was denied service on grounds that, under South Carolina law, no black could eat in the main dining area, and could not eat in the curtained-off "colored" section if a white person was in there. The NAACP had filed suit citing the commerce clause of the Constitution and the Interstate Commerce Act as forbidding South Carolina or any other state to segregate, or otherwise discriminate against, a Negro passenger in interstate travel.

"The Association takes the position that Dr. Mays, who was paying the same charges as were paid by white passengers for similar accommodations, was entitled to be served in the dining car so long as and under the same conditions as white passengers were served."

Here was *Plessy v. Ferguson* revisited, a modern version of the 1896 railway segregation case in Louisiana that led to the Supreme Court decision declaring "separate but equal" constitutional.

Jim Crow was commonplace in transportation across the South, not just on trains, but on city trolley systems, buses, in airports and depots. Marshall had fretted over his difficulties in getting cases with which to challenge the system in court. Virginia was notoriously racist in its statutory requirement of racial separation, but its law enforcement officers were shrewd in avoiding any challenge by the courts or the Interstate Commerce Commission. A black traveler who tried to sit among whites would be arrested for "disturbing the peace," not for violation of the Jim Crow statute.

One day Spottswood Robinson, the NAACP's Richmond lawyer, got an irate call from a black woman, Irene Morgan, who had been arrested when she refused to accept Jim Crow accommodations while traveling on a Greyhound bus from Virginia to Washington, D.C. Robinson was about to dismiss her lightly when it dawned upon him that she had been charged, not with disorderly conduct, but with violating the Jim Crow law. He leaped on the case, but lost in the Supreme Court of Virginia.

Now, in 1945, because Spottswood Robinson was not yet approved for practice before the Supreme Court, Marshall would argue *Irene V. Morgan v. The Commonwealth of Virginia.* This fuming attorney made it clear that he was eager for the legal wars.

"During the past few years," he wrote, "the Association and private attorneys have fought other battles against the Jim Crow statutes of the South, and have won some victories. It is hoped that in the cases involving Dr. Mays and Mrs. Morgan we will get rulings from the Federal courts which will outlaw Jim Crow transportation among the several states. That will, of course, still leave the problem of Jim Crow in transportation which takes place wholly within the boundaries of one state."

On June 3, 1946, Justice Reed delivered the Supreme Court's ruling in the *Morgan* case that Jim Crow statutes could not be imposed upon interstate travelers, or upon vehicles moving across state lines.

Here, with the war ending and many thousands of black GIs coming home, full of new dreams about democracy and justice, Marshall had scored a sweet triumph and delivered a new level of dignity to black travelers. The highest court had wiped away a smidgen of his anger.

"Who the fuck else who's black would have gone into Hugo, Oklahoma, in 1941?" [in the *Lyons* case] Howard president Jim Nabrit once asked me.

That *was* a perilous mission. On the day he arrived, barred by race from staying in the town's hotel, most black families were too frightened to rent him a place to sleep. An aged black widow said, "I ain't scared," and welcomed him in. That first night she snored while Marshall lay awake in fear.

"I never wanted anyone, I mean anybody, to know that during that first night in Hugo I lay on the bed sweating in fear. I think I remembered every lynching story that I had read about after World War One. I could see my dead body lying in some place where they let white kids out of Sunday School to come and look at me, and rejoice."

Marshall's personal courage got a major test in 1946 when the physical harm that he always anticipated occurred in Columbia, a town of eight thousand people in Maury County, Tennessee. A terrible racial blowup had occurred there in late February. It began when a black woman, Mrs. Gladys Stephenson, complained about the radio repair job that a white man named William Fleming had done for her. Resenting Mrs. Stephenson's criticism, the twenty-eight-year-old Fleming slapped her. James Stephenson, Mrs. Stephenson's nineteen-year-old son and a Navy veteran, went quickly to his mother's defense, and knocked the white radio repairman through a plate-glass window. Stephenson and his mother were jailed on charges of assault. Fleming, who was only slightly injured, was not arrested.

Tensions mounted rapidly. One black leader went to Sheriff J. J. Underwood and demanded that the Stephensons be let out on bail because, "Let me tell you one thing, Sheriff, there won't be any more 'social lynchings' in Columbia." The two blacks were released on $3,500 bond.

In talking about "social lynchings" this black leader, J. W. Blair, was referring to the fact that two Columbia Negroes had been lynched within the previous two decades and in each case it was an affair to which hundreds of whites had been invited as spectators. One lynch victim was a seventeen-year-old youth named Cordie Cheek, who was slain even though a grand jury had refused to indict him on a charge that he molested a white girl. Blacks in Columbia whispered for years that the car which transported Cheek to the area of the social lynching belonged to the very magistrate who had fixed the bond in the Stephenson case. Less than two hours after the Stephensons were released, some seventy-five men came to the jail and began kicking on the door. Sheriff Underwood leveled a submachine gun at them and ordered them to disperse. Two members of the mob were so drunk they couldn't even leave the jail, and were locked up on charges of disorderly conduct. The other whites began the bedlam.

Policemen and hoodlums spread wanton destruction throughout the black community, claiming they were searching for weapons. A black physician's office was reduced to shambles, with furniture damaged and decorations mutilated. Morton's Funeral Home was ransacked by vandals who used plaster of Paris to scrawl the initials "KKK" on a coffin.

By the end of February, more than one hundred blacks had been arrested, and only four whites, although newspaper photographs showed white hoodlums walking the streets freely armed with sawed-off shotguns. On February 28, two Negro prisoners were shot to death, and one was wounded by policemen who were questioning them. The official explanation was that William Gordon and James Johnson were slain when Gordon reached into a pile of guns, managed to pull out one that matched the bullets that he allegedly had smuggled into jail, loaded the gun, and then fired on his police questioners before they could detect what he was doing. The National Lawyers Guild called the killings "murder."

Ultimately, twenty-five black people went on trial, charged with assault with intent to commit murder. Marshall, Nashville lawyer Z. Alexander Looby, and others from the NAACP intervened, and they got freedom for twenty-three of the black people.

In mid-November 1946, Marshall went back to Columbia to argue in behalf of the last two accused blacks, William Pillow and Lloyd Kennedy. He won an acquittal for Pillow and a limited sentence of five years for Kennedy, which infuriated the police of Columbia. No one could concoct a more chilling story than the one Marshall told to me about his effort to leave Columbia and drive back to Nashville:

"The mob followed me out across Duck River — the mob was a very interesting mob. It was composed equally of state troopers and city police [two state troopers, two Columbia policemen, and four Maury County sheriffs and constables]. They said they had a warrant to search our car. I said, 'Go ahead!' And then I thought for a moment and said to one of the guys in our car, 'Look, let's watch him. Don't let him put any liquor in there, 'cause this is a dry county.'

"Well, they said they couldn't find anything, so then one of the members of the mob whispered loud enough for me to hear it, 'The warrant only covers the car.' He turned to me and the other blacks and said, 'Do you agree to a body search?' We told him, 'Well, hell no, we don't agree to it.'

"He said, 'Go on.' And then we drove about a mile when they pulled us over again.

"I was driving the first time, but I let Looby drive after the first search. The officer looked at me, then said to Looby, 'You weren't driving this car.' Looby said, 'I'm not answering your questions.' He looked at me and said, 'Weren't you driving the car?' I said, 'I'm not answering your questions, either.'

"Then I heard a voice in the back say, 'That's the one! The tall yaller nigger!' So they took me out toward the river and told Looby and the other guys to keep going the other way. Looby wouldn't go the other way. He was one brave man. He followed them as they carried me down toward the river. When we got down to the riverbanks you could see the people for the party. By party, I mean lynch party. But Looby and the others wouldn't leave, so the whites didn't know what to do. So we drove back into Columbia, and the head guy of the group accosting us, the head of the city police, whose name was Lynch — I thought that was a good name — said to me, 'You go across the street and you see that sign that says Justice of the Peace? You go across there and I'll be over there.' I said, 'I'll only go over there if you go with me.'

" 'Why?' the cop said.

"I said, 'I'm not going to go over there so you can shoot me in the back and claim that I was escaping. That's too easy. You come with me.'

"So he went over there with me, where there was this little magistrate, a very short guy — five feet two at the most. The magistrate said, 'What's this guy charged with?'

" 'Drunken driving,' the cop said.

"The magistrate turned to me and said, 'Look, I'm a teetotaler. I've never had a drink in my life. If you're willing to take my test, I'll decide your guilt or innocence.'

" 'What's your test?' I asked.

" 'Blow your breath in my face,' he said. So I blew my breath, and the magistrate rocked a little bit and looked at the cop and said, 'You're crazy. This man hasn't even had a drink. He's certainly not drunk.'

"So I walked out to where Looby and the other Negroes were waiting, and told them what had happened. They said, 'Well, Thurgood, we'll put you in another car,' which they did, and they put another driver in Looby's car. The guy who was in the original car with me was a local guy. After Looby and I had gone, the cops grabbed the local guy and they beat him bad enough that he had to stay in the hospital for a month. I mean, they didn't play around."

Marshall did not become the "treat" at a lynch party because of the protection he got from a group of black men who had shown that they were willing to die before submitting to new social lynchings in Maury County. The field general of the black revolt was Sol Blair, a veteran of World War I, but the enforcer was Milton Murray, an Army frogman who had fought from North Africa into Italy and was then put into a unit that was to help invade Japan. That assignment was aborted when atomic bombs were dropped on Hiroshima and Nagasaki. Murray had returned to Columbia one day before Stephenson had thrown the white man, Fleming, through the plate-glass window. Murray had brought home from the Army a Thompson submachine gun, as had another black called "Popeye." When word spread that Ku Klux Klansmen and police in Maury County had joined forces in a scheme to kill Stephenson and his mother, Milton and Popeye got out their weapons of war.

Tensions mounted, but there was no major violence until an ambulance screamed through the black community and the white men inside it began firing on black people. Suddenly Columbia became Anzio, Okinawa, every battleground ever known. Murray showed me where blacks set up a command post in Blair's barbershop, and how he and others went to the top of an adjacent building, firing furiously at the policemen and Klansmen who were hunkered down in a higher building a block away. Murray said he saw some stricken whites fall from the roof of their building, and that the black group took some casualties. Legend in black Columbia still has it that whites held funerals at night so as to deny Murray and other blacks knowledge of how many people they had killed.

Murray was solemn, but still defiant, last September when he showed me and my Gannett Company camera crew the bullet holes that are still in the bricks, the mortar, the concrete, of two buildings, despite forty-five years of city officials' efforts to plug them and paint them over.

Murray told me that black forces retreated when they got word that the National Guard was coming in. Even his and Popeye's submachine guns were no match for National Guard firepower. Murray said he had just enough time to run and hide his weapon. He was arrested on charges of loitering and spent only twenty-four hours in jail. But twenty-one black men were charged with extremely serious crimes. That is when Marshall, Looby, and others from the NAACP came in to free some and to get reduced sentences for others.

"Until Marshall came, the law in Columbia was whatever a white lawyer or white policeman or white judge said it was," Murray recalled. "These whites were humiliated when Marshall stood in the courthouse and told them what the Constitution said and what the statutes of Tennessee really said. Thurgood had nerves of steel. He just didn't give a damn how many whites he embarrassed. I admired him for that. But I was overwhelmed by the willingness of this man to come into a race-crazy community and risk his life to defend twenty-one black men he had never met."

Murray lifted his shirtsleeve and said: "Look at my skin. You mention Thurgood Marshall and goose bumps come out all over my body. I would lay down my life today for that man because he gave me a renewal of life. He made it possible for me to be a man."

Murray, now seventy-two and on crutches because of two bad hips, took me and my camera crew down to the spot on the Duck River where the lynch party awaited "the tall yaller nigger." He showed us where the sheriff's officers and the Tennessee highway patrolmen had stopped the caravan taking Marshall, Looby, and others back to Nashville. It was too dangerous for Marshall to spend the night in Columbia, so he commuted morning and night from Nashville. Marshall and Looby acceded to a search of their car, Murray recalled, but he and others told the policemen that they had no warrant and no right to search their car (which was full of weapons, including Murray's submachine gun).

Murray said he and another man who was protecting Thurgood spotted some people down by the river.

"Oh, oh!!" he half shouted. "They're trying to lead Thurgood to the river. There's a crowd of Klansmen and others down there who are supposed to overpower the cops and take Mr. Marshall." He said the black men jumped out of their four cars with their mighty arsenal of weapons.

"Gentlemen, the party stops right here," Murray shouted.

"Y'all are free to go on back into town," one policeman replied.

"We aren't going anywhere," Murray said. "The party is over."

The police forces did not want another fierce shootout in which they, and Marshall, surely would have died. A cop or a Klan leader gave a signal that "THE NIGGERS HAVE GUNS," and those who had come to revel in the hanging of Marshall fled in panic.

Murray says that the next morning a group of armed black men went to the river and found the lynch rope and noose still hanging from the tree. They cut it down as a souvenir.

Milton Murray became a marked man, the prime target of a Ku Klux Klan that embraced many members of the law enforcement establishment. Two years after he helped to prevent the lynching of Marshall, his house was burned down. Someone shot dead all the cattle on his farm. Murray got new cattle, but they were quickly slain.

So this incredibly brave black man had to go to Nashville, and then Chattanooga, to find work. He finally came back to a Columbia where he says he still is not safe.

"Why do you still run the risk of white vengeance?" I asked him.

"Because I don't want my son to think I'm a coward," he said. "And because I owe a debt to one of the bravest, proudest men this country ever produced — Thurgood Marshall."

There, alongside the Duck River, I noticed tears in Murray's eyes.

"Tears of joy," he said, "that somebody has finally given me a chance to talk about what that marvelous man Marshall did for me, and this town, and all the persecuted people of the world. Just tears of joy."

Marshall alerted White, Wilkins, and everybody in the NAACP headquarters about how close he had come to being lynched. Angry NAACP officials fired off the following letter to their branches asking them to:

Write or wire President Harry S. Truman and U.S. Attorney General Tom Clark. In your communications demand:

A. *An immediate investigation by the FBI* of the incident and urge that criminal charges be pressed against the officers participating in November 18th's outrage by the Department of Justice.

B. Ample protection of lawyers and participants in subsequent trials to be held in Tennessee.

No officers were ever prosecuted.

Hollywood has done its *To Kill a Mockingbird* and *The Intruder* and a score of other movies about lynchings and brutalizations, but I found that no movie was as compelling as just sitting and listening to Marshall tell stories of his journeys into the land of Jim Crow where, in some communities, he would go into one house to have dinner and pretend to go to bed, then sneak into the darkness and shift to some black family's house on the other side of town.

"If the Klan and the other violent crackers were on one side, we had to move to the other side," he explained.

Marshall recalls that when he went to the Deep South in the late thirties and forties, he had to go alone. Because of the NAACP's lack of funds there were no aides, no secretary, "nobody but me — I don't know how I did it."

But somehow this young lawyer managed to stay in black homes when no hotel dared give him shelter, and he lay awake nights wondering when the lynch mob might come.

In telling that Columbia story, Marshall repeated to me what he had said in 1955 and would say until his death: "I don't deserve the credit. The people who dared to stand up, to file lawsuits, were beaten and sometimes murdered after I spoke my piece and took the fastest goddamn train I could find out of the area."

Sometimes the train didn't get there fast enough. Marshall tells of the time that he was in Mississippi, in a little town where he had to change trains, standing on the platform alone, just waiting:

"I was hungry. It was the middle of the day. I looked over and saw across the street that there was a restaurant. I said to myself, 'You've got better sense than to go in the front door, but you probably can go and see if they'll sell you a sandwich through that back door.' Then I insisted on my civil rights, to myself, as I got hungrier. So I started down the platform to go over there and get a sandwich. All of a sudden this big white man came up who was about two inches taller than me — a big feller with no uniform on, but a noticeably long pistol on his side. He said, 'Nigger, what are you doing here?' I said, 'I was going' — and he interrupted me to say, 'What did you say?' I said, '*Sir*, I'm changing trains.' And he said, 'Well, there's only one more train coming through here today and that's at four o'clock, and you damn sight better get on it, 'cause the sun is never going down on a live nigger in this town.'

"I wasn't hungry anymore. I was going to catch the next train that came by, even if it was a freight. I was going to get on it. He could have pulled that gun and blown my brains out, and he wouldn't have had to explain it. People just don't know that those guys down there in those days were rough people. They killed many a Negro. All down there I saw Negroes with courage. I remember this man — I don't remember his first name — a little gentleman in West Palm Beach, Florida. He was about five feet two or three, he was really a great leader, and he went in the polling booth. He was trying to get Negroes to vote, and he ended up in an argument with a white man who said, 'Nigger, you have no business here.' And this man, this tiny guy, looked at this great big guy and said, and this I remember verbatim, 'I don't doubt you can whip me. I don't doubt you *will* whip me, but so help me God, if you reach toward me, I'll spit on you.' I've never forgotten this guy, and you know what? The white man turned on his heels and walked out. And this little black guy just stood there like he wasn't surprised. *I* was surprised!"

I asked Marshall if his wife, Buster, worried when he was on these kinds of trips.

"How the hell should I know? I think she took it the same way I did. If it happens, it happens," he replied.

Then Marshall launched into a story about an NAACP official in

Columbia, South Carolina, who came within a phone call of being lynched. This was in 1953, when Marshall and the top NAACP man in South Carolina, James M. Hinton, were fighting for equal pay for black teachers.

Marshall was in Washington at the time, working diligently with Nabrit, Hastie, and other key black lawyers in the Charles Hotel. They had stopped for a late poker game. Fortunately for Hinton, Buster always had a pretty good idea as to where Thurgood was. When a woman, Jessica Simpkins, called from Columbia to say that she had to talk to Thurgood urgently, Buster told her to try the Charles Hotel. An irritated Marshall left the poker table to hear her say that a mob had Hinton, somewhere in or around Macon, Georgia, and that they were going to lynch him.

Marshall telephoned Robert McC. Figg, Jr., the white lawyer who was his opponent in the school segregation case *Briggs v. Elliott,* and the South Carolina teacher pay case. Marshall knew Figg had contacts — and clout — and was a decent man.

Figg called the FBI in South Carolina and was told that the Bureau didn't investigate crimes until after they had occurred. Figg decided he had more influence in Georgia than he did in South Carolina. He placed a crucial call to an unrevealed source. All of a sudden, as Marshall recalled the story, FBI agents and other policemen reached the place where the lynch party was going to occur. The black victim-to-be, Hinton, was a minister, so even as the lynch mob was trying to put the rope around his neck, he had stalled them by asking for time to pray. They granted it. While Hinton was praying, he later told Marshall, a car rolled up with sirens blaring, and somebody yelled to the leader of the mob, "You've got the wrong man!" The mob leader walked over to the praying black man and said, "Nigger, what is your name?"

"The Reverend James N. Hinton," their prisoner said.

"Hell, you're not the nigger we want. Get out of here," the mob leader said.

Marshall leans back, somewhat misty-eyed in recalling that Figg, the lawyer who had opposed him in South Carolina, had saved the life of a colleague.

"Everybody we normally could have expected help from didn't give it to us," Marshall said. "The one white man we shouldn't have expected anything from saved Reverend Hinton's life."

Marshall told me the Hinton story, and that put him on a roll, inspired him to ask for a glass of Wild Turkey so he could tell me his other stories about his flirtations with death in pursuit of the constitutional rights of black people.

He got great joy out of telling me about going to Louisiana to fight Jim Crow, and pay discrimination against black teachers, and learning that the archsegregationists' political boss, Leander Perez, supposedly had put out a $10,000 contract on "that burr-headed nigger lawyer from New York." Marshall said that when he arrived in Louisiana the press was waiting for him, asking what he had to say about the alleged death threat.

"I told the press, 'Hell, I'm not burr-headed,' and they went into hysterics. But the situation in Louisiana was a mess, because Perez was a vicious racist. He got away with it because he bulldozed his way along. The only guy I knew that he couldn't bulldoze was Skelly Wright — Judge Skelly Wright. One other guy who stood up to him was John Minor Wisdom, another very brave guy down there." [The late Skelly Wright was a renowned federal appeals court judge in Washington, D.C., when he died, and John Minor Wisdom was one of the most celebrated federal judges in the nation's history.]

Marshall sipped his bourbon as he talked sentimentally about the greatness of these two men. Then he moved on to another story about the perils of being a black lawyer, trying to change the social structure, the laws, manners, and mores of an America still steeped in the notions and customs of slavery.

I learned, not just from Marshall, but from talking to Judge Skelly Wright and others, that the Thurgood who went to Louisiana to pry open that state's university was profoundly different from the lean and mean fledgling lawyer who had sued the University of Maryland Law School out of personal revenge. The lawyer whom Perez stereotyped as "burr-headed" now had a head full of concerns about a nation's willingness to adhere to its Constitution. Marshall had wrapped the parchment around his heart, and was exposing his body to every conceivable danger in order to prove that the words of Jefferson, Madison, Hamilton, Ben Franklin, Lincoln, were a living legacy.

Physical bravery is one thing, but political and social bravery is at a still higher level — especially when it incurs the wrath of presidents, or an unforgiving, brutal foe such as J. Edgar Hoover, an American icon who headed the FBI for forty-eight years.

Marshall challenged Hoover privately, as Martin Luther King, Jr., did publicly, as an enemy of black people and the civil rights movement. Hoover despised Marshall, but he never could get tapes or salacious bits of evidence with which to attack him publicly or try to assassinate his character.

A postwar spate of lynchings, of beatings of returning black GIs, so infuriated Marshall that he knew he had to challenge the Justice Department, even if it meant incurring Hoover's enmity.

A relationship of controlled hostility, of latent fury, had existed between the NAACP and the FBI for many years. Walter White was diplomatic, using the salutation, "My dear Mr. Hoover," when he wrote on June 17, 1941: "Over a period of some months this office has had inquiries regarding qualified Negroes being accepted in the F.B.I. The general impression seems to be that the F.B.I. does not employ Negroes, whatever their ability.

"Would you be good enough to advise me as to the Department's policy with respect to employment of Negroes. . . . It would be helpful if you also informed me of the capacities in which Negroes are employed. . . ."

Hoover replied that "this Bureau has no ban on the employment of Negroes . . . there are a number of Negroes . . . employed in both investigative and clerical capacities." Hoover later wrote that the FBI was so color-blind it did not even keep records of the race of its employees. He said he "wouldn't know how to get along" without the black man who sat outside his office. The truth was that the FBI had not a single black special agent, and put theater greasepaint on the faces of white agents when investigative work was required in all-black communities.

It was the eruption of lynchings and murders of blacks that produced a rift that White wanted to avoid. On August 21, 1946, White wrote Marshall's deputy, Robert Carter, requesting a memorandum citing "instances known to us where FBI operatives have shown themselves to be anti-Negro or pro-mob." White said he wanted the memo to accompany a letter that he would write to Hoover and the attorney general. Carter replied that any such memorandum should "await Mr. Marshall's return." White said that he didn't want any delay because "actions of the FBI in so many of these cases where they have shown open sympathy with the mob is such that we need . . . to keep them from messing up other cases."

Two weeks later White got a memorandum from Frank Williams of the legal department, alleging FBI collusion with antiblack elements, especially in a notorious case in which the eyes of a returning GI, Isaac Woodard, had been punched out. Williams wrote that Woodard had sworn that two FBI special agents had tried to force him to sign a blank piece of paper on which his "statement" about the South Carolina atrocity would be typed.

On September 17 White forwarded this charge, and others, to Hoover, who denied them all. He accused Williams of obstructing the FBI investigation.

"It has always been and will continue to be the policy of the Federal Bureau of Investigation to conduct all investigations in an entirely impartial, unbiased and factual manner," Hoover concluded.

"Bullshit," Marshall shouted loudly when he read that. He confided to Buster that he didn't like the underlying coziness that seemed to attend these exchanges between White and Hoover. He was going to "grab the bull" with his own hands.

On December 27, 1946, Marshall wrote to Attorney General Tom Clark saying:

> You will remember that sometime ago, I agreed to bring to your personal attention matters which affect Negroes in connection with the Department of Justice. The Federal Bureau of Investigation has done a good job on *average* in the South. . . . [But] the record of the F.B.I. in investigating cases involving Negroes has been notably one-sided. The inability of the F.B.I. to identify any members of the lynch mob in the Monroe, Georgia, lynchings is the latest example of this. In the disturbance at Columbia, Tennessee, on February 25th and 26th of this year, it is reported that F.B.I. agents were sent in almost immediately and were supposed to have made a thorough and complete investigation, yet, they were unable to produce the name of a single individual responsible for the acts of violence and the destruction of the property of the Negroes in that town.

Marshall went on to cite a *New York Times* editorial that was harshly critical of the FBI. This really got Hoover's attention. He had his agents prepare a reply which Clark sent to Marshall on January 13, 1947, the very same day that Hoover tried to go over Marshall's head by writing a letter of protest to Walter White. Clark's letter was a total and incredible defense of the FBI. (It was probably written by Hoover's aides.)

Clark said that after four Negroes were killed near Monroe, Georgia, the FBI interviewed nearly 2,800 people, including 106 who testified before a Federal grand jury in Athens, Georgia. Clark said, "The jury did not see fit to return an indictment against any of the individuals suspected of complicity in this crime."

Regarding the Columbia, Tennessee, cases where Marshall was almost lynched, Clark again blamed a grand jury that "concluded that there had been no violation of a Federal statute [and] commended the law enforcement officers for their handling of this case." Clark cited several cases in which he said the FBI had helped obtain convictions and sentences of people committing violence against Negroes. He repeated almost verbatim the Hoover claim that

Marshall's "NAACP associates" had refused to cooperate with the FBI.

If Marshall had any illusions that anyone in the Justice Department would dare to accept any criticism of Hoover and the FBI, they were wiped out when he saw Clark's whitewash — and what Hoover wrote to Walter White:

> In accord with our understanding, I wanted to bring to your attention a situation which is causing me increasing concern. It relates to the repeated efforts upon the part of Mr. Thurgood Marshall, Special Counsel of your Association, to embarrass the Federal Bureau of Investigation and to discredit its investigation, particularly of cases involving the civil rights of Negroes.
>
> I, of course, recognize the right of Mr. Marshall to have a personal opinion about the Bureau and I recognize his right to express that opinion. I do think, however, that when Mr. Marshall, in his official capacity, addresses a letter to the Attorney General of the United States relating to the work of the Federal Bureau of Investigation he might reasonably be expected to be truthful as to the facts in the situation about which he complains. . . .
>
> I do not believe it is ethical or fair of Mr. Marshall to charge the Bureau with dereliction of duty when a grand jury finds that a Federal statute has not been violated or a petit jury finds a defendant not guilty of a violation of a Federal statute, despite the fact that the Bureau has conducted a complete and thorough investigation of the facts in a particular case.
>
> It is a fact, as you know, that Mr. Thurgood Marshall and his associates in the Legal Branch of your Association have not rendered full and complete cooperation to the Federal Bureau of Investigation, and this lack of cooperation has not served to facilitate or improve the work of the Bureau. As a matter of fact, I don't think that the attitude and actions of Mr. Marshall and some of his legal associates measure up to the standards of cooperation which have been set by you in your very efficient administration of the affairs of the National Association for the Advancement of Colored People.

White was not at all pleased with the brouhaha that Marshall had stirred up. White had, in fact, tried in several ways to cozy up to Hoover. So on January 20 White sent this memorandum to Marshall:

> Attached is a self-explanatory letter from J. Edgar Hoover received today. Will you give me a reply which I suggest be temper-

ate and documented? I would also like to see copy of the letter
you wrote to him on December 27, 1946.

That "temperate and documented" phrase intensified Marshall's
suspicions that White was in truth "sucking up" to Hoover.
On January 23 Marshall answered White:

> The only thing about Hoover's letter that to my mind is worth
> noting is that he charges me with not cooperating with the FBI.
> [That] is just not true. . . .
> I will talk to Clark personally about it, and I am more than
> anxious to have him do something. I, however, have no faith in
> either Mr. Hoover or his investigators and there is no use in my
> saying I do.

The next day White wrote to Hoover that "much could be done
in arriving at an understanding on both sides if you and Mr. Marshall sat down and talked frankly with each other."
On January 28 Hoover sent back a surly letter saying:

> I note that you suggest that much good might come if Mr. Mar-
> shall and I sat down and talked frankly with each other. I think
> that this would have been indeed the proper procedure to follow
> in the original instance, before Mr. Marshall resorted to gross mis-
> statements and unfounded accusations against the Federal Bureau
> of Investigation and my administration of it.

Hoover made it clear that he didn't want to meet with Marshall.
Meanwhile, Marshall had written Clark, who set up an appointment for January 27. He found Clark to be a very decent man, tilted
toward racial justice, so long as he was not squeezed into a spot
where he had to defend Hoover. He would not be the last of attorneys general who felt they had to crawl in bed with a law enforcement legend that many of them despised.
Marshall had developed a profound distrust of Hoover, but
White clung to the belief that he somehow could win over this
power-hungry, thin-skinned man. In April White wrote asking Hoover for an endorsement of the NAACP to be used in an Association
pamphlet. Hoover wrote back this encomium:

> Equality, freedom, and tolerance are essential in a democratic gov-
> ernment. The National Association for the Advancement of Col-
> ored People has done much to preserve these principles and to
> perpetuate the desires of our founding fathers.

"Pure bullshit!" Marshall exclaimed. Dismay was rising among blacks at every level of the NAACP regarding the policies and practices of the FBI. Hoover became apoplectic when in August 1947, the Washington Bureau of the NAACP issued a press release protesting what it called the FBI's "lily-white hiring policy." Hoover immediately fired off an air mail, special delivery letter to White asserting that the press release "in and of itself is a blanket charge against the FBI, and I cannot reconcile myself to the belief that it was issued with your approval. . . .

"It does seem to me that if the NAACP lives up to its objectives of protecting civil rights it would also endeavor to present the truth in its statements. . . . I must insist upon receiving the data upon which the charges in your press release are predicated."

Meanwhile, the CIO-United Public Workers union lashed out at the FBI for continuing a policy long abolished by the Civil Service Commission: the requirement that job applicants submit a photograph. The union said that the photos "provided an avenue through which prejudiced government officials were able to discriminate against Negro job applicants."

Informed of this exchange, White wrote to Roy Wilkins: "I think it would be a good thing for Leslie Perry and Clarence Mitchell [of the NAACP Washington office] to arm themselves with as much information as possible and go see Hoover." Mitchell replied that he did not think the Washington office had enough firepower with which to confront Hoover.

Hoover by this time was livid, personally watching and reading every secret FBI account of meetings in which he was criticized by blacks, and articles in the press accusing the FBI of bigotry in hiring. He was especially stung by a letter from Roy Garvin, general manager of the *Afro-American* newspapers, to John H. Johnson, publisher of *Ebony* magazine, in which Garvin suggested *Ebony* had been suckered by FBI propaganda about the role of blacks in the agency. "There are no Negro FBI agents," Garvin wrote.

"You are inaccurate," Hoover said in a letter to Garvin. "Sam Noisette has been in charge of my reception room for many years. As such he takes care of many matters for me in connection with the official conduct of the Bureau's business. These include conveying my opinions and instructions to other Bureau officials and handling matters that come up in my office. If I did not have Sam Noisette in my office I frankly would be sorely handicapped." Noisette had been Hoover's "spook" who sat by the door, and his claim to fair employment in 1941, six years earlier.

No one in the NAACP wanted to humiliate Noisette, but they

knew that he was to Hoover what Rochester was to Jack Benny. They knew that this black FBI receptionist-gofer-handyman was not giving orders to other Bureau officials. Hoover's letter to Garvin demonstrated Hoover's master-slave mentality, but beyond that it revealed his belief that he could delude black leaders into believing that a black "third banana" was a meaningful force in an overwhelmingly Jim Crow law enforcement agency.

Outraged, Marshall set up an October 22 meeting with a reluctant Hoover, who simply repeated his litany about his and the FBI's fairness. He called Marshall uninformed.

Marshall told Hoover that he knew how grand juries decided to indict or not to indict, especially if the grand jury was composed only of southern whites. The forcefulness of testimony by FBI agents, and the U.S. attorney's trust in the information produced by FBI investigators, were powerful influences on a grand jury.

Hoover's jowls ballooned into the face of a mad bulldog, because he knew that Marshall was accusing the FBI of manipulating grand juries considering the fate of whites accused of beating or killing blacks. He made one point that Marshall knew was correct: new and stronger, more specific federal statutes were needed to stop lynchings and deter policemen from violating the civil rights of any American citizen.

Marshall held Hoover in such contempt that he wouldn't give him the satisfaction of agreement on this point. He figured Hoover "knew damn well that the NAACP had called for a federal antilynch law and other statutes for three decades."

That session did not diminish Marshall's view that Hoover and the Bureau were hostile to black people, or Hoover's view that Marshall and other NAACP officials were uncooperative, and out to smear him and the Bureau. About all they agreed on was that they would stay in touch.

While thousands of Americans had for years dealt with Hoover with trepidation, it was 1950 before racist forces began to speak of the NAACP as a power to be feared and resented. In October of that year, after a Ku Klux Klan show of force near Myrtle Beach, South Carolina, someone attacked the home of Judge J. Waties Waring with pieces of mortar. Walter White asked Attorney General J. Howard McGrath to give immediate protection to this federal judge who had outlawed South Carolina's whites-only primary elections. The *Charleston News and Courier* blasted McGrath in an editorial, saying he had forced Hoover to give Waring around-the-clock protection.

"McGrath is the former chairman of the Democratic National

committee," the newspaper said. "White, probably more than any other man in the country, controls the negro bloc vote. [Is] McGrath . . . the yes-man for Walter White and the NAACP?"

As the NAACP became the great bugaboo of the Jim Crow South, communism was becoming the great fear of the entire nation. Senator Joseph McCarthy of Wisconsin would become the public accuser of many Americans, but in his secret FBI domain Hoover was compiling dossiers and lists of Americans suspected of being communists and treasonous friends and supporters of the Soviet Union. Hoover seemed to get great pleasure out of tarring the NAACP and other black activist groups with slick intimations of doubt about their loyalty.

White's "defense" was to take an anticommunist tack himself and make sure that Hoover knew of it. On June 13, the NAACP secretary asked to see Hoover, and upon finding Hoover was not available, wrote the director asking for "authentic and publishable facts" about how "communist and communist-front organizations" were exploiting Negroes.

This occurred just a couple of weeks after Marshall and that remarkable band of lawyers and social scientists had gone to Charleston to argue the *Briggs v. Elliott* school segregation case, and just days before the NAACP was going to hold its national convention in Atlanta — the first time in the Deep South. White's anticommunist caper got him one thing he wanted. He told assistant FBI director Lou Nichols of rumors that goons associated with Georgia's Governor Herman Talmadge might create racial disturbances and blame them on "communists." Nichols promised to send several of his "most alert" agents to Atlanta to check out the situation.

Nothing White or anyone else did would mollify Hoover. As Clarence Mitchell became one of the most prominent and beloved of NAACP officials, with remarkable access to key members of Congress, Hoover began a series of angry exchanges with Mitchell. When Hoover called Mitchell's criticisms "presumptuous," Mitchell replied, "It is never 'presumptuous' for a private citizen to make suggestions to a government official."

It would become clearer during the McCarthy era, and especially during the civil rights movement of the late 1950s and the 1960s, that Hoover believed he was not just "a government official," and that black people were not "private citizens" from whom he was obligated to take advice.

Fortunately for Marshall, White, Mitchell, and others in the NAACP, the Reverend Martin Luther King, Jr., would become the prime target of Hoover's enmity, provoking an FBI campaign to destroy his reputation and, in my view, to bring about his assassination.

By the time Hoover died in May 1972, most Americans knew that the distrust and hatred of him by Marshall and others were well placed. It had been documented that Hoover was a monstrous abuser of his and the FBI's power. He had hated blacks and the civil rights movement. He had tried to destroy the reputations of many prominent Americans whom he regarded as "liberals." He was an obdurate foe of the personal liberties, press freedom, judicial protections, that made America unique in the entire world.

Hoover was a destroyer. One of the enduring questions about Thurgood Marshall is how he survived Hoover's wrath.

CHAPTER NINE

WINNING THE RIGHT TO VOTE

How CAN ONE LAWYER simultaneously defend a man accused of rape in Connecticut, try to rescue a young black accused of a triple murder in Oklahoma, and struggle in the courts to win equal pay for black teachers and wipe out Jim Crow at law schools in Maryland and Missouri at the same time that he pursues what till then was the biggest prize of all: the right of blacks to vote?

Marshall had marvelously able deputies in Robert Carter, Jack Greenberg, Constance Baker Motley (who had risen from clerk to full-time lawyer and would become a noted federal judge), and a few other brilliant lawyers on his staff, but it was Thurgood himself who wrote the briefs, oversaw every word of briefs written by others, and traveled from city to city and into the small towns and rural areas, seeking to broaden the parameters of justice.

When he decided to fight for the full right of African-Americans to vote in any and all elections, some of his friends told him that he was biting off more than he could chew, or the NAACP could digest. Since the Reconstruction days following the Civil War, whites in Texas, Alabama, Mississippi, Louisiana, Florida, South Carolina, Arkansas, and Georgia had fashioned schemes through which they barred blacks from voting in Democratic primaries, which were tantamount to the final balloting in areas where no Republican could get elected spittoon cleaner.

Marshall and the NAACP Legal Committee decided to go all out and challenge Texas, partly because it was a citadel of electoral bigotry, but also because half a million blacks in Texas were denied the vote, and their leaders were furious, spoiling for a legal fight.

The history of the disfranchisement of blacks in Texas made this appear to be a foolhardy choice. Black hopes had soared in 1926 when, in *Nixon v. Herndon,* Justice Oliver Wendell Holmes ruled that a Texas statute which barred blacks from participating in Democratic primaries violated the equal protection clause of the Fourteenth Amendment. The Democratic party of Texas then tried to have its executive committee exercise the role that had been given to the primaries, but in *Nixon v. Condon* the U.S. Supreme Court ruled in 1932 that the prohibition of blacks from the Democratic primaries by the executive committee was also unconstitutional. Writing for the majority, Justice Benjamin N. Cardozo said, "The executive committee of the Democratic Party was an instrumentality of the government of Texas. Hence, the committee's action barring blacks was violative of the 14th Amendment."

But in 1935, in *Grovey v. Townsend,* the Supreme Court, by unanimous vote, dealt blacks seeking the right to vote a major setback. White Democrats in Texas had decided that they could assemble in convention and make a decision as to who could vote in the Democratic primary. So in 1932 they passed a resolution limiting the right to vote. In 1935, a group of citizens carried the case of *Grovey v. Townsend* to the Supreme Court, where, in an opinion written by Justice Owen J. Roberts, the Court held that the Democratic convention was indeed a private group and that the barring of all but white citizens was not an act of the state and therefore was not in violation of the Constitution.

In 1941, Marshall and other lawyers went back to the federal court in Houston challenging the "white primary." This was the NAACP's first frontal assault on Jim Crow in Texas, a move many Texans regarded as a greater peril than anything that had happened at the Alamo. At that trial it was established that the primary in Texas was an integral part of the election machinery of the state and that the Democratic primary determined the final election. It was also established that all white citizens were permitted to vote in that "Democratic" primary regardless of whether they were Democrats, Republicans, Socialists, Communists, or Independents.

But Judge T. M. Kennerly dismissed the case on May 11, 1942. The NAACP appealed to the United States Circuit Court of Appeals for the Fifth Circuit, which affirmed Judge Kennerly's decision. In June 1943, the U.S. Supreme Court granted the NAACP a petition for writ of certiorari, and the case was argued in November by

Marshall and Hastie, who then was chairman of the Legal Committee of the NAACP.

On April 4, 1944, headlines across the nation declared, "HIGH COURT RULES NEGROES CAN VOTE IN TEXAS PRIMARY." The 8 to 1 majority opinion was written by Justice Stanley F. Reed, a Southerner from Mason County, Kentucky. This historic decision would go into the lawbooks as *Smith v. Allwright,* in the name of Dr. Lonnie E. Smith, a Negro dentist who tried to vote in the 1940 Texas primary, presented a poll tax receipt, but still was denied the ballot because of his race and color. With encouragement of local NAACP leaders, Smith sued two election officials of Harris County, asking for a declaration of judgment upholding the right of Negroes to vote in the primaries.

In the majority opinion, Justice Reed said: "The right to vote in such a primary . . . without discrimination by the state . . . is secured by the Constitution."

Part of the drama of that decision was that Reed had voted nine years earlier with Justice Roberts in *Grovey v. Townsend* to give Texas the right to keep black voters out of the primaries.

The impact of *Smith v. Allwright* was felt across the land. As NAACP officials had made clear four months earlier in a letter to A. Maceo Smith, secretary of the Texas state conference of branches of the NAACP: "The winning of the primary fight is the most important item before Texas Negroes today. It truly does mean whether or not we will be secondary or primary citizens. By all means we cannot allow anything that may mean defeat in this effort. We are the custodians for a million people in Texas. Our acts now will be scrutinized by future generations. Therefore, no stones should be left unturned that could possibly mean defeat."

No stones were unturned, but in the wake of what the press called a "monumental decision," a lot of rocks were hurled in anger. Here was a ruling that carried implications far beyond Texas, because the Supreme Court was also saying to other southern states that they could not use the ruses of "private parties" running the election system to exclude blacks or anybody else they wished. Congressman John Elliott Rankin of Mississippi erupted angrily: "The Negroes are having their hope of peace and harmony with their white neighbors destroyed by . . . parlor pinks in the Department of Justice who are already starting to harass the Southern states as a result of the blunder by the Supreme Court." Louisiana senator John H. Overton declared, "The South, at all cost, will maintain the rule of white supremacy." Senator Edward D. ("Cotton Ed") Smith of South Carolina, asserted, "All those who love South Carolina and the white man's rule will rally in this hour of her great Gethsemane to save her from a disastrous fate." Even Senator Claude Pepper of Florida, the consummate New Dealer, yielded to the racial passions by saying, "The South will allow nothing to impair white supremacy."

The *Charleston News and Courier* called for abolition of the primary and a return to the convention system of choosing political candidates. It said: "Conventions and caucuses to nominate may meet in private houses, in sitting rooms, or around supper tables.

"The South Carolina Negroes are even now preparing to crash the white primaries . . . there should remain no South Carolina primaries to crash.

"To retain the primary system and admit 300,000 Negro men and women to vote in it, would make South Carolina uninhabitable by decent white people."

Those screams were not representative of all of the South. The *Louisville Courier Journal* said: "The Supreme Court . . . has upheld logic, justice, and the plain intent of the Constitution."

The *New York Times* said simply that "the present decision is remorselessly logical."

In April of 1944, in the wake of that stunning decision, Texas governor Coke Stevenson and other officials discussed every step imaginable that might keep blacks from voting. There was talk of white citizens taking it upon themselves to keep blacks from voting. Thurgood Marshall issued a statement saying, "If citizens try to keep Negroes from primary polls we are going to take them to federal court. Such persons will be violating the Supreme Court decision just the same as election judges."

That Marshall statement provoked the following headline in the *Cisco* [Texas] *Press:* "COCKY LAWYER TELLS TEXANS TO BEWARE."

Marshall was not only warning Texans, he was putting pressure on the Justice Department to ensure that the new law of the land was obeyed. He sent a letter to U.S. Attorney General Francis Biddle saying: "We are sure that the Justice Department will now recognize that criminal jurisdiction over interference with the right to vote extends to primary elections.

"The decision in this case . . . clearly establishes the illegality of the practice in most of the states of the Deep South, of refusing to permit qualified Negro electors to participate in party primary elections."

Marshall pointed out that the NAACP had sent to the Justice Department a large number of affidavits from Negroes in Texas,

Arkansas, and South Carolina who had been denied the right to vote in the 1942 primaries. Marshall concluded: "We urge you to issue definitive instructions to all United States attorneys, pointing out to them the effect of these decisions and further instructing them to take definite action in each instance of the refusal to permit qualified Negro electors to vote in primary elections in states coming within the purview of the Supreme Court's decision."

Marshall would tell me years later that "Biddle wasn't worth a damn," and that he was pleased that the response to the above-mentioned letter came from a new attorney general, Tom C. Clark, who asked Marshall to forward to him immediately all evidence that Texas officials were flouting the Supreme Court decree.

The state of Texas asked the Supreme Court for a rehearing in the case of *Smith v. Allwright,* but on May 8, 1944, the high tribunal denied the petition. With that incredible victory, Marshall, Hastie, and others on the NAACP legal team thought they had succeeded in changing profoundly and forever the citizenship status of black people in America. This was heady stuff, and it blinded Marshall to the brutal reality of an editorial in the *Jackson* [Mississippi] *Daily News* that said:

> NOT IN THIS STATE
>
> The United States Supreme Court rules that Negroes can vote in party primaries — including Democratic party primaries. They can't in Mississippi. The Supreme Court may think so, but it is quite wrong, insofar as Democratic primary elections in Mississippi are concerned. If anybody doubts that, let 'em try.

NAACP leaders were dismayed to learn that for at least four years the Democrats of Texas would pass convention resolutions of defiance, would resort to circumventions and subterfuges, and even violence, to keep blacks from voting. But time proved that Marshall and his team had opened the door to the ultimate in "black power," the ability to decide at the ballot box who would manipulate the levers of power. It would take another thirty-five or forty years to see the real harvest of this judicial triumph, when more than eight thousand blacks would hold elective office in America, some as mayors of the nation's greatest (and most troubled) cities, and one, incredibly, as the governor of Virginia, the Cradle of the Confederacy.

The tirades of Rankin, Overton, and others from the states that had installed the white primaries were not to be taken lightly. Many a black person would be murdered, as would some whites of great conscience, before the entire nation would accept the constitutional mandate that every citizen had a right to participate in the choosing of his or her leaders.

The celebration over *Smith v. Allwright* at NAACP headquarters was incredibly restrained — mostly because the organization was still impecunious — hell, impoverished. Marshall, nobody's version of a humble, shrinking violet, was generous in his praise of the many unpaid lawyers and volunteers who had helped him to achieve his most important victory yet. He knew that among the things that made for first-class citizenship, the right to vote was at or near the top. But some at the NAACP, especially Walter White, were a lot more jealous of the credits for this judicial victory than Marshall. In April 1947, a group headed by Atlanta's future mayor, Maynard Jackson, the National Progressive Voters League, sent out a meeting notice in which it pointed out that the group was formed "immediately after we won the Supreme Court decision in the Texas white primary case." White took offense at the "we won" and on April 16, 1947, sent a sarcastic memo to Marshall "and other paid members of the legal department staff." It said: "I am seriously considering asking the board to have all of you refund salaries paid you for winning *Smith v. Allwright,* since you will note in the attached letter from Maynard Jackson of the Progressive Voters League that they, and not the NAACP, won the decision in that case."

Marshall was proud, but ambivalent, every time I talked to him about *Smith v. Allwright* and the voting rights cases he won in South Carolina and other places.

"I don't know whether the voting case or the school desegregation case was more important," he once said to me. "Without the ballot you've got no goddamned citizenship, no status, no power, in this country. But without the chance to get an education you have no capacity to use the ballot effectively. Hell, I don't know which case I'm proudest of."

History shows that in winning this Texas case, Marshall delivered a right, a power to America's outsiders that would forever change the faces of city halls, state legislatures, governor's mansions, the leadership of political parties and their nominating conventions, and eventually American concepts of blacks running for seats in the House and Senate — and for the presidency.

Smith v. Allwright brought to blacks "power" that no bigots would ever be able to strip away.

CHAPTER TEN

"LADY BIG HEART"

Marshall came to learn during the hard times of the 1930s and the war years of the 1940s that this nation was not moved by Supreme Court decisions alone. His life was defined in many ways by the allies he found, the white people who would share his dreams. None was more important to Marshall and the NAACP than the wife of President Franklin D. Roosevelt (whom Marshall bad-mouthed wherever he got the chance): Eleanor Roosevelt.

I must tell a personal story here about some extraordinary days that I spent with Mrs. Roosevelt at Hyde Park in order to give fair emphasis to her support of Marshall, the NAACP, and civil rights and human rights in general. It is crucial that we remember now what Marshall learned two generations ago: that the First Lady can be the catalyst for incredible social change, for a nation's embrace of justice, if she is dedicated to such purposes.

The executive branch of the federal government had always been less than a friend to Marshall and to the NAACP and their expanding endeavors in the field of human rights and civil liberties. Woodrow Wilson had ousted the top twenty-nine black federal officials as soon as he took office. He had been a brazen advocate of racial segregation, his views manifested by his wife, Edith's, overt attempts to impose Jim Crow in every area of Washington life that she could influence. Herbert Hoover and Calvin Coolidge both presided over administrations in which, to quote Marshall, "we didn't have a chance."

In 1932, singing "happy days are here again" after FDR's election might have had meaning for millions of poor white Americans, but not for the constituents of the NAACP. White racists still dominated virtually every committee of the House and Senate by virtue of their control of voting constituencies that were limited to white Anglo-Saxons and mostly the few propertied white people in Dixie. Roosevelt was so dependent upon these southern leaders in Congress, especially in his efforts to prepare for an inevitable new world war, that he refused to antagonize them by bold, open displays of support for America's nonwhites.

Marshall would look back at the turbulent 1930s and 1940s, and attribute most of the grim difficulty in changing racial patterns in America to the terrible economy that not only impoverished the NAACP but created a dog-eat-dog atmosphere in which it was easy for the bigots in Congress and the demagogues in the press to pit poor blacks against poor whites so as to maintain the power and privilege of the plantation owners and the other tycoons of Dixie. But Marshall heaped most of the blame upon the White House leadership of those decades.

"The biggest trouble of all was [Franklin D.] Roosevelt," Marshall said to me. "I am not one of those who thinks he was worth a damn so far as Negroes were concerned. The things he did for me were incidental to what he did for everybody else. When it came down to just the Negro, Roosevelt was not a friend. You cannot name one thing he ever did to solve the antilynching problem. He was threatened by Senator Tom Connally of Texas about what the Southerners would do [to the war preparation effort] if Roosevelt backed an antilynching bill. So Roosevelt never said one word in favor of it. He was not the great friend of Negroes that some people think.

"Now Eleanor Roosevelt did a lot; but her husband didn't do a damn thing.

"The Negro never had a fair shake in the War Department. I don't know of anyplace in government in Roosevelt's time where the Negro really got what he was entitled to."

Marshall mentioned that Roosevelt had his "kitchen cabinet" of Negroes with whom he occasionally met in secrecy so as to avoid offending Southerners.

"When they did give Negroes some jobs in the Roosevelt years, it was always as an assistant to somebody. I remember that when Biddle was attorney general, he offered me a job in the Justice Department. I inquired in detail about it. It eventually ended up with me being offered the title of assistant solicitor or something like that. But all I would be doing would be to sign my name to things that were decided and done by somebody else. I will never forget that my wife, Buster, and I had lunch with Biddle about the job, and when he answered my questions, he finally said, 'Well, Mrs. Marshall, what do you think?' Buster said, 'Well, I have no problem. I think in less than a week Thurgood would tell you, one, to go to hell, or two, where you could put this job, and that would be the end of it.' That's all they ever offered me.

"One night we were playing poker in Bill Hastie's apartment — Bob Ming, Bill Hastie, Jim Nabrit, and me, and I don't remember who else. The phone rang, and this person asked for Hastie. We shouted, 'Tell 'em Hastie's busy.' The person on the other end says, 'He can't be busy! This is the White House calling!'

"We shouted back that we didn't give a good goddamn what house was calling, they'd just have to call back. A little later they did call back, and Hastie answered the phone. It was the White House offering him the job of civilian aide to the Secretary of War." Hastie accepted.

Drifting back to the contempt he had for FDR, Marshall told of a case in Virginia in which a black man had been accused of shooting and killing a sheriff. This provoked widespread protest among Negroes. They called asking Marshall what the NAACP was going to do about it. Marshall said that he read the whole record and saw the coroner's report showing that the sheriff was shot in the back. "I couldn't see how in the world you could shoot a man in the back and call it self-defense," Marshall said. "I didn't get into it, but everybody else, all the other big Negro leaders, got into this case. They came to Washington and I sat up all night seeing what could be done with the people in the Department of Justice about this case. Early that morning I went to see Biddle, and he asked me if I would defend him in front of the angry Negro leaders. I said, 'No.' He asked why, and I told him, 'Because I don't get paid to defend you.' "

Marshall recalls that at about 7:00 A.M. Biddle called President Roosevelt in New York and began to talk about the pressures over the case of the black man in Virginia. Marshall says Biddle asked him to listen in on the extension phone, and that he heard the president say to his attorney general: "I warned you not to call me again about any of Eleanor's niggers. Call me one more time and *you* are fired."

"Roosevelt only said 'nigger' once," Marshall recalls, "but once was enough for me."

"Eleanor's niggers?"

Marshall resented a president of the United States using the word "nigger" to an attorney general, especially when he thought he was doing it secretly. He resented almost as much this evidence that FDR did not comprehend what his wife meant to black people and others who were groping their way out of the Great Depression and trying to cope with the denials and sacrifices brought on by a world war.

Marshall had learned that in many ways a first lady could change a nation profoundly, for good or ill. Thurgood would never forget that Eleanor Roosevelt used her White House status to become a great force for justice in America and many places beyond.

"Eleanor's niggers?"

Marshall remembered that in its 1939 report on "NAACP Gains" his organization had cited "a dramatic spotlight in progress at the annual conference in Richmond, Virginia, when Mrs. Roosevelt presented the Spingarn Medal to Marian Anderson." He recalled that when racial hostilities were at their peak in Detroit, *the president's wife* — repeat, *the president's wife* — had the guts to speak at that city's huge NAACP Freedom Fund Dinner.

No one can write of the life of Thurgood Marshall without telling of his white foes, who were numerous, and his white friends, who were scarce. Those trying to break Marshall's dreams had awesome power. But there was one dream maker, Eleanor Roosevelt, who gave Marshall and the NAACP a reach that exceeded the mean clutches of all the racists combined.

There was hardly a cause that Marshall and the NAACP espoused that Mrs. Roosevelt did not embrace courageously.

I lucked upon a chance to learn firsthand why Marshall regarded Mrs. Roosevelt as one of the greatest of dream makers — and why Thurgood and Eleanor were molded from the same special cast.

William P. Steven, the "idea man" editor of the *Minneapolis Tribune,* where I worked, had a passion for ensuring that I was never without a challenging assignment. So I was not surprised when, in late April of 1957, Steven said to me at a dinner party, "Eleanor Roosevelt is the first lady of the world. She clearly is the most remarkable of all the Roosevelts. If you were the reporter I think you are, you'd get her to let you write her life story."

The following Monday I telephoned Senator Hubert Humphrey and asked for a telephone number for Mrs. Roosevelt. I called her, and to my amazement her secretary Maurine Corr put me straight through.

"What a coincidence," Mrs. Roosevelt said. "I am this moment writing about your new book, *Go South to Sorrow.* I feel personally guilty as I read it, but it is still a very important book."

On April 28 I saw Mrs. Roosevelt's column, "My Day," in which she deplored "our system of states' rights which makes it possible for a state to violate all concepts of justice and decency and still avoid interference by the federal government." She mentioned that my book had forced her "to review what has happened in the South since the Supreme Court decision against segregation in the schools," and concluded by writing: "I shall force myself to read every word of Mr. Rowan's book. I do not have to go South for sorrow. I sorrow here for the shame of these past three years."

"Wow!" I said to myself, figuring that my chances were good for getting the long interview I wanted. I wrote her on May 3, spelling out in detail what I hoped to do — so much detail, in fact, that I feared I might frighten her into saying no.

Immediately, I learned something profound about the practice of journalism in a free society. Access to people who make the laws and structure society is everything. But access can come from being a sycophant, a toady, a quisling, or it can come from being respected.

Mrs. Roosevelt was chafing from my criticism of people of her class and mind, people I assailed as "go-slow moderates," but she still invited me to come to her New York apartment on June 20 and then accompany her to Hyde Park, where she would give her annual picnic for emotionally disturbed children from New York's Wiltwick school.

Before I arrived at her brownstone apartment on East Sixty-second Street in Manhattan, one of her closest friends said to me: "Sometimes I get the feeling that she is not a very happy woman. I get the feeling that she has never conquered her miserable childhood, that she still is a very insecure woman."

I thought about that remark as I wandered about the two-story residence in which she had lived for four years. There was a tiny garden in the rear yard, surrounded by an ivy-draped wall. Reaching out were patches of gay flowers that Mrs. Roosevelt said were her joy.

Her apartment was most unpretentious, cluttered with mementos — a sort of aged decor that was relieved here and there by a modern item like a television set. On the walls I saw four paintings by Louis Howe, the man credited with making her husband, FDR, president, and who most of all had helped to explode the shy reserve that might have kept Eleanor Roosevelt a nonentity all her life. The walls were also dotted with photographs of India's Jawaharlal Nehru, Indonesia's Sukarno, Adlai Stevenson, Bernard Baruch, Winston Churchill, Madame Chiang Kai-shek, and many other great personalities of the world. These photographs hung helter-skelter over what seemed to be an ancient couch, weighted by many soft pillows, and over pieces of random furniture that I would learn had been built by the poor in an old building alongside the Val-Kill Creek cottage that had become her Hyde Park residence.

That June day I arrived at her apartment to find that she had as a special guest the mother of an eight-year-old Hyde Park girl who suffered from a blood ailment that Hyde Park doctors had not been able to diagnose. Upon learning of the girl's condition while shopping at her mother's fruit stand, Mrs. Roosevelt had brought the child to New York City, where she might undergo the most modern — and expensive — blood and other tests. At Mrs. Roosevelt's expense.

Mrs. Roosevelt and I took the train to Hyde Park. I wanted to cram in every precious question that I could during this journey, figuring that this would be the most time that I would have with her alone. But I sensed that she did not want this ride to become a "Meet the Press" quiz. So I shut up and let her reflect, reminisce. She told me that it was on this train, years past, in the early months of the New Deal, that she was thinking of Spain in fraternal conflict. Spain, where bombs and shells were exploding in cities and villages.

"I said to myself," she recollected, "that if reforms do not come peacefully, they have to come through violent upheavals. I said, 'Thank God, this nation has had the courage to face the need of changes before we reached the point where bloodshed was the only way to achieve a change.' " She praised Marshall, White, the NAACP in general, as invaluable instruments of peaceful change.

I was thirty-one years old, and beginning to think of myself as a fairly sophisticated journalist, but the more I listened to this woman, the more I realized my ignorance about human nature, racial passions, American politics, world affairs, and the frailties and foibles of even the most renowned people.

Here I was on a train ride with a woman who was consistently rated "most admired" and "first lady of the world," a woman who had been dubbed "Lady Big Heart" by feature writers because of her constant championing of the underdog, her handouts to the needy, her cries for racial justice, her courage in attacking "reaction and greed." And here she was telling me how she had come to fight for the underdogs of the world because in her rich and powerful milieu *she* had always *been* the underdog.

I strained to hear her extraordinary personal soliloquy above the noise of the train wheels' clatter against the tracks:

"I did not inherit the almost incredible beauty of my mother," she said as I remembered descriptions of her that I had read: skin smooth, eyes lovely, hair beautiful, but protruding buck teeth marring her face. Then, tall, thin, ungainly.

"I was the first girl of my mother's family who was not a belle," Mrs. Roosevelt continued, "and I was filled with shame." She said that she became filled with constant fear of being compared with her mother, and thus became awkward before people, developing a shyness that made her seem older than her years.

This, she said with obvious pain, caused her mother to nickname her "Granny."

So Anna Eleanor Roosevelt was telling me how as a little girl she became a forlorn figure, hiding from public inspection, humiliated by the brace she wore to correct the curvature of her spine, and always wishing for love and affection from a mother whose beauty she envied.

"What children need more than money is love," she said, recalling that with all her family's wealth and prestige, love is what she had least of and wanted more than anything in the world.

This remarkable woman, nearing age seventy-three, said almost in a whisper: "All my life I have fought fear — physical fear, and the fear of not being loved." Here was another version of Marshall's stigmatic injury. Marshall was fighting not for white people's "love" of black children — just respect and fairness.

Abruptly, it seemed, the train ride came to an end and we were on our way to her Hyde Park residence.

The sun reached down fiercely between the leaning birches and the aged elms on a muggy day that would have been completely unbearable but for an occasional breeze that sort of loafed off Val-Kill Creek. Even before the kids from Wiltwick arrived, many of us complained of the humidity, took refuge in the shade, or got dubious relief from a sneaked gin and tonic. Mrs. Roosevelt seemed in her glory, buttering buns. Ernest Papanak, Wiltwick's executive director, told me that on his first trip to Hyde Park, he had urged Mrs. Roosevelt not to butter buns. "The boys will eat them anyway," he had said.

Papanak recalled that "she gave me just one glance and replied, 'When the King and Queen of England had hot dogs here, we buttered the rolls. Why should I do less for the boys from Wiltwick?'"

I scribbled notes furiously as I got an occasional chance to talk to "Lady Big Heart," and as I listened to her talk to these unfortunate youngsters to whom she was bringing so much more than physical nourishment. As the Wiltwick boys and staff began to leave, I expressed my thanks, my good-bye.

"Where are you going? We've had no chance to talk," she said. "Stay for a day or two."

I almost panicked. I had only one day's change of clothing. She had mentioned that she swam every day, so just in case I was invited to her pool, I had gone to Brooks Brothers in New York to buy a swimsuit. But I was embarrassingly short on underwear, shirts, socks. . . .

"That is no problem," she said. When the last guest had gone she beckoned me to her DeSoto convertible and tooled down to the shopping district, her gray hair pushing relentlessly against and through the black net that she obviously hoped would control it. En route, she told me that her son John thought that she had been crazy to buy a convertible.

She had other guests at that Val-Kill cottage — more, as I recall, than she had rooms. But that, I decided, was none of my business. I was an awed reporter who could not believe it when, after dinner, Mrs. Roosevelt and I sat on a porch, listening to frogs croak from the lily pads of Val-Kill Creek, as she again talked openly and honestly to me.

So while I went to Hyde Park on June 20, I did not leave until July 3. I listened to Eleanor Roosevelt speak hilariously of Alexander Woolcott, the celebrated "man who came to dinner," and then say to me delicately, "I'm pleased that you stayed longer than Woolcott did."

I am still moved when I recall, or read my detailed notes, of those long after-dinner conversations when the fireflies gave illumination, and the frogs harmony, to her high-pitched stories of a life that included being wife to the man who held the presidency longer than any other American.

Mrs. Roosevelt talked of her early fears, of becoming an orphan at age nine and going to Tivoli-on-Hudson to live with her maternal grandmother, Mrs. Valentine G. Hall. She recalled the stifling strictness of Grandmother Hall, who sent her to a fashionable New York school where "the director was one of the world's biggest phonies. I didn't learn a blooming thing — a bit of geometry by memory, and nothing more."

Most agonizing of all, she said, was the fact that Grandmother Hall always dressed her in the hand-me-down clothing that her aunts no longer wanted. "Most of the time I went about with my dress above my knees, while other girls wore theirs halfway down their legs," she recalled.

So the teenage years that were glorious to the other girls in High Society were utter misery for Eleanor, who knew that "not by any stretch of the imagination was I a popular debutante."

Still too tall, thin and shy, a very poor dancer, her clothing most inappropriate, Eleanor was the wallflower of her set. She knew that she was "different from the other girls," and just in case she tried to forget it, "the other girls were frank in telling me so." She understood Kenneth Clark's dolls and Marshall's argument about why segregated black children felt "different."

It was at one of those humiliating teenage parties that Cousin Franklin asked her to dance, filling her with "everlasting gratitude."

"I never lost a feeling of kinship for anyone who is suffering," she said. "That childhood did something to me that made me able to understand the fears and needs of other people."

Mrs. Roosevelt explained her support for Marshall and the civil rights movement by telling me that no American was so blessed, so rich, so powerful that he or she didn't need caring support. She noted that her early status of privilege and wealth did not shield her from the agony of watching her father and uncles drink themselves to death. High Society status did not guarantee her a happy marriage.

Mrs. Roosevelt talked openly of her pleasure when in 1903 Franklin Delano Roosevelt looked past the society belles who were all around him and asked his nineteen-year-old cousin Eleanor to marry him. She said she told her grandmother that she was in love with Franklin, only to realize years later that she hadn't understood what love was all about. She talked of how Franklin's mother, Mrs. James Roosevelt, tried to prevent their marriage, prompting Franklin to write his mother:

"Dearest Mama, I know what pain I must have caused you and you know I wouldn't do it if I really could have helped it — *mais tu sais, me voilà!*

"That's all that could be said — I know my mind, have known it for a long time, and know that I could never think otherwise. Result: I am the happiest man in the world; likewise the luckiest.

"And for you, Dear Mummy, you know that nothing can change what we have always been and will always be to each other — only now you have two children to love and to love you. . . ."

I thought I detected lingering bitterness in Mrs. Roosevelt's voice as she told me how Mrs. James Roosevelt "bundled up Franklin, who was her only child, and took him on a cruise of the West Indies, hoping he would 'think things over.' "

Franklin held firm, but the engagement was not announced for a year, and it was March 17, 1905, when the wedding actually took place.

But the sun didn't even shine brightly on the bride that day. She remembered that her uncle, President Theodore Roosevelt, came to the wedding and "stole the show." She said she made sure later that as her children got married, President FDR did not steal the show.

The lonely anguish of this woman really came out when she was asked whether she thought she had been a good mother. She recalled 1920 as the beginning of the tragic years of her "trial by fire" and of dislocations within her family. Her husband, the Democratic candidate for vice president, became ill with "a cold" that turned out to be infantile paralysis. Eleanor learned that her mother-in-law thought she knew more than the doctor, so there were bitter arguments over what was best for FDR.

Mrs. Roosevelt sipped on a little glass of blond Dubonnet as she recalled that daughter Anna was having the emotional problems common to many teenage girls, problems that were worsened, she said, because she had "failed to take her [Anna] into my confidence and consult her about her difficulties."

Her husband's greatest contribution to the nation, she said, was that "Franklin established in the people a belief that government has a responsibility to the people. So this idea is forced on every regime, because the people want it.

"Franklin never intended that the federal government should take over things that can be done by the states. But where there was a need for a uniform policy, or where the states obviously could not do certain things, my husband felt that the federal government must act. It is evident today, for example, that the states simply cannot do the necessary things in education."

Asked about FDR's effort to get rid of "nine old men" and pack the Supreme Court with men who shared his ideology, she said Roosevelt "never regretted his efforts to alter the Court." She agreed with her husband's view that "life implies growth, and the Constitution never was meant to be used as the Bible was used by our most puritanical Puritans." Yet, she said, the attempt to pack the Court was one of FDR's "few ill-timed moves, politically, because if he had waited a while, death would have done the job."

She said she never was ahead of her husband on racial and other social reforms, but there was conflict over timing. She always wanted to move faster than Franklin did.

"He would say to me," she recalled, "that 'a democracy moves slowly, and there is no use in doing things unless you have your following really with you.' "

She recalled that Walter White, "asked my husband to put the antilynching bill on his 'must' list of legislation. My husband said that he couldn't do that because he had to have the southern vote for his rearmament program.

"I said to Franklin, 'Well, how do you feel about my attitude, because I am for the antilynching bill?'

"Franklin looked at me and said, 'You go right ahead and stand for whatever you feel is right. . . . Besides, I can always say that I can't do a thing with you.' "

FDR probably was speaking seriously when he said, "I can't do a thing with you." Mrs. Roosevelt and I spent most of one evening laughing about the legendary stories of her exploits at home and abroad.

A favorite of both of us was told by the late Malvina (Tommy) Thompson, Mrs. Roosevelt's secretary for many years.

Thompson said that one day Mrs. Roosevelt took off in a hurry for West Virginia after receiving complaints about conditions in a jail. When FDR came to lunch, he was irritated that his wife was missing.

"Where's the madam?" FDR asked gruffly.

"Oh, she's in the jail in West Virginia," was Miss Thompson's somewhat absentminded reply.

"Jail in West Virginia," mumbled the president. "What the hell has she done now?"

No one in America could be sure of the answer to that question, and that seemed to please Mrs. Roosevelt as we chatted during one of my last days on the porch of her cottage. She mentioned that since her husband first became a candidate for the presidency, there had not been a single day when she had not been accused of neglecting her children, wasting government money, dying of cancer, loving "niggers," having a nervous breakdown, or looking for another man to marry.

She sipped on the dregs of a daiquiri that she had nursed for at least three hours as she told me: "I got two interesting letters today. One was from a man who said Franklin and I had completely wrecked the country. The other was from a woman who had read that I am going to Missouri to help dedicate the Truman library. She asks how I have "the audacity to appear on the same program with that great man Herbert Hoover." She laughed raucously.

Then, in more somber tones, she talked about how she had been dubbed "Madame Gadabout" and "the first nuisance of the land," partly because she was the most ubiquitous and outspoken of all America's first ladies. She had been criticized for trampling on the idea that a woman's place was in the home, that a president's wife was supposed to be only a dignified social butterfly, and for arguing that the Negroes' "place" was wherever ambition and intellect could take them.

I reminded her that she did a little more than break with convention, having huddled in a White House bathroom to give a reporter an interview even before she had unpacked the first trunk. She was holding press conferences, making radio broadcasts, writing magazine articles and a syndicated column, speaking at political rallies — and beyond that, roaming knee-deep in the mud of foreign battlefields, traipsing through fly-infested huts in Puerto Rico, going into the bowels of coal mines in West Virginia, consorting with the hungry on the breadlines of America.

"Yes," she said, "and for all that they called me a 'fellow traveler,' a 'dabbler in communism,' and in some cases 'an out-and-out communist.'" Westbrook Pegler, the columnist, had labeled her "impudent, presumptuous and conspiratorial," the last word referring to her meetings with Marshall, White, Wilkins.

I thought of my first meetings with Marshall several times during those Hyde Park discussions. Here was a woman with a cause that transcended her personal happiness, her concerns about the attempted insults that some hurled at her. Marshall had the same dedication to a cause. He would never admit that he neglected Buster, or cared less about his personal happiness than he did about wiping out Jim Crow, but the record shows that he did.

Mrs. Roosevelt was castigated in editorials for "fostering communists"; Marshall was accused of being part of "a communist plot to mongrelize America." She was accused of "stirring racial hatreds"; Marshall was called "an outside agitator" by the beneficiaries of racial privilege. Marshall went to Detroit during the nation's worst race riot up till that time and dared to speak the truth about it; Mrs. Roosevelt went to that strife-torn city at the same time to speak to the NAACP convention and put her prestige and that of a reluctant White House behind the cause of racial and social justice. The only thing comparable last year would have been for Barbara Bush to go to South Central Los Angeles to cry out for equal justice for all God's children.

Mrs. Roosevelt and Marshall were embodiments of the fact that, with rare exceptions, people who have suffered show a special compassion for others who need food, shelter, protection — and love.

As I have read the attacks on Marshall, even into his retirement, I have remembered Mrs. Roosevelt telling me of the time Westbrook Pegler came to a picnic at Hyde Park and borrowed her typewriter, upon which he wrote one of his bitterest attacks on the Roosevelt family. Yet, later, his wife ill, his days and prestige waning, Pegler wrote a column in which he called Eleanor Roosevelt the nation's greatest woman "because there is no other who works as hard or knows the low-down truth about the people and the troubles in their hearts as well as she does . . . she knows the country better than any other individual."

Mrs. Roosevelt also knew, and told me, that there wasn't a lawyer in the land who knew the low-down truth about the troubles and injustices heaped upon America's black and poor people better than Marshall, or who worked harder to give them a fair chance.

For Thurgood and his cause, Eleanor Roosevelt helped mightily to keep the dream alive.

CHAPTER ELEVEN

ARMING BLACKS WITH TRAINED INTELLIGENCE

Education is a companion which no misfortune can depress, no crime can destroy, no enemy can alienate, no despotism can enslave. At home a friend, abroad an introduction, in solitude a solace, and in society an ornament. It chastens vice, it guides virtue, it gives, at once, grace and government to genius. Without it, what is man? A splendid slave, a reasoning savage.

Joseph Addison, *The Spectator*
November 6, 1711

DURING ONE HYDE PARK DISCUSSION, Mrs. Roosevelt asked me if I thought Marshall had an agenda, a master plan, during his early years as chief legal officer of the NAACP, or if he was a sort of fireman, flitting from one conflagration to another. I said that Marshall had a plan to achieve one great goal: *to wipe out all the trappings of white supremacy.* He hated the hypocrisy of white Americans talking about "law and order" and "the rule of law" when they tolerated a situation where "the law" for black people was whatever a white man said it was. He was all over the American landscape, defending accused blacks as a way of establishing the principle that "the law" is what is set down in the Constitution and in legitimate statutes and ordinances. That is why he risked his life to go to riot-torn Detroit and Columbia, Tennessee, and why he moved legally against the Atlantic Greyhound Bus Company, charging that its agent, the driver of the bus on which Isaac Woodard was riding,

wrongfully caused Woodard to be ejected from the bus and insti-
gated police to punch out Woodard's eyes with their billy clubs.
Woodard was a black U.S. Army sergeant who had served three
years during World War II, including fifteen months in the South
Pacific. Upon discharge, he was riding home on the back of the bus
and went to a "colored only" toilet at a bus stop in South Carolina.
He stayed there longer than the white driver liked, a quarrel ensued,
and when the bus reached Batesburg, the driver summoned policemen, who beat Woodard mercilessly, blinding him.

Marshall regarded the real estate covenants restricting the rights
of blacks to buy property as grossly offensive, which is why he would
invest some $25,000 of his meager $111,000 budget for 1947 in
McGhee v. Sipes, a lawsuit attacking housing discrimination in Detroit,
and in the far more celebrated case of *Shelley v. Kraemer,* which involved a restrictive-covenant case in St. Louis, Missouri. He called it
an outrage that American courts could enforce bigotry clauses in
housing deeds.

Marshall believed, as in the Texas case of *Smith v. Allwright,* that
there could be no "black power" if blacks did not gain the ballot in
every state. It galled him to see the Democratic party of Alabama
openly using a rooster emblazoned with the words WHITE SUPREMACY
as its slogan. He thought, proudly, that he had made great strides
in winning black people political power by knocking out the white
primaries in South Carolina and Texas.

But still gnawing at Marshall's heart and mind was the gross denial of decent education to black children everywhere, at every level,
especially in the southern and border states. He knew that blacks
could talk about liberation and freedom forever, but without learning, they would remain exactly what Senator Hammond had said
they were in 1861: "We use them for our purpose, and we call them
slaves." Education at the highest level possible was black citizens' only
escape from bondage, their ultimate means of wiping out white supremacy, Marshall believed.

Marshall knew that while the right to vote was precious, only educated black people would have the nerve and the wisdom to use
political power effectively. So he had to do more to open up professional schools — this first, not because it was most important, but
because it was more easily achievable than the desegregation of elementary and high schools. Somehow, the college years, in which
blacks and whites might have sex with each other, did not seem as
dangerous to white racists as elementary and high school integration,
where most children just wanted to learn algebra, become a cheer-
leader, make the football or basketball team.

So in 1946 Marshall intensified his efforts to open up colleges in the South and the near-South. He didn't have to search for people eager to join him in the fight.

Amos Hall and Roscoe Dunjee, the Oklahomans who had begged him to defend W. D. Lyons in the triple-murder case, were now beseeching him to help them get a black woman, Ada Lois Sipuel, into the law school of the University of Oklahoma, and a black professor in his late sixties who wanted to get a doctorate, G. W. McLaurin, into the school of education. Marshall agreed with alacrity, figuring that just as the University of Maryland once "owed him one," so did Oklahoma.

By this time the NAACP had become a feared force, claiming it had more than 430,000 members. It had opened a Washington bureau and a veterans affairs office. W. E. B. Du Bois had returned to the Association, giving at least the facade of new unity. But as a force, the NAACP also was a target, especially of prosegregation politicians who were eager to charge Marshall and his colleagues with barratry — the legal term for soliciting clients who would foment lawsuits. Marshall told Hall that the applicants for the University of Oklahoma had to be "legitimate in every way."

Hall told Marshall that Miss Sipuel had volunteered to be a "guinea pig," and that he had accepted her without hesitation because of her brilliant record as an undergraduate at the all-black Langston University, which had been created to prevent Negroes from enrolling at the all-white Norman campus.

"Thurgood," Hall said, "she's a shy, light-brown-skinned daughter of a minister. She has fetching eyes that seem to have a touch of the Orient in them. No sane person could reject this lovely young lady."

"Shit, they're gonna reject her," Thurgood said. "We just wanna be sure we can prove that they turned her down solely on the basis of her race."

There was Marshall the sagacious strategist. Few of his cases tell more about the skills, the personal dedication, the wit and sarcasm of Marshall than this broadside attack on Jim Crow in higher education in Oklahoma.

On January 14, 1946, Ada Sipuel applied for admission. Marshall knew that an awful lot was at stake. He still fumed over winning a trailblazing case, the *Gaines* lawsuit in Missouri, only to have Gaines vanish. In the case of Sipuel, Marshall, Hall, and the other NAACP lawyers intended to go far beyond *Gaines* and try to use the Fourteenth Amendment as a basis for wiping out not only "We'll give you tuition to go to school in a northern state," or "We'll set up a separate law school for you," but all forms of racial discrimination in graduate and professional education.

Marshall, Hall, and Dunjee conspired to "set up" Dr. George L. Cross, the University of Oklahoma president, and get him to concede in some way that the only basis for rejecting Sipuel was her race. They had no idea that Cross was eager to help them. Dunjee got an appointment with Cross and asked him point-blank if he would admit the Negro woman.

"My hands are tied," Cross replied. "The legislature has made the law very specific. I get fined five hundred dollars a day if I admit a Negro. A professor gets fined up to a hundred dollars a day for teaching a mixed class. A white student gets fined up to twenty-five dollars a day for attending a class with Negroes. I am in no financial position to experiment with, or challenge, that law. Can I be of help in some other way?"

"Yes," Dunjee said, "we would like a letter from you saying Miss Sipuel is being rejected only because she is a Negro. That would give us immediate entry into the courts without our having to fight frivolous and phony claims that she is being denied admittance for some other reason."

In an interview with me years later, Cross would recall the rest of that historic meeting, and subsequent developments, this way:

"I breathed a sigh of relief over Dunjee's request. I sent Sipuel's transcript right off to the registrar, who took a quick look and sent me a message saying, "This girl is qualified for admission to the University of Oklahoma." I called my secretary in and dictated in the presence of Dunjee and Hall the letter they wanted.

"I told my board of regents what I had done, so they called an emergency meeting. It took place on a very cold day, when there were about three inches of snow on the ground. Still, at the time of the meeting three thousand to thirty-five hundred students and faculty members were on the North Oval, demanding the admission of this girl. One student tore up a copy of the Thirteenth Amendment, put it in a cookie can, poured lighter fluid on it, burned it, and put some of the ashes in an envelope and delivered it to me. The students put the rest of the ashes in an envelope and marched to the post office, singing the "Battle Hymn of the Republic," where they mailed the package to President Truman.

"Nevertheless, my regents told me that I could not admit Ada Sipuel . . . a splendid test student, beautiful girl, poised and intelligent."

Cross then gave me his remembrances of what Norman and Oklahoma politicians were like at that time:

I came from South Dakota and had no knowledge of racial problems.

I arrived in nineteen thirty-four on — I think it was the thirty-first of August — and I went downtown to buy some things — you know, refrigerator, stove, and that sort of thing — and my introduction to the problem came in a very shocking way. The salesman in the store, knowing that I was new, undertook to tell me a few things that he thought would be useful to me. One thing he said that really jolted me was, "You'll never have to worry about a nigger problem in Norman." I looked at him inquiringly. He said, "We have an unwritten law that niggers can't be in Norman after sundown."

I said, "Well, just how do you enforce an unwritten law?" And he said, "Oh, we don't have to enforce it. The niggers understand the situation and they don't stay in Norman after sundown."

That was quite true. There was no black in Norman overnight until World War Two, when the Navy moved in with its bases, and the local citizens realized that if they wanted the benefit of these stations, they would need to tolerate the blacks who came as trainees and in many jobs.

So that was a very, very startling thing to me to run into this. I was a little depressed that afternoon. But I did buy a refrigerator and a stove.

I learned in 1945 that there was a specific problem involving the University of Oklahoma. There was a meeting of the NAACP over at McAlester, I believe, attended by Thurgood Marshall, and the Sunday papers announced that a decision had been reached at that meeting to use the University of Oklahoma to test the segregation laws of the states below the Mason-Dixon line.

By the time the *Sipuel* case went to trial, the NAACP could afford one secretary to assist Marshall, Dunjee, Hall, and others. She was Alice Stovall, who was Thurgood's closest assistant for twenty years. She told me:

We were put up in someone's home in Oklahoma City because the Sipuel case was being argued in Norman. Different people would come each morning and drive us to Norman and then they would be back later in the day when court was out to bring us back to Oklahoma City, because at that time a black person could work as a domestic and whatnot during the day, but they said that by the time the sun set we'd better be out of Norman. The first couple of days, we didn't have lunch because there was no place that you could go to have meals.

I recall that when I was there in the district courthouse, I asked Mr. Marshall if it was all right for me to use the ladies' room and he says, "Oh, yeah, baby, this is a federal court." And I went to the ladies' room and I was washing my hands and two young women came in. . . .

They were white. They looked at me and one said, "I don't know if you're with those black lawyers who are arguing the case. If you're black you're not supposed to be in here. And if you're white you're a communist."

I looked at her and I said, "Well, Mr. Marshall told me that this was a federal building from top to bottom and I could be anywhere I chose in this particular building." They just walked out.

Ada Sipuel (later Mrs. Fisher) would later tell me that the first days in court "we were kind of caught shorthanded, and we ate peanuts from a machine and drank Cokes. Thereafter, we carried baloney sandwiches."

When the trial began Marshall was astounded by the state's defense. He recalled its arguments in the Cleveland County (Norman) courtroom this way:

There was an assistant attorney general of Oklahoma arguing against me in the Sipuel case. He said, "You keep talking about equal justice, equal facilities. We're setting up an atom smasher at the University of Oklahoma. Do you mean that we've got to set up an atom smasher for niggers? Everybody knows that niggers can't study science."

It was "nigger" this and "nigger" that. I had to go back to Norman the following year for the second argument, and it was "nigger" this, "nigger" that. When the case reached the Supreme Court I was dumbfounded when this same man said to the justices, "I am defending this [segregation] law only because I took an oath to defend the constitution and the laws of the state of Oklahoma. If you rule against me, I assure you, I will not only follow the letter, but the spirit of the law."

Later, I met this Oklahoma official in the lawyers' lounge, and I said, "You kinda changed your arguments, didn't you? What the hell happened?" He said, "My son's been a student at the University of Oklahoma. He's read about this case. He's been berating me about it, including the question whether I really believe in the U.S. Constitution. He convinced me that I was a jackass."

I didn't convince him! His son did!

Well, no one convinced the court in Cleveland County, or the Oklahoma Supreme Court, that racial segregation was a jackass idea. Both ruled that the university did not have to admit Miss Sipuel.

Marshall said to himself, after those two courts ruled: "Thank God I have a couple of backups." He was referring to the case of G. W. McLaurin; he had also filed a lawsuit demanding that the University of Texas admit a black man, Heman Marion Sweatt, to its law school.

To Marshall's dismay, he had not only lost in the Oklahoma courts but was losing ground in the court of black public opinion. The same old argument about integration versus separate-but-equal that caused Du Bois to leave the Association for a decade had erupted again, threatening the bedrock of Marshall's legal campaign.

Thurgood had seen early that one of the curses of black people in America was that they were so easily divided. When brave men and women tried to rise up during slavery days, there were always a few black spies and cowards who would inform the slave owner, making it easy for the slaveholders to thwart even the mildest efforts of slaves to express their determination to be free. After slavery, there were the black leaders who did not want to stay and fight for first-class citizenship. Some left and founded the tiny nation of Liberia on the west coast of Africa. Marcus Garvey tried to sponsor an even broader back-to-Africa movement. In the period of World War I and afterward, there was a great struggle between blacks who wanted full education and everything else white people had and those who wanted to accommodate the white man, to take a little bit of education, a little bit of economic equality, a tiny bit of civic opportunity, one little piece after another. This pretty well summarizes the classic conflict between Du Bois and Walter White. Marshall was discovering that the old "divide 'em and keep 'em subservient" tactic was working in the 1940s. He had created a tremendous uproar among blacks in South Carolina when he dared to go in and speak against segregation in the public schools, even as he demanded equal pay for black teachers. An NAACP letter of February 18, 1944, from Marshall to the branches, summarizes the dilemma there:

"We have also received newspaper clippings from Hinton and it appears that the State is really in an uproar. In fact, they are again strongly advocating private schools to take the place of public schools, which, as you know would to a large degree deny the great masses of Negro and poor white people the right to an education.

"The road is long and the going is tough and with your broad shoulders, I am sure that the situation in South Carolina will be well taken care of."

As it became more obvious around the nation that the NAACP was not going to compromise and accept *Plessy v. Ferguson* in any way, Marshall began to run into difficulties as he attended NAACP meetings. Some blacks would tell him how much they hated Jim Crow schools, and then suggest that he might want to think twice about having the dual school system declared unconstitutional because "whites in this county can get real mean"; "I worry about economic retaliation, and losing what little I got"; "Can I be sure that if you force integration on these people I can still have a job as a school principal?" "You can be sure that if these white people get real angry they're going to fire the black teachers, and might even close all the black schools"; "Man, you know, we gotta live here, and these white folks are still lynching black people."

Marshall was so dispirited or angered by some of the things he heard that on July 6, 1947, he drafted a memo to NAACP aide Gloster Current, saying something profound about the direction in which the NAACP wanted to go:

> The Branch Department, in planning its field work during the Fall and Winter months, should give as much consideration as possible to doing field work in areas where important legal precedents are being established.
>
> The cases against state universities, which are brand new types of legal action striking at segregation per se, are now pending in Oklahoma, Texas, Louisiana, and South Carolina. In Texas, as a result of the intensive work by the State Conference and others, there is hardly a Negro in Texas today who is not convinced that segregation is not only bad, but cannot be tolerated. It is likewise evident that this sentiment does not exist in any other southern state.
>
> These cases establishing precedents can only be adequately tried when we have the complete support of all of the Negroes in these states on the correctness of our position.
>
> In Southern Illinois, there are completely segregated schools with the approval of Negroes in general and in many instances these Negroes include members of our branches.
>
> The State Conference in Illinois is not worth the paper it is written on. It would be dangerous if we reached the point where we are filing legal cases on matters such as segregation in public schools in areas where our branch people are not whole-heartedly opposed to segregation.

It seems, therefore, to be apparent that we must use additional effort to get our branches sold on the problem, anxious to work on it and determined to fight the matter out.

Just over a month later, Marshall received a copy of an editorial in the *Houston Informer,* a newspaper owned and dominated by one of the most prominent of Houston blacks, Carter Wesley. Wesley challenged NAACP policy in general, and Marshall personally, by asking why they proposed "no action to better the educational lot of Texas Negroes, except fight for admission of Negroes to non-segregated schools." Wesley suggested it might be easier to force Texas officials to equalize separate schools for blacks than to secure the racial integration of existing schools. Wesley said the NAACP was "cuckoo" in fighting solely for desegregation.

That editorial almost provoked Marshall to apoplexy. He was a born arguer. His wife had told him that she had first met him at a restaurant in Washington, D.C., but that he was "so busy arguing with everybody else at the table that you didn't pay any attention to me."

Marshall exploded into a mood to do verbal battle in Texas. He rushed to Denison for the state conference and gave a speech on September 5 that typified the man and his best efforts in or out of court:

Complete equality of American citizens is impossible without equality of educational opportunities. Complete equality of education opportunities cannot be obtained in a dual system of education. There has been some question raised as to the position of the N.A.A.C.P. on this question. Therefore we reemphasize our position as being opposed to all types of segregation, including public education, as being unconstitutional, unlawful, and immoral.

It no longer takes courage to fight for mere equality in a separate school system. Even [Mississippi senator Theodore G.] Bilbo mouthed phrases calling for equality for Negroes as long as there was complete segregation. I think that everyone knew that when the State Legislature in Texas agreed to advance more than three million dollars for a Jim Crow University, there would be Negroes who would be willing to sell the race down the river in order to either get jobs in the school, or to determine who should build the school, or to determine where the school should be built, or any other method whereby the individual could get personal gain.

It was also apparent that there would be Negroes who would attack the N.A.A.C.P. in order to gain these ends. It was also apparent that if they couldn't find anything else to attack the

N.A.A.C.P. for, they would resort to the Rankin Committee's attack of yelling, "There's a Communist in every closet."

The only solution to our problem is that of breaking down segregation in public schools. You cannot accomplish this by giving lip service to opposition to Jim Crow education and then continuing to build monuments to this segregation in the form of Jim Crow schools in order to establish "Jim Crow DeLuxe."

Well, the chips are down, the fight against segregation in the public school system in Texas is on.

Marshall dared to attack Wesley on the publisher's home front:

Mr. Wesley asks whether we believe "it is easier to force Texas to admit Negroes into current white schools than it is to force them to equalize the separate schools." When you realize that Negroes have been fighting for equality in separate schools for more than eighty years and have not obtained a semblance of equality, which is the easier method is not the question before us. I have little faith in opportunists who look for the easy way out. There is no easy answer to segregation and discrimination. We have to decide whether we want separate schools or the end of segregation.

We have found out over a long period of years that segregation has been maintained for the sole purpose of relegating the Negro to a standard of citizenship below that of all other Americans. We must combine idealism and realism. We have whittled away through legal action and other ways at this mode of discrimination and have reached the conclusion that the only sane approach is a direct attack on segregation per se.

The fight is not going to be an easy one. It is going to be just as difficult as you can imagine and I know of nothing that is worth anything which is not difficult to obtain. It might be a long drawn out fight and it might take even more years than the fight against the white primary, but just as sure as we were victorious in the primary cases because of the fullest of cooperation of all parties concerned, I am sure that the same result can be obtained in this fight. The length of time it will take depends upon the amount of cooperation we can get.

I repeat, the chips are down, the lines are drawn. On one side we have the N.A.A.C.P., the Texas Council of Negro Organizations, and most of the Negroes in the State of Texas along with a large and ever growing group of white citizens determined to fight segregation every step of the way; on the other side we have a group who say that although segregation is bad, as well as invalid, we should accept it on one hand and fight for equality on the other hand and hope that by some stretch of the imagination equality will be obtained. We are convinced that it is impossible to have equality in a segregated system, no matter how elaborate we build the Jim Crow citadel and no matter whether we label it the "Black University of Texas," "the Negro University of Texas," "Prairie View Institute," or a more fitting title, "An Apology to Negroes for denying them their constitutional rights to attend the University of Texas."

When southern officials tried to prevent a legal showdown on "separate but equal" and asked Congress to approve and help finance a regional plan for graduate, professional, technical, and scientific schools that would be reserved for blacks, Marshall went before the Senate Judiciary Committee in Washington and restated the NAACP's position:

> Neither Congress nor anyone else can say that you get equality of education in a segregated school. The Fourteenth Amendment requires equality. The only way to get equality is for two people to get the same thing, at the same place and at the same time.

It was clear that somebody would have to out-argue Marshall in some very powerful ways if he were to be swayed from lawsuits that would challenge the basic legal and social fabric of the Southland, in which most American blacks lived. He told one of the great black pioneer newspapermen, Ted Poston: "If we can keep up the educational process and legal suits, Negroes will soon be voting in every community in the South; Jim Crow travel will be abolished and segregation in public education will be broken down, first in the graduate professional schools, and later in the colleges and law institutions. I have no doubt that this will come to pass."

It was four months after that outburst in Texas, in January 1948, that Marshall finally got to the Supreme Court in the *Sipuel* case. Oklahoma's assistant attorney general told the Court that Miss Sipuel could not get facilities anywhere in the state equal to those at the University of Oklahoma, "tomorrow or the next day." He said the regents would open a Negro law school "promptly" if she asked for one.

"She might be an old lady by that time," snapped Justice William O. Douglas.

When one of the state's attorneys complained that Miss Sipuel "is not willing to recognize the state's segregation policy," Justice Robert H. Jackson asked: "Why should she?"

Four days later Chief Justice Fred M. Vinson read the Court's unanimous decision: "Ada Sipuel is entitled to secure legal education afforded by a state institution. Oklahoma must provide it for her, and provide it as soon as it does for applicants of any other group."

Some journalists interpreted this as going far beyond the "separate-but-equal" judgment in *Gaines v. Missouri*, but they made a mistake. The Oklahoma power structure again won through one of the most amusing charades in the history of American education. They asked an Oklahoma City lawyer, Jerome E. Hemry, to set up and become dean of the "Langston University School of Law," a division of the all-black institution that would be located in room 428 of the state capitol. Oklahoma was going to pay three white professors to teach law to one black woman, Ada Sipuel. Five days after Hemry was photographed placing signs advertising the new Langston University School of Law, Marshall was back in Norman arguing that this was not good enough.

The celebrated semivictory had gotten Sipuel in *Time* magazine, the *New York Times*, and other publications across the land, but it was clear that she was a long way from attending her first class in the law school of the University of Oklahoma. Fortuitously, Marshall and Hall still had their backup, G. W. McLaurin, who had applied for study in education at the University of Oklahoma but was rejected also on grounds that the state forbade Negroes and whites to attend the same school. McLaurin went to court, with Marshall and Hall arguing his cause, and they won the following judgment from a three-man federal district court panel: "We hold, in conformity with the Equal Protection Clause of the 14th Amendment, that the plaintiff is entitled to secure a postgraduate course of study in education leading to a doctor's degree in a state institution, and that he is entitled to secure this as soon as it is afforded to any other applicant. . . .

"This does not mean, however, that the segregation laws of Oklahoma are incapable of constitutional enforcement. We simply hold that insofar as they are sought to be enforced in this particular case, they are inoperative."

This was decidedly less than Marshall and Hall had hoped for, because it kept intact the principle of separate but equal. Little did they know that the officials of the university would engage in some absurdities that would give them good reason to go back and challenge the very foundation of racial segregation.

McLaurin was admitted, but the university insisted that he use a separate toilet. When he went to his first class, he was told that he had to sit in what had been a broom closet but suddenly was called an "anteroom." McLaurin was told that at the library he could check out books, but had to read them in a special section reserved for him. There was a snack bar on campus known as The Jug, which white students used most of the day. At noon, however, all white students were barred from the snack bar, which was reserved exclusively for McLaurin. Marshall saw great hope in the fact that the university kept putting up COLORED signs in those special places where McLaurin was supposed to be, but white students kept tearing down the signs. At one point university officials admitted that they had spent $5,000 paying for Jim Crow signs that did not stay up very long.

Marshall and Hall filed to take the *McLaurin* case to the Supreme Court, but before they could get there, troubles were piling up for the regents of the university. They got a legal ruling that Negroes would have to be admitted to all graduate courses that were not provided at Langston, so they opened up ten new courses with a provision that separate courses, or instruction at separate hours, would be the rule. Suddenly, seventy-five blacks had enrolled for those classes, and the problem became acute as the university started looking for new faculty members and was asking for additional state funds with which to pay for this addition to segregation. Then, on September 14, 1949, a Tulsa black man named Julius Caesar Hill came on campus and took his luggage to a men's dormitory, where he asked where his room was. Whites there thought he had lost his mind, but they found out that Hill had a receipt showing that he had applied for a room, been accepted, and had paid his down payment on the spot. Troubled regents met that afternoon and ordered President Cross to find separate dormitories for no fewer than fifty blacks.

The regents had begun to see the impact of the early Marshall strategy of making states and universities spend so much to justify their pretense of "separate but equal" that they would go bankrupt. They might have to build an atom smasher just for "niggers." So the regents decided to abolish the law school that had been set up solely for Miss Sipuel, who by this time was Mrs. Fisher, who won a ruling by the Supreme Court that she had to be admitted to the university for the entering class of 1949.

Embarrassments mushroomed. The University of Oklahoma prided itself on its football team, but everything had been lily-white till then — the players, the coaches, the people in the stands. It was said that no black citizen had ever been allowed to come to the stadium to watch the Sooners play football. But now, with blacks on campus, the university had to set aside a separate area in the stands for black students. In October 1949, one Negro couple petitioned the dean of students for permission to attend the homecoming dance. Lionel Hampton's Negro band was going to play at what was supposed to be a lily-white affair. An official in charge of the homecoming said that Negroes could attend, but they could not dance, so an area to accommodate some fifteen black spectators was roped off. Panic spread across the campus when some white students who objected to Jim Crow declared that they would go over and ask the black students to dance. Newspapers had reporters everywhere at that homecoming affair, but were disappointed when not a single black student showed up.

The Supreme Court took a terrible burden off President Cross and the regents on June 5, 1950, when it ruled that the separate toilets, eating places, classes, classrooms, and housing were illegal. In a unanimous opinion, the Court declared unconstitutional the Oklahoma law that set McLaurin apart from white students. "This modified form of segregation," the Court said, violated the Fourteenth Amendment. Once a Negro is admitted he must receive "the same treatment at the hands of the state as students of other races."

This decision was a harbinger of things to come — a Supreme Court that considered the social, emotional, and other "intangible" factors in determining whether the victim of segregation was having his constitutional rights violated. The Court noted that McLaurin could wait in line in the cafeteria, and talk with fellow students, but that he had to eat apart from them. The Court said that this was bound to "inhibit his ability to study, to engage in discussion and exchange views with other students, and, in general, to learn his profession.

"Our society has grown increasingly complex and our need for trained leaders increases correspondingly," the Court continued. It said the *McLaurin* case "represents perhaps the epitome of that need, for he is attempting to obtain an advanced degree in education, to become, by definition, a leader and trainer of others . . . those who will come under his guidance and influence must be directly affected by the education he receives. Their own education and development necessarily suffers to the extent that his training is unequal to that of his classmates. State-imposed restrictions, which produce such inequities, cannot be sustained."

No one knew the skill, the sharpness of Marshall's mind, the tartness of his tongue, better than the federal district judges who heard him argue, probe, slash, during the basic trials of these university cases. The late J. Skelly Wright, who became a member of the Court of Appeals for the District of Columbia circuit, told me — and later wrote — one of my favorite stories about the way Marshall operated:

Thurgood Marshall played an important role in my judicial education. When I was appointed to the federal bench in Louisiana in 1949, I was only dimly aware of the attacks being mounted against the edifice of segregation. Although I believed that segregation was wrong, I had little sense of the role the courts might play in confronting this injustice. But when Marshall, who was then general counsel for the NAACP, appeared in my courtroom to try the Louisiana State University Law School case, my education began. Pursuant to state law, Louisiana maintained L.S.U. Law School for whites, and Southern University Law School for blacks. *Brown v. Board of Education* had not yet been decided, so the case was being tried under the "separate but equal" doctrine of *Plessy v. Ferguson.* Marshall soon convinced me that Southern University was not only separate from, but also unequal to, L.S.U. Law School. I crossed the Rubicon when I decided that case.

I vividly remember Marshall's cross-examination of one of the deans of Southern Law School. Earlier in the trial, counsel for the state had emphasized that Southern Law School, unlike L.S.U. Law School, was air-conditioned, clearly an advantage in sultry Louisiana. Marshall asked the dean to describe in detail the building in which Southern was housed. The dean testified that it was a large wooden frame structure with five floors housing several parts of the University, and that the law school was on the fifth floor. Marshall then asked the witness to describe what was on each of the other floors, which he did. Marshall then asked the witness whether each of the first four floors was air-conditioned like the fifth. The answer as to each floor was "No." Feigning surprise at the dean's answers, Marshall then asked the witness what was immediately above the fifth floor. His answer: "The roof." Marshall then suggested to the dean that the law school was really housed in the attic of the building. The dean readily agreed, saying, "That's why it is air-conditioned."

Marshall's cross-examination of the Southern Law School dean was typical of his courtroom performances: he was always straightforward, good-humored, and incisive. During my years as a district judge, I encountered few lawyers as skilled in their craft. He had an uncanny ability to identify the crucial facts in a case, and to describe legal issues in clear, commonsense terms. And he was able to do this in a way that conveyed, often quite dramatically, the realities of segregation — how it affected the daily lives of black Americans. His efforts in the law school case, as well as in the other cases he tried in my courtroom, helped persuade me that if the law did not prohibit racial discrimination, then the law was wrong. Two years after the Louisiana law school case the Supreme Court issued its historic decision in *Brown v. Board of Education.*

You begin to understand the energy and dedication of Marshall, the ubiquitousness of the man, when you realize that on the very day the Supreme Court lifted the burden off McLaurin, it was giving Marshall another victory in his case involving the University of Texas and Heman Marion Sweatt. After almost four years, the Supreme Court decided that there was just no way that Sweatt could get a reasonable legal education in Texas without his being admitted to the University of Texas Law School. Still, the Supreme Court, in this decision handed down by Chief Justice Vinson, was dodging the issue of whether "separate but equal" was *ever* permissible under the Constitution. Vinson said: "We cannot . . . agree with respondents that the doctrine of *Plessy v. Ferguson* requires affirmance of the judgment [by the lower court that the separation of black and white students was constitutional]. Nor need we reach petitioner's contention that *Plessy v. Ferguson* should be reexamined in the light of contemporary knowledge respecting the purposes of the 14th Amendment and the effects of racial segregation."

"Oh, boy, was that a disappointment," Marshall recalled. "But I had learned that lawyers couldn't just wallow in disappointment. I told myself that this was the typical caution of Supreme Court justices who wanted to deliver the narrowest opinion they could get away with. This was what some called 'judicial restraint.' I figured we'd just have to go back again and again, however many times necessary, to get the Court to one day recognize the psychological, social, educational, economic damages, done to black people when *the state* imposes the doctrine of *Plessy.*"

Marshall said he and other NAACP lawyers remained confident that one day they would put "stigmatic injury" into the lexicon of American judicial procedures.

CHAPTER TWELVE

SOLDIER TROUBLES

SHORTLY AFTER ITS ARRIVAL in Korea in July 1950, the Twenty-fourth Infantry Regiment won the first notable United States victory of the Korean War, retaking the strategic city of Yechon in a bloody sixteen-hour battle. Then, in the face of superior enemy forces and staggering casualty rates, the all-Negro unit (with mostly white officers) earned even greater acclaim by dislodging the North Koreans from Bloody Ridge, a critical point on the highway to Yechon.

But a few days later American forces began falling back under blistering North Korean attacks. On July 30, 1950, Leon A. Gilbert, one of the few Negro officers of the 24th Infantry, was ordered to take A Company to a ridge to cover the pullback.

Gilbert, a husky, quiet-spoken man, was no newcomer to combat. The thirty-one-year-old Pennsylvanian had earned two Bronze Stars in the Italian campaign during World War II. But the task he had been given was formidable. His company had no machine guns or automatic weapons — only rifles and hand grenades. When North Koreans occupied the opposite side of the ridge, they were able to attack the Americans almost at will. By morning, Gilbert decided his position was no longer tenable or useful, so he ordered what was left of his unit to pull out. As they headed south along a dry river bed, they met up with Colonel Horton V. White, commander of the Twenty-fourth's Regimental Combat team.

White ordered Gilbert to take his men back to the position they had just left. The lieutenant balked and tried to explain that there was no way of getting back on the ridge because the area was overrun with enemy troops. Another officer, a major, suggested that Gilbert might be afraid to go back, and told him to carry out the colonel's order at once. Worn out after a long night and twenty straight days in combat, and convinced it was suicidal and useless to go back, Gilbert again started to explain his concerns. The officers did not listen. They placed him under arrest, charged with violating the Seventy-fifth Article of War, specifically, "misbehaving himself before the enemy by refusing to advance with his command when ordered to do so." That amounted to cowardice, the most serious charge on a battlefield.

Five weeks later, at a forward command post just four hundred yards from the battle lines, Gilbert was tried at a court-martial, found guilty, and sentenced to death before a firing squad.

Before the court-martial, Gilbert's wife, Kay, who was pregnant with the couple's third child, had appealed to the NAACP for assistance. After the conviction, Gilbert himself wrote, asking the organization to intervene. Clarence Mitchell, head of the NAACP's Washington office, wrote Secretary of the Army Frank Pace, Jr., that "the news of the death sentence was a severe shock to colored people throughout the United States. . . . It was fantastic to give [Gilbert] the death sentence in view of his combat record." The NAACP efforts helped convince President Harry S Truman to commute Gilbert's sentence to twenty years at hard labor.

In the wake of nationwide publicity stirred by the Gilbert case, scores of other black GIs began to turn to the NAACP with their complaints about unfair treatment and pleas for help. NAACP files began to bulge with a catch-all category called "Soldier Troubles."

Troubles were nothing new for black soldiers. The U.S. armed forces reflected blacks' second-class status in civilian life, so Negro servicemen had long been victims of segregation, discrimination, scapegoating, false accusations. When World War II broke out, all the services were completely segregated. Negro cavalrymen were used as "officers' grooms," and sea duty for black sailors was almost always restricted to service as mess stewards.

Negro troops were involved in a disproportionate number of courts-martial cases during the war, with charges ranging from rape to cowardice and mutiny. One of the most infamous incidents was the Port Chicago "mutiny" outside of San Francisco. Two ships had blown up in San Francisco Bay in July 1944 while they were being loaded with ammunition, killing 320 men in the grisliest home-front accident of the war. Three weeks later, hundreds of still-frightened sailors refused to go back to loading ammunition on other ships.

Fifty of them, all blacks and over half under the age of twenty-one, were convicted of "making a mutiny." They received sentences ranging from eight to fifteen years in prison.

Marshall, who attended the trial at Yerba Buena Island in San Francisco Bay, contended that "these men are being tried for mutiny solely because of their race and color." At the request of the sailors, he filed a brief for their appeal that was successful in getting the sentences reduced. The NAACP was not as successful in most of the other World War II court-martial cases that it entered. One reason was that, because of lack of funds and staff, it didn't get involved until after the war, by which time the records and witnesses were hard to find.

But there were outrageous cases which convinced Marshall, White, and other NAACP officials that the problems of blacks and the armed forces involved critical issues to which the NAACP needed to pay greater attention. In 1948, A. Philip Randolph, the outspoken head of the Brotherhood of Sleeping Car Porters, created a stir by suggesting that perhaps Negroes should refuse to go along with a new military draft. Randolph argued that segregation in the largest federal enterprise, the armed services, hampered black efforts to make headway in civilian life.

The NAACP rejected Randolph's strategy as self-wounding, but it did offer to provide legal assistance to young men who followed the Randolph boycott, and it put its weight behind the growing move to integrate the military. Those efforts were rewarded on July 26, 1948, when President Truman issued Executive Order 9981 calling for "equality of treatment and opportunity for all persons in the armed services without regard to race, color, religion or national origin."

When the Korean War broke out in mid-1950, about one hundred thousand Negroes were in uniform — sixty thousand of them in the Army, twenty-five thousand in the Air Force, the rest in the Navy and Marine Corps. The Navy and Air Force had already made progress in achieving the integration ordered by Truman, but the Army continued to drag its feet. Units like the 24th Infantry Regiment, whose enlisted men were all black and whose officers were a mixture of blacks and whites, remained the norm. Army commanders still expressed concern that mixing Negro and white soldiers could "impair fighting morale."

That didn't stop the NAACP board of directors from voting to support "the efforts of the United States and the United Nations to halt communist aggression in Korea." But the resolution added, "If America is to win the support of non-Communist Asia and Africa it will have to demonstrate that democracy is a living reality which knows no limitation of race, color or nationality."

And it called on the U.S. government and people to take "prompt and effective action to end all forms of racial discrimination and segregation in our military and civilian life," including "the abolition of separate Army units, the removal of barriers to employment opportunities and the end of segregation."

Stories of "soldier troubles" poured into local and national NAACP offices. From Fort Bliss, Texas, came complaints that white soldiers were being shipped to Europe after their training, while blacks were sent to battle in Korea. From Camp Atterbury, Indiana, there were charges that the commanding officer there had assembled all troops — whites and blacks separately — and told them that there would be no mixing of the races. When Negro soldiers danced with white girls at a post dance at Atterbury, the white hostess complained to the officer of the day, who ordered the Negroes to leave. From Germany, a black soldier asked help in fighting what he insisted was a false rape charge.

One of the most disturbing and revealing reports involved a group of Minnesota inductees who were sent to Camp Rucker, Alabama. The orders for the group stated that all of the men named on the papers were "white, unless otherwise indicated." Asterisks appeared alongside eleven names, with a footnote explaining that those marks "indicate colored."

At Camp Rucker, blacks and whites were segregated, with the blacks given inferior facilities in everything from barracks to post exchanges. One draftee wrote his parents that he and other Negroes had been segregated into a labor battalion, where they were being trained by "Negro-baiting white officers."

The black soldiers were warned to stay away from nearby towns because they would be mistreated there and humiliated, tossed into jail on the slightest pretext. Two of the black GIs complained that military police, all of whom were white, humiliated and abused Negro soldiers if they ventured into surrounding communities.

All of those issues disturbed Marshall and other NAACP officials. But it was the rapidly growing number of arrests and courts-martial of Negro soldiers in Korea that caused the greatest consternation.

Noting that there had been no similar reports of courts-martial of white soldiers, Marshall announced that "the NAACP is ready to defend, with all of its resources, any of those servicemen upon determination that they are victims of racial discrimination." He emphasized that action would be taken only when requested by the soldier or a close relative.

The requests poured in. A Virginia mother passed along a letter from her twenty-three-year-old son, who had been sentenced to twenty years in prison. "There are many more fellows who are being caused to suffer from the injustice practiced in Korea," he wrote. "Tell the National Association of my sentence."

Another letter received by the NAACP from a soldier in the Far East said, "These [courts-martial] records, though filled with legal loopholes and discrepancies, are merely routine and offer little light to the true surroundings. If the whole and true story could be told, your task would be simplified considerably. . . . A complete story of the regiment [24th Infantry] from June 27th to the present day would turn your stomach."

What puzzled and disturbed Marshall and others was the way the same men and units that had been heroic and brave one day somehow became, in white eyes, cowardly and frightened the next. Remembering the difficulties they had encountered in finding records and witnesses to fight courts-martial after World War II, NAACP officials decided that the complete story could only be ferreted out by sending someone to the Far East to conduct an on-the-spot investigation. The task fell to Thurgood.

"We had assumed the responsibility of protecting and advancing the rights of American Negroes," Marshall wrote later in explaining the decision. "Surely in wartime the protection of our men and women in the armed services had first call upon our resources and abilities."

At first General Douglas MacArthur refused to give Marshall permission to make the trip. Walter White shot off a cablegram to him:

ENTIRE NEGRO POPULATION AND MILLIONS OF OTHERS DEEPLY DISTURBED BY REPORTS OF MASS CONVICTIONS OF NEGRO INFANTRYMEN IN KOREA. EXAMINATION OF COURTS-MARTIAL RECORDS INDICATES MANY CONVICTED UNDER CIRCUMSTANCES MAKING IMPARTIAL JUSTICE IMPROBABLE. . . . WE ARE CERTAIN YOU WOULD WANT TO SEE THAT THEY RECEIVE FULL JUSTICE NOT ONLY BECAUSE THEY DESERVE IT BUT ALSO TO COUNTER INEVITABLE COMMUNIST PROPAGANDA THROUGHOUT ASIA.

While denying any evidence of irregularities or injustices, MacArthur ordered his inspector general to start a "thorough investigation" and opened the door for Marshall to come to the Far East.

Meanwhile, Marshall ran into another problem. The always strapped NAACP didn't have enough money in the bank to pay for his trip. But it was considered so critical that checks were drawn anyway, and Marshall knew he had to live "on less than a shoestring."

On January 11, 1951, Marshall took off on what he regarded as "the most important mission thus far of my career." This was typical Marshall hyperbole. He never really considered this mission to Tokyo more important than his trip to Denison, Texas, to defend the NAACP's antisegregation stance, or his 1951 trip to Charleston to argue the *Briggs v. Elliott* school desegregation case. Asked which was his most important case, Marshall always replied: "The next one." The troubles of black soldiers and sailors not only became "the next one," but they were for the moment uppermost in the minds of millions of Americans. Here was the wedge the NAACP needed to begin an overall assault on racial discrimination — especially in the military. Forty-one hours later he landed in Tokyo, spent a day finding a hotel through the Army and settling in, then went to work. He met at once with MacArthur, General Doyle O. Hickey, his chief of staff, and his other top aides.

"I told them frankly that I thought there was a good probability that the men had been victims of racial bias and unfair trials based on conditions inherent in the Army's segregation policies," Marshall reported back to the NAACP. "General MacArthur insisted that I be given the fullest cooperation from everyone under his command."

The first task was to interview the men who were imprisoned. Each day a staff car from MacArthur's headquarters picked Marshall up at 9 A.M. and took him to the inspector general's office, then to the stockade, just outside of Tokyo, where he interviewed prisoners one at a time in a private room until 4:30, with time out for lunch at the officers' club.

He returned to his hotel in the evening, ate dinner, analyzed the information, and on a little portable typewriter he'd scrounged up, prepared a report for the inspector general listing points he wanted checked out.

"It is a much tougher grind than I bargained for," Marshall wrote, "but it is the best way to get the job done."

If MacArthur and his aides had been less than cordial when the trip was first suggested, they showed no sign of that when Marshall was in Tokyo. The IG and his staff were available at any time, as was the judge advocate general. Marshall even had access to MacArthur and General Hickey, and he was permitted to talk freely to all the black soldiers who had been court-martialed, plus anyone else he wanted to see.

All of which prompted the wary lawyer to warn his NAACP colleagues in New York, "Beware, the plush carpet is now out in all its 'glory.'" His "special antennae" told him that MacArthur was a segregationist.

Marshall spent nearly three weeks making his daily forays to the stockade. He interviewed thirty-four of the thirty-six accused men who had written to the NAACP for assistance, along with dozens of other black enlisted men and officers who were witnesses or members of the same outfit as the accused.

Sometimes he would go back to see men he'd already spoken with in order to check out things that didn't seem to jibe. "I separated the gossip from the facts. I separated the hearsay from the facts. I separated the exaggerated statements from the facts," Marshall reported later. "I always do with a case, and any lawyer will do it."

"If one half of what these men tell me is true, this is one of the damndest deals ever pulled," Marshall reported, noting that he had uncovered "one unbelievable story after another."

One involved a young black convicted of cowardice. He had enlisted in the Army when he was only fifteen years old and could have avoided duty in Korea by revealing his true age. Instead, that "coward" stuck it out at the front until he was yanked out on what Marshall called "a trumped-up" court-martial charge. The soldier did not reach his eighteenth birthday until eleven days after he had been convicted, and even then, his real age did not come out until Marshall talked to him.

Another soldier Marshall talked to was Private J. P. Morgan. Although he had proved that he was in an Army hospital during the period when he was charged with not being on duty, he was sentenced to ten years at hard labor.

And Marshall held six meetings with Leon Gilbert, which, together with new information he found in court-martial proceedings, convinced him more than ever that the lieutenant had gotten a raw deal. Marshall learned that the members of the court-martial were all white, and that while defense witnesses were not allowed to appear, the main prosecution witnesses testified in person.

He also learned that a board of three medical officers who examined Gilbert found that at the time of the alleged offense he was able to distinguish right from wrong but was emotionally disturbed. The doctors described his condition as "anxiety reaction, acute, severe." One psychiatrist reported, "I believe that at the time of the alleged offense, Lieutenant Gilbert was suffering from a nervous illness . . . which would prevent him from carrying out his duties as ordered." Gilbert himself explained that he had been without sleep for six days prior to the incident and without food or water part of that time and was suffering from acute dysentery.

Marshall wrote President Truman directly, asking for dismissal of all charges against Gilbert on grounds that by the Army's own definitions the accused officer was not responsible for his alleged misconduct and he had not been given a fair trial.

After three weeks of interviews in Tokyo, Marshall decided that he needed to fly to Korea to talk to men on the front lines and read through the complete court-martial transcripts, investigating reports, orders, and other records that were in Pusan. He spent eight days in Korea, talking with at least two men from every company of the Twenty-fourth Infantry and every battery of its attached unit, the 159th Field Artillery — often within earshot of the battle raging nearby.

"If you don't believe Tokyo is a great place," Marshall wrote back, "just go to Korea, and Tokyo looks like heaven." At one point Marshall flew by helicopter to the farthest forward position of the United Nations forces. They passed over Seoul, which looked rather quiet and peaceful until U.S. artillery began dropping "stuff" on the city. "You should try it sometime," Marshall told colleagues back home. "It is good for my low blood pressure, which is now high."

If the helicopter ride had not raised Marshall's blood pressure, his inquiries and interviews surely would have. Marshall discovered that although there were almost four times as many white soldiers in Korea as blacks, nearly two-thirds of the Article Seventy-five cases taken to trial involved Negroes. Virtually all personnel of the judge advocate general's office were white, as were the trial judge advocates and trial commanding officers.

Many of the trials appeared to have been railroaded. Accused men were pulled out of foxholes at night, brought to the site of the court-martial and put on trial at nine the next morning. It was not unusual for them to meet their counsel for the first time in the courtroom, which meant they had just fifteen minutes to talk before the trial. "No credence was ever given to the story each individual accused man would tell," Marshall noted. "Scant effort was made to find out what was true and what was not."

Marshall learned that the military courts, some of which were only two hundred yards from the battlefield, tried as many as four cases a day. Two men were found guilty and sentenced to life in prison in trials that lasted just fifty minutes each.

One result of this was that many of the accused simply gave up in despair, without even offering mitigating circumstances or legitimate alibis. "It wasn't worth it," one prisoner explained. "We knew when we went to trial that we would be convicted. What could we expect? We knew the score."

Typical was a veteran sergeant, whom Marshall called "one of the finest men I'd ever met." In three months at the front, he had brought wounded buddies out on his back and fought bravely day after day, on at least three occasions assuming command of his unit because officers were killed. During his trial for refusing to obey an order, he never mentioned to his lawyer or the court that he had in his pocket a statement from the medical doctor in charge, saying that he was on the verge of battle fatigue and should be returned to the rear.

In interviews with blacks on the front lines Marshall was repeatedly told that many of the white officers "sneered at their troops who were about to go forth to fight and, if necessary, die for their country." One officer reputedly announced openly, "I despise nigger troops and I don't want to command you. The regiment is no good and you are lousy. You don't know how to fight."

While not every officer acted that way, the attitude was so widespread that it created a lack of confidence between the enlisted men and their leaders. As a result, neither group offered full protection to the other, and so the casualty rates among both the enlisted men and officers were high. That discovery was to prove one of the most significant of Marshall's trip.

Marshall came away with some astounding statistics. During the period from August through October of 1950, thirty-two Negro servicemen were convicted under Article Seventy-five — misbehavior in the presence of the enemy — compared with just two whites. One of the thirty-two Negroes was sentenced to death, fifteen to life in prison. Fourteen got ten, twenty, twenty-five, or fifty years, and two were sentenced to five years. Of the two whites, one got three years, the other five (his defense was that he was a chronic drunk).

In one instance a white soldier who was found by his commanding officer asleep during guard duty on the front lines was charged only with sleeping at his post, not with the more serious Article Seventy-five. Whites charged with leaving a sentry post were acquitted even when they did not put up a defense.

"The unanswered question," Marshall observed, "is why so many Negroes are charged with cowardice and so few white soldiers. No one has given me any answer on this yet. I have maintained that Negroes are no more or less cowards than anyone else."

What had started as a two- or three-week trip stretched to five weeks. And when Marshall returned to the United States in February, he didn't go straight to his New York City home. Instead, he told the "shameful story" of his investigation (and helped raise money to pay for it) to large audiences in San Francisco, Kansas City, Chicago. In these speeches and in a printed *Report on Korea* that the NAACP published a few weeks later, Marshall offered some answers to the questions he had raised about the disparities in courts-martial and the mistreatment of Negroes.

He concluded that the friction between Negro enlisted men and white officers and its deadly effect on both groups was one key. "I believe this condition was the cause of the courts-martial. The high rate of casualties among officers made it necessary to blame someone. The Negro soldier was the convenient scapegoat."

Another factor cited by Marshall was the apparent concern in some quarters about Negro troops looking too able and courageous. This had happened in Italy during World War II and was repeated in the early weeks of the Korean War in the Gilbert case.

First came press reports from the front of heroic deeds done by Negro soldiers, as at Yechon and Bloody Ridge in Korea. "And then suddenly the reports change," Marshall pointed out. "As if in a concerted effort to discredit the record of Negro fighting men, the tales we begin to hear are of incompetence, failure, and cowardice — accounts which would make it appear that Negroes are not capable of combat duty and should be restricted to labor battalions."

Finally, Marshall concluded, at the core of virtually all problems involving blacks and the military were the Jim Crow policies that persisted, primarily in the Army. While exonerating MacArthur from having taken a direct hand in the courts-martial, Marshall did hold him responsible for not implementing President Truman's order for integration. Despite the presence of a few mixed units in the Army, the general practice found by Marshall was one of rigid segregation — glaringly evident at the Tokyo headquarters of the Far East command, to which no Negroes were assigned.

"As long as we have racial segregation in the Army, we will have the type of injustice of which these courts-martial are typical," Marshall warned. "Men who are daily exposing themselves to injury and death at the hands of the enemy should not be subjected to injustice, additional hardship, and unnecessary danger solely because of racial prejudice."

Marshall told the San Francisco audience: "The record in Korea is but one more of the many arguments that the problem of the American Negro in the Armed Forces (at present the Army) will never be solved under a system of segregation and that a beginning toward the building of the proper fighting morale for American forces will never be made until segregation is completely abolished."

Even before Marshall's full report from his Far East trip came out, the NAACP had begun representing Negro servicemen at the U.S. Army's Review Board. It succeeded in getting more than thirty sentences reduced, including one life sentence that was cut to five years and suspended, a second that was reduced to ten years, another to fifteen, and six more that were cut to twenty years.

At the same time that it fought for justice on the battlefield, the NAACP was called on to help servicemen and servicewomen with other problems, many arising out of the stationing of Negro personnel at bases in the South. Five black GIs from Fort Benning, Georgia, were arrested after fighting broke out between the Negroes and white police in Columbus, Georgia. One of the servicemen was beaten about the face until his eyes were closed and his buddies thought he was dead. An Air Force enlisted man who had grown up in the North but was stationed in the South came to the local NAACP office angry and puzzled about the object he flung down on a desk — the leather contraption used to separate black and white passengers on buses.

Ending all types of segregation and racial discrimination in the armed services became the focus of NAACP efforts. Clarence Mitchell, of the NAACP Washington Bureau, put their argument succinctly when he testified before the Preparedness Subcommittee of the Senate Armed Services Committee in 1951:

> It is a frightful thing to contemplate that their government will call upon [blacks] to risk their lives in war and at the same time fail to protect them against undemocratic practices if they are stationed in the South. . . . If the government has the power to draft a man, it also has the power to protect him wherever he may be stationed in the United States.

In a printed interview that appeared in mid-1951, MacArthur disavowed responsibility for the segregation of troops under his command in the Far East. Walter White reminded the general that both the Navy and Air Force had made significant strides in fulfilling President Truman's executive order abolishing racial discrimination in the armed services, but that the Army in the Far East showed little evidence of compliance.

But thanks in large measure to Marshall's efforts in Korea and Japan, the Army had been launched on its way to desegregation and the "soldier troubles" that had become the number one concern of the NAACP were dwindling. Attention could once again be shifted back to the home front, where the old issues of voting rights and school integration were still boiling.

CHAPTER THIRTEEN

A DESTRUCTIVE MARRIAGE

IN mid-1949 Marshall was sweating out the *Sweatt* case at the University of Texas, the efforts to get Ada Lois Sipuel and G. W. McLaurin into the University of Oklahoma, and cases against college Jim Crow in other states. He was already doing research, writing sections of preliminary briefs, for an all-out legal assault on segregation in public schools in particular, and on *Plessy v. Ferguson* specifically.

But Marshall's attention was often diverted by the smell of trouble in the air — not legal problems, but the deeper troubles that often arise from personal and sexual relationships.

Marshall kept getting notes or verbal comments from Walter White about how a woman named Poppy Cannon could get one rich person or another to give big money to the NAACP if Thurgood could get them tickets to this event or that. White would say which rich people he was going to meet at Mrs. Cannon's home in Connecticut. It didn't take much for Marshall to suspect that White was getting more than donations to the NAACP from his frequent trips to Poppy Cannon's house.

Marshall would say bluntly, at a poker game with his buddies Jim Nabrit, Bill Hastie, Bob Ming, and others, that he believed "anybody is free to screw anybody who is willing and of age." Yet, he knew that White couldn't, or shouldn't, do everything he had a right to do. After all, the most passionate attacks against Thurgood and the legal staff were based on charges that they wanted to put black men in the beds of white women, which would "mongrelize" the population and destroy the great society that Anglo-Saxons had built.

Marshall tried to quiet his worries by telling himself that it didn't mean much if White was secretly "getting a little on the side." Fact was, White had had so many spells of illness, with a bad heart, that Marshall and other NAACP males said jokingly, "more power to him" if he could engage in a little extracurricular activity. After all, Marshall figured, "mongrelization" was little more than a propaganda issue, an inflaming figment of the insecurities of white men. Hell, the black men in the NAACP were married almost exclusively to black women. White, who was as fair-skinned as any man claiming to be Caucasian, had been married for twenty-seven years to a woman who was clearly black. It had become a joke throughout the Association, one that White himself told frequently, that on the NAACP leader's speaking trips someone in the audience invariably would turn to Gladys White and ask, "Is Walter White *white?*"

"I'm his wife," ebony-skinned Gladys would reply.

NAACP offices were a beehive of gossip and rumor on March 17, 1949, when Gerri Major, who would become a fixture as a cooking expert in *Ebony* magazine, revealed in print that a white cooking expert for *Mademoiselle* magazine, Poppy Cannon, had gone to the Virgin Islands and secured a divorce from her third husband, Charles Claudius Phillipe, the banquet manager of the Waldorf-Astoria hotel in New York City, on grounds of "incompatibility."

Major raised the question of whether Cannon and White were now married, noting that "although they seldom were seen in Harlem, they were not unknown to show up in smart, downtown rendezvous, and in the Virgin Islands and Haiti." Major said White "used to be a frequent visitor at Mrs. Cannon's home in New Canaan, Connecticut, but a year ago discontinued his visits because of gossip."

Marshall and Wilkins tried vainly to halt the internal whispers, ordering NAACP officials not to talk about the situation publicly.

On July 26, Marshall, who was in charge, issued this memorandum:

Any requests for information or comment from anyone addressed to any executive or staff member of this office concerning the whereabouts of Mr. Walter White or his private life or his marital status must be referred to me. There are to be no exceptions under any circumstances. This, of course, only is in force until the return of Mr. Wilkins, who is expected in the office on Monday, August 1st.

Marshall knew that his fears had more substance than he wished when he saw this big headline across the front page of the *Afro-American:* WALTER WHITE'S DIVORCED! That same day the New York *Amsterdam News* had a bigger headline saying: "HINT WALTER WHITE ROMANCE."

Marshall was shaken when he read a mailed press release saying: "Mrs. Gladys (Walter) White announced that she secured a decree of divorce against Mr. White at Juarez, Mexico, on June 30, 1949."

That item made headlines not just in every black newspaper in America, but also in *Time* magazine and most of the major media. A week later the *Amsterdam News* reported the following:

> Walter White, executive secretary of the NAACP now on leave from his duties, married Mrs. Poppy Cannon, food editor of Mademoiselle Magazine, during the first week in July, according to a report from the Associated Negro Press. The ANP reports that "reliable sources" state they were married in New York, "before both left for Europe during the first week in July."
>
> Whether White's alleged marriage across racial lines will affect his status as head of the NAACP is not known but in a report published in the press over the week end, White is reported to have said that he hopes to return to take up his duties with the Association as soon as his health permits.

Over its four decades of existence, the NAACP had endured crises over white-versus-black domination; over whether to accommodate some segregation for economic reasons; over whether the legal staff should be separated, for tax reasons, from the NAACP itself. But no controversy imperiled the organization more than these 1949 stories that its leader, White, had divorced his black wife of twenty-seven years and married a white woman who was a three-time divorcée.

Marshall virtually abandoned his work on efforts to get *Plessy v. Ferguson* wiped out as he and Wilkins engaged in damage control. But they couldn't control the NAACP staff, let alone its board of directors, and surely not the media. Marshall believed that one person married another, and that nobody married a "race," but he was aware of the explosive public relations potential of the NAACP coming out for "intermarriage" at that time.

The *Norfolk Journal and Guide* was at the time one of the five most influential black newspapers in the nation. On August 6 it said editorially:

Serious embarrassment, if not something worse, is likely to befall the National Association for the Advancement of Colored People as a result of the recent marriage of its executive secretary, Walter White, to a white divorcee.

Of course, as an individual of maturity, the gentleman possessed the legal right to marry the woman of his choice, subject to her consent.

But in view of the nature, character, professed aims and objectives of the NAACP, Mr. White, in his capacity as its most publicized officer, official spokesman, and supposed personification of its ideals might have, for the sake of the organization, used better judgment.

The detractors of the association have made much of the charge that its anti-segregation program is in reality a disguise of the Negro's yearnings to marry whites.

This is a fallacy, of course, which is vigorously denied by friends of the organization, but the denial is subjected to a deflating slap when it is recalled that the association's most vocal official hopped across the race line in matrimony at the opportune moment.

It is not likely, however, that this gentleman, prone as he is to serving his selfish interests, will feel overly concerned about what happens to the NAACP, now that he has attained his latest ambition, but a prompt and official announcement that he will not return to his post at the expiration of his leave is in order.

The record shows that the association has not had statesmanship at its helm since the passing of the late James Weldon Johnson, the astute secretary succeeded by Mr. White, whom, it is hoped will be replaced by someone with more statesman-like perspective.

Wilkins wrote *Journal and Guide* publisher P. B. Young, Sr., an angry letter assailing his "emotional . . . vindictive . . . biased editorial." Wilkins was next in line to succeed White, but he made it clear he did not want a promotion following from an ouster of White because of his marrying a white woman.

In its article on White, the *Afro-American* recalled that President Grover Cleveland had welcomed Frederick Douglass to the White House, despite his marriage to a white woman, and had even invited the couple to receptions attended by distinguished diplomats.

What the *Afro* was printing was not always what its publisher, Carl Murphy, was saying and writing in private. Heretofore closed records in the Library of Congress show that Murphy sent a letter to every member of the NAACP board, of which he was a member (although he rarely attended meetings), saying that White's "sudden divorce and marriage to Mrs. Cannon has so weakened his usefulness that the Association will assume a grave risk in attempting to keep him in office."

Another board member, Palmer Weber of Washington, D.C., put a handwritten note on Murphy's letter and sent it to Wilkins, saying: "Dear Roy: It looks like the pot is boiling. This kind of letter is extremely unfortunate. I am writing Carl to that effect." He did, and only stirred up more anger in Murphy, whose paper suggested editorially that Dr. Ralph Bunche, the black United Nations official, be drafted to replace White.

The controversy grew when C. C. Spaulding, another board member, president of the North Carolina Mutual Insurance Company and a powerful black businessman, told the National Negro Business League: "Walter White has snatched at the rug of economic, social and political advancement upon which the feet of Negroes rest. . . . Moreover, he has given credence . . . to the inaccurate charge of the white South that the highest aspiration of Negroes is to invade the white race."

Murphy and others did not count on the powerful influence of some blacks who were appalled at the extent to which blacks were drowning themselves in passion and rhetoric over White's marriage. Bill Hastie, a towering voice in the Association, who was by this time Governor of the Virgin Islands, wrote Murphy, saying:

> In my judgment the National Board of Directors of the NAACP can no more afford to bow to race prejudice among Negroes than to race prejudice among whites or to the sentiment of those Negroes who approve segregated institutions or any other attitude inconsistent with the principles of the NAACP. The greatest strength of the Association lies in its hard-won reputation — among enemies as well as among friends — for consistency in adherence to basic principles regardless of popular reaction.
>
> I can understand regret that any event should involve the Association in controversy with people who have supported it. It is possible that the "critical attitude of large numbers of colored people" with reference to Mr. White's marriage may, as you suggest, make it impossible for the Association to "expand as rapidly as we would wish." Such an eventuality would, however, be the lesser of evils. If the Board should placate dissidents at the sacrifice of principle, its action would cause lasting and irreparable damage to such

an organization as ours. I have in mind both damage at home and damage through the world wherever the Association is known as the implacable foe of racism in whatever form.

Marshall was proud that one of his most revered mentors, Hastie, had come through just as forcefully in 1949 as he had in 1934 in the war over segregation between White and Du Bois.

A week after Hastie sent his letter, the NAACP board met in New York, faced with a recommendation from its New York branch that the board "request and accept the [proffered] resignation of Mr. Walter White and make known to the public their action." The board tabled this recommendation and announced that White's status as NAACP secretary-on-leave was unchanged. White's leave would not terminate until May 31, 1950.

White and his bride had survived this tempest traveling (some said hiding out) as participants in the "Round-the-World Town Meeting," sponsored by "America's Town Meeting of the Air," a popular radio program. When they came home nine days before the October 10 board meeting that would consider his ouster, White held a press conference:

Q.: Some sections of the Negro press have stated that they feel it is improper for the head of the NAACP to be married to a white woman. Would you comment on this?

WHITE: Throughout my entire life I have lived by one principle — that there is but one race, the human race. I have fought and always will fight against any artificial barriers among the peoples of the world based on race, creed, color, or caste.

Q.: Do you feel that the press handled the report of your divorce and marriage fairly?

WHITE: My wife and I are pleased, and we are grateful to the overwhelming majority of the press in America, as well as Europe and Asia, for their accurate, dignified, even warmly sympathetic treatment of the news of our marriage. As for the small minority of newspapers, which for whatever motives have exploited the news of our marriage, I have only this to say: In this country we, fortunately, have freedom of expression — a freedom which I certainly uphold.

Q.: Do you feel that your interracial marriage has weakened your leadership among Negroes?

WHITE: Time alone will provide the answer.

Regarding his future in the NAACP, White said it was impossible for him to say what he would do until the board of directors made a decision. The board voted to keep White as the NAACP's top man — with some reduction of his duties and power.

You cannot understand the significance of this marriage upon Marshall and Wilkins, or upon the major thrusts of the NAACP, unless you understand White's special relationship to the organization. For all the talk inside and outside the NAACP about White's white skin and blue eyes, his ego, and his eagerness to take credit for Marshall's work, no informed person could deny that White was the great wooer of the media to the causes of racial justice in general and desegregation in particular. Marshall was winning over judges and juries while White was using Marshall's triumphs as a basis for winning over public opinion. One problem was that judges and juries never paid Marshall a dime, whereas the magazines, newspapers, lecture forums, and broadcast stations paid White small fortunes.

After the marriage to Poppy, the conventional wisdom was that White had survived the storm within the NAACP board but could never again deal effectively with the white media, that his relationship with the NAACP could never be the same.

But Marshall and Wilkins knew of the many times people had counted White out in the middle of a fight. They remembered that White had never walked away from confrontation and criticism. But they also knew that this time White was fighting more than political and social foes. He might survive the in-fighting of the NAACP board, but they knew, secretly, that he was a very sick man. Now his marriage had cast an illness upon the NAACP.

Marshall worried every night about the viability of the "man called White" and the organization some wanted him to leave.

Marshall was acutely aware by this time that the NAACP was born in strife, had survived internal brawls, was a legal map of mischief, and faced a threat of internal destruction that was greater than all the anti-NAACP rhetoric thrown out by bigots.

The NAACP's victories in the voting rights cases in Texas and South Carolina, and Marshall's triumphs in the University of Maryland and University of Missouri education cases (*Murray* and *Gaines*), hit the southern and border states like an unprecedented eruption of the San Andreas fault. The politicians who held what for decades had been unchallenged power and privilege, the businessmen whose profits rested on the work of cheap, ignorant black laborers in their cotton fields and peanut patches, suddenly were declaring that the NAACP was an evil force that had to be destroyed, directly or by subversion. But the racists found that there was no "American way" to get federal courts to say that an organization of black and white people could not take legal actions to extend the legal reach of the Constitution.

There were, however, extralegal means through which the South's gendarmes of the status quo could try to render the NAACP impotent. The first step would be to learn the names of the white people, especially "the Jews," who gave the NAACP political and economic support. Given the names, Klansmen and other bigots could impose economic sanctions, boycotts, public humiliation, social pressures, and other measures to intimidate white NAACP members and end their support of Marshall's "subversive" legal activities.

Texas had first tried this in 1919, provoking the NAACP's white secretary, John R. Shillady, to rush to Austin to try to protect the Association's records. That was when bigots beat Shillady to the point of death. But the scheme to hound and harass white NAACP members failed. So in the offices of attorneys general across the South, in state legislatures, in all-white universities, strategies were hatched to cripple the NAACP by charging its lawyers with barratry, the crime of fomenting lawsuits by soliciting clients for litigation. That gambit failed, too.

Eventually, the protectors of the Jim Crow status quo found that they could punish both the NAACP and its donors by denying the Association tax-exempt status, and thus tax deductions to the people who were giving money to this rambunctious civil rights organization. Marshall, Walter White, Roy Wilkins, and the major contributors to the NAACP were shocked in October 1939 when the U.S. Treasury Department refused to grant tax-exempt status to the NAACP. Small wonder that Marshall railed that FDR and his administration were not the friends of black Americans that the media portrayed them to be.

That Treasury Department decision set in motion a string of events and policy decisions through which the segregationists divided and almost destroyed the NAACP. White proposed and the NAACP board authorized the creation of a Legal Defense and Educational Fund. This would be a new corporation, devoted exclusively to education and legal defense, but authorized by the NAACP board to use the NAACP's name. Put bluntly, the Legal Defense and Educational Fund was an instrument designed to get the Internal Revenue Service out of the picture — a way for the Association to get tax-exempt donations, given the reality that even the richest of Americans didn't want to give anything to anybody unless they could deduct it on their income taxes.

This was so crucial to an impoverished NAACP that on October 24, 1939, White sent a telegram from Washington to Marshall in New York saying, "Goodmans' large contribution available when incorporation completed."

This legal maneuver worked. In 1940 the new corporation was granted tax-exempt status.

Marshall, White, and others in the NAACP thought at first that they had perpetrated a harmless tax dodge, a little organizational ruse that would frustrate the bigots and draw desperately needed money into the civil rights movement. This "Inc. Fund" was to be nothing more than a subsidiary, a controlled instrumentality, of the NAACP itself. The Inc. Fund and the NAACP had interlocking boards and staff members to such a degree that any IRS auditor might have said, "This is a conspiracy to evade the tax laws." It may be that the people in Roosevelt's Treasury Department were friendlier, in never ordering such an audit, than Thurgood thought.

The reality was that White and Wilkins were secretary and assistant secretary of the Inc. Fund; Marshall was special counsel of the NAACP and counsel of the Inc. Fund. Marshall's salary was paid in part by the NAACP, and the rest by the Inc. Fund. Other staff members were on the payrolls of both the NAACP and the Inc. Fund.

Here was a map of mischief, not unlike the partitioning of an area into India and Pakistan, or the dividing of an area once called Palestine. Explosions were inevitable. The certainty of personal and bureaucratic wars increased as the legal work increased. The Inc. Fund, because of the publicity that Marshall garnered, was getting many donations compared with the nondeductible money given to the NAACP. So as the legal load increased, new lawyers were put on the Inc. Fund payroll. That created a situation in which the Legal Defense Fund was paying for the courtroom struggles, with little money coming out of the general fund of the NAACP. Yet White was Marshall's boss and the NAACP exercised control over the Fund's decisions about where and when to sue whom about what.

This arrangement was altered in the 1950s when the NAACP became more hated and feared than ever before. Congressional pressures provoked the Treasury Department to scrutinize more closely the cozy structure of the NAACP and the Inc. Fund. The Library of Congress holds a 1961 memorandum in which Robert L. Carter, Marshall's close ally in the *Briggs v. Elliott* case and at the time the general counsel of the NAACP, wrote:

To save the latter's tax exemption, a series of steps were begun which culminated in Board, staff and organizational independence of the Fund. What was done was authorized by the NAACP Board, but with little analysis or understanding of its consequences, as the past few years have demonstrated. The right of the Fund to continue to use the NAACP's name was approved, by inference at least, by the NAACP and by acquiescence since 1957. The separation, however, drastically altered the relationship of the Fund to the NAACP. The Fund was no longer an NAACP instrument; the NAACP no longer had a real legal department or legal program, and whatever legal activities it assumed were now financed from its general funds.

The Special Counsel was completely dropped from the NAACP payroll, and the Assistant Counsel was dropped completely from the Fund payroll and became, as General Counsel, exclusively an employee of the NAACP. Since all other lawyers on the national legal staff were employees of the Fund exclusively, the effect of this change was to transfer the legal department from the NAACP to the Fund.

While these changes were declared to be mere paper changes to conform to tax problems, events demonstrated that they effected very real differences in the Fund-NAACP relationship and in legal activities of the latter.

In effect, two separate legal arms came into being, both purporting to be the legal arm of the NAACP. While the Fund's legal department was no longer the legal department of the NAACP, it acted as such. It initiated legal activity in the NAACP's name and spoke for the NAACP. The greater proportion of legal activity taken in the name of the NAACP emanated in the Fund.

The Fund, while continuing to raise money to finance the NAACP's legal program, has contributed no funds to the Association to meet the costs of the litigation which the latter undertakes. At present the NAACP is spending roughly between $75,000 and $100,000 out of its general fund to underwrite its legal activities.

Legal action which may involve NAACP policy (e.g. decision to put up bail and defend all the Freedom Riders) is now undertaken without clearance with the NAACP Board. In sum, the NAACP has lost control of its main legal machinery and has an insufficient staff or funds to have a legal program in the pre-1956 sense.

Since its legal activities are still regarded as the NAACP's most important function, the Fund has received increasing amounts of public contributions, while the NAACP has shown an increasing deficit.

The NAACP has lost one of its main sources of fundraising — its legal activities.

Carter was recommending in his 1961 memo that the NAACP take legal actions to deny the Inc. Fund the right to use the initials "NAACP" and require the Inc. Fund "to make clear that the funds it raises are to carry out its own, not the N.A.A.C.P.'s legal program." Blacks had criticized each other historically as "a bunch of crawfish," one in a basket of servitude pulling down another who was crawling out to freedom. Marshall clearly was no crawfish. He was the glue between the NAACP and the Inc. Fund because he had no interest in a legal crusade that was bereft of the influence and co-operation of White, Wilkins, Carter. In his memo, Carter noted: "There is, indeed, only one delicate issue involved and that is the relationship of the present N.A.A.C.P. General Counsel [Carter] and the Fund's General Counsel [Marshall] in the reorganized department." Carter took note of the fact that the dilemma might be eased when Marshall resigned to take a seat on the Second Circuit Court of Appeals:

> The harm to the N.A.A.C.P. could not have been seen or understood while the former Director-Counsel headed the Fund, simply because he symbolized the N.A.A.C.P. From its inception the N.A.A.C.P., like all organizations of its kind, has had to struggle with two polar concepts of its role — militancy and accommodation. At least, since the 1940's, the image of the N.A.A.C.P. as a militant and aggressive organization has been exemplified by its legal activities and in the person of Thurgood Marshall as "Mr. Civil Rights." His resignation should remove any deterrent to a clear analysis of the situation in terms of the N.A.A.C.P.'s best interest.

For eighteen years, NAACP officials moaned and groaned about the "independent" status of the Inc. Fund, about the money it raised, about the continuing impecunious status of the NAACP itself, this granddaddy of all civil rights organizations that was caught in the so-called shadows of a spinoff organization that was the illegitimate child of the racists and the IRS.

By 1979 the NAACP's leadership had changed at every level, but that did not mean more unity, just a different basket of crawfish. Frustration over the bifurcation of the legal program that the Treasury Department had imposed forty years earlier became the focus of angry charges and demands. There was, after all, no Thurgood

Marshall at the Inc. Fund who might be insulted. So at the Association's national convention in Louisville in 1979, the board of directors got the delegates to revoke permission of the Legal Defense Fund to use the NAACP initials. Delegates at Louisville had been fired up by what they were told was an attempt by the Fund "to revise history" and portray itself as the triumphant force in winning *Brown v. Board of Education.*" The Legal Defense and Educational Fund (LDF) greeted the Louisville resolution with scorn.

On May 25, 1982, the NAACP filed a lawsuit against the LDF, demanding a halt to the Legal Defense Fund's use of the NAACP initials. Almost a year later U.S. District Court Judge Thomas P. Jackson, in Washington, ruled that the LDF had to "cease and desist from its use of the NAACP initials in any form." The Legal Defense Fund appealed and the Court of Appeals in the District of Columbia restored the right of the LDF to use the NAACP initials. Judge David Bazelon wrote, with judges Robert H. Bork and Abner J. Mikva joining, that the NAACP had waited so long to take this dispute to court that it had waived its right to sue.

The damage to both the NAACP and the Inc. Fund was colossal, as was indicated most tragically when I asked Thurgood in 1986 if he had any interest in joining in a fund-raiser for the Inc. Fund or the NAACP.

"Hell, no. Not to raise a nickel," he said. "We used to do so much with so little. Now they've got a lot of money and are doing nothing."

CHAPTER FOURTEEN

JIM CROW'S LAST STAND?

W HITE'S MARRIAGE to Poppy Cannon did provoke repercussions, especially among white Southerners. Cries about the threat of "race-mixin' " and "mongrelization" increased dramatically, as did charges that the NAACP was a sinister organization controlled by "Jewish agitators" and communists.

But Marshall was pleased to see that the marriage squabble had had little lasting effect among the mass of black people. This was evidenced by the increasing number of cries for help that the Association was getting in 1949 and 1950. Stirrings of freedom were taking on new life in the souls of black people who knew that they needed the NAACP lawyers desperately because they had no one else to whom to turn.

So while a few black intellectuals still lashed each other, Marshall dismissed it as just another temporary black exercise in self-destruction. He had to follow his vision of a new America, to seek a new destiny for America's black people in the marble halls of the Supreme Court.

It was not long before Marshall's no-compromise-with-segregation stance seemed to soak into the hearts and minds of black people across the nation. In Topeka, in the fall of 1950, the Reverend Oliver Brown took his little seven-year-old daughter, Linda, by the hand and walked with her to the Sumner Elementary School, hoping to enroll her in the second grade. Brown was told what he really already knew: that the school board had decreed that even though his little girl lived in an integrated neighborhood, she could not attend the all-white Sumner public school four blocks away; that she would still have to leave her white and Mexican-American playmates and take a bus almost two miles to the "Negro" school. Twenty-four years later, Linda Brown would tell an interviewer for the United States Commission on Civil Rights:

> Both of my parents were extremely upset by the fact that I had to walk six blocks through a dangerous train yard to the bus stop — only to wait, sometimes up to a half hour in the rain or snow, for the school bus that took me and the other black children to "our school." Sometimes I was just so cold that I cried all the way to the bus stop . . . and two or three times I just couldn't stand it, so I came back home.

Angry minister Brown went to his friend and former classmate at Topeka High School, Charles Scott, who was the local attorney for the NAACP, and they agreed to file suit against the Topeka school board.

Just a few months later, in Farmville, Virginia, located in Prince Edward County, fifteen-year-old Joan Johns and her sister Barbara were rebelling in ways that I am sure Marshall had not thought possible when he challenged Houston editor Wesley Carter and other blacks who expressed a willingness to live by "separate but equal." Barbara Johns had become the embodiment of the "new Negro" in the Southland — a young woman who was unwilling to go on tolerating educational deprivation and all manner of humiliations under the phony label of "separate but equal." In 1951, she led the entire student body of all-Negro Moton High School in a walkout, protesting against the tarpaper buildings, which were terribly cold in the winter and into which the rains poured in every other season.

You cannot understand the bravery of Joan and Barbara Johns, who planned and executed the walkout without their parents' knowledge, unless you get a sense of what Virginia, especially Prince Edward County, was like at the time. The area was barely a step away from slavery. J. B. Wall, editor of the *Farmville Herald,* was declaring that "any court order outlawing segregation in schools would set the South back fifty years in education. Our races have gotten along very well over three or four generations, but God only knows what would happen if the court ruled against segregation."

Dr. Dabney Lancaster, the president of Longworth College, in Farmville, who had been Virginia's state superintendent of education from 1941 to 1946, was declaring publicly that "the Court had better leave this matter of segregation to the states. . . . Negroes need to have their own class officers, their own student government, so it's possible for the Negro to advance better under segregation than integration. . . . I've looked these Negro children over from every angle, and I've never seen a happier lot. They're happier than the white children."

Those "happy" black youngsters were placing a telephone call to Spottswood Robinson in Richmond, asking if he and his partner Oliver Hill would drive to Farmville and attend a mass meeting at which the youngsters would spell out their grievances.

Robinson and Hill heard out the students, then listened to the defiant voices of white officials. They knew that, on behalf of all black school children in the state, they and the NAACP would have to challenge Virginia in the federal courts.

Meanwhile, in South Carolina emotions over the mere thought of desegregating the public schools was at fever pitch. In the little town of Summerton, in Clarendon County, black parents who could barely write their names carefully signed slips of paper authorizing court action designed to end the appalling discrepancies in the level of education offered black children and that offered white youngsters.

Mrs. Rebecca Brown, a tart-tongued, grandmotherly proprietor of a little grocery store, represented thousands of blacks when she said, "That Court has got to cut this segregation out, because we Negroes have caught hell long enough."

Harry Briggs talked bravely, too, but he also acted. He asked Marshall to go to court to end segregation in district 22, where his kids went to school. And that is how Marshall and his small army came to take the fateful 1951 journey to Charleston that I have described at the beginning of this book.

Legal wrinkles were developing elsewhere that made it seem certain to Marshall and his team that the Supreme Court finally would have to do what some justices had avoided: decide whether "separate but equal" was a constitutional concept in the education of America's children. In Wilmington, Delaware, in *Gephart v. Belton,* the state supreme court had ruled that blacks had to be admitted to white schools — but only because the schools for Negroes were demonstrably inferior. The Delaware court did not say that Jim Crow schools were an inherent curtailment of the rights of black children.

But even this limited ruling rankled some white education and other officials in Delaware, so *they* decided to appeal to the U.S. Supreme Court.

In the District of Columbia, which was a citadel of racism, a man named Spottswood Thomas Bolling sued C. Melvin Sharpe and other school officials, arguing that the segregation of black school children violated their Fifth Amendment rights to "due process" of law. Advocates of segregation argued that the District schools were the clearest evidence that in passing civil rights laws after the Civil War and the adoption of the Thirteenth, Fourteenth, and Fifteenth Amendments, the Congress never intended to impose integration — otherwise, why had the Congress allowed Jim Crow schools to exist in the nation's capital for generations? This was a challenge that Marshall and the NAACP team took seriously, and worried about.

All of a sudden, the moment of crisis and hope had arrived, with five Supreme Court cases dealing with school segregation generally lumped together under the title *Brown v. Board of Education of Topeka.*

Almost no one in the land was so naive as to think that these cases were simply attacks on Jim Crow schools. *Brown* was clearly an assault on "the southern way of life," an attack on the ingrained racial customs of border states like Kansas and Delaware, and, although few people wanted to talk about it, the de facto segregation in schooling, housing, and almost every aspect of life in even the northernmost communities of America.

Brown v. Board of Education had brought visibility to things that millions of Americans did not know about, such as the crazinesses of United States laws and customs regarding matters of race. Some examples:

• Florida and North Carolina required that textbooks used by Negroes and whites be stored separately, and that they never be interchanged.

• Oklahoma required that separate telephone booths for Negroes be provided wherever whites demanded such separation.

• Louisiana and South Carolina required segregation at the circus.

• Mississippi forbade anyone to print or circulate printed or written matter advocating social equality or intermarriage between Negroes and whites. Penalty: a $500 fine and/or six months in jail.

• North Carolina and Virginia prohibited interracial fraternal organizations.

• Fifteen states required segregation in hospitals.

- Alabama, Mississippi, and South Carolina required Negro nurses for Negro patients and white nurses for white patients.
- Alabama, Arkansas, Florida, Georgia, North Carolina, and South Carolina forbade the chaining together of Negro and white chain-gang prisoners.
- West Virginia and Alabama required separation of Negro and white paupers.

The year 1952 came on brightly for Marshall. *Collier's* magazine did a marvelously laudatory article on him. After citing the flair with which Marshall had won the voting rights and higher education cases, *Collier's* quoted him as saying, "I intend to wear life like a very loose garment, and never worry about nothing."

The author, James Poling, went on to write: "But Marshall, at forty-three, is no dual personality to intrigue the psychiatric-minded. He is a tall, burly, gregarious man, light-skinned and lighthearted, and if he is paradoxical it might almost be said to be deliberate. He has consciously chosen to follow a hedonistic, nonworrying philosophy. And he has, just as consciously, dedicated himself to the extremely worrisome task of fighting racial discrimination.

"Apparently, Marshall's determined gaiety in the face of the gravity of the project he has embarked on has never lessened his effectiveness. He is, as a matter of fact, well aware that it throws many people off guard."

The Clarendon County, South Carolina, and other public school desegregation cases were on a course of certain argument before the Supreme Court. The black press was talking of mounting "educational equality" fund campaigns. Then Marshall discovered that success also brought troubles — that even in a black America that needed unity so badly, every time a real leader stuck his head up, someone would throw a rock at it.

Marshall was astonished to receive a call on January 18 informing him that the *New York Age,* a black-run newspaper, was carrying an article saying that he had been planning secretly to run for Congress against the Reverend Adam Clayton Powell. Marshall wrote to Powell to say that "there is absolutely no foundation [for this story] that could give anyone the slightest impression that I had the slightest idea of running for Congress."

Powell replied, "You really didn't have to write because after all we both know the brother [who wrote the story] and what's more, we know the brother's press."

Marshall went on a long trip to Cairo, Illinois, twice, to Chicago, to South Carolina, then Tulsa, Oklahoma, and Dallas, Texas, to argue or confer on a variety of legal problems. He returned to New York weary as a dog on March 10 to find that the NAACP board had been wrestling with allegations that he was "desperately seeking a federal judgeship."

A black Cleveland lawyer, Chester K. Gillespie, had written to Dr. Louis T. Wright, the board chairman:

> I wish to make it clear that Thurgood Marshall and I have been close personal friends for a great many years and still are and I have a high regard for his ability.
>
> Many people know, however, that Mr. Marshall for years has been desperately seeking a Federal Judgeship from the Democrats. I understand he has recently been able to secure the approval of some of the Democratic leaders in New York for appointment to the Federal bench.
>
> I do not see how it is possible for any official of the NAACP to seek a political position and at the same time do a sound and impartial job for the NAACP and the Negro race. When Mr. Marshall was in Cleveland a few weeks ago he used half of his speech in deriding General MacArthur and the Republican Party in general. Not one word escaped his lips relative to the double talk of the National Democratic Administration with relation to civil rights.
>
> I think the situation is dangerous and the time has come when some of the NAACP officials should desist from playing organized politics and set themselves exclusively to the task for which they have been hired.
>
> Some of us Republicans are substantial contributors to the NAACP. We work hard for our money and unless our organization cleans house, in my opinion, it is going to be increasingly difficult for it to raise funds among some Negroes who are able to pay in a substantial manner.

Gillespie gave his letter to the press before it arrived at the NAACP.

When the item went before the board, Arthur Spingarn moved to table it because it was "silly and impudent." His motion was defeated by members who felt the organization had to respond to "an attack on Mr. Marshall's personal integrity." So Wright wrote to Gillespie:

> . . . The Board knows of no campaign by Mr. Marshall to secure an appointment as a Federal judge. However, the Board does

not deny that Mr. Marshall has been mentioned on several occasions for appointment to a Federal judgeship. The Board does not consider this a sin nor an incident impairing Mr. Marshall's usefulness in the great public service to which he has given unselfishly so many years of his life. The Board goes further. It does not consider that a prominent and superbly qualified member of its staff is debarred from seeking a position of honor and security in his chosen profession.

We are certain it was never contemplated that when a man chose to cast his lot with the work of the NAACP he should be regarded as having gone into a monastery and to have renounced all opportunities that might develop in later years as a result of his outstanding service in this organization. In Mr. Marshall's case no one can accuse him of using the NAACP as a quick and convenient stepping stone to other employment. He has given 16 years to this work. In that time he has become the outstanding authority in civil rights law in this country. He has won significant victories in the courts which have expanded the rights of Negroes and others as citizens and brought them new opportunities in their struggle for full and complete citizenship. . . .

The Board does not feel that in the light of this history of sacrifice and hard work and demonstrated superior ability that it could entertain any protest upon such a public servant being offered a reward in keeping with his achievements. The Board does not believe that the membership of the NAACP or the American Negro public generally would concur in or support such a protest.

Marshall told the press that he wouldn't respond to Gillespie. "But I couldn't hold back my fury over a black Republican who claimed to resent criticism of MacArthur, who was resisting the desegregation of the military," Marshall recalled. "So I fired off a personal letter . . . don't remember what it said."

It said:

Dear Chester:
    . . . I have condemned General MacArthur and will condemn him some more. I have condemned politicians of both parties who are hostile to equality for all Americans regardless of race and color and will continue to do so without regard to what party they might happen to belong to. If in doing so, the person I am condemning happens to be a member of the Republican Party, I am going to condemn him just the same.
    I think, however, that the best answer to your letter would be

to answer the first paragraph. And the answer to the first paragraph of your letter and the rest of the letter is merely to quote a phrase that has been used by some people and which I would like to repeat. "With you as a friend, I don't need any enemies."

Marshall was too harassed on a dozen fronts to keep something as trifling as Gillespie's letter on his mind for long. But it never left his mind that the political system, and who ran it, were crucial factors in his crusade. On June 16 he wrote to White:

> From now until election will be the most important period in our fight for civil rights from a legislative and political standpoint. First the conventions and then the political campaigns. I would say that the period between the NAACP Convention and the November elections would deserve double time from all of us in keeping up the pressure on the delegates and then the candidates. Unfortunately, I doubt that I will be able to help out on this part of our work.
>
> Although I have not had a vacation since 1947 except for a few days here and there (usually from three days to ten days) during a summer, I had hoped to again give up my vacation and be able to use this summer to help in the office (NAACP) while you and Roy did the work on the candidates. However, it is now apparent that the school cases will be up in the Supreme Court in October. This means our briefs will be due in September. This means not only the preparation of these briefs but also the question of getting our experts together several times during the summer. Then, too, there is the problem of getting the legal research department operating on a sound basis. Thus, although once again I get no vacation, I cannot do anything but this legal work.
>
> For these reasons it is apparent that I will not be available for any NAACP work other than legal work set out above until October.

White replied the next day:

> I am genuinely sorry you aren't going to be able to get the rest you sorely need because of the Clarendon County briefs. I hope you will be able to take your vacation right after the argument of the case because no human being could stand up forever under the pace with which you have been going.

Almost laconically, Marshall makes a look-back observation: "How the hell could I 'slow the pace' when the most important case of my life was coming up?"

He became a man driven to write the most convincing brief possible and to assemble an incredible team of lawyers, anthropologists, sociologists, and others who might convince nine men that the Constitution of a democracy could never give license to the stigmatic injuries of insult and exclusion that were being imposed upon Negro school children.

Marshall had been before the Supreme Court before, scared out of his wits momentarily when he soaked in the grandeur of a huge courtroom of more than seven thousand square feet, with its huge marble pillars, its towering velvet drapes, and its thick carpets. The mahogany furnishings, the placement of reporters from the most powerful news media in the world, the whole scene was awesome.

"No matter how many times I argued there, I never got used to it." Marshall told me "Just the voice of the court crier could make your knees shake."

Many lawyers have written about the intimidating majesty of the crier chanting, "Oyez! Oyez! Oyez! [Hear ye! hear ye! hear ye!] All persons having business before the Honorable, the Supreme Court of the United States, are invited to draw near and give their attention, for the Court is now sitting. God save the United States and this Honorable Court."

Marshall did not want to walk alone into this setting.

By his side, during all the planning for arguments that were to take place December 9 through 11, were Jack Greenberg and Robert Carter, his close in-office associates. Carter would take the lead in the Topeka case of the Brown family, whose name got top billing in this legal drama; Spottswood Robinson would argue the Prince Edward County, Virginia, case; Jim Nabrit the Washington, D.C., challenge, along with George E. C. Hayes; Louis L. Redding of Wilmington would try to uphold but broaden a decision by Chancellor Collins J. Seitz that the schools for Negro children in Newcastle County, Delaware, were inferior to the schools for white children and that Negro children had to be admitted immediately to the white schools. Marshall himself would handle the brunt of the argument with regard to South Carolina, and would be the "cleanup" man for all five assaults on Jim Crow schooling.

But also walking with him were Kenneth Clark and his dolls; John Hope Franklin; Robert K. Carr (he would become president of my alma mater, Oberlin College); President Charles Johnson of Fisk; Horace Bond; Walter Gellhorn; C. Vann Woodward; Alfred H. Kelly; Robert Cushman, Jr.; and dozens of other law school deans and celebrated people from academia. They contributed to a massive brief in which it took 235 printed pages to spell out the NAACP version of the history of the Fourteenth Amendment and the intentions of the congressmen who enacted it.

More important, perhaps, than the brief was the number and diversity of organizations that filed amicus curiae, or "friend of the court," briefs on behalf of the NAACP's appeal that the "separate but equal" doctrine be abolished. Of the twenty-four amicus briefs filed, nineteen supported Marshall and the NAACP. Taking a stand against Jim Crow were the CIO (Congress of Industrial Organizations), the American Jewish Congress, the American Civil Liberties Union, the Japanese American Citizens League, the Catholic Interracial Council, the American Federation of Teachers, the American Veterans Committee . . .

Marshall had lined up some very powerful "friends."

The friend he wanted desperately to speak up was the federal government. He knew that it would make a critical difference if Solicitor General Philip B. Perlman, and Attorney General James P. McGranery filed a brief on his side. Perlman argued against such a brief. The Democrats wanted Adlai Stevenson to win the presidential election, and Stevenson's aides had passed the word that he'd just as soon not be burdened with the passions over race and schools. But Robert L. Stern, who succeeded Perlman as acting solicitor, argued that the federal government had to oppose Jim Crow. Truman's secretary of state, Dean Acheson, stated publicly that racism in public schools was a burden on U.S. foreign policy. McGranery ordered Justice Department lawyer Philip Elman to write a brief supporting the NAACP. It was something short of a document of bravery. The brief said that "compulsory" racial segregation was "unconstitutional discrimination" and that "separate but equal" was a farce, but it did not call for the overruling of *Plessy,* primarily because McGranery, Elman, and others thought the Court would never go that far. They counted only Justices Hugo L. Black, Harold H. Burton, and William O. Douglas as being willing to outlaw "separate but equal."

The justice that Elman — and Marshall and others — worried about was "Little Napoleon," Frankfurter, the five-foot-five-inch advocate of "judicial restraint." The word was spread, accurately or not, that Frankfurter believed it was not the Court's role to order monumental social change. Elman was sure, as one of Frankfurter's former law clerks, that this curmudgeon of a justice would say that Congress should pass a law forbidding school segregation. He would say that the executive branch should take the lead since it would have the duty to uphold new anti-segregation laws in Mississippi, South

Carolina, Alabama. Frankfurter would argue that if the federal courts tried to supervise the public schools the judges would get bogged down in interminable lawsuits and violent conflicts.

So the Justice Department took a "moderate" stance that infuriated the segregationists, yet failed to please Marshall, who was in no position to denounce the federal government the way southern politicians did. Marshall didn't know whether to be happy or worried when he learned that McGranery had made an unusual request to the Court that he be allowed to participate in oral arguments. Chief Justice Vinson, who was still wedded in mind to *Plessy*, turned McGranery down, returning his written request with the suggestion that he forget he ever sent it.

The grueling days of Marshall's legal and political planning dwindled into December, when oral arguments were to begin on the ninth. "I was whupped to my socks," he told me. "Dead tired. Going on excitement alone. Well, some anger, too. But I knew that my team and I were ready for the challenge."

A court duel of historic proportions between Marshall, who was operating on a shoestring, and a noted constitutional lawyer, John W. Davis, who had all the resources of the Jim Crow South behind him, was imminent. Dusty and musty boxes in the Library of Congress tell a dramatic story of the conflicts that Marshall oversaw — joustings among his own legal staff, arguments over whether to plead for an immediate end to segregation or tolerate some delay, suggestions that he junk Kenneth Clark's dolls and the sociological approach.

Marshall was not going to abandon his belief that the Supreme Court would accept his argument of stigmatic injury and then interpret the Constitution in ways that would give permanent relief to black children. Yet, when he went before the high tribunal in December 1952, he was armed with cold legal arguments, historical citations, and everything else he thought would win over even someone as unsentimental as Frankfurter. Except in the case of the District of Columbia, a *federal* jurisdiction where Fifth Amendment protections were claimed, Marshall's basic argument rested on section 1 of the Fourteenth Amendment, which he read aloud:

> All persons born or naturalized in the United States and subject to the jurisdiction thereof, are citizens of the United States and of the state in which they reside. No state shall make or enforce any law which shall abridge the privileges or immunities of citizens of the United States; nor shall any state deprive any person of life,

liberty, or property, without due process of law; nor deny to any person within its jurisdiction the equal protection of the laws.

Davis, Marshall's distinguished adversary, who was a former presidential candidate and the most celebrated constitutional lawyer of the era, would ask the Court to say the following:

> The fourteenth amendment never was intended to do away with segregation in schools. It is a proper use of the police powers of a state to separate the races if the state believes segregation to be in the interest of common welfare. Segregation in schools is not in conflict with the Constitution as long as equal facilities are provided for the two races. A state has as much right to classify pupils by race as it does to classify them by sex or age.

Marshall and his legal team were better prepared than Davis or even the members of the Court thought they would be. In their basic brief, the Marshall team made the following points:

> The importance to our American democracy of the substantive question can hardly be overstated. The question is whether a nation founded on the proposition that "all men are created equal" is honoring its commitments to grant "due process of law" and "the equal protection of the laws" to all within its borders when it, or one of its constituent states, confers or denies benefits on the basis of color or race.
>
> The argument that the requirements of the Fourteenth Amendment are met by providing alternative schools rests, finally, on reiteration of the separate but equal doctrine enunciated in *Plessy v. Ferguson.*
>
> Were these ordinary cases, it might be enough to say that the *Plessy* case can be distinguished — that it involved only segregation in transportation. But these are not ordinary cases, and in deference to their importance it seems more fitting to meet the *Plessy* doctrine head-on and to declare that doctrine erroneous.
>
> Candor requires recognition that the plain purpose and effect of segregated education is to perpetuate an inferior status for Negroes which is America's sorry heritage from slavery. But the primary purpose of the Fourteenth Amendment was to deprive the states of *all* power to perpetuate such a caste system.
>
> The evidence, both in Congress and in the legislatures of the ratifying states, reflects the substantial intent of the Amendment's proponents and the substantial understanding of its opponents that the Fourteenth Amendment would, of its own force, proscribe

all forms of state-imposed racial distinctions, thus necessarily including all racial segregation in public education.

The Civil Rights Bill of 1866, as originally proposed, possessed scope sufficiently broad in the opinion of many Congressmen to entirely destroy all state legislation based on race. A great majority of the Republican Radicals — who later formulated the Fourteenth Amendment — understood and intended that the Bill would prohibit segregated schools. Opponents of the measure shared this understanding. The scope of this legislation was narrowed because it was known that the Fourteenth Amendment was in process of preparation and would itself have scope exceeding that of the original draft of the Civil Rights Bill.

While the Amendment conferred upon Congress the power to enforce its prohibitions, members of the 39th Congress and those of subsequent Congresses made it clear that the framers understood and intended that the Fourteenth Amendment was self-executing and particularly pointed out that the federal judiciary had authority to enforce its prohibitions without Congressional implementation.

In short, the historical evidence fully sustains this Court's conclusion in the *Slaughter House Cases* that the Fourteenth Amendment was designed to take from the states all power to enforce caste or class distinctions.

The Court [assuming segregation might be declared unconstitutional] inquires as to whether relief should be granted immediately or gradually. Appellants, recognizing the possibility of delay of a purely administrative character, do not ask for the impossible. No cogent reasons justifying further exercise of equitable discretion, however, have as yet been produced.

. . . Appellants are unable to suggest any compelling reasons for this Court to postpone relief.

There may never have been any days of oral argument before the Supreme Court to equal the depth of passion, the agony of the justices, that erupted in this *Brown* case.

Listening to this debate were nine very troubled white men: Chief Justice Fred M. Vinson, a sixty-two-year-old Kentuckian who had been appointed by Harry Truman; Stanley F. Reed, sixty-eight, another Kentuckian, the man who had delivered the decision in the *Lyons* murder case that crushed Thurgood Marshall's heart for a time; Felix Frankfurter, seventy, a former Harvard Law School professor, the only Jew on the Court and a conservative who showed resistance to "activist" court decisions that changed *anything* unnecessarily; Robert H. Jackson, sixty, the former chief counsel for the United States at the Nuremberg trials; Harold H. Burton, sixty-four, a former mayor of Cleveland, Ohio; Tom C. Clark of Texas, fifty-three, a former U.S. attorney general; Sherman Minton, sixty-two, a former senator from Indiana who had bent toward the conservative side; Hugo Black, sixty-six, an Alabaman and former member of the Ku Klux Klan who had become a liberal and vocal defender of civil liberty; and William O. Douglas, fifty-four, who joined Black as the most conspicuous of the Court's advocates of equality for American Negroes.

Marshall had submitted his brief with delight because it was the product of a team that included his deputy, Jack Greenberg; some of the best black lawyers in America, most of them graduates and teachers of the Howard University Law School; and of some equally brilliant white lawyers, in the ACLU and on law school faculties, most of whom were Jews with a profound desire to see racial justice done in America. Marshall's style was far different from anything his briefs suggested. In all cases, Marshall was the homespun lawyer, appealing to the common sense of the judge or judges, forcing them to think about what they would consider justice if they were one of the plaintiffs or defendants, one of the prosecutors or the accused, in a particular case at issue.

In December 1952, the Supreme Court saw the quintessential Thurgood in action:

> I got the feeling on hearing the discussion yesterday that when you put a white child in a school with a whole lot of colored children, the child would fall apart or something. Everybody knows that is not true. Those same kids in Virginia and South Carolina — and I have seen them do it — they play in the streets together, they play on the farms together, they separate to go to school, they come out of school and play ball together. They have to be separated in school. . . . Why, of all the multitudinous groups of people in the country, [do] you have to single out the Negroes and give them this separate treatment?
>
> It can't be because of slavery in the past, because there are very few groups in this country that haven't had slavery some place back in the history of their groups. It can't be color, because there are Negroes as white as the drifted snow, with blue eyes, and they are just as segregated as the colored men.
>
> The only thing it can be is an inherent determination that the

people who were formerly in slavery, regardless of anything else, shall be kept as near that stage as possible. And now is the time, we submit, that this Court should make clear that that is not what our Constitution stands for.

Members of the Court knew that they were being asked to "legislate," to do what neither the Congress nor the White House had the guts to do. Some members of the Court knew in their hearts that segregation was wrong, but they were not committed to a full range of "racial mixing." Most justices were profoundly troubled when Paul Wilson, the assistant attorney general of Kansas, asked whether the Court was going to say that twenty-one states and the District of Columbia "have been wrong for seventy-five years when they believed that separate facilities, though equal, were legal within the meaning of the Fourteenth Amendment."

Justice Burton articulated the justices' anguish when he asked of Wilson: "Don't you recognize it as possible that within seventy-five years the social and economic conditions and the personal relations of the nation may have changed so that what may have been valid interpretation of them seventy-five years ago would not be valid interpretation of them today?"

"We recognize that as a possibility," Wilson replied. "We do not believe that the record discloses any such change."

"But that might be a difference between saying that these Courts of Appeal and state supreme courts have been wrong for seventy-five years," Burton almost shouted.

"Yes, sir," Wilson replied. "We concede that this Court can overrule the *Plessy* doctrine, but nevertheless, until it is overruled, it is the best guide we have."

Every lawyer, newsman, spectator, stretched forward when Frankfurter intervened: "As I understood my brother Burton's question or as I got the implication of his question, it was not that the Court would have to overrule those [separate but equal] cases; the Court would simply have to recognize that laws are kinetic, and some new things have happened, not deeming those decisions wrong, but bringing into play new situations toward a new decision."

"We agree with that proposition," Wilson replied, "But, I repeat, we do not think that there is anything in the record here that would justify such a conclusion."

Marshall's ears went up like those of a Doberman pinscher hearing a strange sound when he heard Frankfurter say that "laws are kinetic" and speak of "bringing into play new situations toward a new decision."

"I just refused to believe the import of what I was hearing," Marshall told me. "I had learned that in the Supreme Court you had no time to engage in wishful thinking."

The 1952 hearings produced some classic exchanges between Marshall and Justice Frankfurter, who, as almost everyone expected, did more talking and asked more questions than the eight other justices combined. Some viewed Frankfurter as "hectoring" the NAACP attorneys; Marshall saw his questions as eliciting answers that would enlighten the nation about the complexity of the issues at stake.

Marshall walked into the spotlight on December 10, the second day of the hearing, to handle the South Carolina part of the case, which with Virginia was the most vexing for everyone. Both states had promised to equalize black schools, and officials of both states had declared publicly that they would close down the public schools rather than permit black children to study in classrooms with white youngsters. Marshall's first declaration was that the black parents and children were not attacking South Carolina's segregation statutes on grounds that they fostered separation but not equality.

"We told the lower courts that governmentally imposed segregation in and of itself was a denial of equality," he said.

Frankfurter asked if the South Carolina statute was in the same category as one prohibiting blue-eyed children from attending public schools. "You would permit all blue-eyed children to go to separate schools?" he asked.

"No, sir," bellowed Marshall, "because the blue-eyed people in the United States never had the badge of slavery, which was perpetuated in these statutes."

Frankfurter asked if South Carolina had a right to consider the reality that it had "a vast congregation of Negro population. . . . Is this an irrelevant consideration? Can you escape facing those sociological facts, Mr. Marshall?"

"No, I cannot escape it," said Marshall, comfortable and confident now beyond any question. "But I [will not] throw aside the personal rights of [these Negroes] to be considered like any other citizen of Clarendon County — a right that has been recognized by this Court over and over again."

Frankfurter noted that states made many classifications of their people that were not excluded by the Fourteenth Amendment.

"When an attack is made on a statute on the ground that it is an unreasonable classification . . . the least that the state has to do is to produce something to defend their statutes," Marshall replied.

"I follow you when you talk that way," Frankfurter said.

When Frankfurter noted that segregation was ingrained in the South, and that neither the Court nor local officials might be able to contain the hostile reaction to an overturning of *Plessy*, Marshall replied without a pause: "Go back to the case of *Buchanan v. Warley*, where the Court said:

'That there exists a serious and difficult problem arising from a feeling of race hostility which the law is powerless to control . . . may be freely admitted. But its solution cannot be promoted by depriving citizens of their constitutional rights and privileges.'

Frankfurter tried repeatedly to press Marshall to spell out in detail what kind of decree the NAACP wanted to force upon Clarendon County. Marshall replied again and again that "the only thing we ask for is that the state-imposed racial segregation be taken off, and to leave the county school board, the county people, the district people, to work out their own solution."

The prescient Frankfurter was looking ahead: "Nothing would be worse," he said, "than for this Court to make an abstract declaration that segregation was bad and then have it evaded by tricks."

In the flush of advocacy, Marshall did not envision the gerrymandering of school districts, the subterfuges, the violent tactics of obstruction that Frankfurter foresaw.

"I think it is important to know, before one starts, where he is going," snapped Frankfurter.

Justice Jackson got a chance to sneak in a question after declaring that, for tax purposes at least, he wished he had "a little Indian blood." He asked if the Fourteenth Amendment covered the segregation of Native Americans.

"I think it would," Marshall replied. "But I think the biggest trouble with the Indians is that they just have not had the judgment or the wherewithal to bring lawsuits."

"Maybe you should bring some up," said Jackson.

Thurgood replied, "I have a full load now, Mr. Justice."

When Marshall finished, the gray-maned, seventy-nine-year-old Davis, a former solicitor general (1913–18), a former ambassador to Great Britain (1918–21), a lawyer with the most awesome of résumés, stood up.

"May it please the Court," he said with a gallantry mixed of West Virginia, where he was born, and South Carolina, for which he argued, "I think if the appellants' construction of the Fourteenth Amendment should prevail here, there is no doubt in my mind that it would catch the Indian within its grasp as much as the Negro. If it should prevail, I am unable to see why a state would have any further right to segregate its pupils on the ground of sex or on the ground of age or on the ground of mental capacity. If it may classify it for one purpose on the basis of admitted facts, it may . . . classify it for others."

Davis showed that his shrewdness was still a force when he picked up on Justice Frankfurter's questions to Marshall about whether desegregation could be ordered wisely in an area where blacks outnumbered whites in great measure. Davis noted that in district 1 of Clarendon County "there are 2,799 registered Negro students and 295 registered white students. . . . Whether discrimination is to be abolished by introducing 2,800 Negro students into schools now occupied by the whites, or conversely introducing 295 whites into the schools now occupied by 2,800 Negroes, the result is one which one cannot contemplate with entire equanimity."

Davis declared it the duty of the Court to interpret the Fourteenth Amendment by placing itself "as nearly as possible in the condition of those who framed the instrument."

Justice Burton wriggled in his seat in what might have been disbelief, or even disgust, and said to Davis: "But the Constitution is a living document that must be interpreted in relation to the facts of the time in which it is interpreted."

Davis argued that circumstances might change in a century "but they do not alter, expand, or change the language that the framers of the Constitution have employed."

This was carrying the doctrine of "original intent" beyond anything that Frankfurter could stomach. He badgered Davis into an admission that "what is unequal today may be equal tomorrow, or vice versa."

Yet, Davis insisted with rising emotion, "We find nothing in the latest cases that modifies that doctrine of 'separate but equal' in the least."

Davis ridiculed Clark and his dolls, and said that the experts that the NAACP relied on lacked knowledge of life in the South.

With a blow like a karate chop into the back of Marshall's head, Davis wound up his defense of racial segregation by quoting Du Bois:

"It is difficult to think of anything more important for the development of a people than proper training for their children; and yet I have repeatedly seen wise and loving colored parents take infinite pains to force their little children into schools where the white children, white teachers, and white parents despised and resented the dark child, made mock of it, neglected or bullied it, and literally rendered its life a living hell. Such parents want their children to 'fight' this thing out — but, dear God, at what a cost!

"We shall get a finer, better balance of spirit; an infinitely more capable and rounded personality by putting children in schools where they are wanted, and where they are happy and inspired, than in thrusting them into hells where they are ridiculed and hated."

"Here was the Devil quoting phony Scripture," Marshall said. "I was so furious at Du Bois that I just closed my eyes and told myself that I had to stick with our constitutional arguments."

"Oh, my God," Marshall said softly, when Davis concluded by arguing that "the wishes of parents, both white and colored, should be ascertained before their children are forced into what may be an unwelcome contact. . . ."

In rebuttal, Marshall showed a burst of emotion. "The significant factor running through all these arguments," he said, "is that for some reason, which is still unexplained, Negroes are taken out of the mainstream of American life in these states. There is nothing involved in this case other than race and color. . . . If Ralph Bunche were assigned to South Carolina, his children would have to go to a Jim Crow school. No matter how great anyone becomes, if he happens to have been born a Negro, regardless of his color, he is relegated to that school."

Davis had cited a magazine article by Mississippi editor Hodding Carter to justify the continuation of school segregation.

"The article quoted was of a newspaperman answering another newspaperman," snapped Marshall. "I know of nothing further removed from scientific work than one newspaperman answering another."

Frankfurter rocked back and said, "I am not going to take issue with you on that."

Justice Reed, who Marshall assumed was against him, came in at the end of the day, asking if Marshall couldn't accept the proposition that segregation in the schools was legislated "to avoid racial friction."

"I know of no Negro legislator in any of these states," said Marshall, "so the people disadvantaged have had no say in this policy. . . . I know that in the South, where I spent most of my time, you will see white and colored kids going down the road together to school. They separate and go to different schools, and they come out and play together. I do not see why there would necessarily be any trouble if they went to school together."

When Reed pressed his belief that segregation was a matter for legislatures, not the Supreme Court, Marshall replied:

"The rights of minorities . . . have been protected by our Constitution. . . . As to whether I, as an individual, am being deprived of my right is not legislative, but judicial."

Chief Justice Vinson blinked through ever so short a pause and said, "Thank you."

"Thank you, sir," said Marshall as he strode to his seat.

On December 12, 1952, the day after the arguments ended, Walter White sent this memorandum to all NAACP directors:

> . . . The arguments on December 9–11 before the Supreme Court in the school segregation cases . . . marked what may be the most important epoch in the entire struggle against race prejudice. The arguments presented by members of our national legal staff . . . were magnificent. We received the best news coverage of any cases in the Association's history.

"I thought Walter was a helluva lot more optimistic about how well we had done than I was," Marshall recalls, "but at the time I wasn't going to piss on any praise."

Marshall did not believe that he had the five votes he needed. So, as the Court lapsed into months of silence, he told members of his team hundreds of times that "No news is good news" — so often in fact that he came to believe it.

No matter the praise of Walter White and others of his performance before the Supreme Court, Christmas of 1952 was not merry for Marshall, and 1953 did not bring a particularly happy New Year. Dwight David Eisenhower had won the presidency, and Marshall distrusted him as much as he had come to detest General MacArthur. "These white generals all seem to think that their role is to thwart change — especially racial change," Marshall said.

Marshall remembered with some anguish that in 1947, after great internal strife, Eisenhower had, as Army chief of staff, ordered publication of *Army Talk 170*, which said: "The Army is not an instrument of social reform. Its interest in matters of race is confined to considerations of its own effectiveness." Marshall had had no doubt that the Army was saying that a racially segregated force was most effective, and he got confirmation a year later when Eisenhower told a Senate committee that the Jim Crow Army was "merely one of the mirrors that holds up to our faces the United States of America." Eisenhower had gone on to argue that since the society at large was racially segregated, the Army risked riots and other destructive disturbances and disruptions of its security functions if it tried to let soldiers live and socialize together. Eisenhower had voiced without apparent reservation or shame the view of Lieutenant General John C. H. Lee that black and white soldiers, living together, could never handle the problem of "liquor and women"; and the argument of General Omar N. Bradley that powerful congressmen were violently opposed to "mixing the races in the military," and that because of these views, the Army had to go slow and make desegregation in the military part of a national social evolution.

Eisenhower had said: "I believe that the human race may finally grow up to the point where [race relations] will not be a problem. . . . But I do believe that if we attempt merely by passing a lot of laws to force someone to like someone else, we are just going to get into trouble."

"This is the president I'm counting on to help when I'm waiting for the Supreme Court to tell me whether the Fourteenth Amendment really protects Negro people?" Marshall shouted rhetorically.

As Marshall waited and waited for the Supreme Court to rule in the *Brown* case, he got a few glimmers of hope. Senator Hubert H. Humphrey of Minnesota had begun to raise hell about racial segregation in schools on federal property, even in the Deep South. Humphrey reminded officials of the Eisenhower administration that in 1951 Truman had vetoed the education appropriation bill because it required Jim Crow in such schools. Eisenhower was asked about this in a press conference on March 15, 1953, and replied:

> I have said it again and again: whenever Federal funds are expended for anything, I do not see how any American can justify — legally, or logically, or morally — a discrimination in the expenditure of those funds as among our citizens. All are taxed to provide these funds. If there is any benefit to be derived from them, I think they must all share, regardless of such inconsequential factors as race and religion.

Marshall says he knew that Eisenhower was reading copy prepared in advance by advisers who were a lot wiser than Generals Lee and Bradley. Still, it buoyed his spirits a trifle. And even more when the Defense Department ordered an end to racial segregation in military base schools and at the veterans hospitals.

But as much as Marshall was determined to wipe out bigotry against young blacks who fought and died for America, his first priority was to secure equal educational opportunity for minorities. When Eisenhower named Herbert Brownell, Jr., as his attorney general, Thurgood made numerous telephone calls to ask those who knew Brownell whether the newly staffed Justice Department would be his friend in court regarding the school segregation conflict. He accepted, warily, declarations that Brownell was "a good and decent man."

Marshall was feeling physically lousy — again — in part from his continued travel and long working hours, but surely also from incessant worry about whether he would win or lose the *Brown* case. His spirits were lifted in May when the Supreme Court ruled that the Jaybird Democratic Association of Texas, known as "the Jaybird Party," was holding unconstitutional primary elections because they were a "contrivance to deny the ballot to Negro voters."

"This should end all such devices," said Thurgood in another of his overly optimistic pronouncements.

In June 1953, on the next-to-last opinion day of that term of the Court, Marshall and his lawyers, and counsel for the other side, went to the Supreme Court, expecting a *Brown* decision one way or the other. They were astonished when, after a few decisions were announced, Vinson said that "other orders of the Court have been . . . filed with the clerk and will not be announced orally." On the way out of the Court a Marshall colleague looked at a bulletin board and saw an announcement that the Court needed more information on the school segregation cases, and that they would have to be reargued in the fall.

"My heart dropped to my feet," Marshall says. "I knew why I had never trusted Vinson."

On July 17, 1953, Marshall sent off a letter chiding Louis Lautier, Washington correspondent of the National Negro Press Association, for writing a favorable article about Vinson. "I note that you did not mention the fact that he wrote the long dissenting opinion in the restrictive covenant case from Los Angeles," Marshall complained. "I think upon reading this opinion you will agree that it was not a good one and while appraising the Chief Justice in the future you will bear this in mind."

In *Barrows v. Jackson,* Vinson was the lone member of the Court to argue that the courts of California could be used to exact damages from a woman who reneged on a real estate covenant that said the properties owned should never "at any time be used or occupied by any person or persons not wholly of the white or Caucasian race."

Lautier professed ignorance as to whether he had been neglectful of that fact, or been misedited, and told Marshall that he was working on an article on Frankfurter and could use some help. Marshall rushed off a letter to Bill Coleman, now a lawyer in Philadelphia, asking him to help Lautier, saying, "I'm sure you agree that a good job should be done of FF [Frankfurter]."

Chief Justice Vinson and the mystery of his position on school desegregation was an intellectual aneurysm on Marshall's mind. "I thought about him every day and every night," Thurgood told me. "You know how we Negroes claim we have a sixth sense for detecting which white person is for us or against us? My sixth sense told me that Vinson in mind and heart was my enemy."

The first time that I met Marshall under circumstances in which I could talk to him was during the tense hiatus when he was preparing for the December 1953 arguments before the Supreme Court. Marshall was by the summer of '53 an American treasure, at the age of forty-five. I was a twenty-eight-year-old reporter for the *Minneapolis Tribune* who had made a few journalistic forays into the bowels of racism, which earned me Marshall's respect. That is why Marshall invited me into the crowded New York City offices of the NAACP legal staff so I could see firsthand its dedicated but often-scrambling efforts to outwit foes who could throw the weight of city, county, and state treasuries against him. Marshall still had to rely on volunteer college presidents and professors, psychologists and psychiatrists, law school deans and others to give him vitally needed help.

I sat alert when Dr. Charles S. Johnson, the president of Fisk University in Nashville, walked into the room, announcing proudly that his research team had found a document, a precedent, that might ensure an NAACP victory. Marshall and his team rushed eagerly to read what Johnson had brought.

White deputy Jack Greenberg turned to Marshall excitedly and asked, "Who's going to write this up?"

Marshall looked at Greenberg in mock disbelief and said, "I'll tell you who's gonna write *this* up. The head nigger's gonna write this up!"

Nobody in the room lifted an eyebrow. They all knew that Marshall would fight any white man who called him a "nigger" in disrespect. They knew also that Marshall had a sense of security that enabled him to remind the other lawyers, white and black, that in the domain of the NAACP Legal Defense Fund he was what blacks called the "HNIC," the "head nigger in charge." I saw early that Marshall did not put on airs, or posture like some high falutin' dude, when he was in the presence of people who knew where he "was comin' from." He cursed, drank bourbon, laughed raucously at dirty jokes, told great self-deprecating stories of his escapes from potential lynchings, and just let it all hang out with regard to the challenge that was before him. I saw all this as a way of breaking the incredible tension that enveloped almost every moment of his life.

Spending time with Marshall, I also saw that he was swallowed up in a legal challenge that many of his peers thought was impossible to win.

Marshall gave me a quick seminar. He talked first about the circumscribing powers of "precedents," of the fact that one group of Supreme Court justices was always reluctant to overrule an interpretation of the Constitution made by another court. He was doomed to failure if he could not convince Vinson, or at least five of the eight other justices, to overturn *Plessy.*

In the late summer of 1953 I telephoned Marshall and asked if I could come talk to him about the upcoming rearguments.

"Hell, come on, buddy," he said, as though we were fast friends. But those were days in which one black man could take it for granted that another black man was not out to betray his race. Furthermore, Marshall had been reading what I was writing in the *Minneapolis Tribune* and in magazines, simply because I was among only a handful of blacks writing about racial and social issues in the major media.

I found, however, when I got to Marshall's New York offices, that he, like a lot of lawyers, never believed that a journalist knew enough about his cases, or understood the historical perspective and current nuances. So I had to listen to Marshall's lecture:

"Do you know what we're up against?" Marshall asked rhetorically. "The weight of bad court decisions over a century. Hell, we're fighting Chief Justice Roger Taney, who said for seven members of the Court in 1857 that a Negro was not a citizen of the United States, and had 'no rights that a white man is bound to respect.' The problem that we've got to overcome is that millions of white people still believe what Taney wrote. Shit, they've brainwashed some blacks into believing that they are and will always be treated like subhumans.

"Look at what the framers of the Constitution did. For purposes of voting representation, they counted a colored man as three-fifths of a person. Three-fifths, for Christ's sake. And that mentality is alive and well, and it's what we've got to overcome."

Thurgood twisted in his chair, his body language revealing both irritation and frustration. Then he cooled down to talk to me about *Plessy*, the Court decision that he specifically wanted reversed.

In 1890 Louisiana had enacted a law declaring that "all railway companies carrying passengers in their coaches in this state, shall provide separate but equal accommodations for the white and colored races." Black nurses attending white children were exempted. A New Orleans man named Homer Adolph Plessy, who had been declared a Negro under Louisiana law because he had "one-eighth African blood," challenged the law by sitting in a coach reserved for white people. He was ordered to move, and was arrested when he refused to do so. He went to the U.S. Supreme Court, challenging John Ferguson, the Orleans Parish judge who had declared the Louisiana law constitutional, arguing that the Louisiana statute was in conflict with the Thirteenth and Fourteenth Amendments. Speaking for a seven-man majority of the Court, Justice Henry B. Brown said in 1896 in *Plessy v. Ferguson:*

"A statute which implies merely a legal distinction between the white and colored races — a distinction which is founded in the color of the two races, and which must always exist so long as white men are distinguished from the other race by color — has no tendency to destroy the legal equality of the two races. . . .

"The object of the [Fourteenth] amendment was undoubtedly to enforce the absolute equality of the two races before the law, but in the nature of things it could not have been intended to abolish distinctions based upon color, or to enforce social, as distinguished from political, equality, or a commingling of the two races upon terms unsatisfactory to either. . . .

"Legislation is powerless to eradicate racial instincts or to abolish distinctions based upon physical differences. . . . If one race be inferior to the other socially, the Constitution of the United States cannot put them upon the same plane."

Justice John Marshall Harlan, the "great dissenter" from the erstwhile slave state of Kentucky, said: "The white race deems itself to be the dominant race in this country. And so it is, in prestige, in achievements, in education, in wealth, and in power. So, I doubt not that it will continue to be for all time, if it remains true to its great heritage and holds fast to the principles of constitutional liberty. But in the view of the Constitution, in the eye of the law, there is in this country no superior, dominant, ruling class of citizens. There is no caste here. Our Constitution is color-blind, and neither knows nor tolerates classes among citizens. In respect of civil rights, all citizens are equal before the law. The humblest is the peer of the most powerful. The law regards man as man, and takes no account of his surroundings or of his color when his civil rights as guaranteed by the supreme law of the land are involved. It is therefore to be regretted that this high tribunal, the final expositor of the fundamental law of the land, has reached the conclusion that it is competent for a state to regulate the enjoyment by citizens of their civil rights solely upon the basis of race.

"In my opinion, the judgment this day rendered will, in time, prove to be quite as pernicious as the decision made by this tribunal in the *Dred Scott* case."

What had changed in America to lead Marshall and his impecunious little band of lawyers to think that they could reverse the tide of segregation in America? How audacious of this black man and his allies to think they could alter the legal landscape of America!

"I have to keep believing, because I know our cause is right. Justice and reason are on our side. Everybody knows this but those enslaved to customs that say whites are whites and Negroes are Negroes and never the twain shall meet. But I tell you, it isn't easy knowing that we'll be going up against the most renowned constitutional lawyer in American history," said Marshall.

Governor Byrnes of South Carolina had pleaded with John William Davis to argue the South's case for maintaining Jim Crow schools. Byrnes had persuaded Davis to "defend the South" for just a silver tea service — and to satisfy his personal support for "states' rights" and his conviction that race was just a reality of life that could be reflected in statutes.

While Marshall respected his foe — he had cut classes while in law school to watch the brilliance of Davis's arguments — he knew that he had a few advantages of his own. He had, in a short period, won thirteen cases before the Supreme Court while losing two. Years earlier, he had enjoyed the heady compliment of seeing three robed judges of the Fourth Circuit Court of Appeals step off the bench to congratulate him on his successful argument that Virginia had to pay black teachers the same salaries that it paid white teachers.

I left Marshall that fall day of '53 thinking that he believed in himself and his cause so much that it was impossible for me and others not to believe in him.

Still, nothing could wipe out Marshall's personal doubts about Vinson. Marshall lost a lot of sleep tossing and turning and wondering where Vinson really stood.

Then came one of those monumental quirks of fate. On the night of September 8, 1953, Vinson told his wife that his stomach was bothering him and he felt really ill. A few hours later he was dead of a heart attack.

The media had been spreading the word that the Supreme Court was bitterly divided on the explosive issue of separate but equal. Rumors abounded that Vinson lacked the personal commitment and the overall leadership qualities to produce a unanimous ruling against Jim Crow. The general wisdom was that the passions about race were so great that anything short of a unanimous decision would create a calamitous social eruption across the nation, not just in the South. It became obvious that the person President Eisenhower chose to replace Vinson would be a critical figure in the revolution of racial and social progress. Conservatives and liberals squirmed when leaks were put out that Ike's attorney general, Herbert Brownell, Jr., wanted the president to elevate Associate Justice Jackson to the role of chief justice. Conservatives criticized Jackson as a "left-of-center Democrat" who had supported FDR's scheme to pack the Supreme Court with people who shared his views. Liberals considered Jackson to be one of the more conservative members of the Court. Blacks moaned when another leak said that Eisenhower would name Thomas Dewey, who had lost the presidency to Truman.

Not many people even speculated that Eisenhower might turn to Governor Earl Warren of California, who had been on the ticket with Dewey — the only man to be elected governor of California three times, who had won both the Democratic and Republican nominations for governor in 1946, and who had beaten James Roosevelt, the eldest son of FDR, by more than a million votes in the gubernatorial contest of 1950.

Eisenhower remembered that he was to some degree indebted to Warren, because in the brutal battle between Ike and Senator Robert Taft of Ohio in the 1952 Republican convention, when there was a dispute over delegates, Warren had thrown California's support behind the seating of a delegation favoring Eisenhower. After his election, Eisenhower had offered Warren a cabinet post, which the Californian rejected while letting Ike know that he would someday like a seat on the Supreme Court.

Some Eisenhower aides told him that he didn't owe Warren a thing, because in the 1952 convention itself, after the delegate dispute was resolved, Warren held California's seventy votes for himself, and never released them for Eisenhower.

Nonetheless, Eisenhower dispatched Brownell to Sacramento, to talk to Warren; when he returned to Washington Brownell told the president that the California governor was his choice. The maleable Eisenhower approved, and Brownell immediately leaked to the *New York Times* and a couple of other publications the word that Warren was going to be the new chief justice — a leak that infuriated the rest of the American media.

Warren's appointment was of towering importance. While technically the chief justice has only the one vote that associate justices have, the chief justice can be a man of incredible influence. As the chief judicial officer of the land, and as presiding officer over the Court, he gets the first opportunity to say what the issues are in cases coming before the Court. He gets to cast the last vote when it comes to deciding a case, and on a Court that had had so many 5–4 decisions, this was crucial. Then, if his vote puts him in the majority, he designates the justice who will write the opinion. Thus, any chief justice with great leadership qualities, and the guts to use them, could change the central direction of judicial policy in America.

Warren was ensured of confirmation when Adlai Stevenson, the titular head of the Democratic party, expressed his approval, as did the leaders of the labor unions, which in those days had real clout. They approved even though somewhat bothered by Ike's endorsement, because the general assumption among Democrats was that Eisenhower's idea of a "middle-of-the-roader" was a white, socialite, status-quoer, a "solid American" who could be counted on not to "rock the system" in any meaningful way. There was much in Warren's background to suggest that he was just what Eisenhower wanted. Warren had won fame as a sort of law and order man. He had been deputy district attorney for Alameda County (cities of Oakland, Berkeley, and Alameda) from 1920–1925, and district attorney from 1925–1939. He was credited with convicting an average of fifteen murderers a year. He once jailed the county sheriff for gambling and graft, and convicted Alameda's mayor for bribery and theft of public funds. Warren had supported the internment of Japanese Americans during World War II. He had said he favored revising the highly controversial Taft-Hartley labor law, but that he did not favor repealing it, as the labor unions wanted.

Warren's father had been bludgeoned to death in 1938 in what was presumed a robbery, and his killers had never been brought to justice. This, too, led some in the Eisenhower administration to believe that Warren would be very hard on people accused of violent crime.

In a 1952 interview with *U.S. News and World Report* Warren had given his views on the most burning issues in the land — the questions of keeping communists out of government and of the tactics of Senator Joseph McCarthy of Wisconsin:

> *Q.*: To what extent do you believe anti-Communism will be an issue, Governor?
>
> *WARREN*: That's very difficult to state. I am of the opinion, however, that no Administration should have any trouble with Communists in the Government. There is only one way to get Communists out of the Government, and that's to never let them get in. If we never temporize with them, never seek their favor, never coddle them, but on the contrary are always opposed to them, they will never be a problem in Government. . . .
>
> *Q.*: Where do you stand on the McCarthy question?
>
> *WARREN*: If you refer to unsupported accusations made in blanket form, either against a group of persons or an individual, or against our Government, without an opportunity for those involved to have a fair hearing on charges that are made against them, I believe it is not in keeping with the American spirit of fair play. I've been a lawyer, an officer of the courts, for many, many years and have spent many years of my life in court. I have become devoted to judicial processes and to due process of law. I am quite sensitive on that score.
>
> It is my belief that a man's reputation is just as valuable to him and perhaps more valuable to him than his property, and that he ought to have an opportunity to defend it with equal vigor under rules that are fair. To the extent that anyone indiscriminately charges individuals or groups of individuals with dishonesty or subversion, or whatever it might be that would destroy reputation, that is in my opinion not in the American tradition and should not be encouraged.

Neither Ike, Brownell, nor others in the administration really had any idea what Warren's judicial and other beliefs were, nor did the journalistic elite. Arthur Krock, the conservative columnist of the *New York Times*, thought that Warren had taken a properly middle-of-the-road stance in the controversy over whether professors at the University of California should be required to take a special loyalty oath. Warren had opposed a special oath because it singled professors out and was discriminatory, but at the same time he endorsed legislation requiring that all state employees sign a piece of paper declaring their loyalty to the United States and their opposition to efforts to overthrow the government of the United States.

Yet, conservatives should have learned that Warren might be a little troublesome when *U.S. News and World Report* asked him about his stand on a Fair Employment Practices Commission (FEPC) law. He told them that he favored such a law in order "to rid the country of the evil that presents itself" — racial discrimination.

There was another passage in that 1952 interview that should have been a warning signal to Republican conservatives:

> *Q.*: Let's take another issue, Governor, do you believe in federal aid to education?
>
> *WARREN*: Yes, I do. I believe that every child in America should have the right to a sound, basic education. Some of the states are not in a position to afford that kind of education. Some of them devote a very large part of their income to education, and the revenues are still not enough to provide a sound, basic education for the children. No child should be penalized just because his father must work for a living in a particular locality. In my own state, we have tried to equalize education by having an equalization fund for the benefit of poorer districts. I think the same principle can be applied by the Federal Government — provided the Federal Government puts no controls of any kind on education, which is a state function and a state problem.

The greatest indicator that Warren would not be what the Republican party wanted him to be was in his family background. He was born on March 19, 1891, in Los Angeles, the son of a Norwegian railroad mechanic, Methias Warren. Earl's grandfather was Halvar Varran, who Anglicized his name and became Harry Warren. Earl's mother was Swedish-born Chrystal Hernlund. All sturdy working people.

Governor Warren was no Republican snob. He had grown up in a lower-class "railroad section" of Bakersfield, California. He had been a newsboy, a freight hustler, a farmhand, a cub reporter, and attended Bakersfield's Kern County High School, where he played clarinet in the school band and outfield on the baseball team. He had been a social friend of blacks and other minorities at a time when it was decidedly not the popular thing.

As Warren virtually began his tenure as chief justice by presiding over the explosive second hearing of the school segregation case, he watched in astonishment as Davis turned emotional, almost suffering a nervous breakdown, as he abandoned constitutional arguments and pleaded with the justices to preserve "the Southern way of life." Warren and the other justices had expected Marshall and the other NAACP lawyers to deliver sonorous lamentations about what the slave owners and other wicked white men had done to black people over two centuries. But there was Marshall, giving razor-sharp legal presentations about the Fifth, Thirteenth, Fourteenth, and Fifteenth Amendments, and the other provisions of the Constitution that were designed to make ex-slaves full American citizens.

The oral arguments of December 7–9, 1953, were, incredibly, more emotional, more engrossing to the nation, than had been the debates of a year earlier. With Warren as the new chief justice, some in the media argued, the odds had risen that the Court would repeal *Plessy*. But with Eisenhower and the Republicans controlling the White House and the Justice Department, others surmised, the odds had increased that "separate but equal" would remain the law of the land. On November 15 the NAACP had filed a brief that argued forcefully that the Fourteenth Amendment, by its own force, prohibited all state action based upon race and color, and asked the Court to order the admission of black children to schools of their choice.

Then Attorney General Brownell filed the long-awaited "friend of the court" brief for the Eisenhower administration. There had been intense speculation as to whether the Republicans would begin a campaign to woo the white South away from the Democrats or whether they would make an unprecedented GOP appeal for the black vote. Brownell learned that the White House wanted it both ways, supporting the view that the promoters of the Fourteenth Amendment intended "to secure for Negroes full and complete equality before the law and to abolish all legal distinctions based upon race." Yet, the Brownell brief added, complex educational, social, and racial problems were involved, so the Eisenhower administration suggested that the South be given a one-year transition period.

"Give 'em a year and they'll take forever," Marshall said to Spottswood Robinson, who knew that this was an understatement where his case, Prince Edward County, was concerned. But Marshall, Robinson, and the other NAACP lawyers needed the "friendship" of Eisenhower, Brownell, and Assistant Attorney General J. Lee Rankin. So they dared not complain publicly about the government brief. This was good judgment, even though Marshall had no idea that the Justice Department had given Rankin secret instructions that if questioned by the Court, he could go beyond the tepid brief and put the government flatly against Jim Crow. So when Justice Douglas asked Rankin if the Court could properly go "either way," Rankin replied no, that the only proper decision was that segregated schools violated the Constitution.

The ornate courtroom was filled with people, and tension, on December 7. Newsmen noticed that not only did South Carolina have there its big gun, John W. Davis, who had argued 140 cases before the high tribunal, but that Virginia had sent T. Justin Moore and Attorney General J. Lindsay Almond, two of the most prestigious lawyers the state had produced. Marshall and Robinson would lead the NAACP rearguments.

Justice Frankfurter badgered, or "challenged," Marshall as assiduously as he had in 1952. He got Thurgood's repeated and unwavering claim that "any segregation, which is for the purpose of setting up either class or caste legislation, is in and of itself a violation of the Fourteenth Amendment."

Frankfurter's questions, however many, threw no light on his voting intentions. Justice Reed was more transparent. He kept asking Marshall whether the Constitution required only "substantial equality" for black people. Marshall said in many ways that the fundamental purpose of the Fourteenth Amendment was "to raise the Negro up into the status of complete equality with the other people."

Davis, at age eighty, was weary, and it showed through his brilliant efforts to milk the passions of the times. He interjected "delicately" the fact that twenty-nine states had antimiscegenation statutes, suggesting that if the Fourteenth Amendment said that blacks and whites had to go to school together, then laws saying blacks and whites could not fornicate together would become unconstitutional.

In a moment that Chief Justice Warren later called "surprisingly emotional," this esteemed lawyer cried out that all the black plaintiffs were like the dog in Aesop's fable which was carrying "a fine piece of meat in his mouth, crossed a bridge, and saw the shadow in the stream and plunged for it and lost both the substance and the shadow." He said black people were throwing away equal education "on some fancied question of racial prestige."

On December 8, Marshall pounced upon Davis's version of the fable: "Mr. Davis said yesterday, the only thing the Negroes are trying to get is prestige. Exactly correct." Marshall's voice was a baritone boom now. "Ever since the Emancipation Proclamation, the Negro has been trying to get what was recognized in *Strauder v. West*

Virginia — which is the same status as anybody else, regardless of race."

When the Prince Edward County, Virginia, case came up Moore and Almond argued mostly emotional issues. They said that the right of women to vote, the right of racial intermarriage, were not mentioned in the Fourteenth Amendment or the debates attending its passage, therefore unmentioned "mixed" schools could not have been intended. Moore seemed to sense that the Court was going to outlaw Jim Crow, so he asked that the cases be remanded to local federal district courts, with the southern judges given broad latitude to decide how to change things, if at all.

Almond approached the Court as an uncompromising racist. He assailed Thurgood and his associates by declaring: "They are asking you to disturb the unfolding evolutionary process of education where from the dark days of the depraved institution of slavery, with the help and the sympathy and the love and respect of the white people of the South, the colored man has risen under that educational process to a place of eminence and respect throughout the nation. [Segregation] has served him well."

That got Frankfurter's dander up. His "strict construction" and "judicial restraint" leanings were offended by Almond, who went on to ask Frankfurter why "the seceding states . . . have been indicted by the opposition of treachery, of fraud, of conniving to subvert the Fourteenth Amendment."

The transcripts of those oral arguments of 1953 run into many hundreds of pages. After reading them, I have only respect and admiration for nine men whose bladders and brains sustained them through such endless rhetoric of passion, and even hatred. I can understand why, at 2:40 P.M. on December 9, when the Court adjourned, Marshall would walk out with his colleagues without a clue as to whether he should celebrate or weep. The only thing he felt sure of was, he later said, "that Justice Reed will vote against us and, God save him, as many as four other justices."

Those last weeks of December 1953, and the first months of 1954, were not halcyon days for Thurgood Marshall, or his wife, Buster, or the hundreds of lawyers, social scientists, college presidents, law school deans, who had invested their minds, their research, their very reputations, in the efforts to banish school segregation.

Buster was very sick, but Thurgood was too consumed by his legal crusade to realize how ill she was. Marshall himself was ailing, but his commitment to the NAACP was greater than any concern about his health or his economic viability. Even though his pay was still a pittance, in January 1954 he wrote a $100 check as his first payment for a life membership in the NAACP. That same month he was named to the 1953 Honor Roll of the *Chicago Defender,* which vied for recognition as the greatest black newspaper in America. In February he was delighted to learn that he had been nominated to become a trustee of Howard University. In May the *Chicago Defender* and its publisher, John Sengstacke, honored him again with the Robert S. Abbott Memorial Award for fighting to "secure basic human rights guaranteed every citizen."

It was the overoptimistic Marshall who accepted that award with an inexplicable prediction that Jim Crow in America would end "by 1963."

But these things were only temporary boosts for the spirit of a man whose waking and sleeping moments were dogged by one question: "Will the Supreme Court agree with us that the Fourteenth Amendment outlaws Jim Crow schools?"

Only those who lived, or had lived, in the South, where their jobs, their lives, their daily movements, were circumscribed by Jim Crow, could understand Marshall's doubts about the verdict of this Court. Black people didn't have black aides in the Supreme Court building to give them leaks about where a case was going. But some of the law school deans, the former clerks of Supreme Court justices, picked up gossip about the exchanges of memoranda, the devious messages that attended the Court's frenetic efforts to resolve the NAACP challenge to racial segregation. Marshall got tips that justices were sending angry messages through one law clerk to another and were engaging in "off the record" conversations in which one tried to influence the other. He was told that Justice Reed had hired someone to write his support of "separate but equal."

What no leaker told Marshall or any of his allies was that Earl Warren was working in incredible ways to prod the Court into delivering a decision that would have the greatest positive and healing impact upon the nation. Marshall did not know that in early 1954 there had been an attempted intervention by a powerful force outside the Court.

Eisenhower invited Warren to a White House dinner that was blatantly political. Warren went because it is deemed an insult for almost anyone to turn down an invitation to the White House. Warren would later tell members of his family and close friends that Eisenhower had seated him on his right, as protocol required, and had positioned Davis, the counsel for the southern states, close to where Warren sat. During the dinner Eisenhower kept telling Warren what a truly great American Davis was. After the dinner, Warren would later reveal, Eisenhower said that the Southerners "are not bad people" and that all they really wanted was to see that "their sweet little girls are not required to sit in school alongside some big, overgrown Negroes."

Warren was offended but chose not to reply to Eisenhower in any way. Warren never wrote or revealed, as far as I know, whether he informed other justices of this incredible breach of governmental ethics, this gross violation of the separation of the executive and the judicial branches. It is conceivable, however, that this incident turned out to be extremely helpful to Warren in getting other members of the Court to vote to outlaw Jim Crow schools — just the opposite of what Eisenhower wanted them to do.

May 17, 1954, was just an ordinary day at the Supreme Court for all but a couple of reporters who noticed that Justice Jackson, who had been in the hospital with a heart attack, had shown up at the Court. Then even some of the "dumb" newsmen noticed and thought it strange that celebrities such as Dean Acheson, the former secretary of state, Attorney General Brownell, and noted black lawyers such as Nabrit and George E. C. Hayes were there, along with attorneys Marshall and Davis.

But the reporters reverted to boredom when all that happened was that 118 lawyers were admitted to the Supreme Court bar and Justice Clark read a case dealing with alleged monopolistic practices in the sale of milk in Chicago and a couple of cases involving picketing and negligence were announced by Justice Douglas. Then, suddenly, at 12:52 P.M., Chief Justice Warren picked up a document and said: "I have for announcement the judgment and opinion of the Court in *Oliver Brown v. Board of Education of Topeka*." When word of Warren's statement was relayed to the ground-floor press room, where some reporters were sipping coffee, pandemonium broke out. The Associated Press sent out a *flash:* "Chief Justice Warren today began reading the Supreme Court's decision in the public school segregation cases. The Court's ruling cannot be determined immediately."

It did not take the hushed audience long to find out what the ruling was. In a loud and firm voice, silver-haired Warren set the background of the legal dispute:

In approaching this problem, we cannot turn the clock back to . . . 1896 when *Plessy v. Ferguson* was written. We must consider public education in the light of its full development and its present place in American life throughout the Nation. Only in this way can it be determined if segregation in public schools deprives these plaintiffs of the equal protection of the laws.

Today, education is perhaps the most important function of state and local governments. Compulsory school attendance laws and the great expenditures for education both demonstrate our recognition of the importance of education to our democratic society. It is required in the performance of our most basic public responsibilities, even service in the armed forces. It is the very foundation of good citizenship.

We come then to the question presented: Does segregation of children in public schools solely on the basis of race, even though the physical facilities and other "tangible" factors may be equal, deprive the children of the minority group of equal educational opportunities? We believe that it does.

. . . To separate them from others of similar age and qualifications solely because of their race generates a feeling of inferiority as to their status in the community that may affect their hearts and minds in a way unlikely ever to be undone. The effect of this separation on their educational opportunities was well stated by a finding in the Kansas case by a court which nevertheless felt compelled to rule against the Negro plaintiffs:

"Segregation of white and colored children in public schools has a detrimental effect upon the colored children. The impact is greater when it has the sanction of the law; for the policy of separating the races is usually interpreted as denoting the inferiority of the Negro group. A sense of inferiority affects the motivation of a child to learn. Segregation with the sanction of law, therefore, has a tendency to [retard] the educational and mental development of Negro children and to deprive them of some of the benefits they would receive in a racial[ly] integrated school system."

Whatever may have been the extent of psychological knowledge at the time of *Plessy v. Ferguson,* this finding is amply supported by modern authority. Any language in *Plessy v. Ferguson* contrary to this finding is rejected.

We conclude that in the field of public education the doctrine of "separate but equal" has no place. Separate educational facilities are inherently unequal. Therefore, we hold that the plaintiffs and others similarly situated for whom the actions have been brought are, by reason of the segregation complained of, deprived of the equal protection of the laws guaranteed by the Fourteenth Amendment.

Some in the courtroom were stunned. It seemed moments before anybody dared to smile or even tried to applaud. Marshall leaned over to one of his fellow lawyers and said, "We hit the jackpot." Marshall had a penchant for snap, premature celebrations. Little did he realize that he had come close to characterizing the nature of his victory. It was like someone in Las Vegas pumping money into a slot machine and having the bell ring for a colossal payout — but with nobody showing up with silver dollars, a check, or anything that could be spent right away.

I asked Marshall if he entertained some doubts that he would win that case.

"Some doubts? Great doubts. I would have bet all the tea in China that it wouldn't be unanimous," he replied, "because I happened to know that one justice had hired a separate law clerk to write his dissent. That I know to be a fact."

"How did it get to be unanimous?" I asked.

"I don't know, and nobody will tell."

Marshall called Warren "the greatest leader I've ever run across in my life. He was likable, but firm. I know one day he came into my office, my chambers, when I got on the Court, and I said, 'Hey, what's up?' And he said something. I said, 'Well, Chief, look — not to mention that you're the chief judge and I'm just a little old justice. But I mean, I'm a little younger than you are. Why don't you just get your secretary to call me, and I'm on my way?' He says, 'I don't operate that way.'

"He knew the first name of everybody that worked in that building. I mean, he was a great man and he knew exactly where he wanted the law to go, and if your opinion didn't do it, he would come in and sit down and say, 'This is not what I want,' and explain it to you."

Warren, the great dream maker, had pulled off a political-judicial miracle in getting a unanimous vote of the Court, of justices profoundly affected by the appendix to the NAACP brief written by doll-carrier Clark and other social, educational, and psychiatric experts about the terrible damage that state-imposed segregation had been doing to black children. But some of the justices who were voting to outlaw Jim Crow schools were also worried about threats to close the public schools; that blood would run in the streets of Jackson, Mississippi; that all kinds of Southerners were vowing to die before they would let little white girls go to school with "overgrown" Negro males.

The last holdout in agreeing to vote for desegregation had been

Justice Reed, so he was adamant about structuring the Court's mandate in such a way as to make this tremendous change in southern life as painless as it could be. One of the most eloquent advocates of "go slow" was Frankfurter. Eisenhower's people spoke up publicly for a careful and painstaking implementation of the *Brown* decision. Some of Harry Truman's people advocated a process of integrating one grade at a time, an idea that was rejected immediately by Marshall and the NAACP.

The Supreme Court that spoke unanimously was in fact so woefully divided that it said it would take a year before delivering a second opinion, to be known as *Brown II,* in which it would specify *how* the South was going to go about erasing Jim Crow in the public schools.

CHAPTER FIFTEEN

SUDDEN DEATH

After the first *BROWN* RULING, Marshall went home to his and Buster's new apartment on Riverside Drive in New York City, dreading the fact that even after what most of the world thought was a great legal triumph, he had to go through the grueling process of telling the Supreme Court how to put some substance into his victory. His wife was on such a "high" of celebration that he said nothing of his disappointments, his fears that he would be involved in a lifetime of litigation over what the Warren Court had said in 1954.

Marshall had had a good marriage to Vivien Burey for a quarter century, despite the fact that she could not give him a baby, and that his duties made it impossible for him to give her all the companionship that any wife — or husband — must crave.

You ask Marshall if he was disappointed that Buster's pregnancies always wound up in miscarriages, and he replies laconically, "What could I do about it?"

I never met Buster, so I could not ask her how she felt about the fact that Thurgood was so wedded to his obsession with using the law to free black people that she seemed to be number two on his priority list. A look at the records of Marshall's travels, his time away from home and his wife, makes you wonder how the marriage survived.

Consider 1943. Marshall left his wife on May 12 to go to Detroit, where the nation's worst race rioting had broken out. He stayed there four days before leaving for St. Louis. From there he went to

Tulsa, and from there back to St. Louis. On May 25 he returned to New York. On June 4, Marshall left again for a trip to Columbia, South Carolina, where teacher pay cases were pending. From there he went to Atlanta, returning to New York on Sunday, June 20, when he went, not home to Manhattan, but to attend a meeting of the White Plains branch of the NAACP. This was typical over many years, as witnessed by the schedule in April of 1944, when he went to Little Rock, Arkansas, on April 6, to Houston on April 11, to Dallas on April 19, to St. Louis on April 20, returning to New York on April 21. On June 20, 1944, Marshall went to Plaquemine, Louisiana, to Baton Rouge the next day, to Alexandria on June 23 to defend three black soldiers, Lawrence Mitchell, Richard Adams, and John Walter Bordenave, who were at Camp Claiborne and had been convicted of rape and sentenced to death in the electric chair. Then to Jackson, Tennessee, on June 28, where an important teacher pay case was pending. Then to Chicago on July 11, returning to New York on July 17!

Marshall clearly was always aware of the extent to which he was neglecting his wife and endangering his health. On February 10, 1943, he wrote to Walter White: "These changing climates have kept me with a cold. Either the cold or the army will get me, and in case I happen to get by them, Buster should kill me for staying away so long. Oh well, such is life." But Marshall couldn't slow down.

Through all this maddening activity, White and others at the NAACP were themselves worried about the possibility of Marshall being drafted. In a February 16, 1943, letter, White wrote: "Speaking of draft status, what is yours now? Have you been reclassified? Roy tells me that there is no point in filing 42A until one has been classified in 1A. The news out of Washington would seem to indicate that you may be in 1A fairly soon. So hurry on back so we can get the 42A moving. And hurry back for another reason. The office has been too quiet. . . . I do hope, both for your sake and to prevent Buster from killing both of us, that you will be home soon and will be able to stay here for a while."

The truth was that Marshall had been keeping his draft board better informed as to his whereabouts than he had White or his wife. On November 5, 1942, he had written Local Draft Board Number 62:

"Gentlemen: This is to inform you that I am leaving town today for an extended trip in the states of Arkansas, Louisiana, Texas and Georgia. I shall inform you of the date of my return."

Somehow, the draft board never caught up with Marshall.

However, by August 1943, Marshall had caught up with his senses, to a degree. He sent a memorandum to the chairman of the legal committee, Bill Hastie, and to Wilkins:

"Beginning Thursday night, August 5, I will be c/o Charles Jones, 410 Ridge Street, Steelton, Pennsylvania.

"By order of myself and my physician, 'I do *not* care to be disturbed.' "

Marshall had decided to go to his wife's hometown and spend some time with her — and repair his health, which would be a problem for him throughout the rest of his life. Marshall's note about an "order from myself and my physician" illustrated the kind of heavy sarcasm of which he was so wickedly capable. It went back to, or beyond, February 11, 1942, when Wilkins sent out a memorandum laying down strict rules as to when NAACP executives should come to work and when they should leave:

MEMORANDUM TO THE EXECUTIVE STAFF
FROM: MR. WILKINS
Come, children, and let us reason together.

The dance will be over tonight, and tomorrow is a holiday. Beginning with Friday morning, February 13, I am requesting that every executive be in the office at 9:30 A.M.

I am requesting, also, that no executive leave the office during regular office hours without notifying me.

Marshall responded that same day with the following memorandum:

MEMORANDUM TO MR. WILKINS
FROM: MR. MARSHALL:
On your memorandum concerning the keeping of the schedule for executives in the office, I am more than happy to cooperate. It might be quite difficult to get up in time to be in the office at 9:30 o'clock A.M. War time, which is 8:30 Standard time; but I think that Frank Reeves and I have been able to keep pretty good time although I *was* late this morning, teacher. This was unavoidable, because it happened to be Mrs. Marshall's birthday — for which I beg to be excused.

We will be more than happy to notify you whenever we are out of the office during the day, because we have usually done this in the past, anyway; and we have always secured your permission to leave the office before 5 o'clock P.M. when it was necessary to do so.

Teacher, we will continue to cooperate, if for no other reason than that stated in the last paragraph of your memorandum: ". . . because in the event that executives do not report promptly for work, other methods will have to be devised."

Go, children, we have reasoned together.

Buster thought that this was a silly, bureaucratic hassle, considering the amount of time her husband was putting into his job. Marshall had shared with her some of the hundreds of requests for speeches and other appearances that he was getting. A typical, and in one respect pathetic, example was the March 18, 1942, letter that Marshall got asking him to speak at the banquet of the State Negro Business League in Tampa, Florida. The letter said:

The number of guests has been limited to 200 and we are therefore anxious to have your response. If you will favor us with your presence, please fill out the enclosed blank, attach your remittance, and forward immediately.

The reservations are $1.00 each. If you find that you cannot be present, we will greatly appreciate your forwarding to us the amount of your reservation.

Nothing could have indicated more the pitiful economic state of black America than the fact that black businessmen in Tampa would ask Thurgood to send them a dollar if he couldn't show up to speak.

Marshall's reputation was growing, and his impecunious state was well known across the land. This inspired a lot of people to offer him jobs in the guise of helping him out of his economic misery.

On October 29, 1942, White was a little shocked to get the following letter from Morris L. Ernst, the distinguished New York lawyer, the soul of the American Civil Liberties Union, who had been trying to get the Justice Department to give Marshall a meaningful post:

Walter White, Esq.
69 Fifth Avenue
New York, NY

Dear Walter:
Sometime ago I suggested to Justice that Thurgood Marshall ought to be put on the staff. I understand that you are blocking this *brilliant* move on my part. For God's sake, lay hands off. You can pick up a dozen Thurgoods and you can tell him so, but Justice cannot get a guy as good as Thurgood.

Best,

Yours,
Morris L. E.

White responded:

Dear Morris:

Who told you I was blocking Thurgood's appointment to the Department of Justice staff? I don't want to lose him, but I would not stand in the way of any member of the NAACP staff doing a necessary job or advancing himself.

Now that that's off my chest I'd be ever so grateful to you if you would let me know the place where I "can pick up a dozen Thurgoods"!

All the best.

A few months later, in November, Leon A. Ransom of the Howard University School of Law wrote to Marshall:

Dear Turkey:

. . . I have some interesting information concerning the possibilities of your employment here which I would like to discuss with you as soon as you get in town. Please see me before you talk with anybody in the government offices.

Marshall cared infinitely more about what he was doing at the NAACP than about any job he might get at the Justice Department or at his alma mater, Howard. So did Buster. She made it clear that she could live with the long separations because they bore the fruits of political, social, economic, and judicial freedom for blacks and the other "little, down-and-out people of America." What Thurgood's wife could *not* live with was a sickness that crept up like a murderer in the night.

Buster Marshall had never smoked. She had berated Thurgood week after week because he smoked like a barbecue pit. What bitter irony — or early evidence of the dangers of "passive" smoke — that in 1955 she began to have extremely serious pulmonary problems. Marshall called in a close friend, Dr. Walter A. Crump, Jr., a distinguished doctor from a famous medical family whose father had been one of the greatest surgeons in New York City. Dr. Crump examined Buster and thought at first that she might have pleurisy. Marshall recalls:

"They took the liquid out and examined it and realized that it wasn't pleurisy. Then Dr. Crump went back and examined all the X-ray plates from about five or ten years. Then he did something they called 'cross X-ray studies,' and there it was, hiding the way it always does. A terrible cancer."

Marshall canceled all of his appointments, abandoned the writing of briefs on the growing variety of legal battles the NAACP was fighting, and sat at home, looking after his wife.

"That cancer's a mess, I'm telling you," he reminisced to me. "How terrible just to watch her lie there dying. Every day you'd look at her and she'd gone down further. Eventually, Monsignor Drew from the Catholic Church, a very good friend of mine, came by our apartment and asked me, 'How's my baby doing?'

" 'No better, Monsignor. I think even worse.' "

" 'Can I look at her?' he asked, and I said, 'Sure, go ahead.'

"He went in the bedroom where she was lying. She was unaware of anything or anybody. After five or ten minutes he came out and said, 'Thurgood, is it all right if I give her the last rites?' "

"I said, 'I'm sure she'd appreciate it. But why?'

" 'Because she's dying,' the monsignor said.

"I told him that I had been watching her hour by hour, minute by minute, and hadn't seen that kind of change, and he told me that he had seen too many people in her state not to know.

" 'She's got a maximum of twenty-four hours,' the monsignor said."

Marshall told me matter-of-factly: "She died that night [February 11, 1955]. The monsignor knew, and I didn't know. He said he could just look at them and tell — that it was simple when you had dealt with death as much as he had."

I asked Marshall whether the death of Buster was devastating, and he said, "What could I do about it?" This is the Thurgood Marshall who always wanted to pretend that nothing much fazed him, that he could roll with whatever punch Jim Crow lawyers, bigoted sheriffs, or the Fates threw at him.

Alice Stovall, Marshall's secretary, knew better. She told me how "he took it very hard, because it was rather sudden. He had a pretty hard time for a while."

Marshall could not grieve for long. He was in the grip of a quest eternal, so he soon was back in the office, on trains and airplanes, in courtrooms and schoolrooms, trying to establish the Constitution as a bulwark of freedom for blacks and women — the Americans whom the founders had dismissed so cavalierly.

Stovall recalled that a few weeks after Buster's death, she and the other NAACP secretaries would be trying frantically to get out press releases on the growing number of cases being fought by the organization, when they would look up and there would be Wilkins and Marshall helping with the mimeographing, organizing the pages (there were no fancy Xerox copiers with collators then), licking stamps and pasting them on envelopes, eager to ensure that the press releases were ready for delivery to the post office before the next mailing went out.

Work became Marshall's temporary eraser of deep grief.

As Marshall, Wilkins, Stovall, and others struggled to stay on top of the greatest crises of their lives, none could escape the reality that a pale-faced, blue-eyed "ghost" hovered over their work, their every decision. What was their future regarding Walter White? They remembered how White had ultimately outfoxed his foes in the great row over his marriage to Poppy Cannon. In March 1950 he had withdrawn his 1949 letter of resignation with the claim that his staying on would stop the "dissension and disruption" and deprive enemies of an opportunity to divide and conquer the NAACP. When members of the board questioned White's ability to do the job, given his bad health, he said his coronary problem was "more neurogenic than coronary" and that Dr. Arthur Master, a specialist, had assured him that "if I lead a sensible life I can count on a number of years of continued active life."

So in May 1950 a bitterly divided board had voted to have White return as executive secretary, emphasizing that Wilkins would have all administrative authority, but would be "second in command." Marshall and others knew that while White had survived the infighting he probably would not long survive what he was doing to his body — the long trips, the many lectures, the writing deadlines, the pressures of trying to satisfy sexually a woman who reputedly had a very large appetite.

On October 12, 1954, just after returning from a "rest" period in Puerto Rico, Haiti, and Jamaica, which he told the press had put him "in robust health," White had a massive heart attack. He was taken to New York Hospital in "critical" condition, released after four days, then readmitted and placed in an oxygen tent for thirteen days.

The NAACP board had granted White months of time to recuperate in the Caribbean. Now Marshall, Wilkins, Stovall, and others awaited with unease his return as the big boss on April 1, 1955. Would he? If he did, how much would he try to assert himself? Could Wilkins and Marshall handle either coddlings of, or hassles with, White when they were immersed in plans to argue before the Supreme Court the *Brown II* decree concerning how to take racism out of public education in America?

Just over a month after Buster's death, Walter and Poppy returned to an apartment at 242 East 68th Street in New York City. On March 21 the irrepressible White went to the NAACP offices, where he told the staff that he felt "chipper" and just wanted "to get the feel of things" before he retook control of the organization ten days later. White spent two hours in the office and returned to his home. Three hours later he died of a sudden heart seizure.

Marshall had never been close to White. They had, after all, been rivals for the attention of the press and the affection of the black people of America. There was bitterness over the fact that White had gotten rich as the "front man" while Marshall lived in relative poverty, even though he was the one who wrote the briefs, argued the cases, and often put his life on the line.

In one interview with me Marshall said:

"Arthur Spingarn was a great NAACP leader, but the things he let Walter White get away with were unbelievable."

I asked if Walter was "a little like J. Edgar Hoover. . . . I mean, when there was something good to announce, Hoover always managed to get himself to the microphone."

"Or to issue the press release," Marshall added. "Walter was a front-runner. Like racehorses they have to put blinkers on, because if they see another horse gaining on them, they stop. Walter was a front-runner. But when it came to doing something, like working, oh, God, no. For work, he wasn't your man. Still, you can't take away from him all the things he did.

"He used to come to the Supreme Court and sit in the lawyers' section, and I said, 'Walter, you have no damned business down there. You can go to jail for it.'

"Case after case he kept sitting there, and finally I said, 'A key case is coming up. If you show up, I'm gonna tell the marshal, because you're not gonna get me blamed for it.'

" 'You don't mean it,' he said.

" 'The hell I don't! Try me!' I replied.

"The next Monday I went in and looked at the lawyers' section. Walter wasn't there. All of a sudden I looked over, and there he was in the *judges'* box. He just looked at me and laughed. He just liked to get on top of you. I guess we wouldn't have been anyplace without a Walter, but I'm telling you, Roy [Wilkins] did all the work and Walter got all the damn credit.

"Walter wanted to take over all my stuff. I made it clear to him to keep out of my way, and I'd keep out of his way. I told him if he got in my way, I'd walk all over him. Then Roy and Bill Hastie called me into a meeting and said if that confrontation went on, everything would fall apart. So I said, 'Okay, he's the boss.'

"You know," Marshall chuckled, "the dope was that she [Poppy] was really a Negro. But nobody ever proved it. Once, when Walter and his first wife were still married, Walter and Poppy went to the Virgin Islands, the office story went, and when our NAACP messenger went to their door, in the middle of the day, a girl of four or five answered and said, 'Mommy is not available. She and Walter are back having wintercourse.'

"She killed him," Marshall said. "She knew he had a bad heart. She killed him!"

Still, White's death shocked Marshall deeply, coming as it did just five weeks after the heart-searing death of Buster. For Thurgood, there was something eerily worrisome about the coincidence of his wife dying on February 11 and White dying on March 21, already guaranteeing that 1955 would be the worst year of his life. Marshall prayed that the Supreme Court would not deliver him a triple blow.

Marshall had to go before the Supreme Court again on April 11 to argue the most crucial aspect of the school desegregation cases: What should the Supreme Court say in its decree? Should it tell the lower courts and the officials of South Carolina, Virginia, and the other segregating states that they must put black and white children in the same schools immediately? Should the Court, out of consideration for social passions and administrative difficulties, allow a long period of adjustment?

When Justice Reed suggested a twelve-year-plan of integrating one year at a time, Marshall rejected it summarily. "You not only destroy completely the rights of the individual pupils [in this litigation], you destroy the rights of the whole class [of black plaintiffs]. Nobody in that class will ever get mixed education."

Marshall asked for a decree ordering the end of segregation in the school districts involved at the opening of school in September 1955. He said that he could live with a decree that said September 1956.

"The situation needs a firm hand of government to say, 'We are going to desegregate.' And that is that," he emphasized.

But there were lawyers aplenty from several states there to tell the Supreme Court that it could not say that, or do that, and that the president couldn't do it, either. The arguments over the proposed decree, incredibly, became more emotional and bitter than the two hearings leading up to the decision of May 17, 1954.

There was S. E. Rogers of Clarendon County, begging the justices to understand that "our district is composed of the old plantation section of the county, fronting along a deep curve in the Santos River. It is for that reason that our Negro population is so large and our white population so small." Rogers said that blacks and whites in this old plantation area had had a "bi-racial," meaning segregated, existence for a century. "We are faced with problems that cannot be solved except with a change of attitude and those attitudes will have to be changed slowly."

Justice Frankfurter observed that "attitudes are partly the result of action. . . . You do not fold your hands and wait for an attitude to change by itself."

Rogers suggested that it might be the year 2015 or 2045 before attitudes changed enough in Clarendon County for white people to allow their children to go to school with black children.

Chief Justice Warren said: "I wonder if the decision of May seventeen last year would be of much value to these people if they waited until two thousand forty-five for that change in the attitude of [white] people." Still, South Carolina's lead lawyer (Davis had died earlier that year), Robert McC. Figg, told Warren that the South Carolina district involved was one where "it might well prove impossible to have unsegregated schools" unless the Court allowed "opportunity and time for community acceptance of the idea."

Marshall thundered that "they want no time limit," and that when the southern lawyers went back into lower court, their word for when they would desegregate would be "the same thing they are arguing here — NEVER!"

These orals got "down and dirty" when Archibald C. Robertson and Attorney General J. Lindsay Arnold spoke for Virginia and Prince Edward County.

Robertson said that fifty-five of Virginia's ninety counties were on record as opposing "compulsory integration." He declared that "neither a Court decree nor an executive order can produce the result which is opposed by a united majority in the place where it must be enforced."

Marshall said he was shocked by arguments "of the impotency of our government to enforce its Constitution."

Robertson then went into an argument that was supposed to grab even white judges by their guts:

We say that the standards of health and morals must also be taken into account. Tuberculosis is almost twice as prevalent among the

Negroes as it is among the whites. Negroes constitute twenty-two per cent of the population of Virginia but seventy-eight per cent of all cases of syphilis and eighty-three per cent of all cases of gonorrhea occur among the Negroes.

One white child out of every fifty born in Virginia is illegitimate. One Negro child out of five is illegitimate.

Of course, the incidence of disease and illegitimacy is just a drop in the bucket compared to the promiscuity. We say that not as a moral issue, not as to where the fault lies, but that the fact is there and the white parents at this time will not appropriate the money to put their children among other children with that sort of a background.

Attorney General Almond reemphasized this theme when he told the Court:

I am not going further into the matter of health. Mr. Robertson brought it out, but with the same drinking fountain, the same toilets, the same physical daily habits, and all, our problem is increased. The conclusion as a result of these conditions with reference to health is inescapable, that white parents will keep their children out of school. They will withdraw their support. I do not say that as a threat.

Marshall seemed to try to hold back the sarcasm when he replied:

It has always been interesting to me, if the Court please, from the Morgan case involving transportation, that, well, whenever Negroes are separated from other people because of race, they always make an exception as to the Negro servants.

In Virginia, it is interesting to me that the very people that argue for this side, that would object to sending their white children to school with Negroes, are eating food that has been prepared, served, and almost put into their mouths by the mothers of those children, and they do it day in and day out, but they cannot have the child go to school. That is not the point involved in this case. The point is as to whether or not, at this late date, with emphasis, this government can any longer tolerate this extreme difference based upon race or color.

In predicting disobedience by Virginians to the Court's ruling, Robertson said: "I lived through that Prohibition era, and that noble experiment keeps coming back to my mind." Almond waxed more eloquent when he said: "We Virginians lead in giving law and order to the nation. We washed the Eighteenth Amendment out of the Constitution and flooded the Volstead Act to oblivion on the stream of our honest spirits because it affected the way of life of the American people."

Marshall replied with a dubious display of indignation: "I am shocked that anybody classes that right to take a drink of whiskey involved in Prohibition with the right of a Negro child to participate in education."

Without ever arguing that Negroes were inferior, and whites superior, Robertson cited educational tests as a reason why Virginia could not put blacks and whites in the same classrooms:

> In a typical class of thirty-six, according to these tests, accepted, appropriate standard tests, in a typical class of thirty-six, half white and half Negro, the range of comprehension would extend all the way from six Negro pupils with a reading age of nine years and four months to a top group of six white pupils with a reading age of sixteen years and two months.
>
> In dealing with the how of integration, which they tell us we must deal with, how would it be possible to proceed with an effective teaching program on any such basis if the teaching level is pitched for the level of the median Negro child?
>
> Then the education of the white group must suffer. Regardless of why and as to any other reason, it is a fact that these great differences do exist. And these are not intangibles.

Marshall's retort:

> They mention these educational tests. They use figures on a percentage basis. They leave out the fact that in each one of those percentages, there are Negro children that run the gamut in each one of those twenty-five figures, but they try to give the impression that all the Negro children are below all the white children when that is not true.
>
> There are geniuses in both groups and there are lower ones in both groups, and it has no bearing. No right of an individual can be conditioned as to any average of other people in his racial group or any other racial group.
>
> They give tests to grade children, so what do we think is the solution? Simple. Put the dumb colored children in with the dumb white children, and put the smart colored children with the smart white children — that is no problem.

Almond was almost feverish in his cry that the May 17 decision "involved the rights, the mode of life, the customs, the mores of fifty million people and eleven million schoolchildren." He went on:

> Our adversaries ask this Court — and I say without any spirit of bitterness, they ask this Court to arm them with the power to destroy that which this Court has said to be perhaps the most important function of state and local governments.
>
> . . . You will have placed in their hands unbridled power to destroy the most important function of state and local government.
>
> The high schools of Prince Edward County, not in defiance of the mandate of this Court, but under the imperative necessity of relentless circumstance over which they have no control, would cease to operate.
>
> . . . I say, in all candor and frankness to this Court, that solution whatever it may be, will not in my judgment in the lifetime of those of us hale and hearty here, be enforced integration of the races in the public schools of that county.

On May 31, 1955, the Supreme Court, again speaking unanimously, issued its instructions as to how the constitutional procedures were to be implemented:

> At stake is the personal interest of the plaintiffs in admission to public schools as soon as practicable on a nondiscriminatory basis. To effectuate this interest may call for elimination of a variety of obstacles in making the transition to school systems operated in accordance with the constitutional principles set forth in our May 17, 1954, decision. Courts of equity may properly take into account the public interest in the elimination of such obstacles in a systematic and effective manner. But it should go without saying that the vitality of these constitutional principles cannot be allowed to yield simply because of disagreement with them.
>
> While giving weight to these public and private considerations, the courts will require that the defendants make a prompt and reasonable start toward full compliance with our May 17, 1954, ruling. Once such a start has been made, the courts may find that additional time is necessary to carry out the ruling in an effective manner. The burden rests upon the defendants to establish that such time is necessary in the public interest and is consistent with good faith compliance at the earliest practicable date. To that end, the courts may consider problems related to administration, arising from the physical condition of the school plant, the school

transportation system, personnel, revision of school districts and attendance areas into compact units to achieve a system of determining admission to the public schools on a nonracial basis, and revision of local laws and regulations which may be necessary in solving the foregoing problems. They will also consider the adequacy of any plans the defendants may propose to meet these problems and to effectuate a transition to a racially nondiscriminatory school system. During this period of transition, the courts will retain jurisdiction of these cases.

The judgments below, except that in the Delaware case, are accordingly reversed and the cases are remanded to the district courts to take such proceedings and enter such orders and decrees consistent with this opinion as are necessary and proper to admit to public schools on a racially nondiscriminatory basis with all deliberate speed the parties to these cases.

Some legal scholars who looked at *Brown II* and its virtual invitation to segregated school districts to stall, to obfuscate, to resist massively, to inspire violence, concluded that what had taken place in 1955 was not an historic mandate for full black freedom, but something that would turn out to be, as one critic put it, "worse than *Dred Scott.*" That gloomy assessment referred to the fact that while the Supreme Court had declared Jim Crow schools unconstitutional in 1954, it had not really said in 1955 how or when they were to be abolished. This was a point lost on millions of celebrants across America, including this writer, who called the 1954 decision "Jim Crow's last stand."

"I was terribly disappointed that the Court did not set a firm date for desegregation in the fall of 1955, or at worst, 1956," Marshall told me. "But Almond, Rogers, and the others scared the hell out of some justices with their threats of disobedience and school closings. But what was I to say publicly? Hell, I had a hundred other battles to fight in that Court trying to wipe out the vestiges of *Dred Scott, Plessy,* and all the other judicial approvals of ways and schemes to keep black people just a step away from legalized bondage."

Thurgood was not the kind of man who would ever live as a celibate. He loved the presence of females. With his work schedule and lifestyle, he needed a woman to look after him. In fact, women in his offices had for years noticed his wrinkled shirt collars, his baggy trousers, his unkempt hair, and whispered that Buster "should take better care of him."

A few months after Buster's death, Marshall was at the NAACP headquarters office for a meeting when he spotted a petite young woman with mocha-colored skin and large, glowing eyes. She was Cecilia Suyat, a Hawaiian of Filipino descent who had left Maui in 1947 and taken a job as an NAACP secretary. Just looking at her set Marshall's hormones rushing. He said to a staffer whom he knew:

"I'll give you a quarter if you can get that pretty girl over there to give me a little kiss."

Chauvinist, sexist Marshall watched the black aide relay his proposition to Suyat, who looked at him with irritation and dismissed him with a no-deal wave of her hand. In doing so, she became as much a challenge to Marshall as any of his court cases. He finally succeeded in introducing himself and talking her into a date. In just a few months he asked "Cissy" to marry him.

Their wedding, on December 17, 1955, raised anew the bogeyman of miscegenation because some people lamented the fact that this great civil rights hero had "married outside his race."

One office contemporary recalls Marshall making only one comment about the whispers: "I've paid my goddamn dues!"

There was really no office criticism and no big furor anywhere else comparable to the brouhaha over the White-Cannon marriage because (1) whites and blacks alike considered Cissy to be "black at heart" and a member of one of the several "races" Caucasian lawmakers said could not marry whites, (2) Marshall had not divorced a black woman in order to marry her, and (3) Cissy was so beloved by those who knew her that they thought Marshall had had a great stroke of good luck.

I went to New York shortly after their marriage and Marshall invited me to their apartment for dinner. "I'm gonna treat you to some of the best goddamn cooking you ever had," he said.

"Whose?"

"Mine!"

"Should I start praying now?"

"Hell, I make the best fucking beef stew in the world."

I took an immediate liking to Thurgood's bride because she was so unpretentious. But I quickly saw that Marshall was counting on her to "take care" of him in the sense of giving him her judgment on almost everything.

"Can I tell him the joke we heard last night?" Thurgood asked, after pouring each of us a bourbon.

"Why not?" Cissy said. That led to an exchange of "dirty jokes" that lasted through another bourbon or two — or three.

"Aren't you guys ever going to eat?" Cissy asked.

That was signal enough for Thurgood, who got up and walked to a pot in which the meat and vegetables for the stew were simmering gently. Marshall poured a slug of bourbon into the mixture. Then he ham-handedly spread flour into the pot, mixed with a big spoon, took a taste, and pronounced: "Too thick."

He poured in another gurgling slug of bourbon.

After repeating the "too thin" and "too thick" routine one more time, Marshall declared dinner ready. The bourbon I had drunk and the smell of the stew had made me ravenous. It may not have been "the best beef stew in the world," but it sure tasted like it.

Cissy would joke more than thirty years later that it was the only time in history three people got drunk on beef stew.

We didn't really get drunk — just oiled up enough to engage in some serious and, I think, memorable conversation about the status of Marshall's obsession with wiping out the trappings of white supremacy.

I mentioned that I had been naive in calling the 1954 *Brown* decision "Jim Crow's last stand." Marshall said that he had been overly boastful when, shortly after that decision, he said about defiant Southerners: "If they put any plan into effect in the morning, we will have them in court by the afternoon." Neither Marshall nor I had any idea at the time how many napless, trouble-filled afternoons he would face.

But it was obvious already that southern reaction to *Brown* was torrid, with much of the Deep South bitterly assailing both the NAACP and the Supreme Court. Eugene Cook, the attorney general of Georgia, had told the Peace Officers Association of Georgia: "The ugly truth about the NAACP and its origin, aims, and manipulators is so shocking as to stagger the imagination, but it is borne out by incontrovertible facts which can be established as matters of official record. These facts have been uncovered, checked, assembled, and correlated through many weeks of intensive investigation and cooperative effort by my staff and the staffs of Congressman James C. Davis of Georgia and Senator James O. Eastland of Mississippi."

Cook went on to name the vice presidents and directors of the NAACP who, he said, "have records of un-American activity." Among the people he cited (without defining what he called un-American activity) were the late Mary McLeod Bethune, librettist Oscar Hammerstein II, journalist Lewis Gannett, federal judge William Hastie, educators Benjamin E. Mays and Buell Gallagher, diplomat Ralph Bunche, magazine editor Norman Cousins, and former U.N. delegate Channing Tobias. To further "document" his charge, he cited five other NAACP board members as "well-known apologists for left-wing causes." They were Senator Wayne Morse, Eric Johnston of the motion picture industry, Mrs. Eleanor Roosevelt, C.I.O President Walter Reuther, and New York senator Herbert H. Lehman.

Cook's speech was played up boldly in the press of the Deep South. The Association of Citizens Councils printed thousands of copies of it and circulated them about the nation.

Roy Wilkins issued what he called "The NAACP Reply to the Cook Canard," declaring: "Mr. Cook knows that the NAACP is not a Communist organization or a Communist-front organization. He knews also that neither the Attorney General of the United States, the House Un-American Activities Committee nor any other official federal body has ever branded the NAACP as a Communist or Communist-front organization. He cannot show anywhere to anyone a listing of the NAACP as subversive by any responsible body."

In November, shortly after Cook spoke, Senator Eastland went before the Mississippi Association of Citizens Councils, which had been dubbed "the uptown Ku Klux Klan," and said: "The Supreme Court of the United States, in the false name of law and justice, has perpetrated a monstrous crime. It presents a clear threat and present danger, not only to the law, customs, traditions, and racial integrity of southern people, but also to the foundations of our republican form of government."

Then Eastland used the tactic of simply kicking the Citizens Council members in the balls — by playing upon their collective fears that they were caught up in a grotesque plot to put white women in bed with black men. Eastland said: "The court has responded to a radical pro-Communist political movement in this country. I do not have to tell you that this thing is broader and deeper than the NAACP. It is true that the NAACP is the front and is the weapon to force integration. It is the agent. It is the action group. It is backed by large organizations with tremendous power, who are attempting with success to mold the climate of public opinion, to brainwash and indoctrinate the American people to accept racial integration and mongrelization."

There was worse to come, but neither Marshall nor I wanted to believe it that winter night. We preferred to believe that Jonathan Daniels, editor of the *Raleigh* [North Carolina] *News and Observer*, knew more about the white man of the South than did Eastland, or Herman Talmadge of Georgia, or James F. Byrnes of South Carolina. Daniels had told an audience of the National Urban League:

"However sweeping the decision of the Supreme Court, after some dismay and much declamation, it will be met in the South with the good sense and the good will of the people of both races in a manner which will serve the children and honor America."

The Supreme Court had set the stage. The nation and the world could wait to see whether Eastland or Daniels spoke for the American South in the middle of the twentieth century.

When Marshall and I talked that night about the Supreme Court's final decree in *Brown v. Board of Education* — a decree that carried some troublesome language about enforcing the law "with all deliberate speed" — Marshall said to me some things I never heard him say publicly, probably because he could never be on record as criticizing a Court that had given him the greatest victory of his life. "How the fuck do you have 'all deliberate speed'? There's a contradiction in those terms." At one point, I lifted a glass and said to Marshall, "I want to simply congratulate you on your bravery, your willingness to go into these places and put your life at risk to try to save blacks accused of murder, or get decent pay for black teachers, or get blacks into the universities of their states."

"Oh, cut the shit," Marshall responded. With what I was sure was a bourbon slur, he added, "You forget just one little fucking thing. I go into these places and I come out, on the fastest vehicle moving. The brave blacks are the ones who have to live there after I leave."

I should have known better than to talk about Marshall's bravery. I had read in *Time* magazine that September his expression of love and admiration for the local blacks who had filed petitions and complaints, even though they knew they might lose their jobs, or even their lives.

"There isn't a threat known to men that they do not receive," Marshall told *Time*. "They're never out from under pressure. I don't think I could take it for a week. The possibility of violent death for them and their families is something they've learned to live with like a man learns to sleep with a sore arm."

Properly chastised, I told Marshall that I understood what he was saying, because I had just gone back to Prince Edward County, Virginia, to talk to the Reverend L. Frances Griffin, the black preacher who had aroused the black people of Prince Edward to file a lawsuit, to call in Marshall and other lawyers of the NAACP, such as Spottswood Robinson, and Oliver Hill, in order to break the chains of Jim Crow schooling. This Baptist preacher, Reverend Griffin, had said to the mostly timid, unhappy citizens of Virginia's Black Belt, "God helps those who help themselves. Pray! Go ahead and pray till your knees get sore. Then get up, and let's fight for our rights."

"How's Griffin doing?" Marshall asked.

I told him how I had rapped on Griffin's door a few weeks earlier, in November 1955, and seen a man answer who did not resemble the World War II stalwart, the brave challenger of Jim Crow that I had met in 1953. Here was a sad-faced man, coughing and wheezing, his eyes expressing his wish that my photographer and I had not caught him in such humiliating circumstances. Inside Griffin's house, I had stood puzzled. Where were the rugs? Why were the walls bare? What happened to the furniture that was in the back bedroom when I telephoned from there two years earlier? Why was the house so bitterly cold? I looked at his children, their faces marked by what I thought was ringworm. One child ran barefoot. The girls' hair was uncombed. Their clothing bore patches that now showed a need for patches. Over the wailing of the youngest child, who stood with tears streaming down a face marked with eczema, I asked the minister an embarrassedly silly question: "Well, how are things going in Prince Edward?"

Mr. Griffin rubbed his hands as if to warm them, breathing heavily and noisily like an overweight man with respiratory trouble. Then he smiled and said facetiously, "I tell you, foolery has turned to infamy." I smiled, recognizing a spark of the old orator and leader. Obviously, this was his way of saying that white men who had acted "foolishly" in 1953 were doing "infamous" deeds in 1955.

"So foolery has turned to infamy? In what way? What has happened to you?"

Mr. Griffin stared at the floor for a while, then said, "My furnace is out of order and I've got a bad cold."

"Have you been put under some unusual pressure?"

"This cold . . . I'm almost beat down," he said somewhat evasively. "I'd go out into the county with you, but I'd catch pneumonia."

The thirty-seven-year-old preacher went to the telephone to see if he could locate a guide to help us find some county people who might tell what they were experiencing. When he left the living room, his wife spoke: "I used to think I was courageous; now I'm afraid to stick my neck out."

I was still asking myself what had happened to Mrs. Griffin when her husband returned from the telephone to perplex me with these lines:

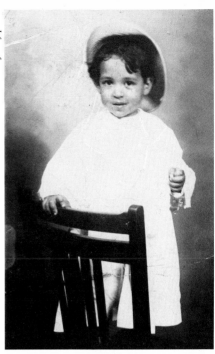

Marshall as a toddler — with the fair skin and straight hair that would cause one pro-segregation editor to denounce him as "that mulatto lawyer."

Marshall at two years old — with a hernia — and a foul temperament that irritated his mother.

Marshall says he got his fighting spirit in the genes of his mother, Norma Marshall (*left*), his father, and his aunt, Denmedia Dodson (*right*).

Hundreds of lynchings of black people during Marshall's formative years fueled his intense desire to deliver constitutional protections to all Americans.

Marshall dressed elegantly as a high school student, but his rascal-like behavior was considerably less than elegant.

Marshall (*right*), and his mentor, law dean Charles Houston (*left*), with Donald Murray, who got into the University of Maryland law school as part of "Marshall's revenge."

In the lean and violent days, Mrs. Eleanor Roosevelt became a staunch supporter of the NAACP and Marshall's fight for racial justice. *Standing, left to right:* Walter White, the NAACP's executive secretary; Roy Wilkins, who would later succeed White. *Sitting, left to right:* Dr. James J. McClendon, president of the Detroit branch of the NAACP; Mrs. Roosevelt, who spoke at the national convention in Detroit in 1943; Thurgood Marshall

Marshall (*right*) discusses anti–Jim Crow strategy with Roy Wilkins (*far left*), Henry Lee Moon (*standing*), longtime NAACP publicist, and Walter White (*middle*).

Among the lawyers recruited to fight Jim Crow in public schools were (*left to right*): Elmwood H. Chisholm, Oliver W. Hill, Marshall, Spottswood W. Robinson III, Harold Boulware of South Carolina, and Jack Greenberg.

Psychologist Kenneth Clark watches a black South Carolina youngster ponder a white doll and a black doll as part of Marshall's effort to prove that school segregation stigmatized black youngsters and damaged their personalities forever.

Marshall outlines his legal strategy for (*left to right*) Jack Greenberg; Derrick Bell, who would become a Harvard law professor; Constance Baker Motley, who would become a federal judge; and James Nabrit, Jr., who with his father fought many legal battles.

An angry Marshall escorts Autherine Lucy away from violence on the University of Alabama's campus after white regents ousted her.

Left to right, Roy Wilkins, Marshall, Walter White, and Marshall's deputy Robert Carter are jubilant after winning the *Brown v. Board of Education* decision declaring public school segregation unconstitutional.

Walter White's marriage to a white woman, Poppy Cannon, caused the greatest internal furor in the history of the NAACP. They are shown here with New York City mayor Vincent R. Impellitteri and Walter F. Shirley while attending a Duke Ellington concert to benefit the NAACP.

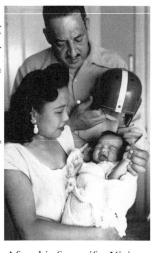

After his first wife, Vivien Burey, died early in 1955, Marshall married Cecilia Suyat, of Hawaii. They are shown here with their first son, Thurgood Marshall, Jr.

The Marshalls later had a second son, John William (*far right*), pictured here with his brother, Thurgood, Jr., and parents.

Thurgood and Cissy Marshall on a 1962 visit to Vermont.

The Marshalls in 1988.

Above: As an NAACP lawyer, Marshall won 29 of 32 cases that he argued before the Supreme Court. He was one of America's staunchest believers in "equal justice under the law."

Left: Marshall wears proudly the monkey-skin cape and headcovering that he got when he was made an honorary chief of the Kikuyu tribe after he went to Kenya in 1961 to help write that country's constitution, particularly the section that protected the rights of the white minority.

Marshall considered *Smith v. Allwright* (1944), in which he won the ballot for Texas blacks, one of the great achievements of his life. Here he sits with President Lyndon B. Johnson, with some of the nation's great civil rights leaders watching, as LBJ signs the Voting Rights Act of 1965.

Marshall wears the fancy garb of solicitor general of the United States, the lawyer who speaks for the U.S. government in cases before the Supreme Cour

Marshall meets with President Johnson in 1967 before the announcement that the president would nominate Marshall to serve on the U.S. Supreme Court.

Marshall as he posed after confirmation to the U.S. Supreme Court.

Cissy Marshall helps her husband to don his robe prior to his taking his seat on the Supreme Court on October 2, 1967.

The Supreme Court as Marshall joined it in 1967: *front row, left to right,* John M. Harla Hugo L. Black, Chief Justice Earl Warren, William O. Douglas, William J. Brennan, Jr. *back row, left to right,* Abe Fortas, Potter Stewart, Byron White, and Justice Marshall.

President Jimmy Carter watches proudly as Marshall swears in the late Patricia Harris as Secretary of Health, Education and Welfare. Harris's husband holds the Bible.

President Reagan poses on the left of Chief Justice Warren Burger in 1982. In ranking American presidents, Marshall said Reagan was "at the bottom."

In 1983 the Marshalls share a laugh with Vice President George Bush. Marshall wasn't laughing after Reagan and Bush packed the Supreme Court with right-wingers.

Justice Marshall chats with author Carl T. Rowan prior to two prize-winning Rowan television specials on the U.S. Constitution and on "Thurgood Marshall the Man."

o person ever took a seat on the U.S. Supreme Court under more humiliating circumances than did Clarence Thomas. Two cartoons by Sean DeLonas of the *New York Post* e illustrative of the ridicule that continues.

"HONEY, IT'S LONG DONG SILVER. HE'D LIKE TO CONGRATULATE YOU ON YOUR CONFIRMATION."

Baltimore, where Marshall once was not allowed to use a downtown toilet, now has this statue symbolizing his greatness.

Marshall family photo

Justice Marshall holds a press conference upon retirement, telling reporters "I'm falling apart."

Prize-winning photo by John McDonnell of the Washington Post

Chief Justice William Rehnquist and Justice Byron White watch intently as new justice Clarence Thomas signs documents at his investiture ceremony.

Photo by Ken Heinen

Chill penury has repressed my noble rage
And froze the genial current of my soul.

Chill penury? Was this the minister's way of saying that he had
run into terrible economic distress? "What has happened to you?" I
asked again.

"Many things have happened since the Court struck down segregation. As a result, my situation has become somewhat impecunious — I think you've noticed that."

The minister strode into the empty bedroom, where he gulped
down two spoons of cough syrup and half whispered to me:
"They've almost beat me down."

Now Mr. Griffin was talking freely, telling of the price he was
paying for being the leader, for telling Negroes to fight as well as
pray, to demand instead of beg.

After the Court ruling, when he led Negroes to reject a plan for
"voluntary segregation," three liberal white men in Farmville called
Mr. Griffin. "They said they wanted to tip me off as a favor that I
would be wise not to buy anything else on credit. But like many other
people, I already was carrying credit to my full limit. Suddenly I was
faced with demands for full payment. I strained in every direction
to find cash.

"Take the fuel companies — they always made it a practice to sell
oil on a yearly basis: you buy what you need this winter, and if you
pay for it by the following September you can get the following winter's oil on credit. Suddenly I was notified that I had fifteen days to
pay my fuel bill.

"When I went to buy clothes for the children or food for the
family I was told I had to have cash. In a country built on credit,
suddenly I had to have cash."

Griffin was paid $175 a month by the church (there was no com-
pensation for his work for the NAACP), so these demands for cash
were more than he could meet.

"All of a sudden, Bruce Oil Company and Brickert Oil Company
and this place and that place and places I can't even remember were
serving warrants on me," Mr. Griffin added. "I had bought a 1949
Buick secondhand. The Brickert people repossessed that.

"First thing I knew I had a warrant sworn out by them to make
me pay for the new tires that they repossessed with the car.

"They didn't even phone me to say that I still was obligated to
pay for the tires. I would have paid them without whimpering. But
they just swore out their warrant."

A lawyer advised Mr. Griffin that he could put an end to all this by declaring bankruptcy, but the minister refused.

"I've never answered a single warrant. I just go on paying them all bit by bit, whenever I get a piece of money. Sure, it means that if the furnace breaks down I may be a while getting it fixed. If shoes wear out or a chair falls apart, I can't replace them. But I didn't give any quarter when I was leading my fight, and I can't ask for any.

"I don't turn a heel to ask for help, because I'd be losing the last vestige of my own character."

Mr. Griffin said he was thinking about a couple of offers he had received from churches in other cities. Then he looked at his wife and his poorly clothed children and added: "But I've got sense enough not to leave in the wintertime. Anyhow, I owe something to the people here. I led the Negroes here into this fight. I owe them something."

As I finished telling Thurgood about the state of this unglorified warrior, this dream maker, Reverend Griffin, I noticed that Marshall was wiping his eyes furtively, as if to preserve the fiction that "real men don't cry." Suddenly my own cheeks were wet.

"I gotta go," I said. "We all got a helluva lot to do tomorrow."

The next morning I awakened early, my mind agitated by the memory of something Marshall had said during dinner. We were speculating about where the next eruption of defiance against *Brown* would occur. We both named a few hot spots, but Little Rock was not among them. The educational, civic, newspaper, and other leadership seemed to guarantee a peaceful transition to integration.

I lay there remembering that Marshall had said, "But I'm watching that new governor of Arkansas. He worries the shit out of me."

I knew in the first days of 1956 that I had to do some research on this governor.

When I got back to Minneapolis, I learned that Orval Eugene Faubus had been born in 1910 on a farm at Combs, in southern Madison County. He had grown up working with his father, Sam, cutting hickory staves for a lumber mill at Greasy Creek, Arkansas. His self-educated father was a known Socialist, an advocate of neutrality in World War I. Orval himself had not finished high school until he was twenty-three, although he had become an elementary school teacher at the age of eighteen. After getting out of high school he had married a young woman named Alta, and the two of them had traveled as "fruit tramps," or migrant harvesters. They had wound up in the Pacific Northwest, and when the fruit had been plucked, he went to work as a lumberjack for a while.

I wondered why in the world Marshall could have any concerns about Faubus, who had gone to Commonwealth College in Mena, Arkansas, a leftist labor school that was the basis of charges in the 1954 gubernatorial campaign that Faubus might be a Communist. Faubus had deflected such charges by telling voters that he had fought in five major campaigns in World War II and had received the Bronze Star and the Combat Infantry badge. Surely he would be no enemy of black people.

As I dug deeper, I discovered some things that Marshall might have known when expressing his concerns. Hugh Patterson, publisher of the *Arkansas Gazette,* told me Faubus had based his 1954 campaign on an ad in which he said "THE TRUTH IS — that Arkansas is not ready for complete and sudden mixing of the races in the public schools" and "THE TRUTH IS — that Communist agitators and prejudicial interests are even now planning to exploit the differences between Whites and Negroes in an effort to create discord, disorder and disunity!"

On May 24, 1955, seven days after the Supreme Court ordered desegregation "with all deliberate speed," the Little Rock school board had approved a desegregation plan under which grades ten through twelve would be integrated in the fall of 1957, with the desegregation of junior high and elementary schools to follow, and the desegregation of the entire school system to be completed by 1963.

A group of blacks went to court claiming that this was too slow, but the federal courts upheld the school board's plan.

Marshall's worries took on substance in January 1956, when Damon Stetson of the *New York Times* interviewed Faubus and asked him: "Do you feel integration is going to come eventually, even if slowly, or that it will never be accepted here?"

Faubus replied: "The Roman Empire integrated the descendants of its Ethiopian slaves, but it took more than eighteen hundred years to accomplish. If complete integration ever comes to Arkansas, it will be a slow process. No one can predict with accuracy whether it will ever be accomplished, or how soon.

"It should be obvious that centuries-old customs, and regional traditions, cannot be changed overnight — even by court edict."

Still, there seemed no major reason to consider Faubus an enemy of black people or of desegregation.

But what neither I nor the NAACP knew was that early in 1956 the segregationist businessmen and planters of East Arkansas had formed a committee to preserve segregation and Faubus had met with them. Faubus agreed to get an appointment for some of these segregationists with Governor Thomas B. Stanley of Virginia, who could explain to them the Virginia theory of "massive resistance," and the thinking behind "interposition," which Virginians thought to mean that the state could interpose itself between its people and the federal government and defy any decision by the Supreme Court.

Marshall would soon see the burdens that *Brown II* had put upon the process of desegregating public schools. The 1954 pledge of obedience by the Little Rock school board became tainted in 1957 when school superintendent Virgil T. Blossom went around the city campaigning for acceptance of the board's desegregation plan by saying that it was "developed to provide as little integration as possible for as long as possible legally."

Segregationists naturally concluded that Blossom's heart wasn't in the desegregation plan. So the racists in the Arkansas legislature got busy, and in the winter of 1957 got four acts passed, one of which made it illegal to require any child to enroll in or attend any school in which both white and Negro children were enrolled. Blossom admitted he had also inspired the formation of a group called the "Mothers' League of Central High School." On August 27, 1957, 250 of these mothers called upon Faubus "to prevent forcible integration."

Meanwhile, Blossom and other school officials had gone through an incredible, and certainly unconstitutional, procedure. They had screened nine hundred black children of high school age and decided that only thirteen would be eligible to go to Central High in the first stage of desegregation. Four of these youngsters said, "No, thanks." The nine black students remaining, all at or near the top of their classes in a new all-Negro school that had been built to prevent desegregation, would be the ones to go to Central High along with nineteen hundred to two thousand white students.

The night of September 2, the day before these youngsters who would make the history books as "the Little Rock Nine" were to enter Central High, Faubus dispatched units of the Arkansas National Guard to the all-white school and placed it "off-limits" to "colored students." Little Rock's mayor Woodrow Wilson Mann, its chief of police, the school board, officials at Central High, were shocked, because none had seen any evidence of potential violence or upheaval at the school. Faubus's action was inexplicable.

The next day Mann told the press:

> . . . The Governor has called out the National Guard to put down trouble where none existed. He did so without a request from

those of us who are directly responsible for preservation of peace and order. The only effect is to create tension where none existed. I call the Governor's attention to the fact that after almost a week of sensational developments brought about by his own actions, the Little Rock police have not had a single case of interracial violence reported to them. This is clear evidence that the Governor's excuse for calling out the Guard is simply a hoax.

Those nine black youngsters went to Central High the morning of September 3 and found National Guardsmen standing shoulder to shoulder to block their entry. Worse yet, they found that they had to run the gauntlet of an angry mob of white people. Elizabeth Eckford, the first black child to arrive, described the mob this way:

"They glared at me with a mean look and I was very frightened and I didn't know what to do. As the crowd came close to me, somebody started yelling, 'Lynch her! Lynch her!'

"I thought I would find safety by running to the bus stop and getting on a bus. As I ran toward a bench at the bus stop, an old woman spat on me.

"When I finally got to the bench, I was so tired and scared that I didn't think I could go another step. I heard the mob shouting, 'Drag her over to this tree! Let's take care of the nigger!' Then a white man sat beside me on the bench and said, 'Don't let them see you cry.' Then a white lady took my hand and led me onto a bus, where she sat next to me. She asked me my name, and tried to make conversation, but I don't think I ever answered her."

Mann was a lame-duck mayor whose term would expire in November. What mattered was the stance that President Eisenhower would take, because this was a historic event — an extraordinary case of a governor defying the federal government, a great constitutional crisis.

Asked about Little Rock in his weekly press conference, Ike said, in his bungling way:

I know this is a slow process. The Supreme Court in its decision of 1954 pointed out the emotional difficulties that would be encountered by a Negro, even if given — or by Negroes if given — equal but separate schools, and I think, probably their reasoning was correct, at least I have no quarrel with it.

But there are very strong emotions on the other side, people that see a picture of a mongrelization of the race, they call it. There are very strong emotions, and we are going to whip this thing in the long run by Americans being true to themselves and not merely by law.

Educators in America were dismayed by Eisenhower's failures to give stronger support to federal judge Ronald N. Davies and the white Little Rock citizens who were trying to obey the law and desegregate the schools. Faubus sent the president a telegram that said:

> . . . THE QUESTION AT ISSUE AT LITTLE ROCK THIS MOMENT IS NOT INTEGRATION VS. SEGREGATION. . . . THE QUESTION NOW IS WHETHER OR NOT THE HEAD OF A SOVEREIGN STATE CAN EXERCISE HIS CONSTITUTIONAL POWERS AND DISCRETION IN MAINTAINING PEACE AND GOOD ORDER WITHIN HIS JURISDICTION, BEING ACCOUNTABLE TO HIS OWN GOOD CONSCIENCE AND TO HIS OWN PEOPLE.

The school board asked the federal district court to allow suspension of the desegregation program. Judge Davies refused, saying: "In an organized society there can be nothing but ultimate confusion and chaos if court decrees are flouted, whatever the pretext."

On September 20, the court enjoined the governor and officers of the National Guard from blocking the attendance of Negro children at Central High. The Guard was withdrawn. But on Monday, September 23, when the black youngsters were escorted to school by Little Rock and Arkansas state policemen, there was such a huge mob around the school that the youngsters had to be withdrawn before they finished a full day.

Ironically, before the Guard was called out, President Eisenhower invited Faubus to his summer home in Newport, Rhode Island, on September 14, where they discussed the school situation at length. Faubus was emboldened by an Eisenhower statement of July 17:

> I can't imagine any set of circumstances that would ever induce me to send federal troops into any area to enforce the orders of a federal court, because I believe that the common sense of America will never require it.

Monday, September 23, brought the greatest turmoil since the *Brown* decision when an angry mob forced the nine black students from the building. That same evening Eisenhower denounced the "disgraceful occurrences" and warned that continued obstruction would bring out "whatever force may be necessary."

Mayor Mann sent a frantic telegram to Ike:

> THE IMMEDIATE NEED FOR FEDERAL TROOPS IS URGENT. THE MOB WAS MUCH LARGER IN NUMBERS AT 8 A.M. THAN AT ANY TIME YESTERDAY. PEOPLE ARE CONVERGING ON THE SCENE FROM ALL

DIRECTIONS. MOB IS ARMED AND ENGAGING IN FISTICUFFS AND
OTHER ACTS OF VIOLENCE. SITUATION IS OUT OF CONTROL AND
POLICE CANNOT DISPERSE THE MOB. I AM PLEADING TO YOU AS
PRESIDENT OF THE UNITED STATES, IN THE INTEREST OF HUMAN-
ITY, LAW AND ORDER, AND THE CAUSE OF DEMOCRACY WORLD-
WIDE, TO PROVIDE THE NECESSARY FEDERAL TROOPS WITHIN
SEVERAL HOURS.

Ike's chief of staff, Sherman Adams, had written that Ike found
the idea of using the military "repugnant." Still, ten thousand Arkansas National Guardsmen were federalized, and one thousand
paratroopers from the 101st Airborne Division were rushed into the
area — incredibly, under the command of Major General Edwin A.
Walker, who later revealed himself as an extreme right-winger and
racist.

In justifying his actions, Eisenhower cited a statute that George
Washington had used to suppress the Whisky Rebellion in 1794:

Whenever, by reasons of unlawful obstruction, combinations, or
assemblages of persons, or rebellion against the authority of the
Government of the United States, it shall become impracticable in
the judgment of the President to enforce, by the ordinary course
of judicial proceedings, the laws of the United States within any
state or territory, it shall be lawful for the President to call forth
the militia of any or all the states and to employ such parts of the
land and naval forces of the United States as he may deem necessary to enforce the faithful execution of the laws. . . .

Regular army troops would stay at Central High for two months
and two days, when they were replaced by members of the federalized Arkansas National Guard.

If Eisenhower was, as Chief Justice Warren and others thought,
a segregationist at heart, why did he send in the federal troops? Why
did he federalize the Arkansas National Guard? In a 1986 interview,
Marshall said to me, "Eisenhower didn't do anything except to undermine the school decision."

"Even though he sent the troops into Little Rock?"

"That was done, believe it or not, by Jim Hagerty, his press secretary. Hagerty was as cold-blooded a bird as you'll ever want to find.
He persuaded Eisenhower to send the troops in," Marshall said.

The Arkansas crisis went to the Supreme Court. Chief Justice
Warren said the Court wanted to make a decision in time for the
Little Rock board to make arrangements for the 1958–59 school

year, so a special term of the Court was convened on August 28. Arkansas lawyer Wiley Branton called Thurgood for help.

The late Wiley Branton told me, and put on paper for the *Arkansas Law Review* in 1987:

> Thurgood could be stubborn and uncompromising where issues of basic civil rights or civil liberties were involved, and he also developed a streak of meanness against organizations and individuals who opposed his views. Unfortunately, this attitude sometimes carried over into areas where there could be a genuine dispute as to strategies or techniques in seeking mutually desired goals.
>
> In my capacity as chief counsel for the black plaintiffs in the Little Rock school integration case, I had very little contact with Thurgood Marshall during the early stages.
>
> In 1957 I phoned Thurgood and requested his personal involvement. I have always felt that it was Thurgood Marshall's stubbornness that caused the United States government to finally enter the case in support of the rights of black children. A high-ranking official from the Department of Justice attempted to pressure me into recommending that the black children who were seeking admission to Central High School return to the all-black schools. He argued that we should allow a year for attitudes to change and tempers to cool before making any further attempts to integrate the schools. Marshall had a verbal clash with the Justice Department official who suggested the delay. When Marshall returned to New York, the U.S. Attorney in Little Rock told me what a fine lawyer he and his colleague thought me to be and suggested that I was really the chief counsel and certainly did not need Thurgood Marshall to tell me how to handle the Little Rock school case. I immediately recognized an effort to create a split between Thurgood and me. Neither Thurgood nor I would agree that constitutional rights should be delayed to allow time for people to accept the law of the land.

Marshall was at his eloquent best in presenting before the Supreme Court an argument that he and Wiley Branton had developed with the help of Jack Greenberg and Bill Coleman. The essence of Marshall's argument was that

> neither overt public resistance, nor the possibility of it, constitutes sufficient cause to nullify the orders of the federal court directing petitioners to proceed with their desegregation plan. This court and other courts have consistently held that the preservation of

public peace may not be accomplished by interference with rights created by the Federal Constitution.

The forces at work to frustrate the Constitution and the authority of the federal courts were deliberately set in motion by the Governor of a state whose school system is under mandate to achieve conformity with the Constitution. Here one state agency, the School Board, seeks to be relieved of its constitutional obligation by pleading the *force majeure* brought to bear by another facet of state power. To solve this problem by further delaying the constitutional rights of respondents is unthinkable.

This case involves not only vindication of the constitutional rights declared in *Brown,* but indeed the very survival of the Rule of Law.

On September 12, 1958, in *Cooper v. Aaron,* Chief Justice Warren spoke for a unanimous Court, saying:

As this case reaches us it raises questions of the highest importance to the maintenance of our federal system of government. It necessarily involves a claim by the Governor and Legislature of a State that there is no duty on state officials to obey federal court orders resting on the Court's considered interpretation of the United States Constitution. Specifically it involves actions by the Governor and Legislature of Arkansas upon the premise that they are not bound by our holding in *Brown v. Board of Education.*

The constitutional rights of respondents are not to be sacrificed or yielded to the violence and disorder which have followed upon the actions of the Governor and Legislature. As this Court said some 41 years ago in a unanimous opinion in a case involving another aspect of racial segregation: "It is urged that this proposed segregation will promote the public peace by preventing race conflicts. Desirable as this is, and important as is the preservation of the public peace, this aim cannot be accomplished by laws or ordinances which deny rights created or protected by the Federal Constitution." Thus law and order are not here to be preserved by depriving the Negro children of their constitutional rights.

Cooper v. Aaron was a profound message that the Warren Court would never permit mobocracy to overwhelm the law of the land. It was a decision hailed by Marshall, but also a decision that further inflamed Faubus and the segregationists of Arkansas and across the land. It intensified the racists' hatred of Warren and the Court.

The reaction in Little Rock was to close the public schools for the

1958–1959 year. Still, the violence intensified. During the year the schools were closed, there were more than five hundred incidents of violence, including bombings of houses, churches, synagogues, and drive-by shootings by half-drunk whites roaming through black neighborhoods. No segregationist target had priority over the home of Daisy Bates, the state chairman of the NAACP, and her husband, L. C. Bates, the publisher of the city's black newspaper. Bombs and gunfire had hit their home several times. On one of my trips to Little Rock in 1958, I stayed with the Bateses. We were so afraid of the bombers and gunmen that we stayed up virtually all night playing poker.

When Marshall and Branton were in Little Rock in connection with the legal struggles, they, too, stayed at the home of the Bateses. Branton told me that he and Thurgood played a macabre little game over who would get the twin bed next to the window that the racists had blown out. He said that he carried two nameplates and placed the one with his name on the bed farthest from the window, only to find that, in the wee hours when he and Marshall got a chance to go to bed, Marshall somehow had had the signs changed so that Branton was sleeping next to the window in the greatest point of peril.

By this time, Little Rock was a city at war against itself. Families were caught up in angry verbal conflict, business partnerships were strained; the *Arkansas Gazette* was waging an heroic, Pulitzer Prize–winning campaign to get the people of the state to "do the right thing"; the rival *Arkansas Democrat* had become a virulent mouthpiece of the segregationists. I went by the *Gazette*, where editor Harry Ashmore and I talked about how terribly wounded economically the state had become because of the blatant attempts to defy the Supreme Court.

From 1954 through 1957, eighteen new plants, valued at over $6 million, with two thousand new jobs, had moved to Little Rock. During the racial strife over schools in 1958 and 1959, not one new plant moved to that city.

My most touching moment was not during an interview with one of the black youngsters, or with Marshall and his associates. It came when *Gazette* publisher Hugh Patterson said to me: "You know, you are my friend, my colleague on the National Citizens Council for Better Schools. You are a journalistic peer whom I respect beyond all bounds. I should be taking you to lunch today at one of the private clubs to which I belong. But they tell me that I am not allowed to bring you or any other Negro to lunch at my clubs. When they told me that it became clear to me that the segregationists have not simply deprived you of freedom, they have stripped my liberty away from me. I don't know why it took me so long to understand that millions of white people are terrible victims of white bigotry."

The 1955 "all deliberate speed" decision generated predictions that it would provoke "a generation of litigation." That turned out to be one of the great all-time understatements regarding the American judicial system. Thirty-seven years after *Brown II,* the Supreme Court still faces myriad lawsuits over such issues as, What is a segregated school? Is it de facto segregation, where the courts cannot become involved, or is it de jure segregation, imposed by some level of government, which makes it a violation of the Fourteenth Amendment? If it is de jure segregation, is it district-wide or region-wide, and how broad must the remedies be? Is busing of children outside of their neighborhoods in order to achieve "racial balance" a proper constitutional remedy? Is it permissible to bus children across city/suburban lines in order to wipe out segregation?

Over the years the Supreme Court created a million headaches and a field day for lawyers when it insisted that those challenging Jim Crow schools were required to present proof that some official moved with *intent* to achieve de jure segregation.

All of a sudden the Supreme Court was besieged by school desegregation cases from Indianapolis, Omaha, Milwaukee, and Dayton, Ohio. And just as suddenly, there was violence, not only in places like Birmingham and Nashville, but in Pontiac, Michigan, in Boston, and other cities of the North.

Richard Nixon had put the word "forced" in front of "busing" and the phrase "forced busing" became a powerful negative factor, working to diminish respect for the Supreme Court and the willingness of Americans to desegregate their schools. It should be noted that many *black* parents spoke out with indignation when they saw that some desegregation plans required their children to take a bus for many miles rather than go to the school nearest their home.

In 1978, Jack Greenberg, who had become director of the NAACP Legal Defense and Education Fund, would assert in an interview that the Supreme Court had become aware of the mood of the American public and that the Court was confronted with the growing doubt in Congress and the White House as to whether the difficulties of integrating the schools were greater than any potential benefit.

Marshall would later recall for me the elation he felt in 1954 when the *Brown* decision outlawing segregated schools was handed down; then the unease he had felt in 1955 when "all deliberate speed" became the form of remedy.

"I knew we had problems ahead," he said to me in 1986, "but I sure as hell never imagined we'd get to this sad state of affairs."

CHAPTER SIXTEEN

DREAM BREAKER GEORGE WALLACE

DURING THE ORAL ARGUMENTS in the *Brown* cases in 1952 through 1956, Marshall was unwavering in his assertions that if a resolute Supreme Court issued a stern decree, and if the executive branch supported it without double-talk, the American people would obey, and desegregation could be achieved without major social conflict. But Marshall — and the justices — had already seen evidence that many people across America were determined to use demagoguery and physical violence to maintain the separation of the races.

When I asked Marshall why, in the face of the angry opposition to desegregating professional schools in Oklahoma and Alabama, he kept telling the justices that integrating the public schools of South Carolina would be "no problem," he said: "I believed, and I still believe, that if the Court had said, 'THIS IS THE LAW! DO IT NOW!' we would have avoided years of strife. In any event, what lawyer goes into a court and says, 'I want you to decree justice, but I want to warn you that the people who hate justice are going to rebel'?"

Marshall had his reasons for dismissing rather cavalierly the politicians who were becoming his angry foes — George Wallace in Alabama, Strom Thurmond in South Carolina, James Eastland in Mississippi. Perhaps because of his success in forcing the University of Maryland to accept black law student Donald Murray; because of his triumphs in getting the Supreme Court to order the University of Oklahoma to admit G. W. McLaurin and Ada Lois Sipuel Fisher;

because he had forced the University of Texas to admit Heman Sweatt; and because the NAACP had helped to pressure the University of Arkansas to admit blacks without a court order, Thurgood Marshall had millions of Americans imagining a new era of higher education.

Marshall would soon learn that the universities and statehouses of the South were full of dream breakers, and that no state would put up more resistance to desegregation in higher education than Alabama. He was elated that the University of Alabama had accepted two black women, Autherine Juanita Lucy and Polly Anne Myers, in 1952. But when Miss Lucy and Miss Myers showed up at the University of Alabama in Tuscaloosa to register on September 20, 1952, they were told that an error had been made in the admissions office — someone apparently was not aware that state laws forbade the university to admit Negroes. The two young black women went to the NAACP, which took their case to the United States District Court in Birmingham.

Marshall soon saw that where university officials are truly devious, and where the commitment to black semislavery is overwhelming, those trying to keep a university all-white could put up a legal fight for years. It was not until October 13, 1955, that the University of Alabama ran out of legal stalls and dodges and saw the United States Supreme Court reinstate an order by federal judge Hobart Grooms in Birmingham that the university had to admit Negroes.

But on January 31, 1956, officials in the university notified Miss Myers (she was now Mrs. Polly Anne Myers Hudson) that the trustees had rejected her application because "her conduct and marital record have been such she does not meet the admission standards of the University," whatever that meant. Miss Lucy was notified that she could register February 1 and begin classes on February 3. On the morning of February 1, both Miss Lucy and Mrs. Hudson went to the campus, but Mrs. Hudson was turned away immediately. Dean of women Sarah Healy took Miss Lucy into her office and gave her "V.I.P." registration procedures, but told her that she would not be given a room in a dormitory or be allowed to eat in the cafeteria. Miss Lucy called this "pathetic and unreasonable" and left campus to see her lawyer, Arthur Shores, in Birmingham.

The next day, the university decided to try another legal stall. It asked the U.S. Circuit Court of Appeals in New Orleans for a new hearing, which was denied. The following day, Miss Lucy commuted sixty miles from Birmingham, necessarily, because she had been denied on-campus housing, and found campus police stationed around and in the corridors of Smith Hall, where her first class was to take place. She took a seat alone, in the front row. When she left Smith Hall for her next class, in Graves Hall, campus policemen went with her. In this class she sat in a row with white students, one of whom leaned over to wish her luck. That night the Associated Press announced to the nation that "the first Negro in history attended the University of Alabama today, a lonely figure accompanied by blue-clad police officers." But that same night, a crowd of some twelve hundred students assembled around a burning cross, exploding fire-crackers, singing "Dixie," and shouting, "Keep 'Bama white." They marched on the residence of the university's president, Oliver C. Carmichael, but learned that he was not at home. Some drunken fraternity members were shouting, "Hey, hey, ho, ho, where the hell did the nigger go? Hey, hey, ho, ho, Autherine must go!" Soon high school students, factory workers, townspeople from Tuscaloosa, and members of the White Citizens Council were at the university, screaming and shouting and inciting each other to violence. They began to throw rocks at buses and cars driven by Negroes. On February 5, Miss Lucy arrived at Smith Hall to find that some fifty men, night-shift workers from the Goodrich Tire Plant and from a nearby foundry, were waiting for her. She slipped past them and got inside Smith Hall, but as she left, escorted by dean of women Healy, and assistant to the president Jeff Bennett, the men began to pummel them with eggs and rocks as they shouted at Bennett, "Nigger-lovin' son of a bitch," and at Dean Healy, "Hit the nigger-lovin' whore." The three jumped into Healy's car as a rock cracked the windshield and smashed one window. The mob chased them across the campus, hurling more eggs and stones and bashing in the rear window of the dean's car, all to chants of "Keep 'Bama white!" and "Lynch the nigger!"

Miss Lucy holed up in Graves Hall until the afternoon, when highway patrolmen whisked her out to an automobile, where she lay on the floor as the car passed through the mob.

The university asked Governor James O. Folsom to call out the National Guard, but Folsom refused, saying, "It's normal for all races not to be overly fond of each other . . . we are not excited."

Three days later, on Monday, as the mob violence continued, university trustees voted to exclude Lucy until further notice. Attorney Shores conferred with Thurgood and said publicly that it was "regrettable that the university would submit to mob rule." He said he would go back to the federal court if Miss Lucy was not reinstated within two days.

On February 9, 1956, NAACP lawyers asked Judge Grooms to order the university to readmit Miss Lucy. But these lawyers made what Marshall later would admit was a serious mistake in claiming that university officials intentionally had plotted and participated in "a cunning stratagem" to have the mob create an atmosphere of danger and thus give the university an excuse for expelling the black woman.

Carmichael called these charges "untrue, unwarranted and outrageous." The board of trustees quickly seized this as an excuse for expelling Lucy, claiming she had made "false, defamatory, impertinent, and scandalous charges." The trustees said, "No educational institution could maintain necessary disciplinary action if any student, regardless of race, guilty of the conduct of Autherine J. Lucy, be permitted to remain."

Marshall flew to Alabama to comfort the young black woman, and to give a plane-side denunciation of the racists before escorting her to New York. But the trustees were winning the public relations battle. Folsom, who had been regarded as a moderate-to-liberal southern politician, accused the NAACP and "professional outside agitators" of making it impossible to quell the Tuscaloosa riot of February 26. He said, "If the professional agitators had been interested only in entering a student at the University of Alabama . . . then they would not have come with their own cameramen and newsmen. They would not have made such an exception out of that student's routine activities . . . the professional agitators are the worst enemies the Negro people have. . . ." It meant nothing to Folsom that cameramen and newsmen came because Autherine Lucy was the first black person to be admitted to Alabama in the history of that institution. Or that the press, lawyers, and police were there because the university and other state officials had made it clear that they wanted to defy Judge Grooms and the United States Supreme Court.

Folsom, university trustees, and others put out a story that ordinary citizens had become inflamed because Miss Lucy "arrived on campus in a Cadillac," as though that were a reason to deny her admission. (She arrived in a Pontiac.) Another story put out was that "Autherine Lucy paid her admission fees with a $100 bill," leading to whispers that no little black gal from Maringo County could have a $100 bill unless the communists had given it to her. Lucy and Marshall had won their battle in the courts, and they were big winners in the eyes of the outside world, but in the propaganda arena of Alabama and the United States, they were losers.

Autherine Lucy was famous in millions of eyes and infamous in others, and that made her a twenty-four-hour-a-day target of many newsmen who meant her well, but hundreds who meant her ill. Marshall tried to find New York housing in which she could hide out on her own. That failed, so he moved her into his apartment with his pregnant bride, Cissy, who welcomed her warmly.

Miss Lucy, twenty-six at the time, would tell me thirty-six years later that "I just felt so secure with Mr. Marshall and his wife. She taught me how to make blueberry muffins. He told me that if the baby was a girl they would name her Autherine . . . but it was a boy. I stayed with them for two weeks while the storm raged in Alabama, and across the nation. Really, I just hope I get a chance to tell him before he dies how grateful I have been over all these years for the protection and the kindness he gave to me."

Marshall's rush to Alabama to rescue Miss Lucy revealed something profound about this man who could and did put on an act of gruffness, rudeness, crudeness, if he thought it necessary to shock someone. The Lucy episode tells us that the sarcastic courtroom lawyer, the hard-drinking, often-bluffing poker player, was a deliberate coverup for a sentimental man whose heart bled in red ruptures for the brave people who joined him in battle . . . and lost. That's why he continued for more than a decade to send bits of money that he could not spare to Oklahoma prisoner W. D. Lyons. That's why, after getting Ada Lois Sipuel and G. W. McLaurin into the University of Oklahoma, and Heman Sweatt into the University of Texas, Marshall felt a special sense of failure and guilt that Wallace and other Alabama racists had outwitted him, had humiliated Autherine Lucy and prevented her from attending the Tuscaloosa institution. Giving safe harbor to Autherine Lucy in those cruel days of 1956 was the essence of a truly caring man.

For the rest of his years, Marshall would look at Alabama as a rock in his craw, because that university stayed Jim Crow until 1963. And even when the next Negroes attempted admission, Marshall would sit outside the fray as a judge and see that the passions of defiance in Alabama were greater than ever. It would really gall him that a little bantam rooster of a man from Barbour County named George Corley Wallace would precipitate a colossal confrontation between the federal government and that state.

Wallace did more than kill a lot of dreams of the black people of Alabama; he ruined the political chances of people like Hubert Humphrey and taught some ugly political lessons that would be used in later years by Richard Nixon, Ronald Reagan, and George Bush. Anyone who wonders how America reached the state of racial polarization that exists today, or wants to know how and why the Democratic party lost the "solid South," must look closely at the life and times of Wallace. This pugnacious Alabaman wrote a long new chapter on the uses of phony populism and racial demagoguery in the gaining of political power. Men who professed to show contempt for Wallace would later embrace his tactics and techniques without apparent shame.

Wallace was born to relative privilege in a little red-clay town called Clio, in Barbour County, in the southeast corner of Alabama. His grandfather, Dr. G. O. Wallace, was a prominent physician in this community of less than a thousand people. He was also the probate judge for six years and is said to have had far more influence on George Wallace than did George's father, George Corley Wallace, Sr. George Wallace, Jr., was virtually weaned on politics, and as a teenager was sent to the state legislature to campaign for a job as a page. He already was declaring his intention to run for political office.

When George was a teenager his father gave him and his brothers Jerald and Jack a set of boxing gloves each, and then gave them a few boxing lessons. George turned out to be a good boxer and was mean as hell in employing his skills. He fought in the bantamweight class at about 118 pounds and, his records claim, won twenty-five fights, lost four, and once boxed to a draw. He was the bantamweight champion in the Alabama Golden Gloves competition two years in a row. Wallace's political skills became obvious when he began to advertise himself as "the Barbour Battler." His shrewdness became even more obvious when he turned down a chance to become an officer in the Army Air Corps in 1942. Friends claim that Wallace said he preferred to be an enlisted man because he would be a politician at war's end, and "there are a lot more enlisted men voters than there are officers."

Wallace knew exactly what he was doing, because in 1952, after three terms in the state legislature, he ran for circuit court judge in an area covering Barbour and two other counties. His opponent was Preston Clayton, a highly-respected state senator who was the favorite. But Clayton had been a lieutenant colonel in the Army, which inspired Wallace to go from one campaign appearance to another shouting, "Now, all you officers vote for Clayton, and all you privates vote for me." Wallace won easily.

Wallace made his first impressions in the national political arena at the 1948 Democratic National Convention in Philadelphia, where Minneapolis mayor Hubert Humphrey set off a bombshell by declaring that it was time "for the Democratic Party to move out of the shadow of states' rights into the bright sunshine of human rights." That was a clue for Wallace to go to battle. When Strom Thurmond and the Dixiecrats walked out of the convention after failing to defeat Humphrey's civil rights plank in the party platform, Wallace stayed, vowing to fight from the floor. He did, and lost, but the word got back to Alabama that their man had waged a valiant struggle against Humphrey and others who were "out to humiliate the South."

In 1958 Wallace ran for governor against state attorney general John Patterson, an avowed racist. Wallace ran a racist campaign, too, but reputedly was more moderate about it than Patterson. After Patterson won, Wallace told a group of his political supporters, "John Patterson out-nigguhed me. And I'm never goin' to be out-nigguhed again." So in 1962, when Wallace ran for governor again, he "out-nigguhed" every politician in the South. After he won, he put in his 1963 inaugural program an anonymous declaration of loyalty to him that said: "We will follow him because we believe. We believe stronger than the Communists, or the pseudo-liberals, or the mongrelizers, or the commanders of crushing military might. We believe. God has given us a man — and we believe."

Was this a case of some overexuberant writer making George Wallace look worse than he really was? Well, let's look at some paragraphs from his official biography in that same 1963 inaugural program: "In 1953, Wallace became the first judge in Dixie to issue an injunction against the removal of segregation signs in railroad terminals. His action set off like examples in other southern states. In 1954, the infamous 'Black Monday' edict of *Brown I* was issued by the Supreme Court and the storm clouds began to gather over the South. In the immediate months and years following, Alabama and the Southland was set upon by professional agitators, revolutionary integration groups and, finally, reminiscent of the 1867 Reconstruction era, by the federal government itself, with socio-engineers at the throttle.

"Schools were invaded, state sovereignties were trampled by politicians in the seats of power, hungry for more power as they sought to outdo each other in gaining the favor of the huge voting blocs of the northern cities and become national darlings of the left-wing press. In the process of this power-drunk orgy, the federal giant, casting about for still more objects to humiliate, set upon the local courts of the South.

"Across Dixie, judge after judge yielded to the threats and

pressure. . . . Through the magic of edict and fear, the disciples of constitutional destruction had discovered the formula for reshaping the federal government with a bloodless revolution. However, for the formula to work, the fear ingredient had to be present and it was here that the giant stubbed his toe over a little country judge named Wallace."

At that inaugural, on January 14, 1963, Wallace stood on the spot on the Alabama capitol portico where Jefferson Davis once took the oath as president of the Confederacy. Wallace made a point of using the same Bible that Davis had used, when he said: "Today I have stood where Jefferson Davis stood and took an oath to my people. It is very appropriate, then, that from this Cradle of the Confederacy, this very heart of the great Anglo-Saxon Southland, that today we sound the drum for freedom as have our generations of forebears before us time and again down through history. Let us rise to the call of the freedom-loving blood that is in us and send our answer to the tyranny that clanks its chains upon the South. . . .

"In the name of the greatest people that have ever trod this earth, I draw the line in the dust and toss the gauntlet before the feet of tyranny. And I say: Segregation now! Segregation tomorrow! Segregation forever!"

Those years following the expulsion of Lucy had "slipped by" because the NAACP was not exactly deluged by Alabama blacks volunteering to risk their lives in the way that Autherine had. But in 1963 two twenty-year-old blacks, Vivian Malone and James A. Hood, did step forward and declare their right to get an education at the University of Alabama — and they did it in a time of incredible racial turmoil in Alabama in general and in Birmingham in particular. These youngsters were just a month away from enrolling at Tuscaloosa when rioting broke out in Birmingham, where the police force and civilian white supremacists had used the most brutal tactics in their efforts to prevent blacks from using public facilities on a nonsegregated basis. On May 12, 1963, a group of segregationists decided that the way to intimidate those pushing for integration was to bomb the black-owned A. G. Gaston motel, and to bomb the home of the Reverend A. D. King, a leader in the desegregation drive and the younger brother of the Reverend Martin Luther King, Jr. These bombings infuriated blacks, many of whom took to the streets in rioting that lasted for more than three hours. President Kennedy also was angered, and immediately ordered federal troops to bases in Birmingham, where fifty people already had been injured. Kennedy also took preliminary steps to call the Alabama National Guard into federal service.

This angered George Wallace, who had been governor for six months, and who declared that Kennedy was usurping his power as governor and taking illegal action for which the president had no authority.

Wallace got the nation's attention by saying: "The timing of the bombings strongly indicates that there are those who are unhappy because of the lack of violence in the last few days. Violence and internal disorder are the stock and trade of the Communists, and in my judgment there has been sufficient activity in Alabama by outside subversives to strongly indicate their involvement in the bombing incident."

In addition, Wallace lashed out at what he called a group of appeasers who were negotiating with Negro leaders about removing some of the segregation restrictions. "I as governor have no part in any such meeting and will not be a party to any such meeting to compromise on the issues of segregation," Wallace continued. "I shall keep the state law enforcement forces in Birmingham as long as Bull Connor [the police commissioner of Birmingham] is of the opinion that they are needed to enforce law and order and to prevent violence."

Wallace suddenly had an opportunity to show his ability to preserve segregation forever. He sent forth word that when the two new Negro students showed up at the University of Alabama he would be in Tuscaloosa to block their admission. He ordered up a National Guard plane to transport him, several aides, and some bodyguards to Tuscaloosa, and he called up some five hundred members of the Alabama National Guard to help him in his show of defiance of federal force. Wallace also ordered 825 highway patrolmen, and deputized game wardens, revenue agents, and others, to go to Tuscaloosa. He said their job was to keep law and order. On June 9, fifteen armed white men were arrested in the Tuscaloosa area, but all were released on bonds posted by Robert M. Shelton, a former Tuscaloosa rubber-factory worker who was Imperial Wizard of the Ku Klux Klan and who had been photographed shaking hands with Wallace and otherwise showing a relationship of friendship with the governor.

Wallace declared that he was only defending the state motto, We Dare Defend Our Rights, against "this omnipotent march of centralized government . . . this military dictatorship."

Meanwhile, the Justice Department had dispatched a team of

officials to prepare for the desegregation showdown. Deputy Attorney General Nicholas deB. Katzenbach headed the group. With him were John Doar, the number two man in the Justice Department's civil rights division, and Edwin O. Guthman, the Justice Department's special assistant for public information.

On June 10 President Kennedy sent a sternly worded telegram to Wallace telling him that his public announcement that he would bar physically the admission of the two Negro students was "the only announced threat to orderly compliance with the law." He told the governor that such obstruction would be "in defiance of the order of the Alabama Federal District Court and in violation of accepted standards of public conduct. . . . I therefore urgently ask you to consider the consequences to your state and its fine university if you persist in setting an example of defiant conduct, and urge you instead to leave these matters in the courts of law where they belong."

But Wallace knew the value of national publicity, of posturing as the savior of states' rights and the "little people" of Alabama.

The great confrontation occurred on the tree-shaded campus alongside the Black Warrior River. The two black applicants, Malone and Hood, arrived at Foster Auditorium, accompanied by Katzenbach, a few other federal officials, and a small group of U.S. marshals. They found Wallace, flanked by state troopers, standing in the schoolhouse door. Katzenbach asked Wallace four times to stand aside and permit Malone and Hood to enter Foster Auditorium and register. Wallace refused.

Katzenbach said to Wallace: "From the outset, Governor, all of us have known the final chapter of this history will be the admission of these students."

Four and one-half hours later, units of the Thirty-first (Dixie) Division, which had been federalized on orders from President Kennedy, arrived on the Tuscaloosa campus under the command of Brigadier General Henry V. Graham. Graham was a real estate executive in civilian life and the former state adjutant general who had enforced modified martial law in Montgomery following Freedom Ride riots in 1961. Graham approached Wallace and said, in almost a whisper, that it was his "sad duty" to order the governor to step aside. Wallace read a prepared statement challenging the constitutionality of the federal judge's order that blacks be admitted to the university, and then he and his aides returned to Montgomery.

Wallace lost that encounter with President Kennedy, but he paved the way for his own candidacy for the presidency, a move that would have a profound effect on the politics of America.

On the Sunday following this doorway confrontation, a bomb exploded in the Sixteenth Street Baptist Church in Birmingham during a children's Bible class, killing four black girls ranging in age from eleven to fourteen, and injuring scores of other innocent children. Later that day, two other black youths were slain.

The Barbour Battler was now a national candidate with a platform from which he could make good his teenage vow that he would run for president of the United States. In the meantime, Wallace's standing in Alabama was such that he had absolutely no trouble winning reelection as governor in 1966.

He obviously was exhilarated by the politics of racism. During the 1970 campaign, he used an advertisement that said: UNLESS WHITES VOTE ON JUNE 2, BLACKS WILL CONTROL THE STATE. This appeal to the racist feelings of white voters was enough to give him another triumph and to intensify his belief that by running for president he could change the nation. Which he did.

Wallace proceeded to rail almost endlessly against the federal government, discovering that an amazingly wide swath of America was eager to hate Washington. He talked piously about law and order, knowing that people in Michigan, Pennsylvania, and Maryland would not know that in Alabama he presided over one of the worst crime rates in America. He waxed eloquent about corruption in Washington, deflecting any attention from the truth that his administrations in Alabama had been among the most corrupt of any state in the nation. He played to fears of violence in the streets and terrorism, even as he buddy-buddied with Shelton, the Klan leader, and ordered the police closest to him to help protect some of the most violent people in Alabama. Wallace was profiting handsomely from practicing the politics of hate and deception. He was clearly one of the great con artists ever to come along in American politics. Wallace ran as a third-party candidate for the presidency in 1968 and got 9,906,473 votes against 31,275,166 for Hubert Humphrey, and a winning 31,785,480 for Richard Nixon. Some thought that Wallace's almost ten million votes were from Democrats, and that he thus denied Humphrey the presidency. My later feeling was that the votes Wallace won would have gone to Nixon, not Humphrey, if the Alabaman had not been in the race, because Nixon's views paralleled those of Wallace, who regarded Humphrey as the greater enemy.

Wallace's presidential campaign record in 1972 was nothing short of incredible. When he went to Laurel, Maryland, on May 15, 1972, he had already won primaries in Tennessee, Florida, and North Carolina, and had finished second, with large numbers of votes, in

Wisconsin, Indiana, and Pennsylvania. He was favored to win the Maryland primary as well as the same-day voting in Michigan. The history of the 1972 election, and of Wallace's life, were changed profoundly that May day in Maryland when Arthur Herman Bremer, a twenty-one-year old student from Milwaukee who had been loudly cheering for Wallace, asked the governor to come over and shake his hand. As Wallace approached Bremer, the young man pulled out a .38 caliber revolver and fired four shots into the governor's body. One of those shots passed through Wallace's right arm and chest and lodged in his spinal column, leaving the governor paralyzed from the waist down.

Nonetheless, Wallace won those primaries in Maryland and Michigan. We will never know how many of the votes he got were out of sympathy for him because of the attempted assassination. We do know that until he was gunned down, Wallace had won 3,300,000 primary votes, 700,000 more than Humphrey had garnered and 1,200,000 more than had been given to George McGovern. Wallace and his brand of politics had become a sensation in the North as well as the South.

In recalling the life of Thurgood Marshall, the world will little remember T. Justin Moore, Lindsay Almond, Robert McC. Figg, or even John W. Davis, among the lawyers who tried to save racial segregation during those dramatic courtroom debates of the 1950s. But Americans will not forget Wallace's efforts to put up oratorical, legislative, and physical barricades to the desegregation of public schools and the University of Alabama.

In 1982, I read that Wallace was running for his fourth term as governor of Alabama, this time as the "candidate of Blacks." There were indeed some black people supporting Wallace who I never would have thought would say a good word about the "Barbour Battler."

Wallace had gone before the Southern Christian Leadership Conference in Birmingham and apologized for his old segregationist politics. He had told newsmen that by then he realized that "racism is a bummer. It pits poor whites against poor blacks and leaves the fat cats with everything." When asked if all this represented a change in his attitude toward blacks, Wallace replied, "No, I have respected and loved them always."

I knew that it was a story of national significance, in another era of other kinds of racial conflict in America, if Wallace was now admitting that he was wrong during all the years when he fought Marshall so doggedly and meanly. I went to see Wallace so as to include the views of his twilight years in this book.

                            *   *   *

Wallace was holding down a little sinecure as chairman of public administration in the Troy State University system. I was told by Wallace's executive assistant, Elvin Stanton, that while the governor had not granted any interviews for years, he would be delighted to see me at 2 p.m. in his Montgomery offices on August 19 of 1991.

As I disembarked in Montgomery that Monday morning, I was reminded that it had, in my first visits there, been one of the most countrified, even backward, of the state capitals of America. It still was. Only a few feet down the concourse, where I had exited from a modern McDonnell-Douglas jet, I had to step over two large dead roaches. A couple of live ones crawled toward me in welcome, something I'd not received in the 1950s.

I was early, at 10:00 a.m., so I decided to stop at the shoeshine stand where a black man whom other employees called "Reverend" was talking just above the rat-a-tat-tat of the shine cloth that he wielded with skill.

When my turn came to climb into the chair, the "reverend" never looked me in the face, even when a well-dressed black man in his forties said, "Mr. Rowan, what are you doing here?"

"Just to have a chat with Governor Wallace."

"Tell him he's what drove me out of this state," he said. "I'm just back here for two days for a funeral."

The "reverend" took notice. "You must be from somewhere?" he half-asked.

"Washington, D.C.," I said.

"Pretty city. I was there once," he said. "Makes this place look like a jungle. But I'm back here because I like to grow things like collard greens, and have lots of dogs around me. I had a wife in Cleveland, Ohio, but I didn't like it there. She had to grow her collards in a box full of dirt that she kept outside a window."

He then looked me over carefully and said: "So you're interviewing old George. He's sure mellowed. Or so he says."

I walked outside and was relieved that there was a single taxicab available. The lean, white, country-boy driver resembled the ones I had seen a hundred times in my boyhood areas of Tennessee.

"I want to go to Troy State University," I said.

His eyes blinked in excitement. "All the way to Troy?" he asked, anticipating at least a $50 fee to take me to the little town where the main campus of the university was seated.

"Hell, no," I said. "The branch in Montgomery where former governor Wallace has offices. . . . You know where the corner of Church and Catoma is?"

"Shore do," he said.

Riding to Wallace's office, I noted the small businesses along the highway, the gangs of black and white men on road-repair jobs, who weren't working much but at least were talking to each other, a distinct change from my earlier times there. I thought I would spot the house in which my wife's grandparents had lived, but it apparently had been torn down, leaving a lot of weeds.

Only a few blocks away I entered the modest funereal-gray building in which Wallace's office was located. His secretary, Helen Hines, had told me that the governor wasn't feeling up to coming into the office, but that I could use it until time to leave for the 2 P.M. interview at his home.

I was astounded that there was no security, no receptionist, nobody guarding the entrance to the building and its elevators. I got to the fourth floor, where I was told I'd find someone to give me Wallace's records and later take me to his home, but saw no one in sight. The place was quieter than a morgue. I turned a corner and there, inside open doors, working away alone, in a no-frills suite of offices, was Mrs. Hines. She led me into Wallace's office, then offered me an adjoining one where there was a typewriter, a telephone, and evidence left by a chain smoker.

"I may leave soon for lunch," Mrs. Hines said. "If *you* leave, just leave the office doors open. The recession and stuff, and people's preference for lunching in the new shopping centers, have forced the restaurants near here to close down, so you might just want to go down to the third floor and get a sandwich or something out of one of the vending machines."

I realized right there that you could never understand Wallace's or Alabama's war with the federal government unless you understood how many worlds away Montgomery was and is from Washington, New York, Los Angeles, and the other great urban areas of America. Who in Montgomery would not cherish "law and order" if it meant that a lone white woman could sit in an open and unprotected office, welcome a black stranger, and tell him to "leave the doors open" if he went to lunch? It seemed foolhardy to me, especially when I knew that in Birmingham and other nearby urban centers of Alabama, violent crime was rampant. Yet, in this little surviving world of George Wallace, trust in neighbors, even strangers, was still a rule of life.

Marshall probably had spent a thousand workdays and lost sleep a thousand nights trying to counter the influence of and undo the damage caused by this Alabaman. I had heard Marshall speak of Wallace in vile words during the 1960s. I could imagine the words in which he would express his disbelief in the former governor's sudden comment about black people: "I have always loved them."

My first reaction on seeing Wallace's office was that I was about to interview a man who still clung to old and deep loyalties and grand notions of patriotism. Behind his desk were four flags — his personal one as governor, the Stars and Stripes, the Alabama state flag, and the battle flag of the Confederacy. Symbolism, I thought, of a mind-set Wallace would never lose. On his unpretentious desk, laid out so immaculately that you knew that Wallace rarely worked there, was a copy of the Bible along with a new book, *Rape of Kuwait*. Flanked by a couple of gavels was a computer printout of the voting in the gubernatorial election of 1982, which Wallace won for his final term.

The widest wall of the office was crowded with photographs of George as a fifteen-year-old prizefighter, as a GI during World War II, of the governor welcoming, or being welcomed by, John F. Kennedy, Chiang Kai-shek, Richard Nixon, Gerald Ford, Ronald Reagan, Jimmy Carter, Sally Field, Barbara Mandrell, Margaret Thatcher, Elvis Presley. In bookcases below the photos on that wall I counted fifty-one black folios full of Wallace's photographs in wider-ranging circumstances, these dramatized by the inexplicable appearance amid them of a red volume, *Who's Who In Japan*.

But nowhere did I spot a photo, or any kind of memento, of the governor blocking the door against two black young people trying to get into the University of Alabama; of Wallace with the state troopers and others he used to try to block public school desegregation; or of any of the other thousands of actions Wallace took in the pursuit of "segregation forever."

Elvin Stanton drove me to Wallace's home in what seemed a nice upper-middle-class neighborhood called Hillwood — decidedly not the home one would have expected for an ex-governor who, according to his worst enemies, had stolen millions in public funds. I was carrying a large black bag full of tape recorders, tapes, batteries, and assorted documents, toilet articles, Delta bags of peanuts, and only God knows what else. Wallace's security people, hangers-on or whatever, sat gossiping in a room near the driveway; they just waved as Stanton and I walked into a room where the ex-governor reclined on a hospital-type bed. He leaned up to shake hands and tell me, "It's so good to see you again. You know, I've always admired you as a journalist."

My mind said "Horseshit!" but my heart told me that at this point in his life, Wallace probably meant it.

I reminded him that we hadn't seen each other face to face since we were on the same platform receiving honorary degrees on the hundredth birthday of Alabama State College.

"WHAT?" Wallace said.

Stanton had warned me that, even though he wore a hearing aid, Wallace had to be shouted to, and that even then he rarely understood. Fortuitously, I had prepared my questions in large type. So I could shout my question, then hold the typed question before his face and wait for his answer, which I recorded. I quickly learned that while his hearing was gone, Wallace's mind was clear, and he knew exactly what he wanted to achieve in, as he kept telling me, "the first interview I've given in eight or ten years — well, at least six."

My mention of our honorary degrees from Alabama State reminded him to show me what he had gathered for my visit. Nothing about his many efforts to defeat or frustrate Marshall. Everything that symbolized what he had done for black children. He had the honorary degree that he had received from Tuskegee University, the predominantly black institution made famous by Booker T. Washington and George Washington Carver. "Blacks there gave me a standing ovation when they put the cap and hood on me," he recalled. "That was the proudest I've ever been."

Then Wallace talked of the blacks who had thanked him for what he had done for black people in terms of vocational education, and training in general. He had a computer printout of the "I'm no racist" elections in which huge majorities of blacks had voted for him. He never mentioned that his Republican opponents were such blatant bigots that they made Wallace look palatable to sophisticated blacks.

Nonetheless, I was acutely aware of the fact that I was interviewing Wallace in a political atmosphere that had been poisoned by Nixon, Reagan, and astonishingly, Bush, presidents who had used, or were using, a politics of bigotry that they had learned from Wallace.

This former governor, long regarded as one of the classic bigots of all time, right up there with Mississippi's Theodore Bilbo and James Eastland and South Carolina's Ben "Pitchfork" Tillman, clearly did not want any association with these racists as he lay on a sickbed, still paralyzed from the waist down by the bullet fired by Arthur Bremer in 1972.

Wallace had granted me an interview in hopes of convincing me that he loved black people, had never suggested that they were inferior, had eaten and lived with them all his life, had lifted the level of their lives, and won praise from them as the best governor Alabama had ever had. Most of all, he was talking to me because he wanted to be rescued from the ignominious label of "bigot," just as Southerners like Lyndon B. Johnson and Arkansas senator William Fulbright had been.

You could gain a positive view of Wallace — perhaps not — but surely a more profound understanding of racism in America, if you absorb my interview with "the Barbour Battler":

"There were people at one time who blamed you for some of the violent atmosphere, the bombing of the church in Birmingham, of the A. G. Gaston Motel, the home of Reverend A. D. King. Did you ever feel that you were in any way to blame for that kind of violence?" I asked.

"No, sir, because every time I went on television, I opposed violence," Wallace replied. "I brought the state troopers to the university for the purpose of preventing violence, in case that group came from Ole Miss — the Socialist Workers Party of America, the old Nazi crowd, and the old Fascist crowd, the Minutemen, the Klan, that killed three people, wounded several, burned babies. I wasn't against somebody, blacks, going to the university. What we wanted to do was set a timetable because the board of trustees had already voted to integrate in 'sixty-four. But they [the Justice Department] said 'sixty-three. We were stubborn, they were stubborn. So I went ahead, but when they wouldn't let me raise the question of who was to set the timetable, the board of trustees or the federal government, I went ahead and did that. But one reason the troopers were there was for the purpose of keeping that crowd off the campus that had erupted at Ole Miss. But I didn't allow any violence, preached against violence every time. In fact, my platform said 'I shall do all I can to maintain safety within the law of nonviolence.' "

"After the 1963 bombing of the A. G. Gaston motel and the home of the Reverend A. D. King, you publicly blamed 'communists' and 'outside subversives.' Did you really believe that?" I asked.

"Well," he said, "I did believe at the time that outside agitators had something to do with it, but there are also a few million people in this state had something to do with it, too, but I don't know who they were. But finally it sickened my mind, especially the church bombing matter, which . . . this was the most terrible thing that happened. And I said they ought to burn the bottom out of the electric chair."

I asked if it was true that after he lost the governor's race to John Patterson in 1960, he said, "John Patterson out-nigguhed me. And I'm never gonna be out-nigguhed again."

"No. I was as strong on segregation as he was," Wallace admitted.

"But the difference was, his father got shot. A sympathy vote elected him. I would have lost under any circumstances, anybody else would have, too, because his father had been assassinated after he attempted to clean up Phenix City."

"What I'm getting at is how much of George Wallace's race baiting was political expediency, and how much reflected your personal support for white supremacy?" I said.

"I don't support white supremacy!" Wallace shouted as he grimaced in apparent pain. "I'm one of the ones that advocated taking the words 'white supremacy' off the rooster that was the symbol of the Democratic party in this state. I said to my friends in the community, 'You've got to get that off.'

"I've never been against any man or woman made by God's hand, whether he was yellow, black, brown, or white or red, because I'm a Christian. I don't defend race baiters a bit, because while I got people riled up about the federal courts, I didn't say a single thing to embarrass a black man unless he was embarrassed by my saying, 'I believe that the best interest of both races is to have segregated schools.'

"Some others used to talk about inferiority and all that kind of stuff . . . NEVER did I use any of that. You can't find a single quote in any paper in the country where I talk about the idea of black inferiority."

"Governor," I said, "in your nineteen sixty-three inaugural, you shouted: 'Segregation now! Segregation tomorrow! Segregation forever!' Was this what you really wanted?"

"Well, that statement I made in 'sixty-three shouldn't have been made," he replied. "I should not have said it. But it was really my vehemence and belligerence against the federal court system for taking over everything. I really shouldn't have said it, because it wasn't true, although at that time I was so cold. It was five below zero chill factor that day. I was not going to say it, but somebody put that in the speech and I got to it. I was going to, you know, slip over it, but I was so cold I just went right ahead reading and forgot about it."

"Did you write those words, or were they sort of put into your mouth?" I asked.

"No, I didn't write those words, no, no, no, no, no," he replied. "You know, Mr. Rowan, that in my presidential campaign, and primary campaign, I never mentioned race at all. Not a time. I always said I'd like to have the vote of any man regardless of his race, color, creed, religion, or national origin. I was gonna be president of all the people."

"Were you aware that you were regarded as the most visible, loudest white supremacist in the land?" I queried.

"No, I wouldn't run an antiblack campaign. Lordy, mercy, that'd be the worst thing a man could ever do."

"Did the tragic incident in Laurel, Maryland, where you were shot, become the catalyst that changed your views?" I inquired.

"No, sir, my being shot in Maryland didn't change my views at all because I knew about blacks," Wallace said. "I love blacks as much as I do whites. That's the reason I've never said an unkind word about any of them, in any speech I ever made. If I had, why did they vote for me from 1974 to 1982? Any self-respecting black person, if a man ever got up and said bad things about them as a person or as a race, they'd never vote for you in a thousand years."

"Governor," I asked, "when did you begin to realize that segregation could not be preserved?"

"In 1964."

"What happened in 1964?"

"Well, I just came to know that a country divided could not stand," Wallace said.

"You were quoted as saying that when poor whites are pitted against poor blacks, the fat cats wind up with all the goodies. Aren't we seeing proof of your warning today?"

"Oh, yes, I certainly do believe that the Republicans under Reagan, the white and black low-income and middle-class people paid through the nose while the wealthy got fat and more millions of dollars were made [by the rich] under Reagan than any other administration. I wanted more blacks to get into the middle class. If every black in America moved to the middle class, this would be a great land to live in, sure enough. Every time I see a black man finish college and get him a job, it makes me feel very good," said Wallace as he asked an aide for an adjustment of his sickbed.

"In 1964, I did say the Constitution provided civil rights for everyone, but I was afraid the bills would damage property owners, and the fair employment laws would hurt the free enterprise system. But I was entirely mistaken. But remember this, now. President Johnson fought civil rights laws for years and years. He filibustered for years. He was also elected to the Congress in an all-white primary. He was a segregationist. *They've* rehabilitated him, but *y'all* haven't rehabilitated me. Would they have given me that [honorary degree from Tuskegee] if I'd been as mean as a lot of people say I am?"

I asked if he has felt all along that the media has been to blame for not portraying him correctly.

"Yes, yes, yes," he said. "I've done no more than Lyndon Johnson's done. He was a segregationist, he fought the civil rights bills, but he changed, like I did. We realized that segregation had to go."

"Of all the things that you have said and done in your remarkable career, of which are you proudest? Which do you now regret most?"

"Well, I regret most that I made that 'segregation forever' speech in my first inaugural. And I'm proudest of the fact that I gave to some blacks real opportunities in education," Wallace replied.

He then gave me a September 1990 letter from A. G. Gaston, the black motel owner, saying, "You have made a good Governor for Alabama. . . . I am now a wheelchair patient as you are. It is my hope that I will live long enough to again vote for a Wallace as governor."

As I was leaving, Wallace asked me to join him in a glass of tea. Two black men lifted him out of bed when he said he would feel less pain sitting in a chair. He lit a cigar and talked about the current politics of race across America.

The tea was, in southern tradition, unbearably sweet. I put it down. The last thing Wallace shouted as I went out the door was: "They rehabilitated [former Alabama senator] John Sparkman, and Bill Fulbright, and Lyndon Johnson. Why won't they rehabilitate me?"

I got back on the airplane that afternoon knowing that my friends and peers would wonder, even ask me, whether I believed Wallace's disavowal of bigotry. I would have to state my view that Wallace was not a black savior, and that he was a revisionist, a modifier of his personal history — although I felt Wallace now truly believed what he was saying.

I remembered the times that I had heard Marshall denounce Wallace as one of "the gatekeepers," the presidents, governors, mayors, and others of political power who decided whether there could be peaceful social change or whether it had to come through violence and insurrection. No one would recall with more bitter memories than Marshall that when Wallace was Alabama's "gatekeeper," he didn't talk the way he did when he spoke to me from his sickbed.

I returned to Washington thinking of a poignant bit of irony rolling around in my head: Autherine Lucy (now Mrs. Autherine Lucy Foster, wife of a Birmingham Baptist minister, the Reverend Hugh Foster) was enrolled at the University of Alabama in Tuscaloosa and would get a master's degree in May 1992, thirty-six years after the cruel ordeal to which Alabama and the university's regents had subjected her. Doubly ironic was the fact that this sixty-two-year-old teacher would graduate alongside her daughter Grazia, on a campus where 1,755 blacks were among the total of 18,096 students.

"We — and fate — finally beat Wallace," Marshall said to me prior to this interview, "but at one helluva cost in human suffering."

CHAPTER SEVENTEEN

MARSHALL THE JURIST — AND HIS NEMESIS

WHILE THE SAGA of George Wallace was being played out, Marshall was involved in a great drama of his own. President Kennedy had looked at the judicial system in America and found it to be among the most Jim Crow of institutions. There was a shameful paucity of female, black, and other minority judges. The bailiffs, the court reporters, just about everybody connected with the judicial system was white. The president decided that he was going to put Thurgood Marshall on the United States Court of Appeals for the Second Circuit, which made rulings for New York, Connecticut, and Vermont, and was the most important of the courts of appeal after the one in the District of Columbia.

Kennedy really wanted to be the president who put the first black on the Supreme Court. He talked to his brother Bobby about naming appeals court judge William Hastie of Philadelphia, the man who had been a Howard University Law School dean and the first black American named to any federal judgeship, to the high tribunal. Bobby, with an arrogance typical of him, went to Chief Justice Warren and asked whether he thought naming Hastie would be a good idea. Kennedy told his brother that Warren urged against it, asserting that Hastie was not a liberal, and that it would be utterly destructive of everything Warren and his allies on the Court were trying to do in the cause of racial equality if Hastie were to be put on the Supreme Court. Marshall would have been apoplectic had he known what Robert Kennedy said, but he did not know.

So President Kennedy went forward with other ways of trying to change the judicial system. He would name ten blacks to federal judgeship posts, but his most sensational appointment was that of Marshall.

Kennedy knew that Marshall's appointment would be highly controversial and had decided that he could not name him to the Supreme Court immediately. It would be hard enough getting him confirmed to the appeals court. It turned out to be more difficult than Kennedy had imagined. He nominated Marshall on September 23, 1961, provoking pro and con headlines across the land. Statements of outrage rippled across the South. But four days after the appointment, Congress adjourned — which Kennedy certainly knew would happen. Eastland of Mississippi, the dictatorial chairman of the Senate Judiciary Committee, announced that there would be no hearings on judicial nominees until after the Congress returned. That gave President Kennedy the chance to give Marshall a recess appointment, allowing him to serve as a judge and display his mettle before the Senate came back and decided whether or not to confirm him for a lifetime appointment. Kennedy resubmitted Marshall's nomination on January 15, 1962, hoping for reasonably prompt confirmation. It was not to come.

Marshall had learned that victory has a million friends; he was about to learn that it also makes powerful enemies, of which he had more than a few in South Carolina. One, J. (for James) Strom Thurmond, had begun to despise him early and would bedevil Marshall until near the end of both their lives.

Thurmond became Marshall's lifelong foe when the NAACP lawyer went to South Carolina to knock out the "white primary" and try to wipe away the other tricks and ruses used to prevent black citizens from voting. Thurmond, a young politician in Edgefield County, saw Marshall as a threat to everything he hoped to become.

The fear of blacks voting in South Carolina was in Thurmond's blood, passed down from his father, the lawyer of former senator Ben "Pitchfork" Tillman, who with other associates in Edgefield County had used extraordinary measures to take away the political power that blacks had gained in the Reconstruction period, right after the Civil War. David Bruck, a Columbia, South Carolina, lawyer, wrote an extraordinary article for the March 13, 1982, issue of the *New Republic* in which he told of Strom's roots. Bruck gave details of the terror of Edgefield's whites in 1867 when they realized that black registered voters outnumbered them almost two to one; and how an ex-Confederate general named M. W. Gary rallied his Edgefield neighbors to do something about it with the warning: "If one

Negro is allowed to vote, you may as well let them all do so, for you have consented to make this a mongrel government, to make the children of your former slaves the successful competitor[s] of your children for the honors of the state."

The whites in Edgefield became so inflamed that they massacred rebellious blacks in Hamburg, ripping away their political rights. Tillman, who would be elected to the U.S. Senate in 1894, "had been in a group that provoked a battle against blacks." As Bruck tells the story,

> Tillman would proudly recall that Edgefield's leading white land-owners had gone to Hamburg looking for a fight, "as it was generally believed that nothing but bloodshed and a good deal of it could answer the purpose of redeeming the state from negro and carpetbag rule." Tillman and his companions counted the Hamburg incident a great success, as "the purpose of our visit was to strike terror, and the next morning when the negroes who had fled to the swamp returned to the town, the ghastly sight which met their gaze of seven dead negroes lying stark and stiff, certainly had its effect."

More than thirty years after that massacre Tillman was using his power and prestige in the Senate to urge the rest of the nation to join Edgefield County's example of disfranchising blacks. In 1900 he stood proudly in the Senate and said, "The state of South Carolina has disenfranchised all of the colored race that it could under the Thirteenth, Fourteenth and Fifteenth Amendments. We have done our level best, we have scratched our heads to find out how we could eliminate the last one of them, and we would have done it if we could. We took the government away. We stuffed ballot boxes. We shot them. We are not ashamed of it."

In 1944, as the NAACP was winning over not just the Supreme Court, but much of America, to the idea that blacks had a right to vote freely in every place in the land, Thurmond was on his way to great political power. He had his eye on the governorship of South Carolina, which he won in 1946. As Thurmond saw Harry Truman siding with the NAACP, moving to outlaw lynchings and poll taxes and asking for fair employment practices, he warned:

> If Congress can [pass a law] to establish the power to deal with the right of the American people to vote, it can establish a form of Federal suffrage. . . . When this occurs, the states could lose their effective voice in the national legislative halls as surely as did

the Southern states in Reconstruction days when our ballot boxes were surrounded by Federal soldiers.

Thurmond was arguing that "states' rights" forbade Washington to say who could vote in Hamburg or Charleston. Even in those days, Thurmond was a master at pretending that he was not doing what he was doing. He tried to let others use the most inflammatory, racist language, and the *Charleston News and Courier* was always willing to oblige. As Thurmond began to talk about the civil rights movement being a communist plot, a threat to states' rights, and an insult to the South, he went so far as to say that no Negro would ever be a guest in the South Carolina statehouse "as long as I am governor." He was a racist's shrewd racist. The *News and Courier* said:

> Some of the men in public life, notably Governor J. Strom Thurmond, have spoken and acted. They are willing to risk their livelihood and their careers for principles they believe to be right. If they fail in their crusade, if negroes are given the deciding vote in electing officeholders in South Carolina, these men are finished politically. They are well aware of this, and yet they are not afraid to speak.

In his first months as governor, Thurmond presented himself as a moderate, as something of a populist. But President Truman's proposals for civil rights legislation so aroused him that he had to reveal his true colors as a segregationist and one of the most radical of states' rights advocates. In February 1948, the southern governors conference appointed Thurmond to head a delegation to ask Democratic national chairman J. Howard McGrath to tell Truman that if he did not withdraw the offending proposed civil rights legislation he would not have southern support in the 1948 presidential election. McGrath rejected the demand on the spot. So the southern governors, urged on by Thurmond, decided that their states would send delegates to the Democratic National Convention who were opposed to Truman, and that they would pick presidential electors who would refuse to vote for any candidate favoring civil rights — which ruled out not only Truman, but Republican Thomas Dewey and third-party candidate Henry Wallace.

The southern governors figured that they could insure that no party got enough electoral votes to win the presidency and that the election would be thrown into the House of Representatives, where one of the southern governors could become the compromise candidate. Thurmond had hooked up with Mississippi's Governor

Fielding Wright to stage the revolt against Truman. After the rejection by McGrath, Thurmond and Wright called a conference in Jackson, Mississippi, to plan for the Philadelphia convention of Democrats. Thurmond gave a speech in Jackson in which he attacked Truman with incredible emotionalism and declared that "all the laws of Washington and all the bayonets of the Army cannot force the Negroes into Southern homes, schools, churches . . . and places of amusement."

By the time they got to Philadelphia, the Mississippi and Alabama delegations were so emotional that they did not recognize that they would have won if they had accepted the weak civil rights plank of 1944. They wanted their own prosegregation plank. They wanted someone with a southern viewpoint to replace Truman at the head of the ticket. The southern delegates had the convention in a chokehold until Minneapolis's Mayor Hubert Humphrey gave his rousing speech in favor of a strong civil rights plank — one that Truman did not even support — and persuaded the convention to adopt it.

Thurmond and other southern delegates walked out. Thurmond told a caucus of southern delegates, "We have been betrayed and the guilty shall not go unpunished."

The "punishment" was for the Southerners to support Senator Richard B. Russell of Georgia. But Truman got 947 delegates to Russell's 263 and became the party's nominee. This provoked Thurmond and Wright to form a States' Rights Democrats party which they got on the ballot in thirteen states. But Truman won a historic victory.

"Man, that's what I like about Truman," Marshall recalled for me. "He was a tough sucker. More than that, he had character. He risked losing his chance at his own term as president rather than swallow the crap that Thurmond and the Dixiecrats were throwing at him. I tell you again that when all the history books are written, Truman is going to come out on top."

Thurmond was not likely to come out "on top" of anybody's ranking of the politicians of that era.

The few blacks in South Carolina who could vote hated Thurmond with a passion. Party-loyal white Democrats and the businessmen and farmers who were getting pork and favors from Washington despised Thurmond as a political traitor. So in 1950, when Thurmond ran for a seat in the Senate, he lost an ugly battle to Olin Johnston, mostly because Johnston, incredibly, could attack Thurmond as a *liberal* and as a man without party loyalty.

But four years later Thurmond defied the Democratic machine, which would not let his name appear on the primary ballot. He ran for the U.S. Senate as a write-in candidate and became the first person in South Carolina history to win in such a capacity.

Thurmond and the Dixiecrats had lost a major battle in 1948, but by the time he won his incredible victory in 1954, he had changed the politics of the South. It would not be many years before Americans began to understand how much Thurmond had weakened the Democratic party and opened the door to Republican triumphs in Dixie.

Thurmond's election to the Senate occurred less than six months after the Supreme Court's 1954 decision outlawing school segregation, with Marshall arguing the specific case that came out of South Carolina. During that campaign of 1954, Thurmond played a major role in inflaming his state in a campaign that showed something of his shrewdness. While other politicians played to Washington and the national audience, Thurmond schmoozed the voters of his state. He went from precinct to precinct, talking to members of the White Citizens Councils that had sprung up all over South Carolina. His message was that "As long as we keep public sentiment strongly against integration in the schools, we will not have integration."

As pressures for desegregation intensified, Thurmond became what some senators said was the most passionate segregationist in that body. But Thurmond was uncanny in knowing how far he wanted to stick out his neck. He would never go as far as Wright of Mississippi, Faubus of Arkansas, Wallace of Alabama — that is, take overt actions that put him in direct confrontation with the federal government. Yet it was Thurmond who masterminded a document commonly known as the "Southern Manifesto," formally titled "Declaration of Constitutional Principles." It was a pamphlet tirade designed to unite the South behind the belief that the racial changes ordered by the Supreme Court were unconstitutional, and that what was passing for "civil rights" was really a communist-inspired subversion of America. Thurmond and the other Southerners sprang the Manifesto on Senate Majority Leader Lyndon Johnson in March 1956, urged him to join John Stennis, Sam Ervin, Walter George, Richard Russell, Harry Byrd, and other prestigious lawmakers from the South in signing a document that said, in effect, "We are not going to obey this edict from the Supreme Court and will do everything in our power to wipe it out."

Three senators from the South refused to sign the manifesto. Albert Gore of Tennessee said the document was "a dangerous, deceptive propaganda move which encouraged Southerners to defy the government and to disobey its laws, particularly orders of the federal courts." Gore was joined by Tennessee's senior senator, Estes Kefauver, in refusing to sign, something that did not surprise Deep South senators who regarded Kefauver as a maverick whom they could rarely count on for anything. The third southern senator who would not sign was Lyndon Johnson, who explained to the Texas press that it didn't mean he was a civil rights advocate, only that in his position as minority leader of all Democrats he could not become too closely identified with any geographical division. Johnson had used the same argument to explain why he refused to join the southern caucus, a group of twenty-two Southerners who met regularly to talk about how to protect the interests of Dixie. Johnson also talked to the Texas press about how he had reverence for the tradition of obeying the laws of the land, a sort of echo of Eisenhower's stance in refusing ever to say whether he thought school segregation was wrong — only that desegregation was the law of the land, and as president he would uphold the law.

Johnson had said publicly that he was not a civil rights advocate, but he beamed proudly and took on the posture of a great human rights leader when anyone told him that he had been courageous in refusing to sign the Manifesto. After Johnson became president, he said to me: "Did you ever notice who signed the goddamned Southern Manifesto and who refused to sign it? You got all those goddamn protesters out there in the streets claiming that I'm a dumb-assed hick; that I'm killing people [in Vietnam] without compassion; that I don't understand anything about the social needs of the country. The damn war protesters are cheering Bill Fulbright because he's a Rhodes scholar, and they think that makes him superior to me, who went to a crappy little college in Texas. Fulbright's got the Fulbright Act, and I've got the Vietnam War. But you look at the record and you'll see that Fulbright signed the goddamn Southern Manifesto. And I didn't sign it, did I?"

It should not go unnoted that at the Democratic National Convention some five months later, three Southerners' names were up for national office — those of Gore, Kefauver, and Johnson.

In 1957, the Eisenhower administration proposed a fairly significant civil rights bill. In the wheeling and dealing in the Senate, with now majority leader Johnson playing a big role, the proposed legislation was whittled down to the point where it was nothing more than a feeble voting rights measure. Most of the southern senators were willing to go along with it. But not Thurmond, who was still living by the dictum of Edgefield County that if you let one Negro vote, you invited catastrophe. So in opposition to the Civil Rights Act of 1957, Thurmond spoke for twenty-four hours and eighteen minutes in what was till then the all-time record Senate filibuster.

No matter where Marshall and the NAACP turned, there was Thurmond, or his surrogates, or the clear influence of Thurmond, blocking the way to racial and social change. Thurmond was proud of what he was doing. In 1957 he declared that "in South Carolina, Negroes are voting in large numbers. Of course, they are not so well qualified to vote as are the white people." What Thurmond called "large numbers" was only a minuscule part of the black population. As Bruck pointed out in his *New Republic* article, at the time of Thurmond's 1957 filibuster the white majority still had 92.4 percent of the votes in Edgefield County. And in neighboring McCormick County, not a single black was registered to vote despite the fact that blacks comprised 61 percent of that county's population.

Thurmond was skilled at citing almost nonexistent racial progress while he maneuvered to prevent any changes in race relations in South Carolina.

In 1960, Thurmond told the Senate that "down South we are having no racial disorders. We are having no racial tension. We are not having crime, or juvenile delinquency. We have a segregated life which both races enjoy."

Marshall could not have imagined that a year later he would be face to face with Thurmond under far different circumstances.

When President Kennedy announced in September 1961 that he was appointing Marshall to the Second Circuit Court of Appeals in New York, Thurmond took it as a personal affront. In his devious way, he moved through the Senate trying to arrange early support to deny Marshall a seat on this federal bench. Thurmond had some heavy weapons — his friendship with Eastland of Mississippi, who chaired the judicial committee in which confirmation hearings would be held, and the fact that the subcommittee that would hold the first hearing was chaired by a South Carolina colleague, Olin Johnston. Thurmond got his point across to both men and was largely responsible for the fact that the Senate would stall for almost a year before Marshall was finally confirmed.

It was soon obvious that Senator Olin Johnston, the South Carolina Democrat who headed the Judiciary subcommittee, had no intentions of holding hearings on Marshall soon, especially when the chairman of the full committee, Eastland, was urging him to stall. Johnston was up for reelection in South Carolina, where Marshall's name was anathema and provoked swear words from thousands of white people, so Johnston had to fight Marshall.

It is probably the greatest testimonial to Marshall's successful work as the chief lawyer of the NAACP, and the best evidence of the extent to which the NAACP was feared and hated by the proponents of segregation, that Johnston and Eastland stalled for seven months before letting even the Senate Judiciary Committee come to judgment on this black man.

When the hearings finally began, Senators Kenneth Keating and Jacob Javits, New York Republicans, praised Marshall effusively, pointing out that he had been rated "well qualified" by the American Bar Association's committee on judicial selection. Javits pointed out that the president of the New York state bar had also given Marshall the unusual rating of well qualified.

Keating confronted Eastland and Johnston, saying: "The controversy about Judge Marshall centers not about the man but about the results he has achieved. I commend him for the part he has played in helping some Americans to enjoy all of their rights under the Constitution."

Marshall was smart enough to know the ways in which they might come after him, so he volunteered at the first hearing on May 1, 1962, that he was once a member of the National Lawyers Guild, a leftist organization, but he said he had quit in disgust in 1949 during the trial of the top echelon communists, when the Lawyers Guild criticized Judge Harold Medina.

There was another long stall until July 12, when the Judiciary subcommittee held a ninety-minute session on Marshall, all of which was taken up by attacks on the NAACP by C. E. Lipscomb, a staff counsel of the full committee who was in Eastland's pocket. Lipscomb was trying to prove that Marshall was not qualified to sit on the court because the NAACP had been found guilty by a Texas judge of "soliciting plaintiffs" and "fomenting litigation," of operating in Texas without a license for a foreign corporation, and of violating the ethics of the American Bar Association.

"We're not here to investigate the NAACP," snapped Senator Keating. "We're here to investigate the competence of the nominee."

Interestingly, Senators Everett Dirksen of Illinois, Roman Hruska of Nebraska, and other Republicans climbed all over Lipscomb. All they got for their trouble was another long delay in permitting a vote on the Marshall nomination. Lipscomb came back with hours of exhibits and arguments about the record of the NAACP in Texas. This brought complaints of "outrageous" from Senators Frank

Lausche of Ohio and Thomas Kuchel of California. The pressure was on Johnston's subcommittee to get to the business of voting. But there was another delay until August 17, when Lipscomb read from a newspaper clipping of a Marshall speech in Memphis, Tennessee, in February 1956. Marshall was quoted as saying, "We've got the law, religion and God on our side, and the devil is on the other side."

"Do you still feel today that you have God on your side, that everyone who opposes the position that you take is in line with the devil?" Lipscomb asked. Marshall replied that, "by the other side" he meant "outfits like the Ku Klux Klan." "Any man who takes a man and lynches him is aligned with the devil," Marshall said firmly.

Lipscomb then cited a speech by Dr. Alfred Kelly, a professor at Wayne State University in Detroit, in which Kelly claimed that Marshall had said to him, "When we colored folks take over, every time a white man takes a breath he will have to pay a fine."

Marshall denied having made such a statement. Kelly expressed outrage that Lipscomb had used the quote without making it clear that he thought that Marshall was using "mordant humor" in making that remark.

When Javits threatened to move, on the Senate floor, to take Marshall's nomination away from the Judiciary Committee, Senate Democratic leader Mike Mansfield of Montana got into the act in a serious way. He pressured Eastland into finally calling a committee meeting on September 7, where the vote was 11 to 4 to confirm Marshall after Eastland had failed to get enough votes to defer action for another week. Voting against confirmation in the committee were Eastland, Johnston, John McClellan of Arkansas, and Sam Ervin, Jr., of North Carolina, all Democrats.

The nomination came up on the Senate floor on September 11, and the debate lasted five hours.

Johnston, declaring that his opposition had nothing to do with Marshall's race, charged that the nominee had practiced law in New York without a license, violated professional ethics by stirring up lawsuits, and "belonged to a communist-dominated organization when others were resigning left and right" — a reference to Marshall's former membership in the Lawyers Guild.

"I want it clearly understood that I do not charge that Thurgood Marshall is a communist," Johnston said.

These remarks irked Keating, who said that the charge of practicing without a license was "totally without merit"; he pointed out that the FBI had checked Marshall's background thoroughly and "if there had been the slightest doubt as to his loyalty, it would have been reported and the president would never have made the nomination."

Senator Philip A. Hart of Michigan said: "In my book, Mr. Marshall will find a place in history along with the great judges."

Thirty Democrats and twenty-four Republicans voted to approve the confirmation. Sixteen southern Democrats from nine states whose leaders had opposed civil rights legislation voted against Marshall, including Thurmond. Democrats William Fulbright of Arkansas and George Smathers of Florida were "absent."

Marshall's confirmation to a seat on the court of appeals was held up for reasons far more profound and enduring than some senator's resentment of his attacks on Jim Crow laws in his state. Then as now a lot of Americans did not believe that a black man had the intellectual qualifications to act as an appellate judge — as any kind of judge — and all the doubters were not in the South. People looked at Marshall and said that "just because a nigger can win cases before this Supreme Court doesn't mean he's as smart as white folks." Georgia's Senator Richard Russell seemed to want people to think that some kind of voodoo would explain Marshall's record as the lawyer who had won the most cases before the high tribunal in modern times. Russell said Marshall exercised "an almost occult power" over the Supreme Court.

Lurking in the minds of many senators and others was the notion of fundamental black intellectual inferiority. Sure, a "nigger" could argue and plead and whine about discrimination against other "niggers," but what could any "nigger" know about tax laws, bankruptcy proceedings, securities and other Wall Street transactions, patent law, and the other critical business-oriented legal conflicts that were the basic issues before the Second Circuit Court of Appeals?

Despite Marshall's angry letter to Chester Gillespie, the Cleveland Republican who had accused him of "campaigning desperately" for a federal judgeship, it had been clear to me for years that Marshall really wanted such a post — for reasons that did not always arise from personal ambition. He had told me in 1955 how "it pains my ass to go from one courtroom after another in one state after another, north or south, east or west, and never see anything but white faces on the bench.

"You goddamn reporters keep writing about how this president or that one is going to change something, but it never happens."

I suspected that Marshall was rankled by the myriad inside stories and gossip articles giving him an immediate seat on the federal bench. I remembered specifically that in late 1949 Cliff MacKay, the editor of the *Afro-American*, had written that President Truman was about to give Bill Hastie (then governor of the Virgin Islands) a spot on the court of appeals in Washington; the distinguished Raymond Pace Alexander a seat on the Third Circuit Court in Philadelphia; and Marshall one of four judicial vacancies in New York. MacKay said New York's Democratic National Committeeman, Edward J. Flynn, had demanded an appointment for Marshall. Nothing happened for Marshall, whose embarrassment almost equaled his rage over the fact that at the time the only two blacks serving in the federal judiciary were Herman Moore in the Virgin Islands district court and Irvin G. Mollison on the U.S. Customs Court.

"Negroes don't have a chance at justice across the boards when all the judges are white, most of them beholden to senators and other politicians who by culture, fear, and personal instinct are committed to segregation and to keeping the Negro down," Marshall said.

I didn't have to guess how proud Marshall felt in 1961 when he heard President Kennedy say: "One hundred years of delay have passed since President Lincoln freed the slaves, yet their heirs, their grandsons are not fully free. They are not yet free from the bonds of injustice, they are not yet free from social and economic oppression, and this nation, for all its hopes and boasts, will not be fully free until all its citizens are free."

Marshall knew that he was to become Kennedy's agent of justice, the first symbol of a judicial system that was about to undergo drastic change.

But Marshall did not say anything publicly in 1961 that would alert his foes to the revolutionary thoughts that ran through his mind. Even in September 1962, when he finally was confirmed, he said simply: "I appreciate the nomination by President Kennedy . . . and the confirmation by the Senate. I will do my level best to live up to their expectations."

Truman did name Hastie to the Third Circuit Court of Appeals in late 1949, so Marshall had become the second black person to serve on any federal appellate court in the 160 years of this judicial structure.

Before the confirmation ordeal began, Marshall was beset by concerns that millions of harassed, anguishing black people across America would think that he was abandoning the civil rights movement for the "glamour" of "sitting up there with some white judges." Black schizophrenia was rampant even then, with some screaming loudly that black people couldn't get any power, and others castigating blacks who won some power as "sellouts." It took only a few hours for Marshall to conclude that he had paid his dues as a civil rights lawyer, and that all blacks would soon learn the importance of his taking the appeals court post. "After all," Marshall said to me, "I had brought together an incredible staff at the Legal Defense Fund. I couldn't have left the legal program in better hands than those of Jack Greenberg, Bob Carter, Connie Motley, and the other lawyers around the country who were sacrificing, and fighting, with unbelievable dedication."

Greenberg had been an Inc. Fund deputy of extraordinary value, first because his dedication to racial equality was beyond anybody's doubt. Lawyers who worked with him just never thought of him as "white" or "a Jew," Marshall told me, because in heart Greenberg was as "black" as Nat Turner, Martin Luther King, Jr., Marshall, or any of the leaders of rebellion against black bondage. But one dare not gloss over the importance of Greenberg's being Jewish. Many of the deans at the greatest law schools were Jewish; a Jew, Simon Sobeloff, was solicitor general during the great *Brown* debates before the Supreme Court; many of the most prestigious sociologists, psychiatrists, and social scientists who supported the argument of stigmatic injury were Jewish. Greenberg was the strongest link in a chain of legal actions in which black and Jewish Americans forged a common army of American freedom fighters.

Yet, even in 1961 the appointment of Marshall exposed some fractures in the foundation of black-Jewish alliance. Lurking in the minds of many senators, many WASPs, and more than a few Jews was the idea of the fundamental inferiority of black people. More Jews than would admit it accepted the view that Kennedy's appointment of Marshall was an act of "racial preference." And that was the beginning of a three-decade rift that has damaged both blacks and Jews.

Even as Marshall was being buffeted by the hot air of bigots for a year, he kept asking himself if he really wanted the judicial post. Some of his closest friends warned that he would be criticized for "abandoning the civil rights movement." Marshall said anew that he had brought together an incredible legal staff at the NAACP Legal Defense Fund, and that the litigations for broader justice were in good hands. When he was finally confirmed, he, Cissy, and their two sons moved into Morningside Gardens, a cooperative housing area near Columbia University.

Marshall was acutely aware that he, like every black pioneer, was being watched closely by his friends, and especially by those who hoped that he would fail. He got a pain in his gut when one writer covering a tax case wrote that he was "embarrassed" that Marshall "didn't seem to know what was going on."

Marshall, in fact, made important law while on the court of appeals. When he took the bench, the principle of "double jeopardy" did not extend to state prosecutions. In *U.S. ex rel. Hetenyl v. Wilkins* Marshall wrote for the court an opinion that the Supreme Court endorsed in *Benton v. Maryland*. His colleagues of the Second Circuit disagreed with him when he argued in dissent that an accused person had a right to counsel even during a hospital bed–identification. The Supreme Court sided with Marshall. While on the court of appeals, Marshall argued, in *People v. Galamison*, that Freedom Riders and black youths who "sat in" at soda fountains and lunch counters, trying to erase Jim Crow, were exercising constitutional rights that gave them protection from federal criminal prosecution. Marshall's view prevailed.

Taking a seat on the same court at about the same time was a distinguished district court judge, Irving R. Kaufman. Long after Marshall had left that appellate court, Kaufman gave the answer to those who had argued privately that Marshall was not up to the job and thus not worthy of the appointment. Kaufman noted that during Marshall's three and a half years on the Second Circuit, he wrote 118 opinions and "not one . . . was reversed."

Kaufman summed up the essence of Marshall's tenure as an appeals judge this way:

> His opinion in *U.S. ex rel. Hetenyl v. Wilkins* presaged the Supreme Court's decision in *Benton v. Maryland*, extending the Fifth Amendment's protection against double jeopardy to state prosecutions [establishing, simply, that a state could not prosecute a citizen twice for the same crime]. His dissenting opinions bore eloquent testimony to his concern for the dignity and inviolability of the individual. Indeed, in one of these, Thurgood's view that an accused had a right to counsel during a hospital bed identification was ultimately adopted by the Supreme Court after the Second Circuit, sitting *en banc*, had disagreed with then-Judge Marshall's stance.
>
> My most abiding memory of Thurgood on this [appeals] court, however, was his ability to infuse his judicial product with the elements of the advocate's craft. As an attorney Thurgood stressed "the human side" of the case. As a judge he wrote for the people. . . . He possessed an instinct for the critical fact, the gut issue, born of his exquisite sense of the practical. . . . Behind his jovial veneer is a precise and brilliant and legal tactician who, to quote

his 1966 Law Day speech, was able "to shake free of the 19th century moorings and view the law not as a set of abstract and socially unrelated commands of the sovereign, but as an effective instrument of social policy." Thurgood was able to sear the nation's conscience and move hearts formerly strangled by hoary intransigence.

Marshall wore the robe with great pride. He knew that it bestowed upon him, his family, and by projection all black people, a measure of wide-ranging respect that he could never have gained as a civil rights lawyer. A friend of the judge's once told me that he and Marshall had gone for lunch at a very popular restaurant and were standing far back in a waiting line.

"Watch how it works," Marshall said. "Now that I'm a judge, they'll treat us nice."

In a minute or so the maitre d' walked past other waiting customers, tapped Thurgood on the arm and said, "Sir, please come with me." As Marshall and his friend were seated at a choice table, the maitre d' said, "And now, Congressman [Adam Clayton] Powell, what would you like to drink?"

As a full-fledged member of the court of appeals, Marshall entered the relative obscurity that goes with such a position. Not many Americans knew about or understood the ramifications of the several cases that Marshall was deciding. But he was not out of the minds of some very important people, one of them being Lyndon B. Johnson, who became president after the tragic assassination of President Kennedy.

Lyndon Johnson was having no problem of misidentification concerning Marshall. He knew not only who Marshall was, but what he was doing. He determined that Judge Marshall was to become the first black justice on the United States Supreme Court. But Johnson was determined not to get involved in the kind of confirmation brawl that attended Kennedy's appointment of this celebrated black man to the court of appeals. Johnson had an advantage that Kennedy did not: the Texan knew where a lot of bodies were buried in the Senate; he knew the skeletons in a lot of closets; he still had a lot of IOU's outstanding from his days as Senate majority leader. He would build a political ski lift for Marshall's ascent to the Supreme Court.

There probably never has been, and never will be, a United States president more given to plotting and scheming, to devious and conspiratorial means of producing a result that he felt was good for the nation, than Lyndon Johnson. His campaign to put the first black man on the U.S. Supreme Court, after ninety-five white men had served on this high tribunal, was LBJ at his scheming best.

Johnson, a Texan who had previously supported segregation, had a passion for proving that he was more liberal than the Kennedys, whom he disliked because he felt they were "uppity" and thought themselves better than a country boy from Texas. Johnson also was determined to prove that he could be a more effective president than Kennedy because he knew how to get legislation through the Congress. LBJ never doubted that he knew how to get a black man past the southern racists and onto the highest court in the land. Johnson's closest aide, Jack Valenti, told me how Johnson went about it:

"Did President Johnson make an early, calculated decision to name a black person to the Supreme Court?" I asked.

"He sure did, and he did it early on," Valenti said. "He was determined that he was gonna put a black on the Supreme Court at the same time that he was trying to pass his monumental Voting Rights Act of 'sixty-five. And I remember that in talking to me about it he determined that he had to get somebody — a black who was going to survive the gauntlet of congressional intervention and hearings for confirmation. He wanted to so certify him that there'd be absolutely no question at all that this black man would be confirmed, even lauded.

"You know," Valenti continued, "today you don't have to be too courageous to vote for civil rights, but in those days Southerners were not given the freedom of maneuver that they have today, nor were there large blocs of black voters pressing for attention. So the blacks were out there all alone in the South and without having the right to vote. It was very, very tough. So President Johnson knew without any question that there was going to be considerable southern opposition to what he was going to try to do."

"Why did he pick Thurgood Marshall?"

"Johnson thought Marshall's credentials as a courtroom lawyer were unsurpassed. He described Marshall as 'a lawyer and judge of very high ability. A patriot of deep conviction, and a gentleman of undisputed integrity.' But he'd determined that he had to outfit Thurgood Marshall and armor him with the kind of battle plates that no opposition could penetrate. I remember he said, 'By God, I'm going to take Thurgood, and I'm going to make him solicitor general, and then when somebody says, "He doesn't have a lot of experience for the Supreme Court," by God, that son of a bitch will have prosecuted more cases before the Supreme Court than any lawyer in America. So how's anybody gonna turn him down?' So he took the fifty-seven-year-old black man off the U.S. Court of Appeals for the Second Circuit and nominated him to be solicitor general of the United States, the first black man ever to hold this third-ranking post in the Justice Department. And so he had a kind of life course all picked out for Thurgood Marshall."

I noted Marshall apparently didn't know this because he told me he was the most surprised man in the world when Johnson told him he was naming him to the Supreme Court.

"Carl, as well you know, Johnson played things close to his vest and he wanted the element of surprise always on his side," Valenti said. "But he was also like a chess player. He played the game six moves down the board, so he knew exactly where he wanted to go. And he knew he wanted to outfit Marshall with all this experience as solicitor general, which is the number one lawyer's job in the government, and the one lawyer whose total practice is before the Supreme Court of the United States."

I asked how much heat the southern senators put on the president.

"I know that Johnston did lay some heat on the president," said Valenti, "but keep in mind that President Johnson had early on in his administration determined to take on the southern establishment, which as you know was headed by the man that Johnson most loved, most revered, Senator Richard Russell of Georgia. Johnson was willing to take on his mentor and his guide, Russell, as he did shortly after he became president by letting Russell know that on the Civil Rights Act of 1964 there'd be no caviling, no compromise. It was all-out, winner-take-all. If Johnson was willing to do that with Russell, he was certainly willing to do it with Johnston, and he made it very clear that he wasn't going to back down or cave in or hesitate or delay — that Thurgood Marshall was going to be solicitor general.

"He knew he had the votes, but the thing had to play out," Valenti continued. "I think each senator had to have his say, because, remember, the confirmation hearings are not only for the record in Washington; you're also playing to the folks back home. But Johnson always believed he had the votes. You can say many things about Lyndon Johnson, but two things you can't say: first, that he was dull; and second, that he wasn't a good vote counter.

"President Johnson was quite proud of his appointment of Marshall [as justice of the Supreme Court]. He counted *that* appointment as one of the two or three greatest accomplishments of his administration. He thought that it not only had symbolism, but it was rooted in the overall cause that he fought for, which was to bring the Negro in America to what he called the front rank of citizenship. And the first thing you do, President Johnson said, was to give people the vote, then they got power; and the second thing is you gotta provide that symbolism of power. There is no greater reward I suppose for anybody than to be one of the nine men and women on the Supreme Court. So President Johnson was justly proud of his appointment of Mr. Justice Marshall. And I think it's fair to say that Mr. Justice Marshall made him proud," Valenti added.

When Marshall got word that Johnson wanted to appoint him as the thirty-third solicitor general of the United States, he felt a sense of unease. He had a lifetime appointment on the appellate court at a salary of $33,000. As solicitor general he would take a $4,500 pay cut — considerable for a black family with no financial reserves — and he would serve at the whim of Johnson, who by this time was in public disfavor and political peril because of the Vietnam War.

But Marshall knew that the post of solicitor general was far more important than the job of any single appellate judge. The solicitor general was more than just the government's voice before the Supreme Court; he was the person who decided which of a possible fifteen hundred or so government appeals would be taken before the high tribunal. The solicitor general had not only a skilled staff of ten of the best lawyers in America, but could call upon the legal staffs of all federal departments and agencies. In short, he ran the greatest law firm in the land. Marshall knew that he would be succeeding Harvard law professor Archibald Cox, who had become something of a legend in arguing a record sixty-seven cases, including critical voter reapportionment cases.

Thurgood's and Cissy's deliberations were influenced most of all by their knowledge that three solicitors general — William Howard Taft, Stanley F. Reed, and Robert H. Jackson — had become Supreme Court justices. Neither Johnson nor Valenti had made him any promises, any intimations, about his eventually being appointed to the Supreme Court. But just as Patrick Henry "smelt a rat" and refused to go to the constitutional convention in Philadelphia, Marshall smelt a bouquet of opportunities, including a powerful Supreme Court seat.

His poker cronies often asked Marshall if he would like an appointment to the high tribunal. He gave a no-fake answer: "Hell, there isn't a lawyer in the country who wouldn't jump at the offer of such an appointment."

He and Cissy had come to a decision, but Marshall had to put on one last show. He knew that by tradition the solicitor general went before the Supreme Court wearing striped pants, a black vest, a swallowtailed coat. Hell, he had bought some of that fancy stuff in 1960 to wear at the inauguration of President William Tubman of Liberia, and he hadn't amortized it worth a damn. He went into a closet, put the fancy garb on, and walked out to show Cissy. "It still fits. Let's go for it."

The next day he initiated steps to buy a new townhouse in Southwest Washington, into which his family would move.

On July 13, 1965, President Johnson announced that his new solicitor general would be Marshall.

Marshall's tenure as an appeals court judge, and most of all Johnson's orchestration and words, disarmed the black man's foes in the Senate. Less than six weeks after the appointment was announced, on August 24, 1965, Marshall was sworn in as solicitor general by Supreme Court justice Hugo L. Black in the White House cabinet room. Johnson said proudly that "our nation has now progressed to the point — in large measure because of what Thurgood Marshall has done — that race no longer serves as a bar to the exercise of experience and skill."

Marshall told me: "I got real shook up when I read that Cox had lain awake every night before a major case, sick to the point of wanting to vomit. I learned that other solicitors general had panicked at the thought of speaking for the country before those nine men. Even though I had been before the Court as a civil rights lawyer, my knees were knocking that first day when I put on that outrageous outfit and stood listening to Chief Justice Warren declare somberly, 'The Court welcomes you.' But I soon found out that I was dealing with, or against, people of pretty much the same abilities as I had, and I learned to relax."

"Relaxing" was a lot harder as solicitor general than it had been as civil rights lawyer because Marshall couldn't always stick to his personal views while speaking for the government. Even before he was sworn in, Marshall discovered that his views did not match those of the American people, and would be disavowed by history. President Johnson named Marshall to head a U.S. delegation to a United Nations Congress on Prevention of Crime, in Stockholm, Sweden. Marshall told reporters that capital punishment would soon be abolished in the United States. He said, "There is a clear tendency to favor abolition [of executions], and the trend tells us that capital punishment is on its way out, although prosecuting attorneys would fight like mad against it."

Solicitor General Marshall pleased liberal lawyers and many millions of ordinary Americans in July 1966 when he disclosed in Court that the FBI was bugging the rooms of people under suspicion in violation of a federal policy that forbade all federal employees to use listening devices, or devices that directly tapped telephones and other wires, except in cases of national security. Even if "national security" was involved, Marshall told the Court, the U.S. attorney general had to give specific approval of any bugging. Several judges applauded when Marshall declared that all eavesdropping was illegal because "it is trespassing" on rights of privacy that had always been protected by the Constitution.

When Marshall took the oath of office as solicitor general the nation was just beginning to see the fruits of his labors against poll taxes, grandfather clauses, property requirements, white primaries, and the brutal violence that had been used to deny black people the vote. Marshall hadn't merely won *Smith v. Allwright* and other critical voting cases, but he; Whitney Young, the great Urban League leader; Martin Luther King, Jr.; Roy Wilkins; Dorothy Height, the ageless leader of the National Council of Negro Women; Rosa Parks of Montgomery bus boycott fame; and others had changed public opinion and emboldened legislators to encode black freedoms in the Voting Rights Act of 1965. That statute said clearly that the Department of Justice had the power to prevent anyone in any state from discouraging potential voters to register and cast ballots. There were to be no more tactics in which registrars disqualified black would-be voters because they couldn't answer questions such as "How many bubbles in a bar of soap?" The 1965 law passed by Congress mandated the Justice Department to impose strict enforcement of the laws in those states that historically had denied otherwise qualified citizens the right to vote because of their race.

Those targeted states sought sanctuary in the 1830 words of Daniel Webster, who declared, "The national government possesses those powers which it can be shown the people have conferred on it, and no more. All the rest belongs to the state governments, or to the people themselves."

South Carolina embraced this argument with passion, arguing that the Voting Rights Act usurped powers reserved to the states by the Constitution, and that it unfairly singled out southern states.

What an irony. As solicitor general, Marshall could, and did, make the Justice Department and White House extensions of the civil rights movement. Sure, those judges in the *Briggs v. Elliott* school segregation cases he argued in Charleston had rejected Kenneth Clark's dolls, and the argument of stigmatic injury, but now as solicitor he could have the last word over judges Parker and Timmerman. This time Marshall would have the government on his side, because when he put on his striped pants and his swallowtailed coat, he was "the government," speaking with awesome authority.

So, in 1966, in *South Carolina v. Katzenbach,* solicitor Marshall led a team that wrote a brief saying that nothing in the Constitution gave South Carolina or any other state or jurisdiction the right to say with absolute authority which group of people would be granted the right to vote. The solicitor argued that the Fifteenth Amendment expressly forbade all states to deny anyone the right to vote on the basis of race, color, or national origin. Marshall said that the Congress was on the soundest of constitutional grounds when it passed the Voting Rights Act.

A unanimous Supreme Court embraced the Marshall brief and said that in passing the Voting Rights Act of 1965 the Congress had not trampled upon the powers or rights of any state.

Solicitor General Marshall didn't just wage war against the South. He hardly had his striped pants on before he was involved in a dispute over whether a New York "literacy in English" requirement was constitutional. The New York law making the right to vote contingent on whether the would-be voter had a level of literacy in English was clearly a ploy to block the enfranchisement of the large and growing Puerto Rican population.

Solicitor Marshall, carrying the weight of the attorney general and the president behind his argument, got the Supreme Court to agree that New York's English literacy requirement constituted egregious discrimination against the Puerto Ricans and violated their Fourteenth Amendment rights.

Marshall told me that he was "in seventh heaven" when he realized that in cases dear to his heart and soul he was no longer just an ill-funded, oft-threatened civil rights lawyer. As the solicitor general he had whatever money was needed; he had the support of brilliant lawyers from every corner of the federal bureaucracy. On the issue of fair housing, for example, as the voice of the government, he could achieve in weeks what he had fought for years to do in winning *Shelley v. Kraemer, Sipes v. McGhee,* and other celebrated housing discrimination cases.

In 1967 the solicitor faced a unique dilemma. California had said in section 51 of its civil codes in 1959 that "all persons within the jurisdiction of this State are free and equal, and no matter what their race, color, religion, ancestry, or national origin are entitled to the full and equal accommodations, advantages, facilities, privileges, or service in all business establishments of every kind whatsoever." Another civil code declared that "whoever denies, or who aids, or incites such denial, or whoever makes any discrimination, distinction or restriction on account of color, race, religion, ancestry, or national origin, contrary [to section 51] of this code, is liable for each and every such offense for the actual damages, and two hundred fifty dollars ($250) in addition thereto, suffered by any person denied the rights provided in section 51 of this code."

It appeared that the law was settled in California in a laudable way. But racists somehow aroused enough passions, especially over "fair housing," that a group managed to put before the people "Proposition 14," an amendment to California's constitution that said, in effect, that anyone in the state who did not want to sell property to any person he or she found objectionable had the shield of the law. The actual words were:

"Neither the State nor any subdivision or agency thereof shall deny, limit or abridge, directly or indirectly, the right of any person, who is willing or desires to sell, lease or rent any part or all of his real property, to decline to sell, lease or rent such property to such person or persons as he, in his absolute discretion, chooses."

Solicitor Marshall didn't need a second to see the terrible implications of Proposition 14. There arose quickly a legal test when a black couple, the Mulkeys, sued a white couple, the Reitmans, for refusing to rent them an apartment. After a spate of conflict, confusion, and reversals in the California courts, the issue went before the Supreme Court. Solicitor Marshall argued in *Reitman v. Mulkey* that Proposition 14 in effect nullified the state's antidiscrimination statutes. The Supreme Court agreed, asserting that the U.S. Constitution does not permit any state to take actions that "make private discrimination legally possible."

Marshall never feasted so unrestrainedly upon the powers of directing and speaking for the mammoth law enforcement machinery of the U.S. government than when he got a chance to use his office to rectify an injustice that wounded his heart. He knew that cases that he had won as "Mr. Civil Rights" had inspired and animated millions of people, especially young people, across America. He knew that the NAACP and the Legal Defense and Educational Fund combined did not have the money or the human resources to bring to practical life the legal victories that he had won. So he pleaded publicly and privately for white and black volunteers to challenge housing and job discriminations locally, to file lawsuits against landlords and employers who practiced bigotry in egregious ways.

In June 1964 Marshall responded, with anger and anguish, to news reports that three civil rights volunteers, James Chaney, Michael Schwerner, and Andrew Goodman, had been murdered outside of Philadelphia, Mississippi.

"It hurt," Marshall told me. "Two Jewish kids and one black one get their lives snuffed out by racists. As an appeals court judge I couldn't say publicly how angry I was. When I read that a police car had taken the kids to the deserted area where they were murdered, I couldn't eat, drink, or do anything."

Marshall found out that as solicitor he could do something: prosecute the three law enforcement officers and their fifteen civilian co-conspirators who had murdered the young civil rights workers so brutally and bulldozed them into a common grave.

The solicitor was pleased when a grand jury indicted the eighteen on charges of "willful deprivation of life and liberty under color of Law without due process of law." Marshall was chagrined when the federal district court declared that the fifteen private defendants were not under "the color of law." The Mississippi district court also dismissed charges against the three officers of the law on grounds that they were indicted under a section of U.S. law that did not include rights protected by the Fourteenth Amendment. A raging Marshall appealed directly to the Supreme Court, which reinstated the indictments. The three law enforcement officers and four of the civilians eventually were convicted in these heinous murders.

In January 1966, Solicitor Marshall filed court papers saying that the Johnson administration was renouncing the portion of the 1965 Medicare law which said that persons filing for Medicare benefits would have to give an oath declaring that they did not belong to any communist or communist-related groups.

But Marshall shocked a lot of people, black and white, in the District of Columbia when in January 1967 he spoke in opposition to efforts to gain D.C. home rule by court order. Marshall urged the Supreme Court to ignore efforts by a Washington, D.C., group to win self-government through a lawsuit. Marshall objected to court-room efforts to limit Congress's authority over the District to national matters. "This Court has said as early as 1838," Marshall said, "that Congress has complete control over the District of Columbia for every governmental purpose. . . . Congress's power to legislate with respect to the District is as great as the power of a state legislature with respect to the state or any of its subdivisions."

Some black residents of the District were appalled to hear those words coming from a black hero. They were seeing evidence that, media reports to the contrary, Marshall was not a knee-jerk liberal. He was in fact conservative in many areas. Marshall was the solicitor who said the federal government could proceed in trying to imprison boxer Muhammad Ali for refusing induction into the Army in April 1967. Marshall defended the right of the president to conduct the war in Vietnam, including Nixon's bombings of Cambodia in 1973, when Marshall was on the Supreme Court.

Those trying to paint Marshall as a mindless, knee-jerk liberal had forgotten, or were ignoring, the fact that his major opposition to confirmation to the Supreme Court came from eleven senators and the Student Non-violent Coordinating Committee (SNCC), popularly known as Snick. The late, great newsman, Ralph McGill of the *Atlanta Constitution* noted in 1967: "The spectacle of the opposition of Southern senators . . . being joined in by Snick's extremists is highly educational. Snick doesn't like the justice because he is too moderate, is middle class and has white friends. They put these, and other, accusations into crude, harshly contemptuous words. . . .

"It is certain, if we speak of a personalized deity, that God in Heaven Himself is laughing loudly at this combination of political opposition."

Marshall argued nineteen cases before the Supreme Court and lost five. When asked once to assess his record, he said, "I volunteered to argue the toughest cases. I guess my record is about as good as anybody else's."

His most galling defeat came when he had to argue against his conscience in confession cases relating to the *Miranda v. Arizona* decision, which declared that suspects had to be warned of their rights before they could be questioned by the police. He voiced the government's opinion that the Supreme Court should not require the appointment of counsel at precinct stations for suspects, or the accused, who could not afford lawyers. "We can't equalize the whole thing," Marshall said.

The Supreme Court shot him down. It is noteworthy that, as this book will later show, some of Marshall's most enduring achievements as a Supreme Court justice lie in his reshaping the law to protect the poorest of Americans accused of crimes.

Marshall recalls his time as solicitor general with special pride:

"It was the best job I ever had. Usually the solicitor general wins on most cases because he takes those that are important and necessary, and he has the full force of great legal minds to work on his cases. The average brief that comes out of the solicitor general's office has been worked on by twenty or thirty people.

"But we never let politics in. When I was solicitor general, a senator who wanted to talk to me had to explain what he wanted to talk about. If he wanted to talk about a case, I didn't discuss it."

Later, Marshall spoke passionately about the extent to which President Reagan and his attorney general Ed Meese had politicized the office of the solicitor general and the Justice Department as a whole. I noted that Meese had led a campaign against "judicial activism" and in favor of a "strict interpretation" of the Constitution.

"People who listen to Meese's statement should bear in mind that they're for the political arena, not the judicial arena," Marshall said. "I don't pay any attention to Meese's statements."

Asked if he thought Meese gave proper respect to the separation of the powers of the executive and judicial branches, Marshall snapped: "I don't think he understands it."

Was this harsh judgment by a Supreme Court justice motivated by a feeling that Meese and others in the Reagan administration were out to undermine and destroy everything that Marshall had achieved?

"I don't think it's aimed at me at all. It's aimed at the Constitution. There are certain movements that the Justice Department is making that could be interpreted as trying to undermine the Supreme Court itself, which is impossible."

When Marshall was told in early June 1967 that President Johnson wanted to see him, he had learned from Attorney General Ramsey Clark that his father, Tom Clark, had given up his seat as a justice "to give the president room to do something he wanted to do badly." Marshall telephoned Cissy to tell her that the high tribunal seat he had said was "not in the cards" just might fall out of the deck that morning — a deck that Johnson had stacked skillfully.

Marshall arrived at the White House at the end of a meeting the president was having with a few members of the cabinet, CIA director Richard Helms, and a few others about the war in Vietnam. The war had drawn Johnson's self-esteem lower than a snake's belly, and he was eager to display his greatness as a human being and as president by showing off his black Supreme Court nominee-to-be. When Johnson told his aides what he planned to do, Helms told me, Marshall tried to fake surprise.

"Oh, boy!" he exclaimed. "Wait till Cissy hears this. Is she ever gonna be shocked!"

"You mean you haven't told her anything?" Johnson asked.

"Hell, how could I tell her when nobody's told me anything?" replied Marshall.

"Well, goddammit, let's get her on the speaker phone and we'll all tell her," said Johnson.

A White House operator, with typical efficiency, had Mrs. Marshall on the line immediately, but totally unaware that she was on a speaker phone.

"It's me, honey," Thurgood said.

"Yeah, honey," Cissy supposedly replied. "Did we get the Supreme Court appointment?"

Even Johnson, who had almost no sense of humor, guffawed.

In 1967, in appointing Marshall to the Supreme Court, Johnson played out his game plan by telling the press:

"I believe it is the right thing to do, the right time to do it, the right man, and the right place.

"Statisticians tell me that probably only one or two living men have argued as many cases before the [Supreme] Court, and perhaps less than half a dozen in all the history of the nation.

"As chief counsel for the National Association for the Advancement of Colored People, Marshall won twenty-nine of thirty-two cases he argued before the Supreme Court. As U.S. solicitor general, he argued the government's case on nineteen occasions and lost but five."

The media was unaware that in order to open up a place for Marshall on the Court, Johnson had played a shrewd game with his fellow Texan, Justice Tom C. Clark. Johnson had named Tom's son, Ramsey, to be attorney general of the United States. This meant that Justice Clark, in order to avoid a clear conflict of interest, had to give up his seat on the High Court.

Johnson talked a lot about "getting his ducks in line" whenever he made an appointment that he thought might be controversial. Now he called Albert E. Jenner, Jr., of the American Bar Association's Committee on the Federal Judiciary and got word that the committee would give Marshall the same rating it had given to Justices Arthur J. Goldberg and Abe Fortas — "Highly Acceptable" — the top rank.

Johnson reached Chief Justice Earl Warren in San Francisco and got him to make a public statement saying that he was "very happy" about the Marshall nomination. "He has had a tremendous amount of experience, of the kind that will be very helpful to the Court," Warren said, adding "I can't imagine better training for the Court than Marshall has had."

While Johnson realized that southern senators would cause him the most grief, he realized that Marshall was opposed by Americans in all regions for reasons other than his espousal of racially integrated schools. Marshall was viewed as a "liberal," a word already falling into political disfavor. It didn't matter that as solicitor general Marshall had ridiculed the efforts to glorify Malcolm X, or that he had spoken out politically against Stokely Carmichael and Rap Brown, the "Burn, baby, burn" black militants. Marshall was opposed, even feared, by some because he scoffed at demands for a "strict interpretation" of the Constitution, arguing that this document was meant to bend, expand, embrace the needs and problems of every generation. Some worried that as defense lawyer and judge Marshall was too inclined to extend too many rights to indigent criminal suspects, or favor defendants over policemen in cases where claims were made of illegal searches and seizures, or that a "confession" was coerced.

Johnson personally telephoned southern senators who, he believed, had walked far enough away from the campaigns of bigotry to have the guts to vote to confirm Marshall.

Still, there was angry opposition from some members of the House and Senate. Some editors in the Deep South expressed outrage. A more "delicate" expression of opposition came from James J. Kilpatrick, the newspaper columnist and former Richmond, Virginia, editor who had been an adamant force behind Virginia's policy of "massive resistance" to the decree ordering the desegregation of public schools. Kilpatrick wrote:

". . . in choosing Marshall to replace the retiring Tom Clark, President Johnson deliberately has moved to upset the rough balance of liberalism and conservatism that recently has prevailed upon the high tribunal. Next term, the forces of judicial restraint will be represented only by [John Marshall] Harlan, [Potter] Stewart, and [Byron R.] White, with an occasional vote from Black. The judicial activists will be in full control.

"By a process of evolution, culminating dramatically in the Warren Court, the tribunal has become the most powerful authority in the whole of our federal system. Its members, serving for life, are in a commanding position to shape national policies as they please. These days, they often are pleased to turn the Constitution into wax.

"At one time, it might have been possible to oppose his nomination by reason of Marshall's total concentration on the narrow field of Negro rights, but his service on the United States Second Circuit and his experience as Solicitor General have removed that objection. Beyond cavil, he is qualified for the high court — more qualified, in truth, than many of his predecessors.

"In *Cooper v. California*, and again in *McCray v. Illinois*, Clark was one of five who voted to strengthen the hand of police officials in securing evidence of crime. The two decisions served to bring some common sense back to the law of Fourth Amendment searches. How would Marshall have voted in these critically important cases? It is a fair surmise that he would have voted with Warren, Douglas, Brennan, and Fortas to reverse.

"What the court and country will be getting in Marshall will be a more congenial Fortas, a less truculent Goldberg, a more disarming Brennan. The appointment is a great tribute to Marshall's own skill and industry; he is the great-grandson of a slave, the son of a Pullman waiter. No critic would wish to take away from the heartwarming success story that came to its climax Tuesday. All the same, in any conservative view of the workings of the court, the nomination is something worse than net no-gain. This was bad news — almost disastrous news — and we shall be living with it for the next ten years at least."

"How did it feel when you heard Johnson say, 'The right man, the right time, the right place' and tell the nation that he was naming you to the Supreme Court?" I once asked Marshall.

"How did I feel?" he replied. "Hell, like any lawyer in America would feel. Real proud — because there is no greater honor a lawyer can get. I felt especially great because I knew President Johnson was using me to say something important to the nation."

Marshall was nominated to the Court at a time when it was already facing serious criticism, not only from politicians, but from thousands of judges and lawyers across the land. Ironically, on August 3, 1967, when Marshall's nomination to the Supreme Court was cleared, 11 to 5, by the Senate Judiciary Committee (all five Southerners voted against him), Justice Byron R. White was in Honolulu at a meeting of state supreme court justices, where he had to defend the Court against some virulent attacks. White ran into complaints that the Court's recent decisions had made it more difficult to obtain criminal convictions, that the Court was giving lawbreakers a legal advantage over those trying to preserve law and order. There was special criticism of the Court's decision in *Miranda v. Arizona*.

White said that he had seen no figures, no research to indicate that *Miranda* had had such a deleterious effect. "But whatever the facts are," he asked, "is the seriousness of the impact of *Miranda* of any relevance whatsoever in determining the proper scope of the Fifth Amendment's shield against self-incrimination?" Judge J. Edward Lumbard of the U.S. Court of Appeals for the Second Circuit followed White with a speech in which he said: "If it should turn out that police adherence to the new ritual makes impossible the solution of many serious crimes," the *Miranda* case could be reversed only through a Constitutional amendment, or having the Supreme Court reverse itself.

The nation was still in turmoil over Fifth Amendment rights, primarily because Senator Joseph McCarthy and those who thought the way he did had made a lot of Americans believe that in giving people the right to "plead the Fifth" the courts were letting communists and criminals hide behind the Constitution. In his confirmation hearings, Marshall was pressed repeatedly by Senator Ervin, a former North Carolina judge, to state emphatically his views on the Fifth Amendment and whether the words "No person shall be compelled in any criminal case to be a witness against himself" applied to testimony or statements that were not compelled. Marshall responded that it would not be proper for him to state his views in the hearings in view of the fact that Fifth Amendment cases were going to come before the Court. That provoked this exchange:

> *SENATOR ERVIN:* I will tell you, Judge, if you are not going to answer a question about anything which might possibly come before the Supreme Court some time in the future, I cannot ask you a single question about anything that is relevant to this inquiry.
>
> *JUDGE MARSHALL:* All I am trying to say, Senator, is I do not think you want me to be in the position of giving you a statement on the Fifth Amendment, and then, if I am confirmed and sit on the Court, when a Fifth Amendment case comes up, I will have to disqualify myself.
>
> *SENATOR ERVIN:* If you have no opinions on what the Constitution means at this time, you ought not to be confirmed. Anybody that has been at the bar as long as you have, and has as distinguished a legal career as you have, certainly ought to have some very firm opinions about the meaning of the Constitution.
>
> *JUDGE MARSHALL:* But as to particular language of a particular section that I know is going to come before the Court, I do have an opinion as of this time. But I think it would be wrong for me to give that opinion at this time. When the case comes before the Court, that will be the time.
>
> I say with all due respect, Senator, that is the only way it has been done before.

The Senate confirmation hearings showed the president's wisdom in setting up the press, getting endorsements of Marshall, and otherwise "getting his ducks in line," because that old nemesis, Thurmond, and some of his pals were still determined to "get even" with Marshall. The Senate transcript shows that in addition to Ervin, Thurmond, Eastland, and John McClellan of Arkansas tried to set booby traps:

> *THURMOND*: On March eight, eighteen fifty, Senator Andrew P. Butler, a South Carolina Democrat and a lawyer, who was John C. Calhoun's colleague in the Senate, stated, and I quote: "A free man of color in South Carolina is not regarded as a citizen by her laws but he has high civil rights. His person and property are protected by law, and he can acquire property, and can claim the protection of the laws for their protection . . . but they are persons recognized by law, and protected by law."
>
> Now, do you believe that this passage shows that the State of South Carolina, while a slave state, was the national leader in giving "civil rights" and "protection of the laws" to colored people, or does it show that these terms had a different meaning a century ago than the Supreme Court has recently given them?
>
> *MARSHALL*: Well, I don't agree that at that time South Carolina was the leader in giving Negroes their rights.

Yet Thurmond had to go after Marshall one more time. On July 19, 1967, he put on a legal show that was either brilliant or disgusting, depending on where one stood on the issue of Marshall's confirmation. Thurmond spent more than an hour grilling Marshall on some of the most obscure and esoteric questions of law that anyone could have imagined.

"Do you know who drafted the Thirteenth Amendment to the U.S. Constitution?" Thurmond asked.

"No, sir, I don't remember," Marshall replied.

Thurmond droned on and on, asking such questions as, "What committee reported out the Fourteenth Amendment and who were its members?" And, "What constitutional difficulties did Representative John Bingham of Ohio see in congressional enforcement of the Privileges and Immunities clause of Article Four, section two, through the Necessary and Proper clause of Article One, section eight?"

"I don't understand the question," Marshall replied laconically.

Through most of the hour, Marshall sat unflappable, mostly saying, "I don't know," often to the amusement of people on the committee and in the hearing room.

There was great laughter when Thurmond asked Marshall:

"What provisions of the slave codes in existence in the South before eighteen sixty was Congress desirous of abolishing by the Civil Rights Bill of eighteen sixty-six?"

Marshall replied: "Well, as I remember, the so-called Black Codes ranged from a newly freed Negro not being able to own property or vote, to a statute in my home state of Maryland which prevented these Negroes from flying kites."

Eastland seemed more coherent, and blunt, than Thurmond:

EASTLAND: Now, you have been in a lot of institutions in the Southern States.

MARSHALL: Yes, sir.

EASTLAND: Are you prejudiced against white people in the South?

MARSHALL: Not at all. I was brought up, what I would say way up South in Baltimore, Maryland. And I worked for white people all my life until I got in college. And from there most of my practice, of course, was in the South, and I don't know, with the possible exception of one person that I was against in the South, that I have any feeling about them.

The "point man" for the anti-Marshall group was McClellan, whose exchanges with Marshall remain fascinating because they deal with issues that even today are part of the great American debate.

McCLELLAN: We regard Supreme Court decisions interpreting the Constitution as being the law of the land, do we not?

MARSHALL: Yes, sir.

McCLELLAN: Whatever they say the Constitution is, we insist that is the law of the land?

MARSHALL: I think that is correct; yes, sir.

McCLELLAN: And we hold, too, that all citizens should be amenable to the law of the land?

MARSHALL: Absolutely.

McCLELLAN: Now, do you feel that that applies to everybody except Supreme Court justices?

MARSHALL: I think that the Supreme Court justices must be more responsive to their oath than any other judge because of that.

McCLELLAN: Then how can they consistently overrule a former decision holding an act constitutional or an act unconstitutional and then say they have been amenable to the law of the land?

MARSHALL: I believe, if you are speaking of stare decisis as such, that the Supreme Court and every member of it has a responsibility, when there is a decision that is up for reconsideration, a sort of flag to slow down and take a real good look and realize what you are actually doing.

McCLELLAN: Then may I ask you, do you feel that they are free to reverse previous decisions that involve constitutional questions?

MARSHALL: Yes, they are free to do it.

McCLELLAN: If you feel they are free, would you have any hesitancy in overruling the *Miranda* decision when it came up for consideration if you became convinced that the decision was wrong?

MARSHALL: If I became convinced that the *Miranda* decision was wrong, I would, of course, vote my conscience, which would say yes.

McCLELLAN: Then the previous Court decision does not bind you, although it is the law of the land?

MARSHALL: It binds the Supreme Court as well as it binds everybody else in the land.

McCLELLAN: That is an inconsistency, is it not? . . . The Supreme Court says so, today, but tomorrow, when you reconsider that decision, in your capacity you do not have to conform to it; you can overrule it and you can change the law of the land. Is that not so?

MARSHALL: I think that is the job of the Supreme Court.

McCLELLAN: To change the law of the land?

MARSHALL: No, sir. You did not let me finish. . . . I can say this, Senator: Number one, I hope you do not interpret me to say it is the duty of the Court to reverse decisions. It is the duty of the Court to keep stability of the law.

McCLELLAN: To what?

MARSHALL: To keep stability of the law.

McCLELLAN: How do you keep it when one year you hold one thing in the Court and next year hold something else? Is there any stability in that?

MARSHALL: It happens often in the exact same Court.

McCLELLAN: That is no stability, is it? You do not interpret that as stability, do you?

MARSHALL: Yes, sir.

McCLELLAN: Then your interpretation and definition of the word "stability" is that one day it is one thing and another day it is something else.

McClellan then sprang on Marshall a series of questions about wiretapping:

McCLELLAN: I am very concerned, as many other people are, about a condition that prevails in our country today, not only with respect to crime generally, but with respect to the tools that are made available to, or withheld from, law enforcement officers to use in their efforts against crime. And wiretapping or electronic surveillance has become a matter of national concern; but I think it is something that is vital. I think under proper regulations and court direction that it is absolutely indispensable to an effective war on organized crime and on some of the more heinous crimes that are committed. . . .

Tell this committee, whether in your own mind you now entertain the fixed belief or conviction that wiretapping or electronic surveillance, where authorized by a court under proper statutes and guidelines, and so forth, whether you have already concluded that the act itself would be an invasion of privacy, that it violates the constitutional rights of the individual.

MARSHALL: [As solicitor general] my position was clearly stated, that if you trespass upon a man's home or his office or any place which means going into his place without permission, and set up an electronic device, it was my interpretation of the Supreme Court decisions that that would be a violation of the man's rights under the Fourth Amendment.

McCLELLAN: And that is irrespective of the procedures by statute, irrespective of a court order directing it under authority of a statute, you would still believe that it is unconstitutional?

MARSHALL: Senator, I was speaking, as I remember, to federal investigators.

McCLELLAN: I don't care whether it is federal or state. We can talk about federal as far as I am concerned.

MARSHALL: Under the rules the federal investigators are not allowed to trespass except on security matters.

McCLELLAN: I am talking about a statute.

MARSHALL: Well, Senator, I would respectfully refer to the latest decision of the Supreme Court, which was the last decision, I think, of Mr. Justice Clark, in the New York case of *Berger,* in which the decision left open to the legislature, the Congress and the state legislature the authority to set up regulations by which eavesdropping could be done by state order.

McCLELLAN: Are you saying that you do not subscribe to the doctrine or the belief that it is unconstitutional to provide by statute for such surveillance?

MARSHALL: I have not made up my mind on that one way or the other. I am only guided by the Supreme Court's decision in the *Berger* case at this time. I believe the legislatures, and I am sure the Congress, will come up with legislation. And I have no fixed view one way or the other how that legislation would stand up against the Constitution. I would have to look at the act once it is passed.

McCLELLAN: What I am trying to ascertain, do you think one could be drawn that is constitutional?

MARSHALL: I think one can be drawn that is constitutional.

McCLELLAN: That would permit surveillance under a court order?

MARSHALL: Not just that. It would have to be more.

McCLELLAN: How much more?

MARSHALL: I don't know. That is my whole point, Senator.

McCLELLAN: That is what we get to. I know we get criticized for trying to find out the philosophy of a nominee for the Supreme Court of the United States. But they are possessed of and they are exercising a power that is lethal in my judgment to the security of this nation. And if we can't get some idea of the nominee's views with respect to the Constitution of the United States, then how am I to exercise my judgment and meet my responsibility in passing upon the suitableness of that nominee? If we can't find out some of the philosophy with respect to the Constitution, what will be constitutional and what will not be, in a matter as grave as the crime crisis in this country, I am in a quandary.

    . . . You can talk about democracy and liberty and all these things; I think they are in jeopardy today in this country. Look at the riots everywhere. A sentiment has been built up over the country to the point where some people feel that, if you don't like the law, violate it. And the Supreme Court takes the position that at its whim it can reverse decisions on constitutional issues, on constitutional questions, constitutional laws that have been the law of the land for a century. And they can change the law. They don't feel very strongly bound to enforce it, to observe it, and to follow it. No wonder the fellow out in the street thinks that, if the Supreme Court has no regard for precedent in law, and can change it when it wants to, why can't I do as I please?

We have an intolerable situation in this country, and I would like to find some way to check it. I would like to start at the top, for I think that is where you need to start.

You may lecture me if you want to. I have told you what I think.

MARSHALL: Far be it from me to attempt to lecture you, sir. I appreciate what you said, and appreciate your problem. And at the same time I am equally certain that you would not want me to prejudge a case that is certain to come up to the Court.

Ervin voted against the confirmation of Marshall, giving this reason:

"Judge Marshall is by practice and philosophy a constitutional iconoclast, and his elevation to the Supreme Court at this juncture in our history would make it virtually certain that for years to come, if not forever, the American people will be ruled by the arbitrary notions of Supreme Court justices rather than by the precepts of the Constitution."

The only non-Southerner who opposed Marshall's confirmation was Robert C. Byrd of West Virginia, who had previously voted to confirm Marshall as a judge on the Second Circuit Court of Appeals and as solicitor general. But Byrd contended that putting Marshall on the Supreme Court would create a "built-in activist majority" that would favor criminal defendants at the expense of the public good.

Obviously, the nomination of Marshall to the Supreme Court was a matter of great pride for black Americans, most of whom saw the seating of Marshall as an indicator of stronger Court support for civil rights and constitutional protections, something that they thought was the desire of most of white America as well.

Fourteen years earlier, when Warren was nominated as chief justice, James Reston had pointed out in the *New York Times* that on civil liberties issues, on such matters as the rights of aliens, loyalty oaths, religion and segregation in the schools, direct restraints upon communists and others regarded as subversive, the Supreme Court trend was toward giving priority to "national security," even if it meant restricting basic liberties. Reston noted that under Chief Justice Vinson, the Court had often voted 6 to 3 or 5 to 4 in favor of curbing civil liberties, and that from 1946, when Vinson was named chief justice, to 1951, he voted sixteen times in support of those who sought civil rights protections from the Court, and ninety-one times against. This meant that Vinson had voted in favor of civil liberties protections in only 15 percent of the cases. During that same period, Justice Reed had voted in favor of a claimed Constitutional right only 16 percent of the time; Justice Minton, 11 percent; Justice Burton, 25 percent; and Justice Jackson, 28 percent. The only justices who voted more than half the time in favor of those seeking constitutional protections were Frankfurter, 53 percent, Black, 79 percent, and Douglas, 83 percent. The oncoming of Earl Warren might make a critical difference, Reston concluded:

"There now seems to be a clear majority on the court in favor of the 'clear and present danger' doctrine first pronounced by Justice Oliver Wendell Holmes in 1919. That doctrine, which he put forward as a sort of 'rule of reason' for the guidance of the Government in the enforcement of legislative restrictions on the First Amendment freedoms, was as follows: That freedom of religion, speech, press and assembly are so uniquely important that legislative restrictions upon them should be presumed to be unconstitutional unless shown to be justified by 'a clear and present danger.' "

At the time of Johnson's appointment of Marshall, some expressed doubt that one black member of the Court could make a difference. But who could doubt that one man, Warren, had made a difference? Or that some occupants of what was considered "the Jewish seat," Brandeis, Cardozo, and Frankfurter especially, had had a great influence.

It is a trite but appropriate figure of speech to say that in 1967 the jury was out regarding Marshall.

The Supreme Court at that time was a virtual oasis of enlightenment compared with the federal judiciary in most of America. Federal judges tended to be ex-politicians, and because of a time-honored tradition known as "senatorial courtesy," they had to have the approval of the senators from their states or there was no way that they could win confirmation in a very conservative Senate Judiciary Committee, headed by Eastland. Marshall and others had seen the magnitude of Eastland's power in 1961 when the Mississippi segregationist refused to allow a vote to confirm Marshall to the Second Circuit Court of Appeals until President Kennedy agreed to name Eastland's law school roommate, Harold Cox, to a federal district court post in Mississippi. Reports at the time were that Eastland had met then-attorney general Robert Kennedy in a Senate hallway and said to him, "You tell your brother that when I get Cox, he gets the nigger."

To understand the importance of Marshall's appointment to the Supreme Court, you must know that for more than 160 years, no black man had served on any federal appellate court in the United States, until 1949, when President Truman appointed William H. Hastie to the Third Circuit Court of Appeals in Philadelphia. Then, in 1961, President Kennedy appointed Marshall to the Second Circuit Court of Appeals. In 1966, President Johnson named Spottswood Robinson III to the District of Columbia Circuit Court, and Detroit's Wade H. McCree to the Sixth Circuit. At the time Johnson appointed Marshall, no black person had ever sat as a federal district judge in Alabama, Arkansas, Florida, Georgia, Kentucky, Louisiana, Mississippi, North Carolina, South Carolina, Tennessee, Texas, or Virginia.

That tells part of the story of a virtually lily-white federal court system, and that is why the appointment of Marshall as a Supreme Court justice was hailed by many as the beginning of a sweeping change of the legal landscape in America. But the changes slowed abruptly when Johnson left the presidency. Neither President Nixon nor President Ford named a single black to any federal appeals court.

The changes, however, became truly significant when Georgian Jimmy Carter reached the presidency. He named eight blacks to serve with 123 white appellate judges, meaning that suddenly one out of fourteen of the federal appeals court judges was black. Carter also named thirty blacks to the federal district courts. His influence spilled over into the states, where blacks suddenly were being seated as judges on local benches.

This kind of progress ground to a halt when Reagan and Bush got to the presidency.

In his eight years as president, Reagan made 360 lifetime judicial appointments to the federal bench, including three Supreme Court justices, the elevation of William Rehnquist to chief justice, and the appointment of nearly half the full-time appeals court judges. Reagan and his advisers, Attorney General Edwin Meese and others, made clear that one of their goals was to achieve a more conservative judiciary — one that was against abortion, passive at best on civil rights, and often mindlessly tough on crime.

People for the American Way, a nonpartisan watchdog organization, studied President Bush's judicial nominations during his first two years in office and came up with a disturbing, though not surprising, conclusion: an overwhelming number of them were wealthy white men.

According to the study, 93 percent of Bush's sixty-nine nominees were white, 88 percent were male, and 64 percent reported a net worth of more than half a million dollars. More than one-third were millionaires.

That record is about the same as Reagan's, but a lot worse than Carter's. Fifteen percent of Carter's judicial nominees were black versus just 4 percent of Bush's and 2 percent of Reagan's. Sixteen percent of Carter's choices were women, compared with 12 percent for Bush and 8 percent for Reagan. Only 3 percent of Bush's and Reagan's nominees were Hispanic, half the proportion of Carter's.

At the time of their nominations, twenty-six of Bush's nominees — well over one-third — belonged to clubs that practiced or once practiced discrimination in choosing their members. On the other hand, not a single one reported membership in the American Civil Liberties Union.

In twelve years, Reagan and Bush appointed 115 appeals court judges, only two of them black, and one being the controversial conservative Clarence Thomas.

Does all this really make a difference? "A judiciary that fails to reflect the diversity of our society is that much more hard-pressed to mete out equal justice," said Arthur J. Kropp, president of People for the American Way.

"Unfortunately," he continued, "in terms of race, gender, and socioeconomic diversity, these [Bush] judges might just as easily have been nominated by Ed Meese and Ronald Reagan. In spite of [Bush's] rhetoric about the opening up of our society, his judicial nominations would suggest that the courthouse is still the province of wealthy white men."

On May 28, 1992, after studying 837 federal district, appellate, and Supreme Court appointments by Reagan and Bush, Kropp issued a massive document claiming to prove that

> the Reagan-Bush court-packing effort is unprecedented in terms of its scope and methods. We've seen political court appointments before, but never such a prolonged and blind adherence to strict ideological guidelines. The architects of this effort, coming from the Republican party's right wing, pulled off a judicial revolution in the guise of judicial restraint.

CHAPTER EIGHTEEN

THE COURT — AND ITS NONVIOLENT REVOLUTION

W HEN PRESIDENT JOHNSON named Marshall to the United States Supreme Court, he was ramming the civil rights leader into the vortex of a gigantic social and legal storm that would buffet Americans for the rest of the century — and beyond.

The nation was in turmoil, with the civil rights movement at a turning point, Lyndon Johnson's Great Society programs starting a social revolution, and the Vietnam War spilling over angrily into confrontations over "loyalty," freedom of the press, the draft, individual rights, and more.

For most of the twentieth century, in fact for most of its history, the Supreme Court had shied away from problems and issues like those. But that had begun to change during the 1940s and had definitely been turned around after Earl Warren became chief justice. By the time Marshall joined the high tribunal in 1967, the Court was well into a period of boldness and reform. One of its members, Abe Fortas, commented that the Warren Court provoked "the most profound and pervasive revolution ever achieved by substantially peaceful means." Fortas was replaced in 1970 by Harry A. Blackmun, who would become a great revolutionary in terms of abortion rights.

The chief revolutionary was Warren. To the surprise, shock, and disappointment of President Eisenhower, who had appointed him, Warren quickly made clear that he would not look at cases in terms of some "strict construction" of the presumed intentions of the framers of the Constitution. "What is fair?" "Where does justice lie?" Those were the hallmarks of Warren's determination to eschew legal technicalities and get to the heart of the issues of human values and personal dignity.

This man, who wanted so much to be president and was a serious contender in 1948 and 1952, inherited from the late Chief Justice Fred Vinson a Supreme Court that was terribly divided on the issue of "separate but equal." The justices had bricks in their bellies from emotional arguments over the intent of those who wrote a Constitution without mentioning slavery, over states' rights, over the predictions of violent upheaval if Jim Crow were to be ruled unconstitutional.

Warren untied the belly knots by simplifying the issue. Having accepted the Marshall-Clark assertions about the black and white dolls and the stigmatic injury of segregation, Warren said privately to each of the eight justices: "Unless you are prepared to say that Negro people, Negro children, are inherently inferior, you cannot uphold laws that decree that colored children may not study alongside white children." Warren got a unanimous verdict declaring Jim Crow schools in violation of the Constitution because no justice was prepared to declare that blacks were inherently inferior. This was leadership that every member of the Court agreed was powerful and rare.

But the storm that was gathering in 1967, when Marshall joined the Court, found devastating energy in other Warren Court decisions that affected the basic fabric of American life. McClellan had lectured Marshall on this.

Under Warren's leadership, the Court had made rulings that brought on the wrath of conservatives regarding justice for those facing criminal charges. In 1961, in *Mapp v. Ohio*, the Court said illegally seized evidence could not be introduced at a defendant's trial. Two years later the justices unanimously declared in the landmark *Gideon v. Wainwright* decision that states had to provide legal help for all defendants charged with serious crimes — meaning that if the defendant was unable to pay for an attorney, the state had to provide one for him or her.

The Court really incurred the wrath of the "law-and-order" forces in June 1966 when it ruled, by a 5 to 4 margin in *Miranda v. Arizona*, that police were forbidden to interrogate suspects in their custody unless they were informed of their right to remain silent, that their words could be used against them, and that they had the right to a lawyer.

All this was occurring while the nation was suffering a crunching hangover from the post–World War II obsession with "loyalty," as determined by Senator Joseph McCarthy, the Subversive Activities Control Board, the House Un-American Activities Committee, and other groups. The Warren Court in 1966 put strict limits on the ways states could impose loyalty oaths and struck down the part of the Subversive Activities Control Act that made it a crime for a member of a "subversive" group to take a job in the defense industry.

Just before Marshall joined the Court, the high tribunal struck down, in a 5 to 4 vote, a loyalty oath requirement for New York State teachers as too vague and declared that membership in the Communist party alone was not a sufficient reason to deny a teacher employment.

Meanwhile, Warren had led the Court to cite the Fourteenth Amendment as requiring "one person, one vote" apportionment on the federal and state levels. In February 1964, in a 6 to 3 vote, the Court said that substantial disparities in the number of voters in congressional districts was unconstitutional and that populations in districts had to be as nearly equal as possible. Four months later the Court held that the same apportionment principle applied to both houses of a state legislature. (Between 1962 and 1970, thirty-six states reapportioned either voluntarily or under pressure of judicial decrees.)

Then, in 1966, after South Carolina challenged the Voting Rights Act of 1965, the Court said, 8 to 1, that this legislation was a proper exercise of Congress's power to ban racial discrimination in voting.

There were no areas of American life into which Earl Warren dared not tread in the name of fairness and justice. In 1965 he led the Court, in *Griswold v. Connecticut,* to strike down as unconstitutional a law forbidding even married couples to use contraceptives. The justices could not agree on what part of the Constitution said the state of Connecticut could not enforce such a law, but they agreed that somewhere in "the penumbra," the shadowy intentions, of the Constitution there is a right of privacy that no state may violate.

Two years later, on June 12, 1967, Warren wrote for a unanimous Court (*Loving v. Virginia*) that a state law that punished persons who entered into interracial marriages violated both the due process and equal protection clauses of the Fourteenth Amendment.

Like most revolutions, the one unleashed by the Warren Court was not welcomed by everyone. After leaving the White House, President Eisenhower was asked if he had made any mistakes as chief executive. "Yes," Ike quipped, "two, and both are sitting on the Supreme Court." (He was referring to Warren and William J. Brennan.) Soon calls went forth to "impeach Earl Warren."

While Warren certainly had led the Court in its new and controversial direction, he had plenty of support, and some opposition, on the bench. Who were these other associate justices that Thurgood Marshall was joining? Which ones would he be aligned with and which would he oppose?

The two senior justices in 1967, the leaders of the liberal bloc, along with Warren, were Hugo L. Black and William O. Douglas. Both had been appointed by Roosevelt; both were brilliant and forceful men who are now ranked among the greatest Supreme Court justices.

FDR's first choice to the High Court, Black had served for thirty years by the time Marshall arrived. Born in a rural, backward Alabama county in 1886, Black grew up playing the fiddle and reading voraciously, everything from Dickens to detective stories to the Bible. He also became an avid tennis buff. "When I was 40," Black wrote, "my doctor advised me that a man in his 40s shouldn't play tennis. I heeded his advice carefully, and could hardly wait until I reached 50 to start again." He didn't stop until he was 83.

After a career as a successful trial lawyer, Black was elected to the Senate in 1926 and re-elected six years later. Black's nomination to the Court in 1937 caused an uproar when the Hearst newspapers disclosed that he had joined the Ku Klux Klan in 1923 in Alabama. The nominee went on radio to explain that he had quit the KKK after just two years and to insist that he was not prejudiced against any race or religion.

Efforts to keep him off the bench failed, and over the next thirty-four years, much of that time as senior justice, Black, with his gentle manner and inner firmness, was one of the tribunal's most eloquent spokesmen for minorities and the disadvantaged. He summed up his judicial philosophy in this passage from a decision he wrote early in his Court career:

"Under our Constitutional system, courts stand against any winds that blow as havens of refuge for those who might otherwise suffer because they are helpless, weak, outnumbered, or because they are non-conforming victims of prejudice and public excitement."

The other steadfast liberal voice of the period was that of William O. Douglas, a Horatio Alger type who overcame polio and poverty to become one of the most colorful, controversial, and influential justices in the Court's history.

Born in Minnesota, Douglas nearly died of infantile paralysis when he was three. His father died when William was six, and the impoverished family moved to the state of Washington, where Douglas early on developed a love of the outdoors that was to be critical in shaping his personality.

Douglas graduated as valedictorian of his high school class in Yakima, worked his way through a local college, and taught high school briefly. Then he rode a freight car to New York and enrolled at Columbia Law School with six cents in his pocket.

It was at Columbia that Douglas was exposed to Louis Brandeis's ideas on the public responsibility of business, which instilled in the young student a greater awareness about the uses of the law beyond business. Douglas spent five years as a professor of law at Yale before joining the staff of Joseph P. Kennedy at the newly created Securities and Exchange Commission (SEC).

Witty, intelligent, down-to-earth, Douglas quickly became part of the New Deal elite in Washington, even to the point of playing poker with FDR. He was named chairman of the SEC in 1936 at age thirty-eight and three years later was appointed to the Supreme Court seat recently vacated by his college-days hero, Justice Brandeis.

Douglas proved a worthy successor, becoming a key part of the activist liberal majority on the Warren Court that backed school desegregation, reapportionment, defendants' rights. Along with Black, he was a ferocious defender of the Bill of Rights, especially the guarantees of expressions of conscience, which he believed were not to be tampered with by government.

His opinions relied less on legal principles than on his own personal involvement in life and his feelings about the condition of society. He believed in "adjusting" the Constitution to the needs of the time.

The Westerner was a maverick both on and off the bench. Law clerks found him cold, sometimes even mean, a man who rarely said hello in the hallways. Douglas's four marriages, his outspoken advocacy of public issues (he urged the admission of Red China to the United Nations), his ties to a foundation that got money from gambling interests, led to a call for his impeachment. But the House Judiciary Committee refused to go along with it, and Douglas went on to serve thirty-eight years on the Court, the longest tenure in history.

A third ally of Warren at the time Marshall came to the Court was William J. Brennan. While Black and Douglas had bona fide liberal and "judicial activist" credentials, Brennan was appointed by

Eisenhower primarily because of his reputation as a court reformer and Eisenhower's desire to demonstrate bipartisanship just before the 1956 election.

A native of New Jersey, Brennan had been on that state's supreme court and brought more judicial experience to the U.S. high tribunal than any other member of the Warren Court. In fact, he was the only one who had served as a state judge.

Short, unassuming, feisty, Brennan was described by one writer as a "sort of leprechaun." His personal warmth, kindness, and honesty proved effective in influencing fellow justices during the Court's internal deliberations. Brennan quickly became Warren's trusted lieutenant and closest friend on the Court, as well as his philosophical ally.

The year before Marshall joined the Court, Warren wrote of Brennan, "He administers the Constitution as a sacred trust, and interprets the Bill of Rights as the heart and life blood of that great charter of freedom. His belief in the dignity of human beings — all human beings — is unbounded. He also believes that without such dignity men cannot be free."

Eisenhower, on the other hand, is reported to have complained about his decisions, and Felix Frankfurter, who had been Brennan's teacher at Harvard, reportedly quipped after they differed frequently while serving together on the Court, "I always encouraged my students to think for themselves, but Brennan goes too far."

A prolific and hard-working justice, Brennan wrote more than 1,250 published opinions, including more than 450 majority opinions and more than 400 dissents. One of his major achievements was to pave the way for applying the Fourteenth Amendment guarantee of due process to curb the exercise of authority by state and local governments, not just federal power. Warren called Brennan's 1962 ruling that led to the "one person, one vote" principle the "most important" of the chief justice's tenure. In later years, Brennan and Marshall were usually aligned together, as Brennan became a consistent supporter of affirmative action programs. He retired from the Court in 1990 at age eighty-four, after serving for thirty-six years.

Abe Fortas was one of Lyndon B. Johnson's closest friends and advisers, a relationship that proved to be both the making and unmaking of his brief Supreme Court career.

Born to a poor Jewish family in Memphis, Tennessee, Fortas studied music and showed talent on the violin. But he also proved to be a skilled debater and headed north to Yale Law School, where he met then-professor William O. Douglas, who stimulated his interest in business law.

Fortas served in government during World War II, then left to go into private practice. There he gained a reputation as a skilled corporate lawyer, but also did pro bono volunteer work in cases involving civil and individual rights.

During the McCarthy era, Fortas successfully defended Owen Lattimore, a State Department policy expert who had been accused of disloyalty to his country. In 1962 Fortas helped make legal history by representing Clarence Earl Gideon, the indigent Florida inmate whose case established the right of an individual accused of a serious criminal offense to be represented by an attorney at trial.

Fortas had first met Johnson during their early years in Washington, and helped him in 1948 when Johnson won a disputed Senate primary in Texas by fewer than one hundred votes. In 1965, after persuading Arthur Goldberg to resign from the Court to become ambassador to the United Nations, Johnson offered the "Jewish seat" to Fortas. Although Fortas balked because he had a lucrative private practice, Johnson twisted his arm and nominated him anyway.

As expected, Fortas became part of the Warren majority, and was especially active in expanding the constitutional rights of criminal defendants. When Warren informed Johnson of his intention to resign at the end of the 1967–68 term, the president chose Fortas to succeed him as chief justice. In the Senate, the nomination ran into charges of cronyism and reports that even after his appointment to the Supreme Court, Fortas had continued to give the president counsel. Troubles multiplied when it was disclosed that Fortas had been paid $15,000 for teaching a seminar at a Washington, D.C., law school.

Republicans and southern Democrats filibustered when the nomination reached the Senate floor, and Johnson eventually withdrew it. Fortas remained as an associate justice but ran into new troubles the following year when *Life* magazine revealed his involvement with an indicted stock manipulator, Louis E. Wolfson. Fortas at first denied the relationship, but, as talk grew of impeachment, he resigned and returned to private practice. For the first time since 1916 the Supreme Court was without a Jewish justice.

The Court that Marshall joined in 1967 was not composed entirely of liberal judicial activists. John Marshall Harlan and Potter Stewart, two Eisenhower appointees, and Byron R. White, a Kennedy choice, were often found in opposition.

Harlan, a New Yorker, was the grandson of the justice with the same name, a judicial maverick who had written the "our Constitution is color-blind" dissent in *Plessy v. Ferguson.* The younger Harlan, a Republican who stayed out of partisan politics, was more cautious than his grandfather.

A graduate of Princeton and a Rhodes scholar, Harlan had been a successful Wall Street lawyer before being appointed to the U.S. Court of Appeals in 1954. He moved to the Supreme Court in March 1955, where he became a friend and judicial ally of Felix Frankfurter.

Harlan dissented from the Warren Court's "one man, one vote" rulings and believed that local government had some latitude for regulating freedom of speech. He practically wrote the credo for judicial conservatism when he said that it was a "mistaken view of the Constitution and the constitutional function" of the Supreme Court to believe "that every major social ill in this country can find its cure in some constitutional principle, and that this court should take the lead in promoting reform when other branches of government fail to act."

Still, Harlan could be liberal in some areas, such as police searches and seizures of evidence, privacy for married couples, and the rights of free speech and association. For example, he upheld the NAACP's right to keep its Alabama membership list confidential and the rights of blacks to desegregate lunch counters in the South, saying that their sit-ins were protected by the right to free expression.

Harlan set high standards of integrity and nonpartisanship. He even stopped voting in elections after he became a justice and refused to attend the annual State of the Union address. Known as "a lawyer's judge," Harlan was one of the best lawyers on the Court and had a great interest in technical aspects of its work. Although functionally blind during the last six years he served as an associate justice, Harlan was active until his retirement, writing opinions by hand, announcing them in public session from memory.

When Potter Stewart was appointed to the Court at the age of forty-three in 1958, he became the second youngest justice since the Civil War. A member of a distinguished and prosperous legal family in Cincinnati, Ohio, Stewart attended private schools and traveled extensively. His nomination triggered lengthy questioning in the Senate, especially about his views on *Brown v. Board of Education.* Stewart told the senators not to assume that he favored overruling *Brown,* and seventeen negative votes were cast against him by southern senators.

On the Court, Stewart pursued a middle ground, becoming the "swing justice" in later years. Stewart tried to keep his own political, religious, and moral beliefs out of his opinions and to decide cases solely on the basis of the law and the Constitution. As a result, he voted to uphold some death penalty statutes, although he opposed capital punishment, and he called the state ban on contraceptive devices "an uncommonly silly law" but voted to uphold it because he felt it was not unconstitutional.

Asked once whether he was a liberal or a conservative, Stewart replied, "I am a lawyer. I have some difficulty understanding what those terms mean even in the field of political life. . . . And I find it impossible to know what they mean when they are carried over to judicial work."

The final member of the Supreme Court at the time Marshall arrived was Byron R. White, who was not the typical justice. A strapping 6-foot-2-inch, 190-pounder, nicknamed "Whizzer," White had been an all-American running back at the University of Colorado and the National Football League's Rookie of the Year in 1938 when he led the league in rushing.

He was also a Rhodes scholar and had met John F. Kennedy while touring Europe between terms at Oxford. White returned to the United States after war broke out in Europe to attend Yale Law School and play professional football in 1940 and 1941. He enlisted in the Navy after Pearl Harbor and became an intelligence officer in the Pacific, where he again encountered Kennedy.

After the war, White got involved in politics and organized a Colorado Committee for Kennedy in 1960. He was rewarded with an appointment as deputy attorney general under Robert Kennedy and became something of a hero when he stood up to George Wallace in Alabama in the spring of 1961.

When Justice Charles Whitaker retired in 1962, Kennedy had his first chance to name someone to the Supreme Court. He passed over three original "finalists" and, surprisingly, turned to White, who had no previous judicial or elective experience.

Although a Democrat, White wound up voting against the Warren majority as often as with it. He wrote caustic dissents in the *Miranda* case and the 1973 *Roe v. Wade* abortion case in which he accused the Court of acting illegitimately and said the decision could be justified only as an exercise of "raw judicial power."

White never could be neatly pegged or assigned to any bloc on the Court. He defies classification when it comes to judicial philosophy. Like Earl Warren, White is prime evidence that presidents don't always know what their Supreme Court appointees will do.

*   *   *

The Supreme Court of 1967 had come a long way since Colonial days, when Alexander Hamilton called the judiciary "the least dangerous branch of government."

The Court first convened on February 1, 1789, under Chief Justice John Jay had so little prestige that it met in the basement of the capitol for a time in the early 1800s, and justices were required to ride circuit. Little of the work involved controversial major issues of public policy.

Between 1790 and 1865 the Court overruled only two acts of Congress and 390 state laws. (By comparison, the Warren Court in sixteen years overruled twenty-nine acts of Congress and 150 state laws, plus reversing forty-six previous Supreme Court decisions.)

Still, there were hints of the clashes to come over philosophy and with other branches of government, as the Court struggled to find its role. In 1803, in *Marbury v. Madison,* the Supreme Court began to assert its right to review acts of Congress. President Thomas Jefferson, expressing exasperation that would be repeated by later presidents, said, "The Constitution . . . is a mere thing of wax in the hands of the judiciary which they may twist and shape into any form they please."

Lincoln also had a run-in with the High Court. After the *Dred Scott* decision, which held that blacks were not citizens, the sixteenth president complained, "If the policy of the government on vital questions is to be irrevocably fixed by decisions of the Supreme Court, the instant they are made . . . people will have ceased to be their own rulers."

Chief Justice Charles Evans Hughes didn't conciliate the other branches of government when, in a 1907 speech, he declared: "We are under a Constitution, but the Constitution is what the judges say it is."

As Marshall joined the Court, the debate about it had increased in intensity. This was because of the Court's new, expanded role. It had moved into political and social controversies where it had rarely trod before — New Deal legislation, civil rights, abortion. It had gained more influence but had brought on more attacks.

The fundamental question then as now involved the Supreme Court's role in America's checks-and-balances system of government. On one side were those who favored judicial activism, who felt justices should not be bound by the precise words of the Constitution, but should interpret it in light of contemporary realities. Brennan expressed this viewpoint when he declared:

"The ultimate question must be, what do the words of the text mean in our time. For the genius of the Constitution rests not in any static meaning it might have had in a world that is dead and gone, but in the adaptability of its great principles to cope with current problems and current needs."

On the other side were and are those who counseled judicial self-restraint and strict construction of the Constitution. Reagan administration attorney general Edwin Meese III reflected this philosophy in a speech to the American Bar Association in 1985 in which he described decisions of the just-ended Court term as a "jurisprudence of idiosyncrasy."

As the importance and power of the Court grew and more attention was paid to judicial philosophy, the selection of justices became more partisan and controversial. Presidents generally wanted justices who agreed with their own philosophy. Congress grew increasingly balky.

The prime example of a philosophical clash between the executive and legislative branches over the judiciary occurred in 1937 when the Supreme Court's "nine old men" frustrated Franklin D. Roosevelt by invalidating his New Deal programs. In the most direct attack on the Court ever launched by a president, Roosevelt threatened to add a new seat to the Court every time a sitting justice reached the age of seventy. His Court-packing scheme failed.

Roosevelt expressed his frustration with the Court at the time when he compared the American government to "a three-horse team provided by the Constitution to the American people so that their field might be plowed. The three horses, of course, are the three branches of government. Two of the horses are pulling in unison; the third is not."

Congress rejected the Court-packing scheme, but that did not end the struggle between presidents and the Senate over Supreme Court nominations.

The Senate rejected two of President Nixon's first nominees — conservative southern jurists Clement F. Haynsworth, Jr., in 1969, and G. Harrold Carswell the following year. In a bitter battle in 1987, it turned down Judge Robert H. Bork, prompting President Reagan to complain that the Court had "improperly set itself up as a third House of Congress — a superlegislature . . . reading into the Constitution words and implications."

Supreme Court confirmation battles are usually couched in terms of "judicial temperament" and scholarly qualifications. But when you strip away the euphemisms, what they really concern is ideology, strict or loose construction, how individual nominees would rule on abortion, affirmative action, and other key issues. In other words, politics.

The politicizing of the Court had been foreseen by Alexis de Tocqueville, who wrote in 1835:

"The Supreme Court is placed higher than any known tribunal. . . . The prosperity and the very existence of the Union are vested in the hands of these seven Federal judges. In other words, the highest court is primarily a political institution."

That conclusion was expressed in pithier form by humorist Finley Peter Dunne's Mr. Dooley, who observed in 1900: "No matther, whether th' constitution follows th' flag or not, th' supreme coort follows th' iliction returns."

Americans will never agree on the proper role of the Supreme Court — whether the Constitution must be dry parchment adhered to faithfully with regard to every bit of language and punctuation, or whether it is a living document that each Court must interpret to fit changing circumstances and concepts of justice.

But few knowledgeable Americans will contest an assertion that Earl Warren did more to change America than most presidents, and so did the first black man to sit with him as one of the most powerful figures in the land.

CHAPTER NINETEEN

MR. JUSTICE MARSHALL'S ROLE

THE STEREOTYPED ASSUMPTION was that Marshall, once on the Court, would stand out as a barrier against racial discrimination. He did. Only a few legal observers expected that Marshall would become a towering symbol of all the fundamental reasons why a United States of America came into being. He became the Court's premier challenger of the powers of the sovereign, of the state, to trample willy-nilly the rights of the people, especially those without wealth, social clout, political power, or any of the armor needed by a citizen under siege by oppressive bureaucrats.

Marshall worked as hard as any justice in the history of the Court to expand the parameters of free speech and the other protections of the First Amendment. Sure, he pressed hard for racial desegregation across the board; for affirmative actions to redress centuries of racial discrimination; for fairness to minorities in housing and many other areas. But he worked to preserve, even extend, the liberties of white people, of every citizen in the land, when he argued that the state could not decree what Americans could read or watch — even porno films — in the privacy of their home. And when he fought government uses of unwarranted searches and seizures, unprecedented electronic surveillance, tainted evidence, to "fight crime." And when he stood up for the rights of the accused to a competent lawyer, no matter how impoverished the criminal suspect, and for sentencing procedures that were not intolerably skewed in favor of the rich and against the poor. And when he struggled, vainly, to pull America away from the emotional belief that state eye-for-an-eye executions would somehow wipe out the crime problem. And when he cried out against discrimination against women in the job market and in most other areas of American life.

Most Court watchers never dreamed that Marshall's crowning moments on the Court would involve, not the issue of race, but of any woman's right to make her own decisions as to whether and when she would bring a child into this world. You will not understand Marshall, or his world, unless you see how he operated in a political and social milieu that was — and is — poisoned by passions over the abortion rights of women. The Court records indicate that no justice ever supported a woman's right to choice as uncompromisingly as Marshall did.

Marshall joined the Court two years after the landmark decision in *Griswold v. Connecticut,* in which the Supreme Court declared that a state could not prohibit married couples from using contraceptives because there was a "penumbra of privacy" in the Constitution that protected women from state interference in their decisions about sex and reproduction. This "penumbra" was something lawyers could not see in written words, but the Court majority just knew that it was there somewhere in the Ninth and/or Fourteenth Amendments to the Constitution.

The "feminist movement" as we know it was not yet alive and kicking in 1967, but the stirrings were vibrant enough to provoke Marshall to say that "it's up to the woman" — that no politician, nobody, ought to be able to coerce a woman into bearing a child she did not want.

Turmoil over the abortion issue escalated across the nation, and came to an explosive semiconclusion when a Texas woman named Norma McCorvey, using the history-making court name of *Jane Roe,* went to lawyer Sarah Weddington in Dallas and said, "I'm pregnant from a rape. I want an abortion, but I can't get it legally in this state. I want to challenge the constitutionality of the Texas law." Norma McCorvey was just what Weddington had been looking for, since the latter regarded the Texas anti-abortion law as a blight upon women. (McCorvey would make all the national TV shows and headlines across America when she confessed to me, in 1987, that she had not been raped, but became pregnant during a love affair in Florida, where she was a ticket seller for the freak animal show in a circus. She said she figured the cry of rape would get Court attention faster. In fact, how "Jane Roe" got pregnant was generally regarded as extraneous to the issue of whether the state could force her to carry the baby to term.)

In the fall of 1972 it became obvious to Marshall that a majority of the Court would side with "Jane Roe" instead of the state of Texas. Thurgood watched what he called "logrolling," through which one justice tried to influence another. Marshall made a contribution to the *Roe v. Wade* decision that most Americans still don't know about because it took place in that secret Supreme Court world of "brokering" and gentlemanly power plays.

Marshall regarded as too inflexible Justice Harry A. Blackmun's formula in which, given the medical judgment of her doctor, a woman could get an abortion without any state interference during the first twelve weeks (first trimester) of her pregnancy. During the next twelve weeks the state could intervene, but ostensibly only to protect the health of the pregnant woman. After twenty-four weeks, in the third trimester, the state could intervene to protect the potential life of the fetus.

There was much about this that Marshall didn't like, including the requirement for a doctor's opinion in the first trimester. But he wouldn't fight that. He zeroed in on the impracticality of the Blackmun formula in a conversation that might have gone like this:

"Harry, baby, do you know anything about the circumstances of life of pregnant women in our pockets of rural poverty, or in the worst of our urban ghettos? The doctor is so many miles away, with no wheels to use to get to him, and he is so expensive that these poor women don't see any doctor during the first trimester. Some don't even know they're pregnant. It may be twenty weeks before some show up in a doctor's office weeping, saying 'I just gotta have an abortion.'

"Harry, you gotta protect the absolute right of poor or rural women way into the second trimester, and always be aware that some states will concoct phony restrictions in the name of protecting the health of the pregnant woman.

"The key point you've raised, Harry, is viability of the fetus. The state ought not be able to forbid an abortion willy-nilly unless it is clear the potential baby can survive outside the womb. And 'viability' may be one thing in Boston or Rochester, Minnesota, where they have high technology and doctors tripping all over each other. A fetus of an early age is 'viable' in great medical centers. But viability would come many weeks later in poor rural areas."

Marshall had a law clerk put his soliloquy into written legalese and deliver it to Blackmun.

Blackmun listened to Marshall intently, partly because of a precious quality that the black justice had brought to the Court. Marshall was the only justice who had ever defended a murder suspect. He was the only justice who had defended and worked with so many poor women that he actually knew how they suffered financially, were pained emotionally, often became psychological wrecks over knowledge that another baby was on the way.

Blackmun emphasized "viability of the fetus" in the Court's landmark decision, announced on January 22, 1973. This historic decree of enduring controversy was overshadowed by the death of Lyndon Johnson that same day. It would be some time before the average American realized what Blackmun and six other justices — Lewis F. Powell, Douglas, Brennan, Stewart, Marshall, and Chief Justice Warren E. Burger — had done. Many Court observers were shocked that Blackmun, Burger, and Powell, the three appointees of Nixon, an anti-abortion man, had rejected Nixon's views. Critics said that Burger had hemmed and hawed and stalled till the last minute because he was to swear Nixon in for a second term as president on January 20, and didn't want the awkwardness of facing the man who made him chief justice in the midst of stories about how he had rebuffed Nixon on abortions. They said Burger gave a feeble excuse for joining the Blackmun-written majority opinion by saying that the Texas law was unconstitutional because it forbade abortions in case of rape or incest (perhaps Norma McCorvey's false cry of "rape" did have legal consequences). They criticized Burger for saying that he wasn't voting for "abortion on demand." The critical reality was that Burger voted for a woman's constitutional right to choose regarding abortion — which set him apart from Nixon.

In that opinion that was overshadowed by Johnson's death, Blackmun wrote:

> The Constitution does not explicitly mention any right of privacy. In a line of decisions, however, the Court has recognized that a right of personal privacy, or a guarantee of certain areas or zones of privacy, does exist under the Constitution.
>
> This right of privacy, whether it be founded in the 14th Amendment's concept of personal liberty and restrictions upon state action, as we feel it is, or, as the District Court determined, in the Ninth Amendment's reservation of rights to the people, is broad enough to encompass a woman's decision whether or not to terminate her pregnancy.

The hands of Marshall and Brennan were evident in Blackmun's construction of the damages done when the state imposes upon a woman a requirement that she have a baby she does not want.

Blackmun spoke of the woman's "distressful life and future" and of "the problem of bringing a child into a family already unable, psychologically and otherwise, to care for it."

Blackmun dealt with the issue that has not gone away, and never will: when does a fetus become a "person," entitled to every protection of the Constitution and the statutes? The Court majority said:

"The Constitution does not define 'person' in so many words. The use of the word is such that it has application only postnatally.

"All this, together with our observation that throughout the major portion of the 19th century prevailing legal abortion practices were far freer than they are today, persuades us that the word 'person,' as used in the 14th Amendment, does not include the unborn.

"Texas urges that, apart from the 14th Amendment, life begins at conception and is present throughout pregnancy, and that, therefore, the state has a compelling interest in protecting that life from and after conception.

"We need not resolve the difficult question of when life begins. When those trained in the respective disciplines of medicine, philosophy and theology are unable to arrive at any consensus, the judiciary, at this point in the development of man's knowledge, is not in a position to speculate as to the answer.

"The unborn have never been recognized in the law as persons in the whole sense."

But does the state have no compelling interest in outlawing what some called the "murder" of babies? Blackmun adopted the compromise that Marshall suggested when he wrote:

"With respect to the state's important and legitimate interest in potential life, the 'compelling' point is at viability. This is so because the fetus then presumably has the capability of meaningful life outside the mother's womb. If the state is interested in protecting fetal life after viability, it may go so far as to proscribe abortion during that period except when it is necessary to preserve the life or health of the mother."

The dissent, written by Justice White, concurred in by Justice Rehnquist, was equally forceful:

"At the heart of the controversy in these cases are those recurring pregnancies that pose no danger whatsoever to the life or health of the mother but are nevertheless unwanted for any one or more of a variety of reasons — convenience, family planning, economics, dislike of children, the embarrassment of illegitimacy, etc. The common claim before us is that for any one of such reasons or for no reason at all, and without asserting or claiming any threat to life or health, any woman is entitled to an abortion at her request. . . .

"As an exercise of raw judicial power, the Court perhaps has authority to do what it does today, but in my view its judgment is an improvident and extravagant exercise of the power of judicial review which the Constitution extends to this Court.

"I find no constitutional warrant for imposing such an order of priorities on the people and legislatures of the states. In a sensitive area such as this, involving as it does issues over which reasonable men may easily and heatedly differ, I cannot accept the Court's exercise of its clear power of choice by interposing a constitutional barrier to state efforts to protect human life and by investing mothers and doctors with the constitutionally protected right to exterminate it. This issue, for the most part, should be left with the people and to the political processes the people have devised to govern their affairs."

Few Americans noted that the Court had decided a companion case, *Doe v. Bolton,* which forbade states to try to block abortions in the guise of protecting the health of women — for example, by requiring that abortions be performed in accredited hospitals with the concurrence of two physicians and a hospital committee.

Neither Johnson's death nor anything else blinded leaders of the Catholic Church to the enormity of what Blackmun, Marshall, Brennan, and others in the Court majority had done. Terence Cardinal Cooke of New York said, "How many millions of children prior to their birth will never live to see the light of day because of the shocking action of the majority of the United States Supreme Court today?

". . . seven men have made a tragic utilitarian judgment regarding who shall live and who shall die."

John Joseph Cardinal Krol, the Archbishop of Philadelphia and president of the National Conference of Catholic Bishops, said the *Roe* decision was "an unspeakable tragedy for this nation. It is hard to think of any decision in the 200 years of our history which has had more disastrous implications for our stability as a civilized society."

Clearly, no decision except the 1954 *Brown v. Board of Education* ruling that outlawed Jim Crow in schools has subjected the Court to so much vituperation and threats of violence. Blackmun got — and read — thousands of the meanest-spirited letters that he could imagine. They were counterproductive blessings because they drove Blackmun further away from Burger and the Court's conservative bloc, and closer to Brennan and Marshall.

Brennan became the target of years of unremitting enmity, hatred, death threats, from anti-abortion forces. In 1986 he went to Los Angeles to deliver the commencement speech, outdoors, for the

Loyola Marymount Law School. Brennan was told that at the morning prayer services at the Fundamentalist Baptist Tabernacle, the Reverend R. L. Hymers, Jr., had asked some four hundred parishioners to pray and ask God to take Brennan's life so President Reagan could replace him with a justice who would oppose abortion. Reverend J. Richard Olivas, the associate pastor, told the congregation that Brennan was responsible for "the murder of fifteen million U.S. citizens . . . as a result of abortions."

When Brennan got up to speak, suddenly there was a plane overhead with a trailing banner that said: PRAY FOR DEATH: BABY-KILLER BRENNAN.

I asked Marshall how many threats on his life he had received because of *Roe*.

"Dunno," he replied, "but more than I've ever wanted to count."

"Did you turn them over to the FBI?"

"Hell no! I never wanted the creeps to know that I ever read one. All I'm sure of is that somebody with big money is behind it. Because we [justices] get mailings of two to three thousand from one little town with a population of five hundred people. A typical letter says, 'My name is so-and-so. I'm in the eleventh grade, and I know all about abortions, and you baby killers are. . . .' Well, somebody's putting that kid up to write that letter, so I give it what it's entitled to. The wastebasket."

But Marshall and the other justices could not dismiss with a toss at the wastebasket the many briefs, writs, appeals of the anti-abortion forces. Their challenges of the assumptions of constitutional law in the *Roe v. Wade* decision took an inordinate amount of the time of the justices and their clerks, but they also gave Marshall a chance to carve out a special niche in the history of justices who fought courageously for what they regarded as a compelling cause.

A verbal and legal war-to-death between the pro-choice and pro-life forces produced a Supreme Court decision in 1974 that mortified Marshall. In *Geduldig v. Aiello* the Court said that while "only women can become pregnant, it does not follow that every legislative classification concerning pregnancy is a sex-based classification, and that exclusion of pregnancy-related disabilities from coverage of a state's disability insurance program is unconstitutional." It galled Marshall that a state could on the one hand force some women to carry a pregnancy to term while at the same time saying that an employer could deny work benefits to those women.

Marshall became a special advocate, or "defense attorney," inside the Court for poor women, black or white, but especially for minority women, who were likely to know both racial discrimination *and* poverty.

This became universally clear in 1977 when the Supreme Court considered three cases — *Beal v. Doe, Maher v. Roe,* and *Poelker v. Doe* — all of which involved challenges to, or efforts to limit the sweep of, the *Roe* decision. In these cases Marshall tried repeatedly to educate the Court and the country to the "human dimension of these [abortion] decisions" because of the reality that it did no good to demand that poor and minority women show "good citizenship" if they were deprived of a fundamental right to control their reproductive systems — a right without which they could never display the ultimate in responsibility. In *Poelker,* Marshall said:

> An unwanted child may be disruptive and destructive of the life of any woman, but the impact is felt most by those too poor to ameliorate those effects. If funds for an abortion are unavailable, a poor woman may feel that she is forced to obtain an illegal abortion that poses a serious threat to her health and even her life. . . . If she refuses to take this risk, and undergoes the pain and danger of state-financed pregnancy and childbirth, she may well give up all chance of escaping the cycle of poverty. Absent daycare facilities, she will be forced into full-time child care for years to come; she will be unable to work so that her family can break out of the welfare system or the lowest income brackets. If she already has children, another infant to feed and clothe may well stretch the budget past the breaking point.

To further illustrate his conviction that it was wrong, legally and morally, for the state to force into motherhood the women who least wanted, least could afford, and were less likely to care properly for a child, Marshall said:

> The enactments challenged here brutally coerce poor women to bear children whom society will scorn for every day of their lives. Many thousands of unwanted minority and mixed-race children now spend blighted lives in foster homes, orphanages, and "reform" schools. . . . Many children of the poor, sadly, will attend second-rate segregated schools. . . . And opposition remains strong against increasing Aid to Families with Dependent Children benefits for impoverished mothers and children, so that there is little chance for the children to grow up in a decent environment. I am appalled at the ethical bankruptcy of those who preach a "right to life" that means, under present social policies, a bare

existence in utter misery for so many poor women and their children.

But for millions of Americans "the human dimension" would never take precedence over their belief that life begins at conception, and that abortion at any time under any circumstance is murder. They kept chipping away at *Roe*, kept putting psychological, political, and even physical pressures on the justices who supported privacy rights, which included abortion. In 1978, Aleta Wallach, a senior judicial attorney in the California Court of Appeals, wrote an angry article for a special edition of the *Black Law Journal* at UCLA (the University of California, Los Angeles). She said:

> When the Supreme Court abnegates its responsibility to protect the basic individual right and responsibility of each woman to choose her own future against the tyranny of the masses, it gives control of the female body back to the popular will of the "democratic processes" and the brutal politicization of the institution of motherhood. The magnitude of this danger to the lives of all women was not lost on Justice Marshall:
> ". . . I fear that the Court's decisions will be an invitation to public officials, already under extraordinary pressure from well-financed and carefully orchestrated lobbying campaigns, to approve more such restrictions. The effect will be to relegate millions of people to lives of poverty and despair. When elected leaders cower before public pressure, this Court, more than ever, must not shirk its duty to enforce the Constitution for the benefit of the poor and powerless."
> Marshall is obviously aware that the ultimate goal of the immensely powerful and seemingly limitlessly resourceful "prolife" movement is a constitutional amendment prohibiting all abortion. This is a serious threat not to be scoffed at as improbable. Already the use of federal Medicaid funds for abortions has been restricted. And the zealous "prolife" forces have caused the House Education and Labor Committee to attach anti-abortion language to legislation designed to repeal the pregnancy exclusion in *General Electric Co. v. Gilbert*, by forbidding an employer to deny sick pay and other insurance benefits to pregnant workers. The amendment to the bill stipulates that eligibility benefits extended to pregnant workers not include abortions. And now abortion clinics are being burned.
> In *Beal, Maher* and *Roe* the Supreme Court did not only disgrace the principle of equal citizenship and the right to be treated

as a person. Nor did it only weaken its own institutional authority: if the enduring values the Court finds for the society are not binding on the Court itself, all judicially ascertained values are endangered with transience and disobedience. But the Court, in addition, committed an intemperate act of deference to the political bodies which threatens to vitiate the separation of powers that underpins our tripartite system of government. The Supreme Court's final word is: "We . . . hold . . . that the Constitution does not forbid a State or a city, pursuant to the democratic processes, from expressing a preference for normal childbirth."

Although the decision in *Geduldig v. Aiello* previewed the great difficulty the Court has with the subject of pregnancy, the decisions in *Roe v. Wade* and *Doe v. Bolton* had already given us false assurance and put us off guard. In retrospect, the Court has been fickle and cowardly. When all is said and done, the Supreme Court does knuckle under the sway of public opinion and well-organized, well-financed special interests. The lesson is this: the independence of the judiciary is a much exaggerated notion, and we must look elsewhere for our freedom.

But Marshall knew that there was nowhere else to look.

In 1987 I asked Sarah Weddington, the lawyer for "Jane Roe," if she feared that a newly configured Supreme Court would soon reverse *Roe*. (Justice Powell, who had replaced Black in 1972, was eighty, and ready to retire.) "Yes," she replied, "I think that with one more Reagan appointee to the Court, women will be thrown back to the days of illegal, back-alley butcher abortions."

I later said to Justice Marshall: "There are people saying this very day that when Reagan replaces Justice Powell, the abortion ruling will be in grave jeopardy, since it has been hanging by a five to four thread. They say affirmative action will be in trouble, and the *Miranda* rule will be wiped out. Do you fear that any of these things will happen?"

"Nope."

"You say no?"

"Because I believe in the Court."

"So you think that Mr. Reagan cannot be sure what his new appointee will do?"

"The only sure way would be to get on the Court himself."

Historians will scratch their heads a century from now as they note that Powell did retire in 1987 and that Reagan named Anthony M. Kennedy to replace him after failing to secure the confirmation of Robert Bork; and that the Court's most powerful liberal member, William J. Brennan, Jr., retired in 1990, and was replaced by a so-called stealth conservative, David H. Souter; and that Marshall himself retired in 1991 and President Bush replaced him with a black conservative, Clarence Thomas. Yet, when the Supreme Court decided in 1992 on a very restrictive Pennsylvania abortion law, in *Planned Parenthood v. Casey*, there was no majority willing to say that Blackmun was wrong in writing that "the unborn have never been recognized in the law as persons in the whole sense." This Court that even I had scorned as "troglodyte" would not renounce the *Roe* conclusion that privacy rights in the Fourteenth and Ninth Amendments were "broad enough to encompass a woman's decision whether or not to terminate her pregnancy."

Millions of women found the Pennsylvania decision onerous and tragic, a "gutting" of *Roe v. Wade*, but the Reagan-Bush Court had left the basic premises of *Roe* standing.

To the astonishment of lawyers — and politicians — across America, Justices Kennedy and Souter had joined Reagan appointee Sandra Day O'Connor (who took Potter Stewart's seat in 1981) as a triumvirate that would stop the Court from disgracing itself and losing its moral force by summarily wiping out abortion rights that women had held to their breast for two decades.

Marshall must have sensed something profound when he said to me, "I believe in the Court."

I began warily to believe a trifle in the current Court when it stood up in its way on an issue to which Marshall devoted much of his life as a lawyer. Just three days before it declined to wipe out abortion rights, the Court told the state of Mississippi that it had to move affirmatively to change its system of higher education so as to remedy generations of discrimination against blacks seeking college training. Marshall had another powerful reason to say, "I believe in the Court."

During the late 1960s and early 1970s, Americans of all races seemed to accept the argument that it was to the benefit of all society to draw long-cheated minorities into the mainstream of American life. People saw it as a destructive anachronism that so many police departments were lily-white in their top echelons. They knew that it was absurd that the Alabama State Highway Patrol had not had a black patrolman in the history of that state. Americans regarded it as ludicrous that institutions claiming to possess a higher level of intellectualism and morality had so few blacks and other minorities on their faculties. The nation's newspapers, magazines, and television stations launched highly publicized campaigns to recruit blacks, women, Hispanics, Asians, so as to give "diversity" to their staffs.

Then a few anti–affirmative action lawsuits in the 1970s, a couple of recessions in the 1980s, and lingering hard times wiped out a lot of the idealism. White parents began to scream that Stanford, Oberlin, Cornell, had given a scholarship to a black person that should have gone to their child, because their child had scored a bit higher on some standardized test than had the black student. White policemen and firefighters in places such as Detroit and Memphis, who had long controlled the exams, promotions, and almost everything through their "old buddy" network, were suddenly resentful and fearful of talk that "the infusion of blacks into these departments is essential to gaining the respect and help of the people who live in these urban areas." To hell with "social engineering" if it would mean that some black person might get a job or promotion that was coveted by a white person.

The University of California at Davis felt morally compelled to try to make up for centuries of societal discrimination against black people when it chose to factor race in as a part of its admission policy. In addition, the university set aside sixteen medical-school slots for minorities. A white man, Alan Bakke, sued, claiming that the university had set up a quota system that discriminated against him. The Supreme Court had held earlier that affirmative actions in remediation of proven injustices were proper. But the *Bakke* case fractured the Court badly, because the setting aside of sixteen places for minorities was called a "quota," a word that was a red flag to Jews who had over history either been denied admission to prestigious institutions, or limited to a token "quota" presence. Never mind the reality that the medical school was not trying to exclude Jews, or anyone else, but to include blacks, the very odor of a "quota" system offended some members of the Court. Incredibly, Justice Powell cast the key vote in a backhanded 5 to 4 approval of affirmative-action programs that factored in race, and then cast the crucial vote in a 5 to 4 declaration that the setting aside of sixteen slots was an unconstitutional quota. Marshall harrumphed in outrage and wrote one of his most emotional dissents:

> While I applaud the judgment of the Court that a university may consider race in its admissions process, it is more than a little ironic that, after several hundred years of class-based discrimination against Negroes, the Court is unwilling to hold that a class-based remedy for that discrimination is permissible. . . .
>
> It is because of a legacy of unequal treatment that we now must

permit the institutions of this society to give consideration to race in making decisions about who will hold the positions of influence, affluence, and prestige in America. For far too long, the doors to those positions have been shut to Negroes.

Marshall watched in dismay as the conservative members of the Court argued that actions to redress previous racial injustices had to be limited to *individuals* who could *prove* that they personally had been victimized. In the Supreme Court conference room, Marshall became a powerful, almost menacing presence when he bellowed that "racism in our society has been so pervasive that no Negro, regardless of wealth or position, has been able to escape its impact." In privacy, Marshall reminded his colleagues of housing and other discriminations against Dr. Ralph Bunche; of Marian Anderson having to ride the freight elevator in the Radisson hotel in Minneapolis; and of millions of black people being denied the right to vote, to attend the public school nearest their homes, to drink a soda pop in a "white" drugstore. Marshall told his colleagues of more than a few occasions when a racial insult was heaped upon him.

For most of his years on the Court, Marshall kept alive the idea that fairness required affirmative programs not only to make amends for three centuries of slavery, repressions that included lynchings, and racist rules that permeated every aspect of American life. But he began to see that some members of the Court were listening to white Americans who said they "should not be punished for the racist sins of my fathers and forefathers." The argument gained credence that it was unfair to give a black police officer in Detroit a promotion over a white one who scored higher on a standardized test "just because whites had rigged the promotion system in previous years." Suddenly, whites were filing lawsuits against affirmative action in dismaying numbers. In 1973, in *United States v. Stanley,* Justice Harlan had written a dissent that foreshadowed a change of mind-set of a majority of the Court:

"When a man has emerged from slavery, and by the aid of beneficent legislation has shaken off the inseparable concomitants of that state, there must be some stage in the progress of his elevation when he takes the rank of a mere citizen, and ceases to be the special favorite of the laws."

Marshall recalled that just eight years earlier the man who appointed him to the Supreme Court, Lyndon B. Johnson, had said in a commencement address at Howard University: "You do not take a person who for years has been hobbled by chains and liberate him, bring him up to the starting line of a race then say, you're free to compete with all the others.

"Negroes are trapped, as many whites are trapped, in inherited gateless poverty. They lack training and skills. They are shut in slums without decent medical care. . . . We are trying to attack these evils. . . .

"Much of the Negro community is buried under a blanket of history and circumstance. It is not a lasting solution to lift just one corner of the blanket."

Marshall rolled the words of Justice Powell and President Johnson around in his mind and obviously sensed that a new measure of insensitivity, even hostility, had crept into relationships between white and black Americans.

"What the fuck is going on?" he once asked me.

I didn't know, so I didn't reply. I did watch the changes in personnel and ideology at the Supreme Court and conclude prematurely that Marshall had been wrong to tell me, "I believe in the Court." Then came the end of the term in June 1992, when the justices had to face up to the question whether the state of Mississippi had taken enough affirmative actions to remediate generations of racial bigotry in its system of higher education. It was established in *United States v. Fordice* that Mississippi had five predominantly white colleges and universities and three that were historically, and still predominantly, black. Mississippi was sanctimonious in saying that it had "equalized" its financial support, spending almost the same dollars on a black college student as a white one.

But Souter, Kennedy, O'Connor, the ones who were expected to protect the devious trappings of racism, saw that the expenditures-per-pupil data were a sham. Mississippi still had a system of keeping the white institutions white (except for the football and basketball teams) and the black institutions black, by setting up a double standard of admissions requirements. At the white colleges and universities there was a test-score factor that let in whites who had gone to the best high schools and came from the most affluent families. A kid from an ill-equipped high school in the ghetto, or even a white kid from a little red barn of a school in a rural area, didn't have much chance of being admitted to Mississippi State or the University of Mississippi. The black schools, Jackson State, Alcorn State, and Mississippi Valley State, were supposed to serve as the "dumping grounds" for blacks.

Hell, the American hierarchy had blinked at this widespread racial sophistry in education, employment, and more throughout the history of America. Why lie awake imagining that a Reagan-Bush Court would challenge "the system"?

Well, lo and behold, as they used to say, on June 26, 1992, thirty years after the University of Mississippi admitted a black student named James Meredith, under pressures and threats from President John F. Kennedy, the Reagan-Bush Supreme Court delivered a shocker. It said plain and simple, in an 8 to 1 decision, that Mississippi would have to come up with more money for the historically black colleges to make up for generations of racial and financial discrimination.

Justice White wrote for the majority that Mississippi had fostered segregation by basing admission to the state's predominantly white schools on standardized tests that were discriminatory. Those tests in effect slammed doors in the faces of poor white and black high school graduates who had been consigned to inferior elementary and secondary schools. Justice White said Mississippi had designated its white colleges as "flagship institutions" that received the most money and offered the broadest and most advanced curriculums. That was why, even in the mid-1980s, more than 99 percent of Mississippi's white students were enrolled in the five historically white schools, while blacks were relegated to the historically black schools.

This decision stunned right-wingers as much as did the Court split in the Pennsylvania abortion case. Justice Antonin Scalia, who had filled the vacancy in 1986 when Burger retired and Rehnquist was elevated to chief justice, the lone dissenter in the Mississippi case, said the ruling would produce years of "confusion and destabilization . . . that will benefit neither blacks nor whites." Bruce Fein, the unbendingly conservative constitutional scholar, wrote that the Court had declared that today's [white] college students in Mississippi "must pay for the racial sins of their parents or more distant ancestors," the standard argument of reactionaries against any programs to redress previous racial discriminations and deprivations.

Fein seemed shocked that *White* would write: "If the state perpetuates policies and practices traceable to its prior system that continue to have segregative effects — whether by influencing student enrollment decisions or by fostering segregation in other facets of the university system — and such policies are without sound educational justification and can be practicably eliminated, the State has not satisfied its burden of proving that it has dismantled its prior system. Such policies run afoul of the Equal Protection Clause, even though the State has abolished the legal requirement that whites and blacks be educated separately and has established racially neutral policies not animated by a discriminatory purpose."

Fein called this "nonsense." He wrote that the *Fordice* decision was "a deplorable and monumental distraction from the imperative of enhancing education for all." But the Court had decided *Fordice* not on the basis of polemics, but on that of a look at the real world. The contiguous state of Tennessee had once been as Jim Crow in higher education as Mississippi. (This writer attended Tennessee State in Nashville as a freshman in 1942–43 when it was a totally black college, and the University of Tennessee in Knoxville was totally white.) After years of lawsuits and costly bickering, Tennessee officials adopted policies that were not driven by racism. The regents of the state institutions declared the same admissions standards for all colleges and universities, whether predominantly white or black. The state legislature appropriated hundreds of millions of dollars to establish courses at Tennessee State that would attract whites — in health sciences, nursing, information systems, agriculture, and more. The result was that whites made up 32 percent of Tennessee State's student body in 1992.

Justice White and other justices, except for Scalia and a concurring but doubting Thomas, knew that if Mississippi had the will it could find a way to combine its black and white colleges in a way that would benefit all its children. The Supreme Court asked Mississippi to find a will. It vindicated Marshall's long struggle in support of affirmative action and made me understand his comment, "I believe in the Court."

Justice Marshall was as passionate in his defense of First Amendment rights as he was in his support of affirmative action. He clearly extended the parameters of freedom of speech in this society. But throughout his tenure on the Court he would fight re-argued wars to preserve the precedents set by the Warren Court, and in the early years of the Burger Court. He tried to sell to the Court and the nation the idea that a parking lot in a shopping center, a prison hall, an army base, was a public forum, and that the government always had to show compelling reasons for limiting free speech there or anyplace else.

Marshall's influence was clear during his first term on the Court. He wrote the majority opinion for the Court in the case of *Amalgamated Food Employees Union v. Logan Valley Plaza*. A union member had picketed a supermarket in this large suburban shopping center, protesting the store's use of nonunion workers. The store sought an injunction against the pickets, claiming that they were trespassing upon private property.

Marshall, always the pragmatist, the jurist looking for common-sense justice, noted that the entire public had free access to the shopping mall. He pointed out that such shopping centers had gained 37 percent of retail sales in the U.S. and Canada. He said that a Court decision to bar picketing at such plazas would have "substantial consequences for workers seeking to challenge substandard working conditions, consumers protesting shoddy or overpriced merchandise, and minority groups seeking nondiscriminatory hiring policies. . . ."

In the 6 to 3 opinion, Marshall wrote that businesses in the great new shopping centers might try to immunize themselves from picketing and protests by creating a *"cordon sanitaire"* of parking lots around their stores. But, he said, "neither precedent nor policy compels a result so at variance with the goal of free expression and communication that is at the heart of the First Amendment."

Marshall's triumph of reason in *Logan Valley* was shortlived. During the next four years Richard Nixon appointed four men to the Supreme Court: Burger, Blackmun, Powell, and William H. Rehnquist. So in 1972, in *Lloyd Corp. v. Tanner,* when the issue involved the right of anti–Vietnam War protesters to leaflet a private shopping center, the Court engaged in what Marshall described bitterly as an attack on "the rationale of *Logan.*"

Justice Marshall tried in creative and imaginative ways to extend the scope of the First Amendment. His daring view of the breadth of "free speech" protections was illustrated in 1974 in *Village of Belle Terre v. Boraas.* This village had foreshadowed the "family values" conflict now raging in America by adopting a zoning ordinance that limited one area to "single family" residences. The ordinance defined a "family" as "any number of persons related by blood, adoption or marriage, plus any domestic servants," or "up to two but no more than two persons not so related." Marshall took the view that the ordinance violated the First Amendment because it outlawed a form of personal association:

> The instant ordinance discriminates on the basis of . . . a personal lifestyle choice as to household companions. It permits any number of persons related by blood or marriage, be it two or twenty, to live in a single household, but it limits to two the number of unrelated persons bound by profession, love, friendship, religious or political affiliation or mere economics who can occupy a single home. . . . The village has, in effect, acted to fence out those individuals whose choice of lifestyle differs from that of its current residents.

Marshall lost that battle against an ordinance that said effectively that three college students, or secretaries, or whatever, who were not blood related could not own and live in the "single-family" area. Only he and Brennan dissented from an opinion written by William O. Douglas, who refused to see freedom of association as a First Amendment issue.

Unlike other members of the Court, Marshall was energized by his last case as attorney for the NAACP Legal Defense and Educational Fund. It was *Garner v. Louisiana*, in which sixteen sit-in demonstrators argued that their "direct action" at lunch counters was a First Amendment form of protected expression. Marshall and his team had argued Louisiana was the constitutional violator because it had used state powers to shelter private racial discrimination when state officials enforced anti-trespass laws. As a backup, the NAACP had argued that the evidence did not support charges that the sit-in demonstrators had "disturbed the peace."

The Supreme Court majority gave Marshall only a slender victory on the last point. But in a concurring opinion, Harlan, one of the most conservative members of the Court at that time, filed a concurring opinion that, since the demonstrators were at the lunch counter to convey the message of their hatred of racial discrimination, i.e., using their freedom to speak out — Louisiana was at odds with the Constitution when it used a general breach-of-peace statute to protect the interests of those who owned and ran the lunch counter.

Thanks to Marshall, Brennan, Harlan, and others, "speech" took on an almost breathtaking new meaning. It embraced such forms of expression as picketing, sit-ins, waving a red flag, wearing armbands against the draft or against United States involvements in war. Even the burning of the American flag, the wearing of long hair by a male, became forms of transmission of ideas that Marshall wanted protected under the First Amendment.

With both exasperation and dedication, Marshall continued to fight for his view that many nontraditional areas where free speech was suppressed were, by constitutional standards, *public forums*. Marshall believed, for example, that the country and the courts had shown a deference to the military that could not be justified under the Constitution. In the Pentagon Papers case he had stood firm for the right of the *New York Times* and the *Washington Post* to tell the American people what they had learned concerning U.S. government lies about the United States involvement in Vietnam. In 1976, in *Greer v. Spock*, a Court majority held that an Army base was not a "public forum," as Marshall would construe it, and said in effect that military commanders need not be burdened by concerns about freedom of speech. Brennan wrote a dissent in which Marshall concurred, but added his own brief, angry dissent:

> The First Amendment infringement that the Court here condones is fundamentally inconsistent with the commitment of the Nation and the Constitution to an open society. That commitment surely calls for a far more reasoned articulation of the governmental interests assertedly served by the challenged regulations than is reflected in the Court's opinion.

A good look inside Marshall's mind, his thinking about press freedoms, is shown in his response when I said to him, "The Supreme Court has no troops. The Court is at the mercy of the attorney general and the Justice Department and the president of the United States."

"Not as long as a free press is alive," Marshall countered.

I asked if he was telling me that the press was a "great keeper of freedom."

"What else have we got?" Marshall replied. "I've been disturbed by recent efforts to curb the powers of the press . . . except at times I get worried about the press when they publish stories that I'm dead, or dying, or terribly ill, or something like that. For those brief moments when I'm angry, I wonder how much free press I'm for."

Marshall brought measures of humor and sarcasm to the conference room that were unprecedented, and for some shocking, as he tried to deliver common sense to the Court's deliberations.

Just what was the personal philosophy of this new justice, this grandson of slaves who suddenly held power beyond that of all but a handful of white men? Conservatives distrusted him profoundly, regarding him as a social revolutionary whose beliefs were akin to those of P. J. Proudhon, who wrote in 1849:

> To be governed is to be watched, inspected, spied upon, directed, law-ridden, regulated, penned up, indoctrinated, preached at, checked, appraised, seized, censured, commanded, by beings who have neither title, nor knowledge nor virtue. To be governed is to have every operation, every transaction, every movement noted, registered, counted, rated, stamped, measured, numbered, assessed, licensed, refused, authorized, indorsed, admonished, prevented, reformed, redressed, corrected.

In fact, Marshall held no such cynical view of government and would never have endorsed Proudhon's assertion that "whoever lays his hand on me to govern me is a usurper and tyrant." Marshall's entire life had taught him that only good government could tame the jungles of racism, greed, and the trampling of the weak by the strong. Yet, Marshall could see enough reality in Proudhon's views to make him hold a healthy measure of distrust of American governments. Thomas Jefferson had expressed the need for vigilance against the excessive reach of government when he said in 1798: "Free government is founded in jealousy, and not in confidence; it is jealousy, and not confidence, which prescribes limited constitutions, to bind down those whom we are obliged to trust with power."

Marshall's crusade as NAACP lawyer, as solicitor general, and as a Supreme Court justice was to "bind down" those who wielded immense power, and who so often abused it in their dealings with the poor and with racial minorities — especially in the criminal justice system. In one of the cases where the Court was trying to define, or redefine, "pornography," the justices decided to view some porno films to see if they saw any redeeming social values, or the extent to which such films offended community values, or how they appealed to prurient interests, or whatever. Justice Harlan was almost blind. "No problem," Marshall said, "I'll sit beside him and interpret what's on the screen.

"That was a fun assignment," Marshall said to me. "Lots of fun. I really enjoyed it."

He enjoyed even more turning to Justice Blackmun at the end of the movies and saying, "Did you learn anything new from that one, Harry? I didn't."

More solemnly, in *Stanley v. Georgia*, he said for the Court in overturning that state's law: "The states retain broad power to regulate obscenity; that power simply does not extend to mere possession [of pornographic materials] by the individual in the privacy of his home."

As solicitor general, Marshall tried to "bind down" the agencies of government that were tapping telephones of Americans, putting electronic listening devices in sofas and walls of private homes, planting cameras *and* listening devices in hotel rooms. Marshall's stance against such illegal intrusions caused him grief in his confirmation hearings for a Supreme Court seat, because Senators Thurmond, Ellender, Eastland, and others regarded an objection to widespread wiretapping and electronic surveillance as being "soft on crime."

Once on the high tribunal, Marshall moved with disdain against senators who loved bugs, wiretaps, and illegal entries as he tried to consolidate the constitutional protections of those accused of crimes.

Marshall had deep concerns about how people get arrested in this country — that is, whether they know their rights against self-incrimination — and how they get indicted through perjured statements by law-enforcement officials, or because of "evidence" secured through illegal searches and seizures. He had a fierce determination to ensure as a constitutional right that even the poorest of the accused has counsel. He moved to cleanse the jury-selection system of the taint of egregious racism. Marshall insisted that sentencing procedures be freed of class, caste, and racial bigotries.

Marshall had not been on the Court long before he saw the impact of Nixon and others screaming that a majority of the justices were favoring "criminals" over the police. In 1972 Thurgood saw the magnitude of the Court's bending to a public clamor about crime when, in *Adams v. Williams,* the majority held that a policeman could make a reasonable investigatory stop of any automobile and conduct a "limited protective search" for concealed weapons. Any weapons or contraband discovered in the "limited" search could be used in a subsequent trial of the motorist, the Court said.

"This decision expands the concept of warrantless searches far beyond anything heretofore recognized as legitimate," Marshall protested. A year later he came close to apoplexy when the majority held that it didn't matter constitutionally if someone consented to a police search without knowing of the right to withhold consent. Under this Court construction, Marshall wrote, "all the police must do is conduct what will inevitably be a charade of asking for consent. If they display any firmness at all, a verbal expression of assent will undoubtedly be forthcoming."

Here, again, Marshall was bringing commonsense fairness into the law. He knew that the highly educated, the wealthy and powerful, the crooks who had many lawyers, would know that they could send the police packing. The poor, the racial minorities, the American underclass, would meekly submit to searches. Marshall continued: "Permitting searches without any assurance at all that the subject of the search knew that, by his consent, he was relinquishing his constitutional rights, is something that I cannot believe is sanctioned by the Constitution." Marshall was aghast when, in *United States v. Donovan,* in 1977, six members of the Court said that the 1968 Omnibus Crime Control and Safe Streets Act required that when applying for a federal judge's order authorizing electronic surveillance, the government was required to tell the judge the names

of all individuals suspected of criminal activity who would be overheard; and that after the surveillance the government had to tell the
judge the names of all persons overheard so that the judge could
decide who ought to be informed of the eavesdropping — but, the
Court majority said, if the government failed to meet these requirements of law, evidence acquired by the surveillance could still be
used in a trial. The Court said, incredibly, that government failure
to comply with the law did not make an otherwise lawful surveillance
unlawful. Marshall, Brennan, and Stevens dissented forcefully.

Marshall had seen, in every week of his work as a civil rights lawyer, that a sickening number of poor, uneducated Americans were
charged with crimes, indicted by grand juries, because they were
coerced into submitting to searches, or tricked into making self-
incriminating remarks. And the injustices were intensified by the fact
that many Americans faced prison terms without the benefit of a
competent defense lawyer. This wasn't supposed to be, because the
Court had declared in the capital case of *Powell v. Alabama,* in 1932,
that the Sixth Amendment required that the defendant be properly
represented at trial. Justice George Sutherland of Utah was both
plain-speaking and eloquent:

> The right to be heard would be, in many cases, of little avail if it
> did not comprehend the right to be heard by counsel. Even the
> intelligent and educated layman has small and sometimes no skill
> in the science of law. If charged with crime, he is incapable, gen-
> erally, of determining for himself whether the indictment is good
> or bad. He is unfamiliar with the rules of evidence. Left without
> the aid of counsel he may be put on trial without a proper charge,
> and convicted upon incompetent evidence, or evidence irrelevant
> to the issue or otherwise inadmissible. He lacks both the skill and
> knowledge adequately to prepare his defense, even though he
> have a perfect one. He requires the guiding hand of counsel at
> every step in the proceedings against him. Without it, though he
> be not guilty, he faces the danger of conviction because he does
> not know how to establish his innocence. If that be true of men of
> intelligence, how much more true is it of the ignorant and illiter-
> ate . . . ?

Then came the celebrated case of *Gideon v. Wainwright,* in 1963,
in which the Court extended the right to counsel to all criminal defendants.

The very first opinion that Marshall wrote for the Supreme
Court, *Mempa v. Rhay* in 1967, involved the right of an indigent

defendant to defense counsel at sentencing. The Court agreed with Marshall that it was obvious that a convicted person needed a lawyer at sentencing because of "the necessity for the aid of counsel in marshaling the facts, introducing evidence of mitigating circumstances and in general aiding and assisting the defendant to present his case as to [a fair] sentence."

But Marshall knew from his courtroom experiences that prosecutors did not always honor with good faith Justice Sutherland's 1932 command, or the Court's decisions in *Gideon* and similar cases. Thurgood was incredulous in 1972 when the case of *Dukes v. Warden* came up to the Supreme Court. Here was a man who had pleaded guilty to a crime under pressure from his attorney while he was recovering from a suicide attempt. At the trial, Dukes tried to withdraw his plea of guilty. His attorney admitted that he might have laid on too much pressure to get his client to plead guilty. There was evidence that the attorney might be using Dukes's admission of guilt to protect two other defendants who blamed Dukes for their activities. The trial court refused to let Dukes withdraw his plea, and the Supreme Court upheld this refusal. Marshall sizzled.

An even more stupefying case, *Brescia v. New Jersey*, came before the Court in 1974. The trial court had appointed a lawyer for Brescia from the office of the public defender. But on the first day of the trial the appointed lawyer announced that he was not sufficiently prepared to argue the case. The judge decided to replace this public defender with a lawyer from the same firm, ordering that the trial would go ahead that day. He gave the new public defender the time of the noon recess to prepare a defense of Brescia, who was soon convicted.

A majority of the Supreme Court danced around the question whether Brescia had received effective assistance of a lawyer. It thrashed around the issue of whether the public defender, the judge, or someone else was to blame for having the trial go forward under such unusual circumstances. Marshall could get only Brennan to join him in saying:

> Timely appointment and opportunity for adequate preparation are absolute prerequisites for counsel to fulfill his constitutionally assigned role of seeing to it that available defenses are raised and the prosecution put to its proof.
>   . . . The issue in determining whether a defendant has been deprived of the effective assistance of counsel is not whether the defense attorney is culpable for the failure but only whether, for

whatever reasons, he has failed to fulfill the essential role imposed on him by the Sixth Amendment. No matter upon whose doorstep the judge cared to lay blame for counsel's lack of preparation, the cost of the failure should not have been visited upon the defendant — who was without responsibility.

The justice once said to me: "This is still a society in which justice is more easily available to the wealthy than to the poor. The disparities are narrower because of government action and because private organizations help make it possible for a truly poor person to get legal aid in America. The people who are really getting squeezed are the ones making just enough money not to be poor, but who don't make enough money to pay the high, exorbitant rates that lawyers are charging. Those people are suffering, and the only way I know to help them is to bring lawyers' fees down. But that's a free enterprise proposition, and it has to be done by lawyers, not government.

"You take the Brown girl in Topeka, or the other poor blacks involved in *Brown*. They never could have gotten to the Supreme Court if there hadn't been an NAACP Legal Defense Fund. Those cases cost around a million dollars. There were no black parents who could have put up that kind of money."

Other members of the Court learned quickly that Marshall would lash them verbally and in a written dissent if they showed what he considered a gross lack of sensitivity to the special problems of the poor. In 1973, in *United States v. Kras*, Blackmun wrote for a five-man majority that refused to extend the equal protection of the laws to the right to receive relief from one's debts through bankruptcy. Blackmun held that even pauper debtors had to pay a $50 filing fee to get bankruptcy relief. He argued that the indigent debtor involved in this case could save up the $50 fee by forgoing a weekly movie or giving up two packs of cigarettes each week. Marshall thundered: "It is disgraceful for an interpretation of the Constitution to be premised upon unfounded assumptions about how people live. . . It may be easy for some people to think that weekly savings of less than $2 are no burden, but no one who has had close contact with poor people can fail to understand how close to the margin of survival many of them are. . . . A pack or two of cigarettes may be, for them, not a routine purchase, but a luxury indulged in only rarely. The desperately poor almost never go to see a movie. . . . They have more important things to do with what little money they have."

Marshall's greatest goal was to humanize the criminal justice system. In November 1973 he said to the Association of the Bar of the City of New York:

> In our hurrying to erect a more sufficient system of justice, we must not forget that our system derives its strength from the fact that it deals with individuals. To mechanize the system, to make it lose its human element, to forget that in every case we are dealing with a human being who, before the law, deserves to be treated as an equal of any man, is to lose that which gives any judicial system its very life.

But how to humanize a system in which the selection of juries was skewed by racism? In 1972 Marshall tried to demonstrate that his passions related not to a concern just for blacks and other minorities, but to the integrity of the heart of the American system of justice. A case, *Peters v. Kiff*, involved the right of a white defendant to challenge the constitutionality of his conviction on the grounds that blacks were excluded from both the grand jury that indicted him and the petit jury that found him guilty. Here Marshall wrote for the Court in saying that all Americans were entitled to trial by a jury that was not skewed by racial manipulations:

> [T]he exclusion . . . of a substantial and identifiable class of citizens has a potential impact that is too subtle and too pervasive to admit of confinement to particular issues or particular cases.
>   . . . When any large and identifiable segment of the community is excluded from jury service, the effect is to remove from the jury room qualities of human nature and varieties of human experience, the range of which is unknown and perhaps unknowable. It is not necessary to assume that the excluded group will consistently vote as a class in order to conclude, as we do, that its exclusion deprives the jury of a perspective on human events that may have unsuspected importance in any case that may be presented.

The Court faced a unique charge of discrimination in the selection of jurors in 1977 in *Castaneda v. Partida*. A Texas prisoner of Mexican descent petitioned for a writ of habeas corpus on grounds that Mexican-Americans had been discriminated against in the selection of the grand jury that indicted him. The prisoner's lawyer pointed out that while Mexican-Americans made up 79 percent of the population of Hidalgo County, where the indictment occurred, over an eleven-year period only 39 percent of grand jurors had been Mexican-Americans. Justice Blackmun wrote for a Court divided 5 to 4 that the grand jury selection process in this case was in violation of the Constitution.

Justice Powell wrote a dissent in which he expressed doubt about a claim of discrimination by a Mexican-American defendant when Mexican-Americans controlled the jury selection and other political processes in Hidalgo County. Marshall joined Blackmun, but felt compelled to give Powell a little lecture about the behavior of minorities. So he wrote a concurring opinion in which he said that it was not unusual for members of oppressed minority groups who gained acceptance and power in the larger society to try to disassociate themselves from their minority moorings and indeed adopt negative attitudes toward members of their own race. So Mexican-American jury commissioners might very well stack the deck against a Mexican-American defendant whose alleged criminal behavior embarrassed them.

Marshall had found probably the very worst of times in which to try to meet Jefferson's mandate to "bind down those whom we are obliged to trust with power." The American people had entrusted Richard Nixon with the ultimate in power, and he was abusing it, warping the FBI, the CIA, the IRS, and other instruments of government in all the ways that Marshall opposed and deplored. With a majority of justices bending to Nixon's harangues against the Court and "activist judges who legislate," Marshall was thrown into the role of a "great dissenter." Did he like this, or did it diminish whatever joy he once felt over being named to the highest Court in the land?

"I love a dissent," he told me. "You have to get real mad to write a good dissent. I love a war. When young lawyers apply to clerk in my office, the first thing I ask is, 'Do you like writing dissents? If you don't, baby, this is not the office for *you.*' Yep, get my juices jiggling and I'll write a helluva dissent. I admit, though, that I sometimes wonder what a difference it might make for the country if I were writing for the majority."

CHAPTER TWENTY

A NATION OF MEN, NOT LAWS

As MARSHALL WATCHED Prince Edward County close its public schools, Wallace stand in the doorway at the University of Alabama, Governor Orval Faubus precipitate a national crisis over Central High School in Little Rock, he said his faith in the rule of law was not shattered. But he would look with a jaundiced eye on the myth that we are a nation of laws, not men. Marshall was observing a harsh reality: that American society had been molded, manipulated, intimidated, warped, and sometimes enobled by men and women who could be classified as heroes or scoundrels, dream makers or dream breakers. He looked at the friends and foes of his struggle and could not escape the truth that in this democracy, strong men and women turn laws into fragile webs that catch gnats and small spiders, but let the wasps and tarantulas break through.

On dozens of occasions Marshall spoke of Truman as a man larger and more forceful than the written statutes. He noted that Truman in 1947 and early 1948 had believed that he was one man who could change the laws. He appointed the president's Commission on Civil Rights to tell him what legislation was needed to halt lynchings, police brutalities, and other violence and oppressions that were being visited upon the Negro people. Truman had risked his political life to send to the Congress a legislative program based upon the recommendations of his blue-ribbon commission.

"Truman proved that one man can be bigger than the statutes of his time — more forceful than the lawmakers," Marshall told me.

Truman illustrated the fact that a man need not have great vision, just a great sense of justice, as Truman did, to change a society. Marshall noted that Truman was no firebrand liberal. He wasn't treading any farther into the waters of racial passion than the more timid NAACP leaders who were reluctant to declare that they were for "social equality" or that they accepted interracial marriages. "I wish to make it clear that I am not appealing for social equality for the Negro," Truman said in 1948. "The Negro himself knows better than that, and the highest types of Negro leaders say quite frankly they prefer the society of their own people. Negroes want justice, not social relations." But that same year, Truman would also say: "In giving Negroes the rights which are theirs, we are only acting in accord with our ideals of a true democracy. If any class or race can be permanently set apart from, or pushed down below the rest, in political and civil rights, so may any other class or race when it shall incur the displeasure of its more powerful associates, and we may say farewell to the principles on which we count our safety."

Truman suddenly was beloved by the black people of America. The *Chicago Defender*, then one of the foremost black newspapers in America, chose to give Truman the annual Robert S. Abbott Award for "the most significant contributions to democracy in 1948." As publisher John H. Sengstacke said to the president in presenting the award: "You, like the man in whose memory it is presented, were faced with an uphill battle at a crucial period of your career. But the 'underdog' role only served to spur you on. Hardship gave birth to determination, and obstacles became milestones along the path of progress. After a hard, tough fight you triumphed to win our nation's highest honor. We are proud of you as Americans. We like a fighting man."

Truman replied that the principles for which he was fighting "are as old as the Constitution and as new as the Democratic party platform. I vow that I shall never stop fighting for those principles."

It is important to note that this president, who Marshall says "will come out on top and in time . . . will be judged the greatest," was pushed and aided immensely by Hubert Humphrey, who turned out to be one of the most fertile-minded of lawmakers, and one of the greatest public officials in American history.

"Negroes never had a better ally," Marshall said of Humphrey. He said that Humphrey was the soloist in "that small choir of white Americans who sang us closer to the Promised Land."

Marshall recalled how White, Wilkins, and he all worked on the presidential candidates and the delegates before each presidential convention. In 1948, only a few paid-off blacks were supporting Thomas Dewey. What the Democrats said, and whom they elected, was crucial, although many blacks were fascinated by the leftist lure of Henry Wallace. But except for Du Bois, NAACP leaders White, Wilkins, and Marshall felt that they had to go with Truman, especially if he demanded a platform that promised greater rights to black people. Platforms seemed to mean something in those days.

When the NAACP hierarchy began to wonder whether Truman could impose his will upon the convention with regard to civil rights, or whether he would even want to in the face of polls showing Dewey defeating him, Marshall and others asked for help from the young mayor of Minneapolis, Hubert Horatio Humphrey. This native of Doland, South Dakota, where there was not a single black resident, was fast becoming the symbol of civil rights activism among white politicians. He had lashed out at the American Automobile Association of Minneapolis because it barred Jews — and, of course, blacks and Native Americans.

The NAACP had been fighting FDR and state governors, demanding fair employment practices laws, and Humphrey had been the first major city mayor to get his city council to pass such a law.

When Thurmond and Russell declared that Eisenhower was a "states' rights man," and was their candidate for the Democratic nomination, Marshall knew that it was time to ask Humphrey for help at the 1948 convention. Humphrey responded with startling fervor.

Suddenly there were Humphrey and members of the newly formed Americans for Democratic Action (ADA) pressing for bolder actions to desegregate colleges and schools. The ADA made a compelling argument that the ten million black people living in the South had not a single delegate representing them at the convention. Truman was pressed forcefully to order immediately the desegregation of the nation's military forces. Humphrey, again with the private urging of Marshall and White, was eager to embrace all these in a civil rights plank.

A new "war of the states" was played out at that Philadelphia convention on the afternoon of July 14, when Cecil Sims of Tennessee begged the delegates not to embrace the liberal platform plank on civil rights.

"If we from the South, having extended the hand of friendship to this convention, if we are defeated," he said, "then I say to you that you are witnessing here today the dissolution of the Democratic party in the South."

Whispers went forth that Truman wanted to heed Sims's warning, and there is evidence even from Truman that this was true — that he did not want his presidential campaign crippled by what he knew would be a tumultuous Deep South reaction to endorsement of the "liberal" civil rights plank. Then came rumors that Humphrey, now fearing defeat in his Minnesota race for a seat in the U.S. Senate, had decided to placate Thurmond, Russell, and the other Southerners. That canard was refuted when Andrew Biemiller of Wisconsin, the former congressman and by then the AFL-CIO lobbyist, introduced the liberal plank and asked Humphrey to speak:

"Friends, delegates, I do not believe that there can be any compromise on the guarantees of the civil rights which we have mentioned in the minority report. . . . To those who say that we are rushing the issue of civil rights, I say . . . we are a hundred and seventy-two years too late. . . .

"The time has arrived for the Democratic party to get out of the shadow of states' rights and walk forthrightly in the bright sunshine of human rights."

The convention adopted the "Humphrey plank" 652½ to 582½.

That provoked Thurmond and the Dixiecrats to walk out. Truman told friends that he was "pissed off" by this upstart from Minnesota who had further burdened his campaign. It is noteworthy that volume two of his memoirs, *Years of Trial and Hope*, Truman wrote at length about that 1948 convention without ever mentioning Humphrey's name. Truman took total credit for the adoption of the bolder civil rights plank, and responsibility for the Thurmond walkout.

Truman often told with gusto the self-glorifying story of a reporter asking Thurmond why he was walking out, given the fact that Roosevelt supposedly had always stood for a strong civil rights plank.

"I know. But that son of a bitch Truman really means it," Thurmond allegedly replied.

History denies insinuations that Truman tried to prevent what Humphrey achieved in Philadelphia. After all, Truman returned to the White House from that convention and on July 26, 1948, signed Executive Order 9981 ordering the immediate end to racial discrimination in the military.

It is remarkable that while the convention events made Humphrey the bête noir of Democratic politics in the South for most of the rest of his life, they did not prevent Truman from defeating Dewey in 1948 and then setting America on a course of legal and moral change that would last for decades.

Yes, I am willing to allow that while Democratic liberals won an astounding triumph at the convention that July day in Philadelphia, history suggests that it *was* the beginning of the dissolution of the Democratic party in the South. I know that while Dixie has produced hundreds more congressmen of the mentality of Thurmond and Eastland, the rest of the nation has produced few men of the caliber of Humphrey, which is why the Democratic party has foundered in the South, consigning the nation to presidents like Nixon, Reagan, and Bush — at least until the 1992 elections.

A nation of laws rather than men? Nonsense! Even Marshall seemed to persist in believing this for years. Some of us knew that there would have been no civil rights laws passed in the 1960s but for the leadership of Humphrey, who marshaled the votes to pass the Public Accommodations Act of 1964, the Voting Rights Act of 1965, the Fair Housing Act of 1968, and so much more.

But Humphrey's extraordinary mind . and broad heart gave America more than civil rights legislation. Credit him for the leadership during the Kennedy administration that brought forth a nuclear test ban agreement which stopped the poisoning of our atmosphere by above-ground tests of nuclear weapons by the United States and the Soviet Union. Not many of today's young adults realize that they didn't ingest strontium 90 and other nuclear poisons in their milk because of Humphrey's tenacity in getting that test ban agreement. Here was a dream maker whom Marshall revered.

Marshall said to me that Humphrey lost the 1968 election because of his patriotism — because he did not possess the ruthlessness that Nixon had shown in a Senate race in which he ran against Helen Gahagan Douglas, or in gaining the vice presidency. Humphrey was destined to become proof of the cynical truism that in American politics, nice guys finish last.

Humphrey refused to say anything publicly in criticism of Johnson, whom he regarded as the greatest of American presidents in terms of social legislation. He knew that the Vietnam War was destroying Johnson emotionally and physically, and probably destroying his place in history. He refused to add to the abuse of a president who was seen by so many Americans, even Democrats, as a blight upon the nation.

"It was a tragedy for the civil rights movement," Marshall told me, "that Hubert was denied the presidency through quirks of politics and fate, and that after these terribly disappointing moments his voice would be stilled by cancer."

There was no consolation for NAACP officials in reading the eulogies, the encomiums in Congress, to this great dream maker.

There was the utterly sincere pap of Barry Goldwater, the ultimate symbol of conservatism at the time, saying that "heaven is going to be a better place to go to . . . because Hubert will be there awaiting us." Hawaii senator Daniel K. Inouye lamented that "never before has our party handed to any man such a tarnished prize," referring to the 1968 nomination amidst tear-gassing of war protestors and other circumstances that "made his election almost impossible."

John Lewis, the black Georgia congressman who had been battered physically during civil rights activities, said simply: "Humphrey demonstrated to all of us, as Martin Luther King, Jr., did, that one man can, indeed, change the world."

By the time of Humphrey's death, Marshall was a Supreme Court justice, quarantined from the often-sick world of politics. He watched in sad silence, repeating a line from his boyhood: "There were some really good white people around." He had also seen some terrible new dream breakers.

In fact, Marshall was a Supreme Court neophyte when Nixon stunned the Republican national convention in 1968 by declaring that the governor of Maryland, Spiro Agnew, would be his running mate — the candidate for the vice presidency of the United States.

"Spiro who?" delegates shouted, as if they felt they were the victims of some grotesque political joke. They were, but they did not realize it fully until Agnew had become a household name, served as Nixon's verbal hatchet man, won the hatred and support of millions, and then resigned the vice presidency after pleading "no contest" to federal tax evasion charges — this to avoid going to prison on charges of extortion and bribery.

In five years this second-generation Greek, "Ted" Agnew, went from political assassin to national laughingstock, but during those five years as the self-styled voice of middle America, Agnew changed the mind-set of this country dramatically, to Marshall's dismay. America still carries the wounds of Agnew's anti-black and anti-poor utterances, of his "southern strategy" for vote getting, of the media bashing that he engaged in unashamedly. No crooked vice president in history ever did so much to make America mean-spirited.

"Agnew bothered me as much as Wallace, Faubus, Thurmond, and the Southerners ever did," Marshall told me. "Americans knew that they were bigots posturing for southern constituencies. But Agnew was speaking to the nation with the prestige of the vice presidency and the White House. And there I was, a new justice, forbidden to say publicly what I thought about him."

Spiro was that rare bird who postured as a liberal Republican, but his actions and statements were reactionary, except when he saw political opportunities for which he changed his tune — temporarily. The record was clear that he was a mediocrity — the kind of second-rate politician who would claim that "blacks aren't ready." He became a college dropout because, as he put it, he paid too little attention to his studies. Agnew sought a new route out of poverty by attending the University of Baltimore law school at night. He graduated in 1947 and opened a law firm, which flopped miserably. He wound up working in a food market. Then Agnew, a Democrat until 1946, began dabbling in Republican politics and land deals, the former eventually bringing him fame, the latter disgrace.

Agnew's fortunes soared on a political fluke in 1966 when an ultraconservative segregationist, George P. Mahoney, came out of a three-way primary with the Democratic nomination for governor of Maryland. Suddenly Agnew, the Republican, was the savior of Democratic consciences, of blacks, and of the state of Maryland. He spared nothing in exploiting the contempt many voters felt for Mahoney, tying the perennial candidate to the Ku Klux Klan. He called Mahoney "a devil that sits holding a two-pronged pitchfork of bigotry and hatred." Agnew won the governorship handily.

Maryland Democrats soon learned that they had bought a pig in a poke. Agnew did not like being challenged. When some two hundred students from Bowie State College protested outside his Annapolis office, Agnew had them arrested and ordered Bowie State closed down. When Dr. Martin Luther King, Jr., was assassinated in Memphis and violence erupted in Baltimore in which six people died, seven hundred were injured, and five thousand were arrested, Agnew sent in the National Guard. On April 11, 1968, Agnew invited one hundred of Baltimore's most prominent black leaders to a meeting at which, to their astonishment, he began to scold them for "knuckling under to black fomenters of violence." Almost every black walked out in anger.

But the national publicity told Agnew that he had struck a political lode of gold. Yet even he did not know that a young right-wing speech writer for Nixon — Patrick J. Buchanan — was reveling in what Agnew was doing, and telling Nixon that Agnew was a man he should keep his eye on.

Nixon's big challenge at the 1968 Republican convention, in Miami Beach, was to keep his southern delegates in line, lest Governor Nelson A. Rockefeller (for years Agnew's personal preferred candidate) or someone else should wrest the nomination from him. Nixon met with the Southerners and made a secret pledge not to pick any running mate who would be offensive to the South. Nixon chose Agnew and consummated a political marriage that was born in hell.

Eight days after Agnew was named, his personal aide on civil rights, Gilbert Ware, resigned, saying that "the governor's thrust onto the national scene has put me in an even more intolerable position. . . . Disillusionment has come, leaving me no choice but to remove myself from an increasingly agonizing situation."

Marshall and others at the NAACP knew that Nixon was bad news and that Agnew would be a bitter pill.

On September 8, 1968, in his campaign for national power, Agnew went on NBC's "Meet the Press," and was asked if student protesters against the war in Vietnam were "under the control or direction of the Communist party, U.S.A., or under the control of Moscow."

"I think they are under the influence of them without any question," Agnew replied.

Shortly after his nomination he told the *Philadelphia Sunday Bulletin* that "housing occupancy cannot be legislated without invading the rights of privacy guaranteed by the Constitution."

Marshall told me that he was "personally offended" by Agnew's virtual endorsement of racial discrimination in housing. "After all our struggles to win *Shelley* and stop the courts from enforcing restrictive covenants, here was the number two guy in government going against us."

In October, when Agnew declared that "the civil rights movement went too far the day it began," a furious Marshall said, "I don't recall a vice president saying anything like that, even in the days of Wilson and Coolidge and Hoover, when Negroes didn't have a chance."

Marshall and millions of other black people agonized through that 1968 campaign, which had so many elements of tragedy. Humphrey and one of the finest politicians in our history, Edmund Muskie, were locked in battle with two of the sleaziest politicians in the world, Nixon and Agnew. But it was far from a fair or even battle. Humphrey carried the heavy baggage of loyalty to Lyndon Johnson, and the stench of tear gas used on war protesters in Chicago. Muskie brought no rescue to the ticket in a time of wretched divisions. Black voters were saying in anger, "All these honkies are alike." Nixon and Agnew had the advantage of both widespread disillusionment over the lingering war in Vietnam and voter anger aimed at those who were demanding an end to the war.

And then there was the destabilizing factor of George Wallace running as a third-party candidate.

Marshall and I discussed the 1968 election and the possibility that in history it might become the greatest blot on the political participation of Negroes. Rap Brown, Stokely Carmichael, and other self-styled militants had counseled blacks to "go fishin' " rather than vote for "either of the honkies." Enough blacks stayed away from the polls to enable Nixon to win with 31,785,480 votes, with Humphrey getting 31,275,166 — and Wallace getting 9,906,473 ballots.

Marshall repeated what he had told a Muskogee, Oklahoma, audience in June 1967: "I'm afraid our young people are getting the wrong people to be their heroes." He added, "And that election tells me that some older Negroes are taking the advice of some damned fools."

Marshall noted that all the civil rights and civil liberties leaders, and many educators, black and white, were worried about the role Agnew would play, since he was Nixon's payoff to Southerners who still fought doggedly — and viciously — to ward off racial integration. Agnew wasted no time confirming the fears of the civil rights and education communities.

He began to pander to bigotry, greed, fear, as no vice president ever had during my lifetime. His hatred of war protesters seemed limitless. In 1969 he told an Ohio State University commencement audience that "a society which comes to fear its children is effete. A sniveling, hand-wringing power structure deserves the violent rebellion it encourages." He told a Harrisburg, Pennsylvania, audience that "America cannot afford to write off a whole generation for the decadent thinking of a few. America cannot afford to . . . be deceived by their duplicity . . . or let their license destroy liberty. We can, however, afford to separate [the protesters] from our society with no more regret than we should feel over discarding rotten apples from a barrel."

The delicate smell of Patrick Buchanan's venom oozed from every such Agnew utterance, especially when Agnew was attacking members of the media who figured he sounded more like a Soviet dictator than an American who understood constitutional rights. Agnew called his press critics "nattering nabobs of negativism."

In 1970 ex–college dropout Agnew began a crusade to stop colleges and universities from giving some benefit of the doubt to poor, black, and other youngsters who saw a college education as their route out of poverty and hopelessness. Marshall knew that elitist Agnew was bent on destroying the fruits of his long legal campaign to get qualified blacks into all colleges. Agnew went to Chicago and Des Moines to give speeches about how a "natural aristocracy" was meant to populate university campuses. "Preparatory and compensatory education do not belong in the university," he said. The record showed that at the University of Maryland in 1968, Agnew's last year as governor, there were only 484 black students out of 24,222, which indicated that Agnew had not let any quota system or anything else clutter up the Maryland campus with blacks. He had enfeebled the effects of Marshall's triumph in the Donald Murray lawsuit.

Still, Agnew went around declaring that no one in his audience would want to be cared for by a doctor who got into medical school under a quota. He completely ignored the fact that doctors must pass college and state examinations certifying that whatever the program that got them *into* medical school, learning and achievement give them the right to practice medicine.

In April 1970, I wrote a column that got Agnew's attention. The following month he went to a Republican fund-raiser in Houston, where he called *Washington Post* editorial cartoonist Herblock "that master of sick invective." He referred to the *Washington Post* and the *New York Times* as "the Washington–New York axis." Tom Wicker of the *New York Times* was labeled "the soft-spoken boy wonder of the opinion molders," and the journalist and commentator I. F. Stone was castigated as a "strident voice of illiberalism."

After also assailing the *Atlanta Constitution,* the *New Republic,* the *Arkansas Gazette,* and Hugh Sidey, who then wrote for *Life* magazine, Agnew got serious . . . and made my year. He told the Texans:

> But for pure unbridled invective, you will have to look far to beat that of the excitable columnist, television commentator and former Ambassador to Finland, Carl T. Rowan. Mr. Rowan might once have used diplomatic language, but he long ago lost the art and his rhetoric is anything but cool.
>
> In one recent column about me, he employed these phrases:
> ". . . rose above his own laziness and ineptitude"
> ". . . a dumb joke — a sort of aberration of history"
> ". . . he has come to personify all the class conflict, the racial hostility, the cultural generational gaps that have transformed this society into a tinderbox"
> ". . . calculated maliciousness"
> ". . . prefers to pander to the prejudices of the most ignorant and selfish elements in society"

Yes, I wrote all that, and I thought it a commentary on Agnew's intelligence (he boasted that he had an IQ of 135 and was five points short of being a genius) that he would stand before an audience and *rebroadcast* my indictments of him. Marshall asked me sarcastically, "This dude is the former governor of my home state?"

It turned out that my criticisms were trifling compared with what was in Agnew's future. The cliché that "it takes a thief to catch a thief" was proven a truism when Nixon and some of his cronies maneuvered to expose Agnew in their desire to ensure that no matter what happened to Nixon, Agnew would never become president.

Marshall said he had "rarely enjoyed another man's discomfort" the way he did watching Agnew squirm during the weeks when the U.S. attorney for Maryland, George Beall, and U.S. Attorney General Elliot L. Richardson were establishing the fact that this smarmy, hypocritically moralistic, minorities-bashing vice president was just a two-bit crook. On October 11, 1973, many Americans read with pleasure the *Washington Post* headline:

> VICE PRESIDENT AGNEW RESIGNS,
> FINED FOR INCOME TAX EVASION

On October 10, Agnew had stood in the courtroom of Federal District Judge Walter E. Hoffman and pleaded nolo contendere to a single charge of income tax evasion. Judge Hoffman said the "no contest" plea was "the full equivalent of a plea of guilty."

More important and shocking was a forty-page "exposition of evidence" that Beall and Richardson had submitted to the court showing that for at least ten years Agnew had sought and accepted at least $87,000 in bribes and extortion money paid by engineers eager to do business with the state of Maryland.

President Nixon was sinking fast in the dirty waters of Watergate. Richardson felt a critical need to get Agnew out of a position where he might ascend to the presidency. So to get him to resign, a plea bargain deal was cut under which the government agreed not to prosecute Agnew on myriad corruption charges, and Richardson urged Judge Hoffman not to send Agnew to jail. Hoffman said in open court that he generally imposed some time in prison on any lawyer found guilty of evading federal income taxes, but in this case would yield to the argument of the attorney general. For a decade of crookedness and corruption, Agnew got off with resignation, a $10,000 fine, and three years of unsupervised probation. In May 1974, Agnew was also disbarred — prohibited from practicing law — by the Maryland Court of Appeals, which said:

"It is difficult to feel compassion for an attorney who is so morally obtuse that he consciously cheats for his pecuniary gain that government he has sworn to serve, completely disregards the words of the oath he uttered when first admitted to the bar, and absolutely fails to perceive his professional duty to act honestly in all matters."

Agnew departed in shame, but he left a legacy of dog-eat-dog meanness regarding affirmative action, shameless appeals to bigotry in political contests, and the cynical exploitation of fear and hatred that undermined Marshall's triumphs and left America with a political system beclouded by the darker side of man's nature.

"Every time I hear the name Spiro Agnew, which is rare now, I lift a glass of anything and say good riddance," Marshall said to me.

Agnew was no wild man, no crazy "second banana." He was Richard Nixon's alter ego, the guy who said the nasty things and did the dirty work when Nixon found it expedient to be "statesmanlike." It was Nixon who put together the most devious, dirty, dishonest presidential ticket in America's history. Nixon was the most ruthless dream breaker.

I had suspected this before August 5, 1968, when I sat with basketball legend Wilt Chamberlain on the bow of a posh yacht that was plowing the blue waters off Miami Beach, where the GOP national convention was being held. Salty mist sprayed our faces, but I didn't mind because I was fascinated with this tall, powerful superstar who was talking intensely and endlessly about why he had entered Republican politics — in support of Nixon.

"It's just common sense," Wilt said, "that the black American must stay in a position to talk to and influence any man who has a chance to become the next president of the United States.

"I can influence Nixon," Chamberlain said, adding that when he telephoned Nixon's office and said, "I want to talk to Dick," all the people around Nixon knew that they had better put Wilt Chamberlain through.

With some trepidation, I said to this giant of a man, "Are you sure you aren't being conned by 'Tricky Dick'? What makes you think this Nixon is not the same one who thumbed his nose at Negroes in 1960?"

"What about 1960?" Chamberlain asked.

The seas were getting a bit heavier, causing the yacht to lurch. But I concentrated on what I remembered about an election in which Nixon had made almost no serious effort to win Negro votes. I told Chamberlain that Negroes in Chicago had voted 20 to 1 for John F. Kennedy, wiping out the lead Nixon had built up in the rest of Illinois. I said that in Missouri Nixon built up a 91,000-vote margin in 114 counties, but lost it when Negroes in St. Louis gave Kennedy a 100,000-vote margin.

"Nixon lost the presidency in 1960," I said, "because neither he nor the Republican party gave a damn about winning black votes."

"He learned his lesson," Wilt said. "He now knows that he has to have black votes."

"You really believe that Wilt? Out of thirteen hundred thirty-three fucking delegates here, only twenty-six are black Americans. I have here in my pocket Ray Bliss's [the GOP national chairman] assertion that the Republican party had found disaster in courting Negroes." I handed Chamberlain the Bliss figures showing a terrible erosion of black support for Republicans:

Chicago: Eisenhower got 33.4 percent of the black vote, Nixon got 19.2 percent in 1960, and Goldwater got 3.6 percent in 1964.

New York: Ike, 35.1 percent; Nixon 26.8; Goldwater 8.2.

The pattern across the nation had been about the same, so Bliss was making a case for the GOP to "write off" the black vote.

"I know Nixon a helluva lot better than this joker, Bliss, does," Chamberlain said. We agreed to let time tell the truth about the "new" Richard Nixon.

Nixon had previously paid lip service to the cause of racial justice. But despite the assurances that Chamberlain offered me, the Nixon-Agnew campaign consisted mostly of attacks on welfare recipients and on crime in the streets. White Americans believed the insinuations that welfare cheats were robbing them. They cheered when Nixon promised to "take crime out of the streets," never imagining that he would give crime a safe harbor in and around the White House Oval Office.

Nixon won the presidency with 43.4 percent of the votes, as against 42.7 percent for Humphrey and 13.5 percent for George Wallace. I should have understood in November 1968, but did not, that I had witnessed a sea change in American attitudes toward personal liberties, the right to dissent, racial justice, and more — on all the issues on which Thurgood Marshall and the NAACP, Martin Luther King, and others had fought so bravely. How could I have missed the far-reaching implications of the fact that an arrogant avowed racist, Wallace, could poll 487,270 votes in California, 390,958 in Illinois, 331,968 in Michigan, 358,864 in New York, 387,582 in Pennsylvania? Well, I missed it, and it would be a year or two before I understood fully the magnitude of the "white backlash" that Nixon and Agnew had exploited so shrewdly.

Marshall and others on the Court knew in 1973 that power-hungry Nixon didn't care about what the Congress said, what the Supreme Court ruled, or anything else. He thought his views ought to be the law, and he marked anyone who disagreed with him as his enemy.

Nixon had so effectively empowered the white backlash that most white Americans were not going to give a damn about his social policies. There was hope, however, in the fact that the American people had begun to understand that Nixon's abuse of IRS powers, illegal use of the FBI, illegal involvement of the CIA in domestic affairs, including politics, constituted a grave threat to them and to constitutional rule.

They became uneasy at whispers about this incredibly insecure, emotional president who, under the unbalancing effects of a few martinis, would scream that opponents of the Vietnam War were all foes of America. Nixon figured that students and others could not be protesting the war out of their devout sense of patriotism; in his mind they had to be in the pay of the Kremlin, Arab terrorists, Chinese communists, or some group hostile toward the United States. That is why he set up the "Huston Plan," named after one of his White House aides, Tom Charles Huston, who joined Nixon in believing that America was bursting at the seams with foreign agents, and that the FBI, the CIA, and other police-intelligence agencies were not doing enough about it.

The Huston Plan, which was issued secretly to all U.S. intelligence agencies, under Huston's name but invoking the authority of President Nixon, gave the National Security Agency, the supersecret cryptographic, code-cracking organization, authority to intercept and read all overseas calls and correspondences of any American citizen. The FBI and CIA, and apparently local police or anyone allied with them, were given the power and right to enter or burglarize any American's home. Law enforcement officials were authorized to open and read any citizen's personal mail.

Here was a superpolice, superspy arrangement, with Tom Charles Huston the master, that virtually nullified the Bill of Rights and much of the rest of the Constitution.

Ironically, of all the intelligence honchos Huston had called together, only FBI director J. Edgar Hoover saw the plan as a territorial threat to him and as a potentially embarrassing scheme to effectively suspend the U.S. Constitution.

"I found a way to answer Agnew, and more importantly, Nixon," Marshall said. "I fought to get the Court not to be intimidated by them, and when the others [on the Court] didn't side with me, I wrote some really angry dissents."

Nixon's outbursts gave Marshall a backdoor way to reply to the president's assaults on almost everything Marshall had worked for, and stood for.

During the 1968 presidential campaign, Nixon ran as much against the Supreme Court as he did against Humphrey, because he knew that "the Warren Court" was anathema in Dixie. When Nixon adopted the "southern strategy" at the Miami Republican convention, he set up a watershed change in American presidential politics. Some of us knew that he had delivered up Agnew to the South; few knew that he had pledged to give "the South" a seat on the Supreme Court. And almost no one believed that Nixon would carry his southern strategy to a point where he would convince Americans to turn their backs on much that had been accomplished by Marshall and the NAACP.

But Chief Justice Warren knew what was going on. He knew because of the former vice president's personal hatred of him that Nixon could attack the Supreme Court with gusto. Nixon realized that in the minds of millions of Americans, Warren exemplified integrity and guts but considered Nixon to be devoid of principle and character. Warren knew better than most of us reporters the ways in which Nixon had shifted his public utterances in order to con the voters. In the mid- and late 1950s, when Nixon still had some hope of winning over millions of black voters, he posed as a great advocate of civil rights. On October 19, 1956, he spoke of the Supreme Court decision in *Brown v. Board of Education:* "[This] is but one step in a continuing process of giving substance and vitality to our democracy. . . . America cannot afford the moral, the economic and the international cost of prejudice and discrimination . . . the American Revolution will not be complete until the ideals of independence, equality and freedom . . . are a reality not only for Americans but for peoples throughout the world. . . . Most of us here will live to see the day when American boys and girls shall sit, side by side, at any school — public or private — with no regard paid to the color of their skin. Segregation, discrimination and prejudice have no place in America."

On April 18, 1959, as he got closer to a presidential campaign, Nixon the statesman became all the more eloquent about the effects of bigotry in America: "The people (of Asia, Africa and the Near East) are different in many ways. . . . But they are alike in one way — they are not white. And, having traveled abroad and having spoken to these people in terms of the traditional beliefs of the United States of equality of opportunity . . . dignity of a man . . . it is most difficult for a representative of this country to talk one way abroad, and then to explain our practices at home."

In early 1960, Nixon was a rousing advocate of voting rights for all Americans. He said: "Whatever we may think of the question of civil rights, I think the great majority of Americans will agree that there is no moral justification for denying any American the right to vote."

But Nixon apparently was terribly disillusioned by the vote of blacks in the 1960 presidential campaign, which he lost to John F. Kennedy. That was clearly when he decided that it was folly for the Republican party to believe that it could effectively woo black voters. He determined that the future of the Republican party rested on wresting away from the Democrats the white ethnics and blue-collar workers, and especially the white males of the South, who had for so long been so loyal to the Democratic party.

Nixon was smart enough in 1964 to let Barry Goldwater take the fall for the GOP, but he was mapping his strategy for a run at the presidency in 1968. Earl Warren and others watched his public statements, his attacks on Supreme Court decisions, and knew that Nixon would do anything to defeat the Democrats. On August 15, 1966, in an interview with *U.S. News and World Report,* Nixon was obliquely, shrewdly critical of the first great piece of civil rights legislation of the Johnson years — the 1964 Civil Rights Act. He said:

> Not all the police in the nation could enforce the public-accom-modations section of the 1964 Civil Rights Act if there were not a commitment on the part of the people to accept it as law. If Ne-groes must repeatedly haul restaurateurs into court before they can be served a meal, then the guarantee of equal accommodations is illusory. [Senate candidate George Bush also opposed this civil rights law.]

Nixon began to reveal his strategy of wooing the white South. America and the South began to see the new dimensions of it when Nixon unleashed Agnew for speeches all over the South in which the vice president said unashamedly that his party was the party of the segregationists. On the eve of the 1968 elections, Nixon went all-out in assailing "the role some of the decisions of the High Court have played in weakening the peace forces in our society in recent years." He lashed out against the justices as "activist" social engineers who had usurped the authority of the Congress and imposed their social views on the nation.

"I believe in a strict interpretation of the Supreme Court's functions," Nixon shouted.

He focused on two controversial cases, *Escobedo v. Illinois* in 1964, and *Miranda v. Arizona* in 1966, as examples of High Court decisions "seriously hamstringing the peace forces in our society and strengthening the criminal forces." The Court had said in *Escobedo* and *Miranda* that before interrogating suspects, the police had to advise them that any statement they made could be used against them, that they had a right to remain silent, and that they had a right to counsel.

Voting for those protections of the accused in 1964 were Warren, Black, Douglas, Brennan, and Arthur Goldberg; dissenting were White, Stewart, Harlan, and Clark. In 1966, in *Miranda,* the lineup was the same, except that Abe Fortas had replaced Goldberg and voted with Warren and the "activist" majority. These two controversial cases galled Nixon mightily, because to him they symbolized "the Warren Court." Nixon was an instigator of the campaign to impeach Justice Douglas, and he smiled upon those commissioning highway billboards that said IMPEACH EARL WARREN.

By early 1969, Nixon's man on the Court, Warren Burger, was trying to appease his Republican benefactor, Nixon. He said:

"The seeming anxiety of judges to protect every accused person from every consequence of his voluntary utterances is giving rise to myriad rules, sub-rules, variations and exceptions which even the most alert and sophisticated lawyers and judges are taxed to follow. Each time judges add nuances to these 'rules' we make it less likely that any police officer will be able to follow the guidelines we lay down. We are approaching the predicament of the centipede on the flypaper — each time one leg is placed to give support for relief of a leg already 'stuck,' another becomes captive and soon all are securely immobilized. We are well on our way to forbidding *any* utterance of an accused to be used against him unless it is made in open court. Guilt or innocence becomes irrelevant in the criminal trial as we flounder in a morass of artifical rules poorly conceived and often impossible of application."

With strident attacks on the Supreme Court as his centerpiece, Nixon sold American voters a "law 'n' order" bill of goods that would prove salable for at least two decades. He also became relentless in his efforts to exploit white fears of the civil rights revolution led by Marshall and others. In 1966 Nixon said:

"Across this nation today civil disobedience and racial disorders are building up a wall of hate between the races, which, while less visible, is no less real than the wall that divides freedom and slavery in the city of Berlin. . . . The recent riots in Chicago, Cleveland, New York and Omaha have produced in the public dialogue too much heat and very little light. The extremists have held the floor for too long. One extreme sees a simple remedy for rioting in a ruthless application of the truncheon and an earlier call to the National Guard. The other extremists are more articulate, but their position is equally simplistic. To them, riots are to be excused upon the grounds that the participants have legitimate social grievances or seek justifiable social goals. I believe it would be a grave mistake to charge off the recent riots to unredressed Negro grievances alone. To do so is to ignore a prime reason and a major national problem: the deterioration of respect for the rule of law all across America."

"I resented that crap," Marshall told me. "Nixon surely knew that I, the NAACP, all the traditional civil rights groups and leaders, had stood up against rioting. I knew that he wasn't trying to promote peace in the streets; he was playing politics with a volatile situation."

In 1966, when he was solicitor general, at a lawyers conference at Howard University, Marshall assailed the spirit of violence of those crying "black power." He said he would "take Stokely Carmichael and the boys who threw rocks in one group, and the Ku Klux Klan in another group, put them on an island somewhere, and let them fight it out." He then told a black fraternity meeting in St. Louis that "the rock throwers and the Molotov cocktail throwers" were impeding black progress. "We are going to increase our lawful protest in order to counteract the unlawful protests that get in our way," he said.

Two years later, in New Orleans, he warned that "nothing will be settled with guns, firebombs, and rocks." He begged Negroes not to let cries of "black is beautiful" blind them to the truth that many skin colors are beautiful.

"I think we Negro Americans have just as many beautiful people in mind and body, as well as skin, as any other group," he said, "and we have just as many stinkers as any other group."

"Nixon didn't care about what any responsible Negro leaders were saying," Marshall told me. "He was simply willing to suspend the Bill of Rights, the Fourteenth Amendment, and more in the name of 'law and order.' I was praying that the Court would not become intimidated."

Marshall politicked assiduously inside the Court to get some help in responding to Nixon. He rejoiced in 1972 when four justices joined him in holding unconstitutional Georgia's death penalty statute. This decision, *Furman v. Georgia*, effectively wiped out all capital punishment statutes in all states — for a few years. In 1972 it was a bitter pill for Nixon to swallow.

This death penalty decision had come just a year after the Court, through Nixon's appointee, Chief Justice Warren Burger, had defied the rhetoric of Nixon and Agnew.

While Nixon was shouting publicly that the Supreme Court was giving unfair advantages to "criminals," Marshall was arguing inside the Court that when the government accused a citizen of a crime, it became an "adversarial proceeding," and that the Constitution required that the accused start out on a plane of equality with the government.

Marshall fought to get the Court to stand up for the right of a defendant to competent counsel in the case of *Tollett v. Henderson,* in which the lawyer for the accused, Henderson, entered a guilty plea without challenging the racial makeup of the grand jury. Henderson had been indicted in 1948 by a grand jury for the crime of first-degree murder. After a questionable guilty plea he was sentenced to ninety-nine years in prison. After twenty-five years, with the help of the NAACP Legal Defense Fund, including lawyers Jack Greenberg and James M. Nabrit III, Henderson contended that the police had coerced him into a confession, that he had been denied the effective assistance of counsel, and that he was deprived of his constitutional rights because Negroes had been excluded from the grand jury.

Marshall noted in his dissent that

> Henderson was indicted in March 1948 by a grand jury in Davidson County, Tennessee. Although Negroes constituted 25% of the population of the county in 1948, not a single Negro had served on the grand jury in the years before 1948. In addition, whenever the name of a Negro appeared on the lists from which members of the grand jury were chosen, the letters "c" or "col" were marked next to the name. In the words of the Court of Appeals, "officials were thus provided with a simple means of determining which citizens might be appropriately 'excused' from grand jury duty. It is apparent from the absence of any Negroes on the grand jury panels that the means were used and the impermissible end of exclusion accomplished.

The Sixth Circuit Court of Appeals decided that Henderson had been improperly convicted. But in April 1973, Justice Rehnquist wrote, with the concurrence of Burger, Stewart, White, Blackmun, and Powell, that there was insufficient reason to concede that Henderson had had incompetent counsel, relying in part on the statement by a judge on the Tennessee Court of Criminal Appeals that "no lawyer in this State would have ever thought of objecting to the fact that Negroes did not serve on the Grand Jury in Tennessee in 1948."

Justices Douglas and Brennan joined Marshall in arguing that Henderson had inadequate counsel — that "an attorney of minimal competence would have realized that, where no Negroes had been summoned for service over many years and where racial designations were used, the Tennessee Supreme Court would very probably have held the [grand jury] selection system unconstitutional."

But the Court majority, pressured by Nixon, was unbending, so Henderson had to endure his ninety-nine-year sentence.

Still, Marshall never stopped "answering" Nixon and Agnew on issues involving the Court's adherence to the Bill of Rights. Marshall was saying, "No matter what others on this Court may do in terms of bending to political winds or public passions, I shall not be moved."

There arose in 1972, at the height of Nixon's diatribes against the Court, the fascinating case of *United States v. Mara*, in which Richard J. Mara, an Illinois suspect in the thefts of interstate shipments, was forced to give voice and handwriting exemplars. Mara objected, saying that the prosecution wanted to use his handwriting and voice exemplars as testimonial evidence with which to convict him, and that this was an illegal search and seizure that violated his Fourth Amendment rights. The issue also was whether the Fifth Amendment forbade only the prosecution's compulsion of "communications" and "testimony," or whether it also protected a criminal suspect from providing "real or physical evidence."

The Supreme Court had, in 1967, in *United States v. Wade* and *Gilbert v. California*, agreed that there were limitations to the Fifth Amendment privilege. "That limitation," argued Marshall, "is at odds with what I have always understood to be the function of the privilege. I would, of course, include testimonial evidence within the privilege, but I have grave difficulty drawing a line there. For I cannot accept the notion that the Government can compel a man to cooperate affirmatively in securing incriminating evidence when that evidence could not be obtained without the cooperation of the suspect. . . .

"The Fifth Amendment provides that 'no person . . . shall be

compelled in any criminal case to be a witness against himself. . . .'
Nowhere is the privilege explicitly restricted to testimonial evidence.
To read such a limitation into the privilege through its reference to
'witness' is just the sort of crabbed construction of the provision that
this Court has long eschewed."

Marshall quoted Chief Justice Warren and Justices Douglas and
Fortas as saying in *Wade* in 1967: "Our history and tradition teach
and command that an accused may stand mute. The privilege means
just that; not less than that."

But "taking the Fifth" had been made a traitorous phrase during
the era of McCarthyism, and Nixon and Agnew had worked to see
that "hiding" behind the Fifth Amendment remained an odious
proposition. So Marshall lost that argument badly. He was not surprised.

"It's hard to beat the gatekeeper," he said by way of admitting
that he had known since Nixon won the presidency that there could
be no greater dream breaker than the man who occupied the Oval
Office, if he passionately sought that goal. Marshall recalled the en-
thusiasm that Nixon had brought to dream breaking.

After Nixon won the presidency in 1968, he watched the Democratic party agonize over the issues of race and gender and finally
resort to "quotas" for members of its deliberative committees and
for delegates to the 1972 convention. Nixon, Agnew, and their political advisers knew that "quotas" was a dirty word in America, and
that most Americans would not distinguish between the old "quotas"
that excluded Jews, blacks, women, and others from the educational,
legal, and other power centers of the land and the new "quotas" that
were designed to bring "outsiders" into the circle of political decision
making.

In exploiting the issue of quotas and racism, Nixon and his
friends were doing extremely well. But they got some unexpected
help from the Supreme Court. The high tribunal had laid down the
law to the lower courts that "all deliberate speed" meant "right now,"
"immediately." U.S. District Judge James B. McMillan in *Swann v.
Mecklenburg* took the Court at its word and ordered that the public
schools of Charlotte, North Carolina, and surrounding Mecklenburg
County had to desegregate totally. He set a quota of 71 percent white
and 29 percent black for each school, this to square with the racial
breakdown of the population in Mecklenburg County. This meant
that attendance zones had to be changed, with many children, black
and white, no longer permitted to attend their neighborhood
schools, and with thirteen thousand children to be bused every day
to meet the decree of Judge McMillan.

Here was an instance of one of the first great public relations mistakes of the NAACP Legal Defense Fund, which of course was no longer headed by Marshall, who by then had been on the Supreme Court for almost three years.

The 1954 *Brown* decision had said that state-imposed *segregation* was unconstitutional, and while it dealt heavily with the sociological effects of racial separation, it did not say that *integration* of all schools had to be achieved even if the racial patterns were not imposed by any arm of government. The Supreme Court decision was a clear blow against the George Wallaces and Orval Faubuses, but there was nothing in it to say that a local federal judge had to remedy the effects of white flight to the suburbs, or of whites sending their children to private schools. The *Brown* decisions of 1954 and 1955 did not say that the federal courts had to issue orders that school officials "reach out and grab" some white kid and use him or her to establish "racial balance," whether at a 71 to 29 percentage or at some other ratio. Here was a case that pitted the federal government against the NAACP in an unprecedented way. School busing was a time-honored part of the American reach for better education. Some eighteen million kids, most of them white, were being bused out of the small towns of America to new schools, the emporia of education that had replaced the little red schoolhouse, in order to supply those youngsters with the best in facilities and teachers. A bus ride had become the passport to meaningful learning of physics, English, math, for all these youngsters, including those in Charlotte, one-third of whom went to school by bus.

But it was the concept of busing to achieve some mathematical formula of "racial balance" that aroused so much of white America. Nixon shrewdly put the word "forced" in front of "busing" and made "forced busing" an American abomination. Nixon sent his solicitor general, Erwin Griswold, one of the most decent men in America, and a stalwart supporter of civil rights and racial justice, to argue before the Supreme Court that in remedying previous discrimination there should be no "quotas," no abandonment of the principle of "neighborhood schools," and only the minimal use of busing to achieve desegregation.

The NAACP Legal Defense Fund sent James Nabrit to the October 12 and 13 oral arguments to take an opposite stand. Nabrit tried to convince the Court that it was feasible, legal, reasonable, to bus thousands of students to distant schools in order to achieve desegregation. He supported the order by Judge McMillan with no reservations.

This drove Chief Justice Burger into agony. He felt it necessary to say angrily to his colleagues that he was not a "toady" of the White House. Burger knew the Nixon stand on busing, but more importantly had come to his own honest conclusion that McMillan's order had gone beyond anything the Supreme Court had ever said.

I asked Marshall about reports that a literal war had erupted in the conference room over the Charlotte dilemma.

"I've told you a thousand times that I ain't gonna talk about conference room deliberations," he said with extra surliness. "Just ain't gonna talk."

I learned enough from other sources to determine that Marshall, Brennan, and others had convinced Burger that *Swann* was as important as the *Brown* decisions in giving the nation's school officials a sense of direction. So, on April 20, 1971, Burger issued a unanimous decision in words almost as incredible as those of Earl Warren in 1954:

> Absent a constitutional violation there would be no basis for judicially ordering assignment of students on a racial basis [Burger wrote]. All things being equal, with no history of discrimination, it might well be desirable to assign pupils to schools nearest their homes. But all things are not equal in a system that has been deliberately constructed and maintained to enforce racial segregation. The remedy for such segregation may be administratively awkward, inconvenient, and even bizarre in some situations and may impose burdens on some; but all awkwardness and inconvenience cannot be avoided.

Here Burger and the brethren spoke a truth that Nixon would seize upon to change the political face of America.

Swann said, in layman's language, that where a long history of state-imposed school discrimination existed, the remedies could include inconvenient, unpopular, costly, and even "bizarre" steps for such time as it took to remedy the old injustices.

The Court outlined the following techniques, in addition to transportation, which were permissible and appropriate:

"A frank — and sometimes drastic — gerrymandering of school districts and attendance zones," resulting in zones "neither compact nor contiguous; indeed they may be on opposite ends of the city."

" 'Pairing,' 'clustering,' or 'grouping' of schools with attendance assignments made deliberately to accomplish the transfer of Negro students out of formerly segregated Negro schools and transfer of white students to formerly all-Negro schools."

The Court found that the use of a mathematical ratio of white to black students in the schools was "no more than a starting point in the process of shaping a remedy, rather than an inflexible requirement." The Court continued: "Awareness of the racial composition of the whole school system is likely to be a useful starting point in shaping a remedy to correct past constitutional violations." If the ratio has been read as requiring "any particular degree of racial balance or mixing," the Court said, "that approach would be disapproved and we would be obliged to reverse."

Nixon had weighed in personally on the issue of busing and school desegregation in a public statement on March 24, 1970. He said that in a free and open society, "it is natural and right that we have Italian or Irish or Negro or Norwegian neighborhoods." Yet, he said, Americans should make their schools "places of equal educational opportunity." Then he sneaked in the dagger: "I am opposed to busing for the purpose of achieving racial balance."

Marshall could not block the efforts of Nixon to reverse his victories in the field of civil rights. Marshall detested Nixon, but he saw that even a Supreme Court justice with a lifetime appointment was no match for a hostile president and his bully pulpit. Especially when justices traditionally took the position that custom decreed they must always avoid all pulpits.

But Marshall still had a few salvos to fire. Rioting over school integration in the Detroit suburb of Pontiac, Michigan, and other eruptions of resistance and violence, produced a federal court challenge that involved the manipulation of school attendance zones, inner city–suburban demarcations, "white flight," residential segregation, and many other factors of racial isolation and polarization that had become commonplace in metropolitan America.

Detroit was — and is — one of the most residentially segregated cities in America. That was enough to produce great imbalances in the populations of the public schools. But the federal district court judge found, in *Milliken v. Bradley,* that the Detroit school board had deliberately drawn "attendance zones" in a way that produced more segregation. Special rules were drawn up to allow white children in areas of "racial transition" to be transported to school zones where few blacks lived. Black children in overcrowded schools were transported past white schools with vacancies to distant schools that were predominantly black.

The district and appeals courts in the area ruled that under Michigan law every school district was an agency of the state government, and that when the Detroit school board practiced racial discrimination, it was state discrimination that was forbidden by the Fourteenth

Amendment. The district and appeals courts further declared that a Detroit-only decree would not produce the desegregation that *Brown I* and *Brown II* supposedly had commanded. These courts called for busing and other programs that would mix the children of the city of Detroit with those in the adjacent suburbs.

Marshall knew that the Detroit cross-boundaries proposal would be viewed by some Americans — especially Nixon — as revolutionary.

"Here was a chance to short-circuit Nixon's transparent attacks on school desegregation," he said, "so I made a commitment to try to get the Court to help me defeat him."

In the hallowed conference room, Marshall used intellect, resorts to Court precedents, the guile of telling stories that were supposed to make his colleagues feel guilty, but there was little inclination on the part of his brethren to decree that the suburbs were not a "hiding place" for those engaged in white flight.

Remarkably, Marshall was persuasive enough to get Justices Douglas, Brennan, and White to join him in dissent in a 5 to 4 loss. The majority had swallowed whole the arguments of Solicitor General Robert Bork, who argued for the government against any interdistrict remedy for school segregation in Detroit.

The Court held in *Milliken* in 1974:

A federal court may not impose a multidistrict, areawide remedy for single-district *de jure* school segregation violations where there is no finding that the other included school districts have failed to operate unitary school systems or have committed acts that effected segregation within the other districts, there is no claim or finding that the school boundary lines were established with the purpose of fostering racial segregation, and there is no meaningful opportunity for the included neighboring school districts to present evidence or be heard on the propriety of a multidistrict remedy or on the question of constitutional violations by those districts.

. . . School district lines may not be casually ignored or treated as a mere administrative convenience; substantial local control of public education in this country is a deeply rooted tradition.

Before the boundaries of separate and autonomous school districts may be set aside by consolidating the separate units for remedial purposes or by imposing a cross-district remedy, it must be first shown that there has been a constitutional violation within one district that produces a significant segregative effect in another district; i.e., specifically, it must be shown that racially discriminatory acts of the state or local school districts, or of a single school district have been a substantial cause of interdistrict segregation.

We conclude that the relief ordered by the District Court and affirmed by the Court of Appeals was based upon an erroneous standard and was unsupported by record evidence that acts of the outlying districts effected the discrimination found to exist in the schools of Detroit. Accordingly, the judgment of the Court of Appeals is reversed and the case is remanded for further proceedings consistent with this opinion leading to prompt formulation of a decree directed to eliminating the segregation found to exist in Detroit city schools, a remedy which has been delayed since 1970.

In a separate dissent, Justice Douglas said:

Today's decision means that there is no violation of the Equal Protection Clause though the schools are segregated by race and though the black schools are not only "separate" but "inferior."

So far as equal protection is concerned we are now in a dramatic retreat from the 7-to-1 decision in 1896 that blacks could be segregated in public facilities, provided they received equal treatment.

Justice White dissented, saying:

Given the State's control over the educational system in Michigan, the fact that the black schools are in one district and the white schools are in another is not controlling — either constitutionally or equitably.

. . . The Court fashions out of whole cloth an arbitrary rule that remedies for constitutional violations occurring in a single Michigan school district must stop at the school district line.

I am surprised that the Court, sitting at this distance from the State of Michigan, claims better insight than the Court of Appeals and the District Court as to whether an interdistrict remedy for equal protection violations practiced by the State of Michigan would involve undue difficulties for the State in the management of its public schools.

Here Marshall got a chance to answer Nixon without losing the "dignity" of his position as a justice. He lectured the nation, and especially Nixon:

Desegregation is not and was never expected to be an easy task. Racial attitudes ingrained in our Nation's childhood and adolescence are not quickly thrown aside in its middle years. But just as the inconvenience of some cannot be allowed to stand in the way of the rights of others, so public opposition, no matter how strident, cannot be permitted to divert this Court from the enforcement of the constitutional principles at issue. . . .

In the short run, it may seem to be the easier course to allow our great metropolitan areas to be divided up each into two cities — one white, the other black — but it is a course, I predict, our people will ultimately regret.

History would show that we were more a nation of men such as Nixon than of the laws and principles of justice that Marshall had articulated. So we got a generation of tragedy in Bensonhurst, Central Park, Los Angeles, and more places where "regret" is to come.

Still, on the issue of busing, Nixon achieved just what he had hoped to. He got Marshall's eternal nemesis, Strom Thurmond, to denounce the Supreme Court while stating that "the Nixon administration stood with the South in this case." He provoked George Wallace to denounce the members of the Burger Court as "a bunch of limousine hypocrites."

But Nixon was doing more than arousing criticism of the Court. In keeping with his promise at the Miami convention, he was trying to pack it, beginning with the appointment of a Southerner. First he nominated a conservative South Carolinian, Clement F. Haynsworth, Jr., the chief judge of the Fourth Circuit Court of Appeals, to fill the seat vacated by Abe Fortas, who had to step down in a scandal that Nixon had worked hard to intensify. But Haynsworth was viewed as anti-labor and anti–civil rights and ran into stiff opposition. His critics discovered that Haynsworth had been indirectly involved in a company in which he held stock. It seemed to many a trifling incident but it was enough to give cover to senators who wanted any excuse to vote against a Nixon nominee. Haynsworth's nomination was rejected 55 to 45. Still trying to keep his promise to the Southerners, Nixon turned to Floridian G. Harrold Carswell, a member of the Fifth Circuit Court of Appeals. It did not take long for opponents to dredge up a 1948 speech in which Carswell said that "segregation of the races is proper and the only practical and correct way of life in our state. I have always so believed and I shall always so act."

This was enough to turn many senators against Carswell. But Carswell's fate was surely doomed when the dean of the Yale Law School testified that the Floridian "presents the most slender credentials of any man put forward [for the Supreme Court] in this century." That brought forth from Senator Roman Hruska, the right-wing Nebraska Republican, a historic assertion that "there are a lot of mediocre judges and people and lawyers, and they are entitled to a little representation, aren't they?"

Carswell was rejected, 51 to 45, provoking Nixon to great anger. But Nixon thought he had the last laugh when he nominated and got confirmed Harry Blackmun of Minnesota, who would vote so often as a clone of Chief Justice Burger that for years the two men were called "the Minnesota Twins." Later, Blackmun jumped the traces and cast a lot of votes that did not please Nixon — or Burger.

The bottom line, however, was that Nixon was ultimately successful in discrediting the Supreme Court — and Marshall's crusade to preserve a reverence for the Bill of Rights — in the eyes of millions of Americans. Nixon set in train a process in which he, Reagan, and Bush turned the Court into a fiefdom of right-wing ideologues.

CHAPTER TWENTY-ONE

MARSHALL WITH AND WITHOUT LAW CLERKS

GIVEN MARSHALL'S BRILLIANT RECORD as the lawyer for the NAACP and the Legal Defense and Educational Fund, it is not unreasonable to assume that history will regard him primarily as "Mr. Civil Rights." He will, as he should, be seen as the most dogged and sacrificing of all the battlers for black freedom. That does not mean that historians ought to gloss over his tenure on the Second Circuit Court of Appeals, where he dealt with issues involving the technical aspects of economic law that are contested in New York and New England, perhaps the most litigious area of the worst "I'll sue you" society on earth. As solicitor general, this imposing black man was awesome when he donned his striped pants and swallowtailed coat and displayed his forensic skills. Some conservatives have tried to characterize Marshall's years on the Supreme Court as a period when some mediocre black token became "the spook who sat by the door." I have written in an earlier chapter of Marshall's powerful role in his first years on the Court — about how this persimmon-hued Marylander was a relentless advocate of constitutional protections for all the people. I think I have not said enough about his early years on the Court, when he made powerful and irreverent statements that never got the publicity accorded to his words regarding *Roe* and abortion, but were nevertheless new declarations of freedom.

There was the 1971 California case in which a young man had been convicted of disturbing the peace and of "offensive conduct" because he was seen in a courthouse corridor wearing a jacket emblazoned with the words "Fuck the Draft." During the oral argument, Marshall asked the prosecutor whether, in that same community, an individual walking the street saying "fuck" might be arrested.

"Yes," said the lawyer.

A scowling Marshall asked, "Are the jails big enough?"

More than any justice on the Court during his tenure, with the possible exception of Brennan, Marshall fought to expand the concept of the right to privacy and freedom of expression. He rejected the argument that watching obscene materials in the privacy of one's home might lead to criminal conduct. Brennan had evaded the issue in an earlier case, by saying that the sociological claims need not be dealt with because obscenity was not protected speech. But Marshall met the issue head-on in writing, in *Stanley v. Georgia:* "Given the present state of knowledge, the State may no more prohibit mere possession of obscene matter on the ground that it may lead to antisocial conduct than it may prohibit chemistry books on the ground that they may lead to the manufacture of homemade spirits."

Marshall recalled for me with pride his assertion that "whatever may be the justifications for other statutes regulating obscenity, we do not think they reach into the privacy of one's own home."

Perhaps Nixon's lawyers still thought, in 1974, that they didn't have to worry about Marshall if no racial issue was involved. They learned better when they went before the Supreme Court to claim that this embattled president, now facing impeachment, had a constitutional right to absolute executive privilege regarding his taped conversations. Marshall threw out the hypothetical question of whether a taped conversation by a president was to be privileged if it showed the president offering to appoint someone to a judgeship in exchange for money.

Nixon's lawyer said that there already was a constitutional remedy: impeach such a president.

Gruffly, Marshall interrupted him, asking: "How are you going to impeach him if you don't know about it? If you know the president is doing something wrong, you can impeach him. If you can't listen to the tapes and hear that he's doing something wrong, you can't impeach him. You lose me someplace [in your argument]."

The Supreme Court, with even Burger going along, decided that Nixon did *not* have absolute executive privilege, an unfettered right to keep his Watergate tapes secret. That doomed Nixon as the nation's leader.

The journalistic and legal professions have long raised questions about how much of Marshall they were seeing and hearing, and how much reflected the bright law clerks that he hired. Some simply doubted any black man could be so smart. No testimonial by one, or all, of Marshall's clerks would induce these doubters to believe that the phraseology, some esoteric references to previous Court decisions, might not be those of a clerk. But clearly the moral content, the bottom-line decision, was always that of Marshall.

The rumors and doubts about justices and their clerks were not directed at Marshall exclusively.

It has always been commonplace for clerks to write briefs after consultation with their justice. It was taken as common knowledge that Chief Justice Warren did not write his own opinions — that his law clerks did. It was also accepted as true that the second Justice Harlan, although nearly blind, squinched inches above a yellow pad as he scribbled his own opinions in an almost illegible hand. Clerks whispered that Burger wielded the pencil, or sometimes delegated brief writing to his clerks, but that on the crucial issues Burger's briefs were dictated by Nixon's White House legal advisers. Which I don't believe.

As the gossip went, Marshall could not possibly have written his briefs, because he didn't put in enough working hours. In their book, *The Brethren*, Bob Woodward and Scott Armstrong told an anecdote about how Stewart would come into the Court around 10:00 A.M. and put in a couple of hours, and as he headed home he would meet Marshall coming to work. The implication was that Marshall was very lazy, given to watching soap operas or snoozing unless some civil rights issue came up that got his adrenaline going. Those who had known Marshall during his days as chief counsel for the NAACP's Legal Defense Fund could not imagine the word "laziness" ever being used about a man who had devoted such incredible energy to the pursuit of legal action in almost every state in an effort to secure the rights of black people.

A couple of Marshall's former clerks scoffed at the printed rumors that the justice was lazy and let his clerks do the thinking and the writing. The clerks said they knew that, while they might *write* an opinion or a dissent, the views expressed had better be those of Marshall. I was told that in one very controversial case, a clerk walked into the chambers and said, "Judge, you *have* to come down on this side of this case."

"Say what?" screeched Marshall. "Step closer so I can be sure you're hearing me. I don't *have* to do a damned thing except stay black and die!"

Clerks who knew that Marshall was in total control laughed some, and cursed a lot, over what they regarded as ignorant, mischievous, malicious, and even racist reports that "The Judge" was addicted to "General Hospital," manipulated by clerks, or in some way less than a real jurist.

How many briefs did Justice Marshall write himself? We shall never know. But what we can do is engage in what I find to be a really thrilling exercise of looking at Justice Marshall *with* law clerks, and Justice Marshall *without* law clerks, something that I can do because, while the record is clear on what he said about the great issues of our time in his majority opinions, his concurrences, his dissents, I have also been fortunate enough to interview and talk informally with Marshall for dozens of hours and have his straight-from-the-heart, sometimes from-the-hip, opinions on those same important issues that have absorbed the Court in this century.

So let us take a look at Marshall talking officially, and Marshall just talking.

AFFIRMATIVE ACTION

Marshall took his seat on the Court at a time when the medical and law schools, universities at large, great corporations, were as a matter of conscience opening long-closed doors to blacks and other minorities and to the women of America. He soon saw the mood of the white majority change as America went through a serious recession during the tragic last months of Nixon's presidency and throughout the lackluster tenure of Gerald Ford in the presidency. Marshall saw a dog-eat-dog atmosphere permeate white America, provoking people to claim that some black or Hispanic or some woman had gotten a place in a class, a job, a promotion that should have gone to a white Protestant male or to a Jew.

Soon this issue was before the Supreme Court in the case of *Regents of the University of California v. Bakke.* The background of the case was clear. The University of California Medical School at Davis set up a two-tier admission system under which one hundred students would be admitted. For eighty-four of those slots whites, minorities, and all other applicants would compete on an equal basis. But the institution at Davis reserved sixteen spots only for minority students. Allen Bakke, a white man, filed suit after he was rejected for admission to the medical school in 1973 and 1974, even though his test scores were higher than those of some minority students who had been admitted. Bakke claimed that the affirmative action system

at Davis violated the equal protection clause of the Constitution and
Title VI of the Civil Rights Act of 1964. The California Supreme
Court said Bakke was right. In 1978, the U.S. Supreme Court split
all over the lot, with a basic decision that the University of California
Medical School at Davis was practicing preferential racial quotas,
which did indeed violate the Civil Rights Act of 1964. Justice Lewis
Powell spoke for the Court in saying that the clear quota of sixteen
seats for minorities at Davis was forbidden, but did not say that the
Court was striking down all racial preferences. In his half concurrence, half dissent, Marshall said:

> I agree with the judgment of the Court only insofar as it permits
> a university to consider the race of an applicant in making admis-
> sions decisions. I do not agree that petitioner's admissions pro-
> gram violates the Constitution. For it must be remembered that,
> during most of the past 200 years, the Constitution as interpreted
> by this Court did not prohibit the most ingenious and pervasive
> forms of discrimination against the Negro. Now, when a State acts
> to remedy the effects of that legacy of discrimination, I cannot
> believe that this same Constitution stands as a barrier. . . .
>
> It is because of a legacy of unequal treatment that we now must
> permit the institutions of this society to give consideration to race
> in making decisions about who will hold the positions of influence,
> affluence, and prestige in America. For far too long, the doors to
> those positions have been shut to Negroes. If we are ever to be-
> come a fully integrated society, one in which the color of a person's
> skin will not determine the opportunities available to him or her,
> we must be willing to take steps to open those doors. I do not
> believe that anyone can truly look into America's past and still find
> that a remedy for the effects of that past is impermissible.

It was in this case, showing the divisions of the Court that would
soon divide the entire nation, with ugly repercussions, that Justice
Blackmun made the following classic statement:

> Despite its two-track aspect, the Davis program, for me, is within
> constitutional bounds, though perhaps barely so. . . .
>
> I suspect that it would be impossible to arrange an affirmative
> action program in a racially neutral way and have it be successful.
> To ask that this be so is to demand the impossible. *In order to get
> beyond racism, we must first take account of race.* [Emphasis added.]
> There is no other way. And in order to treat some persons equally,
> we must treat them differently.

THE DEATH PENALTY

Marshall had been very influential in getting the Supreme Court to rule, in *Furman v. Georgia,* that the death penalty was unconstitutional.

In *Furman* and for all of his years on the Court, Marshall opposed the idea of punishment for the sake of retribution. He said repeatedly that "the Eighth Amendment itself was adopted to prevent punishment from becoming synonymous with vengeance."

In a 5 to 4 vote, the Court ruled that, as applied to Georgia and Texas, and in nearly all other jurisdictions, the death penalty constituted cruel and unusual punishment because judges and juries were allowed to use "whim even unfettered" discretion as to whether to impose capital punishment. The Congress and some thirty-five states had revised their statutes, bringing them into conformity with the *Furman* decision, when the Supreme Court was faced with the 1976 case of *Gregg v. Georgia,* involving a man who had been convicted of murder and sentenced to death. Here again we got a widely divided Court, with Justice Stewart speaking for the Court:

"There is no question that death as a punishment is unique in its severity and irrevocability. When a defendant's life is at stake, the Court has been particularly sensitive to insure that every safeguard is observed. But we are concerned here only with the imposition of capital punishment for the crime of murder, and when a life has been taken deliberately by the offender, we cannot say that the punishment is invariably disproportionate to the crime. It is an extreme sanction, suitable to the most extreme of crimes.

". . . We hold that the death penalty is not a form of punishment that may never be imposed, regardless of the circumstances of the offense, regardless of the character of the offender, and regardless of the procedure followed in reaching the decision to impose it.

". . . We hold that the statutory system under which Gregg was sentenced to death does not violate the Constitution."

Marshall had grown up in a time when lynching was commonplace in America. He had great difficulty viewing a state execution in Georgia, Mississippi, or any of the places where racism was virulent, as little more than a lynching. This fact would surely color his attitude on capital punishment for the rest of his life. This was reflected in his dissent:

"In *Furman* I concluded that the death penalty is constitutionally invalid for two reasons. First, the death penalty is excessive. And second, the American people, fully informed as to the purposes of the death penalty and its liabilities, would in my view reject it as morally unacceptable."

FIRST AMENDMENT FREEDOMS

Marshall's dedication to the First Amendment, without which he felt the Constitution was no great document at all, showed up in a wide variety of his opinions. One of the first was the case of the *New York Times* against the United States government on the issue of prior restraint of the *Times* regarding the printing of the so-called Pentagon Papers. In this case the *New York Times* and the *Washington Post* had gotten their hands on a document called "History of U.S. Decision-Making on Vietnam Policy," quickly dubbed "Pentagon Papers." The newspapers proposed to publish these materials although they were classified. The government tried to enjoin the publication of the documents on the grounds of national security. There was some division in the lower courts, but the general thrust of the rulings was to say that there could be no prior restraint on the newspapers. The Supreme Court voted 6 to 3 against the Nixon administration, holding that the government had not provided enough evidence to make the Court walk away from its general rule that any prior restraint on publication bears a heavy presumption of unconstitutionality. Burger and Blackmun, who at the time were still called "the Minnesota Twins," and Justice Harlan, one of the most conservative members of the Court, went along with the government. In a separate concurrence, Marshall made some telling points about the effort of the executive branch to get the Court to do what Congress has refused to do.

"Either the Government has the power under statutory grant to use traditional criminal law to protect the country or, if there is no basis for arguing that Congress has made the activity a crime, it is plain that Congress has specifically refused to grant the authority the Government seeks from this Court. In either case this Court does not have authority to grant the requested relief. It is not for this Court to fling itself into every breach perceived by some Government official nor is it for this Court to take on itself the burden of enacting law, especially a law that Congress has refused to pass."

COERCION

Use of the blackjack, "the nigger beater," the rubber hose, the electrical prod to the genitals, in order to coerce a confession out of a person believed guilty of a crime, would always be a horrible thing to Marshall, especially since the Court had saddled him with defeat in a case that nagged at him most — the *Lyons* case in Oklahoma. In 1973, in *United States v. Dionisio*, Marshall entered a twenty-page dissent from the Court's approval of a grand jury's right to compel handwriting and voice exemplars from a defendant. Marshall argued that this was coercion that violated both the reasonableness requirement of the Fourth Amendment, and the self-incrimination protections of the Fifth Amendment. He said: "I cannot accept the notion that the government can compel a man to cooperate affirmatively in securing incriminating evidence when that evidence could not be obtained without the cooperation of the suspect."

Marshall said he would compel the government to show that its request was reasonable. "To do less is to invite the very sort of unreasonable government intrusion on individual liberty that the Fourth Amendment was intended to prevent," he added.

FREEDOM OF EXPRESSION

Marshall made it clear that he did not think the First Amendment protected only the freedom of expression of artists or preachers or newspapermen. He probably never was more eloquent about this cherished right than in 1974 in his concurring opinion in *Procunier v. Martinez*, which dealt with the requirement for a "humane environment in youth corrections institutions," and specifically with whether prison officials have a fundamental right to read inmates' mail. Marshall wrote:

"The First Amendment serves not only the needs of the polity but also those of the human spirit — a spirit that demands self-expression. Such expression is an integral part of the development of ideas and a sense of identity. To suppress expression is to reject the basic human desire for recognition and affront the individual's worth and dignity. . . . When the prison gates slam behind an inmate, he does not lose his human quality; his mind does not become closed to ideas; his intellect does not cease to feed on a free and open interchange of opinions; his yearning for self-respect does not end; nor is his quest for self-realization concluded. If anything, the needs for identity and self-respect are more compelling in the dehumanizing prison environment. Whether an O. Henry authoring his short stories in a jail cell or a frightened young inmate writing his family, a prisoner needs a medium for self-expression. It is the role of the First Amendment and this Court to protect those precious personal rights by which we satisfy such basic yearnings of the human spirit."

ABORTION

Marshall's most powerful words on this nation-rending subject are probably ones that never made it to any official brief, or into any majority opinion or dissent. In 1973, when the Supreme Court was anguishing over how to deal with the issue of a woman's right to an abortion, Justice Blackmun, no longer a "Minnesota Twin," departed from Burger again and made it clear that he and a majority of the Court would vote to say that under rights of privacy implied by the Constitution, a woman had a personal right to choose, to decide whether she would carry a pregnancy to term or not.

I have written earlier about Marshall's influence in the *Roe v. Wade* decision. But nothing illuminates more brightly his belief in a woman's right to control her body, her reproductive organs, than the words he wrote in 1990 in the case of *Jane Hodgson, et al, v. Minnesota.* That state had a statute providing that "no abortion shall be performed on a woman under 18 years of age until at least 48 hours after both of her parents have been notified." The statute contained a "judicial bypass" that a pregnant woman under age eighteen could avoid telling her parents if she got a judge's permission to undergo an abortion.

The Court was, as has often been the case recently on this issue, crazily divided into factions. Marshall was unwavering in writing of the majority compromise: "This scheme substantially burdens a woman's right to privacy without advancing a compelling state interest. More significantly, in some instances it usurps a young woman's control over her own body by giving either a parent or a court the power effectively to veto her decision to have an abortion. . . .

"This scheme forces a young woman in an already dire situation to choose between two fundamentally unacceptable alternatives: notifying a possibly dictatorial or even abusive parent, and justifying her profoundly personal decision in an intimidating judicial proceeding to a black-robed stranger. For such a woman, this dilemma is more likely to result in trauma and pain than in an informed and voluntary decision."

We may discover a special sense of humanity, a common man's sense of justice and fairness, in the written opinions of Marshall, but anyone who has shared a few "snorts" with him, or engaged in a truly informal interview, realizes that he had that special knack of bringing the majesty of the law down to the level of the needs of common Americans, whatever their race, color, or financial circumstances. Marshall dealt with legalisms only when the constrictures of his profession forced him to. His preference was to talk about the law and about justice in terms of every person's understanding of what is decent and fair.

It was this Marshall that the other justices saw inside their sanctum, their conference room. They came to know a Thurgood who could be just as prim, proper, scholarly, as he felt he needed to be to prove his right to sit there. But Marshall could suddenly be as rambunctious, irreverent, outrageous, as he knew he needed to be to make the other members of the Court understand that they didn't know a damn thing about being a poor, pregnant woman, white or black, living in Appalachia or the poorest precincts of the District of Columbia, with no fancy hospitals, no high-falutin' doctors, no medical technology, to nourish the futures of babies kicking in their undernourished wombs. Marshall could make the other justices understand what it meant to be poor and poorly educated, cheated on almost every level of life, and suddenly have to face the awesomeness of a courtroom appearance on a charge, genuine or trumped up, without a relative who knew how to speak up, or dared to, or a lawyer well enough prepared to protect that person's rights. Marshall could try to make his colleagues understand that if a police officer boarded a Greyhound bus and asked the passengers if he could search their luggage and see if they were carrying any drugs, most of those passengers would be so poorly educated that they would not understand their right to simply say no and send the officer packing. Marshall tried to convince that Court that any officer requesting the right for such a search should be obligated to make a *Miranda*-type declaration to the people on that bus saying, "Each of you must understand that anything I find in your luggage that suggests you have committed a crime can and will be used against you."

Marshall was exasperated that some justices felt that nothing took priority over catching and locking up dumb drug couriers — not even the Constitution's prohibition against illegal searches and seizures.

In the America of Marshall's last decade on the Court, when the executive branch was moving with shameless abandon to pack the high tribunal with troglodytes, Marshall became an anachronism, a non-salmon swimming hopelessly against the tide.

But he became a powerful voice *without* law clerks.

*   *   *

You cannot understand a lot about the character of Thurgood Marshall, his moral impact upon other justices, or how he painted delicate touches of humanity into the landscape of the law, unless you have had the chance, as I did, to listen to Marshall unvarnished by law clerks. When the man himself talks, you sense the fierce pride of self and race that made it impossible for him to sell out the rights of black people just to become a dinner favorite at the White House, or anyplace else. In the free-spirited talk of an octogenarian I saw the qualities that led some critics to call him an iconoclast, provoked a Mississippi editor to try to demean him by calling him "that mulatto," and drove Eastland, Thurmond, and others to try to brand him as an agent of communism.

During several interviews, I got to hear more of Marshall-without-clerks than any journalist, law professor, or anyone else ever would — except perhaps Cissy and their two sons. Following are excerpts from those interviews, in which Marshall offered some timeless wisdom about some of the most controversial issues of our day:

THE DEATH PENALTY

"People nowadays ask you, are you for capital punishment or not? It's not that simple.

"The difficulty is, if you make a mistake, you put a man in jail wrongfully, you can let him out. But death is rather permanent. And what do you do if you execute a man illegally, unconstitutionally, and find that out later? What do you say? 'Oops'?

"I'm not going to be swayed by this emotional business. I think it's cruel and inhuman to kill somebody. They say, well, we had the death penalty when the Constitution was written. That's true. You also put people in jail for debt. We did a lot of other things that we don't do now.

"It's the old story about the man who was arguing with the hunter, and he said, 'It's a shame, the way you shoot these poor little rabbits.' He said, 'Well, what do you complain about? You go fishing every weekend.' And the guy said, 'Yeah, but the fish, it doesn't hurt the fish.' And he said, 'Have you ever asked a fish?'

"Well, it's the same way about these people that are electrocuted and gassed and all. Some say it doesn't hurt them. Has anybody asked them? How do you know?

"This deterrent thing? I don't know of a single person who, when he committed a crime, thought he was going to get caught. His whole theory is he's smarter than the next guy, not that if he gets caught he'll be hung. He says, 'I'm too smart to get caught. So why do I worry about getting hung?'

"You remember the story in England when they made pickpocketing a capital offense? When they were hanging the first pickpocket, people were picking pockets in the crowd!"

PRIVACY

"My dad always said nobody could come in his house without a search warrant, or other than at his request. I guarantee if anybody had tried to come in my father's house without a warrant he'd kill him. Fortunately, he died before any of this happened.

"But I think a man's home is his castle, and goodness knows, if his home is his castle, his bedroom is the middle of it. Nobody snooping around in my bedroom. I don't have a gun, but I might be tempted.

"A couple more decisions like that Georgia sodomy case and we won't have any privacy left. But I'm going to raise my voice against it as long as I got breath.

"This privacy thing is unbelievable. Everything now has your serial number. I mean, you even got your Social Security number on drivers' licenses now.

"It's obvious — everything is going to be put in one place. So Big Brother's right with you now. Now that they've let Big Brother in the bedroom, I don't know anyplace else that you can keep Big Brother out of."

WOMEN'S RIGHTS

"We have progressed from the stage of keeping them barefoot and pregnant. We have escaped that stage. But I think there's a lot further on that we have to go.

"I mean, like I voted for having women guards in the prison, and I, for the life of me, can't imagine why a woman would want to be a guard in a prison. I wouldn't be caught dead in a prison. But they want to do it, let them do it.

"I have always been in favor of women's rights, of complete and absolute equality, and that is to bring my wife down to my level.

"I had a very independent mother. Her mother was a suffragette. She believed in that stuff. So I guess I had it beat into me."

AFFIRMATIVE ACTION

"I have no trouble with affirmative action. I think they [fellow Supreme Court justices] honestly believe that Negroes are so much better off than they were before.

"They didn't know what Negroes were doing before. They thought they were out digging ditches. And when I tell 'em, for example, in the legal profession, in the thirties when I came along, a Negro in Chicago represented either Swift or Armour. Those weren't bad companies to represent. Another in Charleston, West Virginia, represented the coal mines.

"I mean, the Negroes weren't out in the cold. They talk about how blacks have made so much progress. Against what? Yeah, *everybody's* made progress.

"As I told one member of the Court, 'Ain't you making more money than your father made? Well, if you make more money than your father made, then the Negroes ain't really doing too much now. I make more than my father made.' "

RACISM

"The biggest thing we brag about in this country is that it's a great melting pot. Well, as I sit and look at it now, at this late date, I have come to the definite conclusion that if the United States is indeed the great melting pot, the Negro either didn't get in the pot, or he didn't get melted down.

"Years ago, a Pullman porter told me that he'd been in every state and every city in the country and he'd never been anyplace in this country where he had to put his hand up in front of his face to know that he was a Negro. I agree with him.

"You know, everybody quotes Martin Luther King saying, 'Thank God, we're free at last.' We're not free! We're nowhere near free.

"Segregation — in general we still have it. I still know when I'm in certain places — I know that there are clubs here in this town that invite everybody but me. I don't have any honorary membership in any club, anyplace, under any circumstance. How come?

"The trouble is — if you haven't been a Negro, you don't understand. They think you're just 'sensitive' about something. Well, let's find out what you're sensitive about. When you're not eating, or you can't find a place to sleep, sure you get sensitive.

"They think that segregation is just a little something aside, a little inconvenience. Segregation is the worst thing that ever happened. Apartheid is an example of it."

"Do you think some members of the Court think you're oversensitive?" I asked.

"Absolutely. They say so," Marshall replied.

"So the business of having a black person on the Supreme Court has a particular value of sensitizing some of the whites on there?" I continued.

"Oh, I should imagine so. I should imagine so. You don't hear certain words there at least."

PRESIDENTS AND CIVIL RIGHTS

"I call him the gatekeeper. I don't care whether he's the president, the governor, the mayor, the sheriff — whoever calls the shots determines whether we have integration, segregation, or decency.

"That starts exactly with the president. I don't know the last president that came out fully, four-square for ending all segregation everyplace. I think it would be good for the president to say people are all people, take the skin off, there's no difference. I think it'd be good to say so.

"The first time I met Bobby Kennedy was when he was attorney general. He ended up by telling me the trouble with 'you people' — and I never like anybody to call me 'you people,' 'cause I know what they're talking about — he said, 'you people oughta get out the vote and get something done.' I said, 'Why, I thought we did turn out a little vote to get your brother elected.' And then he said, 'You all go around begging all the time.' So I said, 'What did I beg you for?' He was always patronizing. Always.

"When my appointment came up on the Second Circuit, Bobby tried to block it. But the president said no. I thought the president was great myself. I think Ted Kennedy was a lot like him — great. But I didn't like Bobby. I don't know of anybody that did like Bobby. He was as ruthless as anybody ever said he was, except his father was more ruthless.

"Lyndon Johnson — his plans were unbelievable, the things he was going to do."

THE CONSTITUTION

"I think it's the greatest body of laws set out ever, and what to me, and to many people, is so extraordinary about it is that at this late date you find that it works. And when you dig down into it, I don't know of any better job that could have been done. I have studied it considerably, along with constitutions of other countries, and compared it with Britain, which has no constitution, and I think we've just got a great body of laws.

"There's hardly anything it doesn't cover. I mean, it's just unbelievable that a constitution written in the horse and buggy days will cover outer space.

"We are celebrating a Constitution that didn't do what you and I would want it to do. It did not free all men. It didn't say that all men were free. It didn't say that all men were equal. It said all except slaves. And we have to recognize that they deliberately left out the slaves and that, to that extent, the Constitution was not as good as it could, or should, have been.

"Somebody months ago made the suggestion that this present Court should sit in Philadelphia like it did two hundred years ago, and I made the point, 'Well, if you're gonna do what you did two hundred years ago, somebody's going to give me short pants and a tray so I can serve coffee.'

"I don't back off that [criticism of the Constitution] at all. I think we have a great Constitution today. I've defended it all over the world and I'll continue to defend it, but it didn't start out that way. It has become a great Constitution by considering it as a living document. And the legislature passing amendments, and this Court issuing judgments. That's what's made it a great Constitution."

JUDICIAL RESTRAINT

"I don't know of any person who is worth their salt who goes on simple emotion, except maybe actors. When you take an oath to hand out justice, you in your own mind have to take any prejudice you have, or predilection that you might have, and push it back, out of your mind until after you decide the case, and then go back and pick it up, if you want.

"The British system is not based on precedents. Ours is based entirely on precedents, except this — that there's no precedent that binds me unalterably. If I think the precedent is wrong, I can vote that way. But unless I decide to reverse it, it's binding.

"I would say that, ninety-nine and forty-four one hundredths of the time, we follow precedents. Once in a while, we will reverse it. I've been party to some of that."

ORIGINAL INTENT

"I wish somebody who raised that point of 'original intent' would tell me what did the framers mean in that Constitution that would apply to rockets. If they'll tell me what there is in the Constitution that applies to rockets, then I'll understand it.

"So Chief Justice Hughes was right. It's this Court's job to interpret."

STRICT CONSTRUCTIONISTS

"That is when I don't do what you want. If I roll with you, I'm an absolute straight-arrow constitutional lawyer. If I don't, I'm a congressman making law. So I prefer not to join them.

"You see it almost every day. You see the majority opinion and the minority opinion, both saying, 'We strictly construe the Constitution'! The same words! One saying yes, and one saying no, but both doing it *strictly.*"

CONFIRMATION OF SUPREME COURT NOMINEES

"I think that protest is a part of the American way of life, and the right to petition Congress is in the Constitution. So I think any individual, any group, has a specific duty — not only a right, but a duty — to present to the Congress their views on any matter that's before Congress.

"I want you to remember that when my nomination was pending to the Court of Appeals for the Second Circuit, the senate committee held hearings for eleven months before they got around to confirming me, but I still think they had that duty."

I asked if Justice Marshall thought presidents would ever stop looking at ideological viewpoints.

"Oh, I think the founding fathers meant for the president to have that," he replied, "because they batted that around back and forth and they ended up — somebody had to put the name up. And when they said the president, I think that, number one, they didn't expect the president to appoint somebody that was opposed to him. I imagine that any president would prefer to put on the Court somebody that thought like he did and acted like he did.

"But President Harry Truman had some very disrespectful words to say about Justice Clark when Clark issued the steel decision against him, and President Eisenhower had some disrespectful words about Justice Brennan, whom he appointed. They don't all turn out the way you want 'em to turn out."

DEATH THREATS

"If I worried about every letter that came across this desk — well, you'd be surprised at what some people can say. But they get the correct treatment — waste can. They're fun to read though. They shouldn't write to me. They should write to a shrink. He could help 'em more than I can."

Thurgood had been ill, injured, hospitalized, so many times, going back to his birth, that I had to take him seriously in 1987 when he told me that he had two years to live. Ignoring the evidence that the man had shown a capacity to overcome myriad physical adversities, I was brazen enough to ask him what he wanted as an epitaph.

Displaying no noticeable fear of death, Marshall said, half belligerently: "He did the best he could with what he had. That's it. I can't beat that."

CHAPTER TWENTY-TWO

DISILLUSIONMENT AND RETIREMENT

IN THE LATE 1970s the sense of the power and glory of being a Supreme Court justice began to fade for Marshall. He had begun to see the impact of the departure of Earl Warren, the effect of Burger, and of Nixon's and Reagan's appointments to the high tribunal.

Marshall's dissents began to take on an edge of anger, sometimes outrage, but in his public utterances he stifled most of the fury that was welling up inside him. He did not betray his feelings that political change toward activist conservatism in America threatened to wipe away every protection that he had won as a civil rights lawyer for the "ordinary people" of America.

But in 1979 Marshall decided he could no longer anguish in silence. In a May 27 speech to the annual meeting of judges and lawyers of the Second Judicial Circuit, which is made up of New York, Connecticut, and Vermont, he attacked the Supreme Court in a speech that the *New York Times* described this way:

BUCK HILL FALLS, PA. — In a rare display of sarcasm, bitterness and pique at his Supreme Court colleagues, Justice Thurgood Marshall attacked the court yesterday for affording "insufficient protection to constitutional rights" in two recent cases.

Marshall objected almost venomously to the Supreme Court's overruling Judge Irving R. Kaufman, chief judge of the Second Circuit, in cases involving the rights of prisoners in a Manhattan jail, and the First Amendment protections of journalists. The

Supreme Court majority had said that placing more than one prisoner in a cell was not unconstitutional because "There is no one-
man, one-cell principle lurking in the due process clause."
Deriding this as "an enduring legal homily," Marshall ad-
libbed: "For a prisoner in jail, that ain't funny."

The Court had also upheld a rule subjecting inmates to body cav-
ity searches after every visit with a relative or lawyer. Marshall said
he could "think of no more degrading experience" and suggested
that prison wardens who did not dislike conducting such searches
"should visit a psychiatrist."
Rehnquist had written for the majority in the jail case (*Bell v.
Wolfish*) that the presumption of innocence has "no application" to
someone whose trial has not begun. Marshall was vitriolic in saying
that pre–trial detainees "are clothed with a presumption of innocence. . . . That is, before the Supreme Court decided the presumption didn't exist at all."

The *New York Times* said the audience gasped when Marshall said,
"Ill-considered reversals should be considered as no more than temporary interruptions." The newspaper quoted several unnamed lawyers and judges as saying that Marshall "was feeling increasingly
frustrated and isolated."

Concerning an earlier First Amendment case (*Herbert v. Lando*),
Marshall said reporters ought not to be forced to testify as to what
they were thinking, or what their conversations with colleagues were,
when they wrote an article that someone considered libelous. "Pre-
serving a climate of free exchange among journalists is essential to
sound editorial decision-making," he said. "Such collegial discussion
will likely be stifled unless confidentiality is guaranteed."

"Scandalous!" for a justice to go public, some Court watchers
screamed. "I think Marshall did the nation a service," I wrote in my
column, adding:

> He peeled back the cloak of stuffy arrogance under which our
> highest tribunal operates almost as free of public scrutiny and ac-
> countability as do the revolutionary tribunals in Iran.
> The Burger court, more than any in my time, has employed
> aloofness to nurture the myth that Supreme Court Justices are a
> nobler breed of men who have thrown aside political bias, racial
> prejudice, social preference and individual idiosyncrasies so they
> can sit in imperial isolation and hand down pure justice.
> Surely no one on or around the court dares to remind the pub-
> lic that Burger is a conservative Republican who dislikes the press

intensely, that William Rehnquist is an ultra-conservative who votes his reactionary glands, or that Marshall is a liberal whose votes will reflect the years he spent leading the NAACP's legal battles against racial and social injustice.

Marshall must have decided before going to the meeting of the Second Judicial Circuit, "Hell, they psychoanalyze U.S. presidents; they search the past and pockets of our lawmakers; it's time the public got a chance to see the human side, the frailties, the mindsets, of the nine men whose judgments affect the lives of all Americans." Marshall violated the "old boy" rule that justices see no evil, hear no evil and surely speak no evil of each other.

And Marshall has challenged us to stop swallowing the nonsense that nine powerful justices can "hide out" from the American people, pretending that to reveal their human qualities would be to imperil their integrity. I say bravo!

Marshall would lapse back into silent deference for the customs and traditions of the Court and then, when it was least expected, let go another verbal cannonade. In September 1984, when he spoke at the Second Circuit meeting in Hartford, Connecticut, he assailed the Supreme Court for approving a New York law for the detention of juveniles which he said exposed children to prisonlike conditions, violence, and possible sexual assault. In 1985 he went to Hershey, Pennsylvania, to tell Second Circuit judges and lawyers that "capital defendants do not have a fair opportunity to defend their lives in the courtroom. . . . Recent decisions of the Supreme Court have taken their special toll on capital defendants. . . . I continue to oppose [the death penalty] under all circumstances. But as long as our nation permits executions, lawyers, judges and public officials have a duty. They must assure that people who face the ultimate sentence receive the same opportunity to present their best case that non-capital defendants receive."

The going had become tougher for Marshall with Reagan's 1981 appointment to the Court of Sandra Day O'Connor, who Marshall thought was overly fond of the death penalty. Yet Marshall continued to win a few judgments in this area.

The "law 'n' order" fever that was sweeping America in an era of horrible crimes had produced a groundswell of opinion in favor of "victim impact" statements before a jury that was to decide whether someone convicted of a particularly heinous crime would get a life sentence or the death penalty. Beyond his absolute rejection of the death penalty, Marshall found revolting the idea that a jury that already knew the character of the crime and the criminal should be emotionalized at sentencing time by relatives telling of their anguish. In his days as a lawyer, Thurgood had seen numerous black men consigned to death not by intellectual or legal considerations, but by pure, racial emotion on the part of jurors.

When the victim impact issue arose in 1987 in *Booth v. Maryland*, Marshall was on the winning side of a 5 to 4 vote that relatives could not be allowed to put on heart-rending theater before jurors in hopes of inspiring a death sentence. In 1989, in *South Carolina v. Gathers*, Marshall again was in the majority in a 5 to 4 decision to forbid victim-impact statements.

Whatever his misgivings about continuing the Court grind, by 1989, when he was eighty-one, tired, often ill, *Booth* and *Gathers* told him that his vote was decisive. He had to hang on. Yet his nights, even his dreams, were spoiled by his sense that some of the justices were ripping gaping holes in the safety net he had helped to build for the weak, poor, virtually defenseless people of America. He remembered how he had learned that Chief Burger was not so bad when he saw the far-right opinions and leadership of Rehnquist. But he was adamant in telling friends that he could live with Rehnquist, especially when he got a chance to compare him with Reagan's 1986 appointee, Antonin Scalia. Then came Anthony M. Kennedy, the substitute for Robert Bork, who seemed at first to be more illiberal than Bork, and David H. Souter, the nominee who was becoming visible in ways that disturbed Marshall.

Marshall got some consolation out of his knowledge that most politicians and Court watchers did not expect him to still be on the Court into the 1990s. On November 4, 1980, the day Reagan won the presidency over Jimmy Carter, ABC Supreme Court reporter Tim O'Brien broadcast a rumor that Marshall would resign immediately so that Carter rather than Reagan could choose his successor. Marshall, who pitched a tantrum every time he saw someone on TV predicting that he was resigning, or dying, telephoned O'Brien immediately to say, "I was appointed for life, and I intend to serve out my full term!"

In 1987 I asked Marshall: "Are you deliberately dedicated to hanging in there, as we say, until Reagan's out of office?"

"Oh, longer than that," he replied.

"Longer than that?"

"Yeah, I mean I'm not going to leave until I die — unless I become senile, or something like that. And I don't have to worry about that, because my wife has promised she'll tell me when I get [senile], and when she tells me that I'll retire. But until then, UH-UH!"

I was one of only a few people who knew, in 1987, that Marshall had a serious aorta problem, and that because of this heart ailment his doctor had given him only about two more years to live. But Marshall beat the aorta problem, as he had whipped so many spells of bad health in his lifetime, beginning with the hernia problem as a child.

Nixon's flacks had spread rumors every time Marshall was hospitalized that alcoholism was the justice's problem. Members of even the black media spread these "leaks," even though none had ever seen Marshall intoxicated in any situation, let alone at work. Yet, those of us who had drunk with him knew that he could put the bourbon away, so the Nixon rumors would be plausible throughout much of the press corps.

This was especially so, given the frequency of Marshall's bouts with ill health. He had been forced by his doctor to hide out in Steelton, Pennsylvania, in 1943, because of sheer exhaustion. He had been hospitalized with unannounced problems in early July of 1946, was away from the office for two months, and then was ordered by his doctor to go to the Virgin Islands and not return until mid-October. In 1948, as he left for a meeting in Los Angeles, he begged publisher Loren Miller for "a suggestion as to a good place . . . where one can go and rest and hide." A year later he apologized to William G. Nunn, managing editor of the *Pittsburgh Courier*, that he could not come to Pittsburgh because "one of my eyes has gone bad." In October 1946 he became suddenly ill in Kansas City, causing White to wire the superintendent of St. Joseph's Hospital:

> PLEASE SEND ALL CHARGES FOR THURGOOD MARSHALL AFTER BLUE CROSS OR OTHER ADJUSTMENT TO OFFICE OF NAACP. . . . WE FEEL CONFIDENT YOUR HOSPITAL WILL RENDER EVERY SERVICE BUT THIS IS AUTHORIZATION TO FURNISH AT OUR EXPENSE EVERYTHING RE-QUIRED FOR MR. MARSHALL'S COMFORT AND RECOVERY.

Marshall's bouts with illness did not become a matter of national concern until after he became a Supreme Court justice. His every sneeze and cough provoked some Americans to hope he would die and others to pray fervently for his recovery. As in February 1975, when he checked into Bethesda Naval Hospital with a respiratory infection that became pneumonia. And in 1976 when he was hospitalized for "a mild heart disturbance" that later was called a myocardial infarction, or heart attack.

Marshall had been smoking two packs of cigarettes a day and had been ordered by his doctors to lose forty pounds, but after two more

mild heart attacks in three days, and not experiencing another predicted attack within six weeks, he declared, "I'm okay."

Marshall's biggest health problems probably arose from the fact
that black people wouldn't even let him be sick in peace. The pressures put on him are illustrated in this October 31, 1954, letter from
the Reverend Jerry Drayton, minister at the New Bethel Baptist
Church in Winston-Salem, North Carolina:

Dear Mr. Marshall:

I regret so very much to hear of your illness and would not
wish, under any ordinary circumstances, to impose upon you at a
time when you are not strong physically.

In the light of your physical condition, I wonder if you would
consider this plan:

You could fly here and come straight to my home, eat, and go
to bed and rest until time to appear on the program. We can cut
our program short, have you speak for seven minutes, rest and
then answer a few questions at the end of the program. We could
even cut out the question period and settle for a seven minute
speech. I could meet you at the airport.

The people are more interested in seeing you than anything
else. You are a symbol for us, and your presence will mean more
than your speech. I can explain your illness, and everybody will
understand; but I cannot very well explain your absence in the
light of the widespread publicity given your appearance prior to
this time. . . .

. . . NO SPEAKER WANTS TO SUBSTITUTE FOR THURGOOD MAR-
SHALL, because he realizes that the audience would be so greatly
disappointed that it could never recuperate from the great let
down. It is impossible to build up a suitable atmosphere for a
substitute. Besides we have collected money from several hundred
patrons, and some might feel that the whole thing was a fraud.

Mr. Walter White came to us against his doctor's advice in 1952,
and we did everything humanly possible to keep from placing him
under any strain whatever. His coming did not make him any
worse, because of our careful planning.

I have prayed over this affair, and I believe that it is the will of
God that you come to Winston-Salem. I shall continue to pray that
God will give you the strength and the determination to make the
trip.

Marshall's sense of being put upon, his mastery of sarcasm, are
evident in his reply:

Dear Rev. Drayton:

. . . I simply have to give up everything other than preparations for the December 6th argument of the school segregation cases. This is not only the orders of the three doctors involved but I am most convinced that this is the only way I will be on my feet when the [*Brown II*] arguments start.

The other point is that as I came out of the hospital my wife went in another hospital and will be there for weeks, and her condition is such that her doctor insists that I not leave the city at any time in the near future. You see that these two reasons add up to just a complete impossibility of my coming to North Carolina. I have had to give up all of the other engagements as well.

Incidentally, you mention the fact that Walter White was able to come to Winston-Salem over his doctor's objections. As a result of doing that over a period of time, Mr. White has now been in the hospital for three weeks, was in an oxygen tent for one week at which time he was at the point of death.

When he turned eighty, in 1988, Marshall made mental notes of the conference room arguments that he was losing, the dissents that became more bitter, the ways in which the Court had changed so profoundly since that day in 1967 when he had taken his seat with such pride for himself, and so much hope for his country.

Marshall got a clear picture of what the future held when he read the decision in *Holland v. Illinois*, weeks before it would be officially decided on January 22, 1990. Daniel Holland, a white man, had been charged in Cook County, Illinois, with aggravated kidnapping, rape, deviate sexual assault, armed robbery, and aggravated battery. Holland alleged that the state had used peremptory challenges to strike the only two black members from the pool of possible jurors, and that this was a violation of his Sixth Amendment right to be tried by a jury that was representative of the community. Holland's clever lawyers saw a chance to claim jury rigging. Scalia wrote the opinion, joined by Justices Rehnquist, White, O'Connor, and Kennedy, saying that Holland was not entitled to a *representative* jury, but only an *impartial* one, and that striking the only blacks from the jury pool was not a violation of his Sixth Amendment rights.

Marshall wrote a dissent in which he defended Holland's Sixth Amendment protections as zealously as he would have had the accused been a black man. In his majority opinion, Scalia made ad hominen attacks on the black justice. "Justice Marshall's dissent rolls out the ultimate weapon, the accusation of insensitivity to racial discrimination — which will lose its intimidating effect if it continues to be fired so randomly," Scalia wrote. "It is not remotely true that our opinion today 'lightly . . . sets aside' the constitutional goal of 'eliminating racial discrimination in our system of criminal justice.' . . . Race has nothing to do with the legal issue in this case. . . . All we hold is that [Holland] does not have a valid constitutional challenge based on the Sixth Amendment."

Justice Stevens filed his own dissent. Marshall's was joined in by Justices Brennan and Blackmun, who wrote angrily:

"The court decides today that a prosecutor's racially motivated exclusion of Afro-Americans from the petit jury does not violate the fair cross-section requirement of the Sixth Amendment. To reach this startling result, the majority misrepresents the values underlying the fair cross-section requirement. . . .

"The majority today insulates an especially invidious form of racial discrimination in the selection of petit jurors from Sixth Amendment scrutiny."

The years 1990 and 1991 became the most frustrating, angering, disillusioning years of Marshall's entire legal life. There was a string of Supreme Court decisions that challenged, and mostly ran counter to, everything that he had fought for as lawyer and judge. Here is a chronological sampling:

April 18, 1990 — *New York v. Harris*

On January 11, 1984, Ms. Thelma Staton was found murdered in her New York City apartment. Police had reason to believe that a boyfriend, Bernard Harris, was the murderer. On January 16 they entered his apartment without a warrant and arrested him, apparently in violation of a 1980 Supreme Court decree in *Payton v. New York* that "the Fourth Amendment prohibits the police from effecting a warrantless and nonconsensual entry into a suspect's home in order to make a routine felony arrest." Police took Harris to a police station, where they got him to admit guilt. Harris's lawyers claimed that the confession was the result of an illegal search and arrest and should be suppressed.

But Justice White wrote for a majority, including Chief Justice Rehnquist and Justices O'Connor, Scalia, and Kennedy, that "where the police have probable cause to arrest a suspect, the exclusionary rule does not bar the State's use of a statement made by the defendant outside his home, even though the statement is taken after an arrest made in the home in violation of *Payton*."

Marshall wrote a dissent, joined in by Justices Brennan, Blackmun, and Stevens, saying:

"The majority's conclusion is wrong. Its reasoning amounts to nothing more than an analytical sleight-of-hand, resting on errors in logic, misreadings of our cases, and an apparent blindness to the incentives the Court's ruling creates for knowing and intentional constitutional violations by the police." These four justices were deploring a frightening shift in which a Court majority suddenly found excuses to give a blind eye to police violations of the Constitution.

June 4, 1990 — *Illinois v. Perkins*

After police got a tip that prisoner Lloyd Perkins might be guilty of murdering an East St. Louis, Illinois, man, they put an undercover agent named John Parisi in the cell block with him, hoping Perkins would make self-incriminating statements, which he apparently did. The trial court suppressed the statements made by Perkins on grounds that Parisi had not given him the warnings required by *Miranda*. The appellate court of Illinois agreed that Perkins's rights had been violated.

But Justice Kennedy wrote, with Rehnquist, White, Blackmun, Stevens, and Scalia concurring:

"An undercover law enforcement officer posing as a fellow inmate need not give *Miranda* warnings to an incarcerated suspect before asking questions that may elicit an incriminating response. . . . *Miranda* does not forbid mere strategic deception by taking advantage of a suspect's misplaced trust."

Brennan filed a concurring opinion, leaving Marshall in lone dissent:

"The exception carved out of the *Miranda* doctrine today may well result in a proliferation of departmental policies to encourage police officers to conduct interrogations of confined suspects through undercover agents, thereby circumventing the need to administer *Miranda* warnings," Marshall wrote. "The Court's adoption of the 'undercover agent' exception to the *Miranda* rule is necessarily also the adoption of a substantial loophole in our jurisprudence protecting suspects' Fifth Amendment rights."

June 21, 1990 — *Illinois v. Rodriguez*

Chicago police entered the apartment of Edward Rodriguez without a warrant after his former girlfriend Gail Fischer used a key to open the door. The police seized cocaine and arrested Rodriguez for drug possession. The trial court and the appellate court of Illinois ruled that this was an "illegal search and seizure" under the Fourth Amendment, because Fischer had no authority to consent to the police entry and search of Rodriguez's apartment.

Justice Scalia wrote, with Rehnquist, White, Blackmun, O'Connor, and Kennedy joining, that "a warrantless entry is valid when based upon the consent of a third party whom the police, at the time of the entry, reasonably believe to possess common authority over the premises, but who in fact does not." What the "police believed" had become a cover for all manner of searches and seizures.

Marshall dissented, with Brennan and Stevens joining, arguing that "by allowing a person to be subjected to a warrantless search in his home without his consent and without exigency, the majority has taken away some of the liberty that the Fourth Amendment was designed to protect."

It was clear by this time that the Court fashioned by Reagan and Bush had tilted dramatically in favor of the police, and that the clamor for law and order was prevailing over Marshall's interpretations of the Bill of Rights.

The decision that destroyed Marshall's hope, broke his spirit and heart, was *Payne v. Tennessee*, decided 6 to 3 on June 27, 1991. It was a victim-impact case.

On June 27, 1987, in Millington, Tennessee, Pervis Tyrone Payne murdered twenty-eight-year-old Charisse Christopher and her two-year-old daughter, Lacie. He wielded a butcher knife mercilessly on her three-year-old son, Nicholas, who miraculously survived. Payne was charged with two counts of first-degree murder and one count of assault with intent to commit murder in the first degree. After hearing the grisly details of this crime, a jury convicted Payne on all counts.

In the sentencing phase of the trial, Payne did what convicts long had been allowed to do: present witnesses with mitigating testimony. His mother and father, and his girlfriend, testified that he was a "very caring person" who didn't drink or use drugs and had never been arrested. The horrifying murders, they said, were alien to Payne's character. Dr. John T. Huston, a clinical psychologist, told the jury that Payne was "mentally handicapped."

The judge permitted the state to bring in Charisse Christopher's mother, Mary Zvolanek, who told the jury how Nicholas had been affected by the slayings of his mother and sister.

"He cries for his mom," she said. "He doesn't seem to understand why she doesn't come home. And he cries for his sister Lacie. He comes to me many times during the week and asks me, 'Grandmama, do you miss my Lacie?' And I tell him yes."

The jury imposed a sentence of death. Payne appealed, arguing that Zvolanek's highly emotional statement to the jury violated his Eighth Amendment rights. The Tennessee Supreme Court held that the trial judge was right in allowing the victim-impact statement.

Payne then appealed to the Supreme Court, producing one of the most divisive brawls in the history of the high tribunal, on the issue of victim-impact statements. Late in the 1990–91 term it became obvious to Marshall and his clerks that the Rehnquist Court was going to use the *Payne* case to trample over the principle of stare decisis — that is, once the Court has decided an issue, that becomes the "law" that Americans can count on.

On June 27, the Court announced in a decision by Rehnquist that it was reversing the decisions in both *Booth* and *Gathers* and declaring victim-impact statements constitutional.

But that was not the big news of the day. The top headlines blared forth the shocking message that Marshall was retiring. The media carried a simple — and misleading — letter from Marshall to George Bush:

June 27, 1991

My dear Mr. President:

The strenuous demands of court work and its related duties required or expected of a Justice appear at this time to be incompatible with my advancing age and medical condition.

I, therefore, retire as an Associate Justice of the Supreme Court of the United States when my successor is qualified.

Respectfully,
Thurgood Marshall

That letter was the epitome of diplomatic departure. It told nothing of the rancor, the personal insults, that had befouled the conference room, or energized the nasty little secret memos that preceded the final Court alignment on *Payne*. Rehnquist wrote the basic decision asserting that "the Eighth Amendment erects no *per se* bar prohibiting a capital sentencing jury from considering 'victim impact' evidence. . . ." But the blood on the conference room floor was evident in the fact that while Justices White, O'Connor, Scalia, and Souter joined in Rehnquist's majority opinion, O'Connor felt compelled to write a concurring opinion in which White and Kennedy joined, Scalia filed a concurring opinion, in part two of which O'Connor and Kennedy joined, and Souter filed a concurring opinion in which Kennedy joined. Marshall wrote a furious dissent in which Blackmun joined, and Stevens filed an emotional dissent in which Blackmun joined. This judicial mess seemed incredible, though it was not unprecedented.

Ironically, precedents lay at the heart of the searing controversy.

Two hours before he announced his retirement, Marshall released his dissent, which said: *"Power, not reason, is the new currency of this court's decision making. Four terms ago a five-justice majority of this court held that 'victim impact' evidence of the type at issue in this case could not constitutionally be introduced during the penalty phase of a capital trial. By another 5–4 vote, a majority of the court rebuffed an attack upon this ruling just two terms ago.*

"Neither the law nor the facts supporting Booth *and* Gathers *underwent any change in the last four years. Only the personnel of this court did."* [Author's emphasis.]

Rehnquist knew in advance the scope and force of Marshall's dissent, and he tried to preempt it in the majority decision by writing that *Booth* had turned the victim into a "faceless stranger" at the penalty phase of a capital trial. He said *Booth* deprives the state of the full moral force of its evidence and may prevent the jury from having before it all the information necessary to determine the proper punishment for a first-degree murder.

As for the honoring of Court precedents, Rehnquist said that "stare decisis is the preferred course [but] stare decisis is not an inexorable command; rather, it is 'a principle of policy and not a mechanical formula of adherence to the latest decision.' "

Rehnquist argued that *Booth* and *Gathers* were decided by the narrowest of margins, were "wrongly decided," and had to be overruled.

Marshall thundered in his dissent that "this truncation of the court's duty to stand by its own precedents is astonishing. . . . The majority sends a clear signal that essentially all decisions implementing the personal liberties protected by the Bill of Rights and the Fourteenth Amendment are open to reexamination. . . . The continued vitality of literally scores of decisions must be understood to depend on nothing more than the proclivities of the individuals who now comprise a majority of this court."

The gray-maned, obese, wheezing old civil rights warrior then ticked off seventeen "endangered precedents." He said Americans could expect the Bush Court to overrule *Roe v. Wade,* which said a woman has a constitutional right to abort a pregnancy; *United States v. Paradise,* in which the Court upheld an Alabama federal judge's decree that that state promote one black state trooper for every white trooper promoted in order to remedy "long-term, open and pervasive discrimination" against blacks; *Ford v. Wainwright,* in which the Court said the Eighth Amendment forbids execution of the insane; *Metro Broadcasting v. FCC,* in which the Court upheld Federal Communications Commission regulations setting aside some broadcast licenses for minority applicants. . . .

Scalia wrote that "the response to Justice Marshall's strenuous defense of the virtues of *stare decisis* can be found in the writings of Justice Marshall himself. That doctrine, he has reminded us, is not 'an imprisonment of reason.' "

Some on the Court argued that Marshall wanted it both ways — on one hand a walking away from the 1896 precedent of *Plessy*, which gave a constitutional blessing to Jim Crow, but when it suited Marshall, an endless Court adherence to decisions that gave "unfair" economic and other preferences to minorities, or courtroom "advantages" to criminals.

Others countered with the argument that in effectively (but not specifically) reversing *Plessy* the Court was simply acknowledging, after fifty-eight years, an egregious error made manifest by changes in America's customs, mores, beliefs — but that there was no historical justification for the Court to reverse arrogantly and summarily a ruling made only two years earlier.

Columnist James J. Kilpatrick wrote that in his explosion over *Payne*, Marshall had "effectively disrobed his colleagues and stripped away some of the mystique in which the justices historically have wrapped themselves. Justice Marshall was honest. He was always honest. Here he was saying what Charles Evans Hughes said in an unguarded moment eighty years ago: 'We live under a written Constitution, but the Constitution is what the justices say it is.'

"Is ours a government of laws? Nonsense! In this regard ours is a government of men. This is the way the system was meant to work. . . .

"Let us thank Thurgood Marshall for his last cannonade. Nothing in his judicial life became him like the leaving it."

Most of conservative America was not so thoughtful or charitable as Kilpatrick. In fact, there was a cascade of caustic and cruel comments by those who were delighted to see Marshall retire.

Richard Viguerie, chairman of United Conservatives of America, said: "This is the moment for which conservatives have toiled for decades. . . . With one more conservative vote on the Supreme Court, the criminals' lobby will be on the run. Those who put the rights of criminals ahead of the rights of victims will be on the run."

"I was beginning to think he would never leave," exulted Gary Bauer, president of Family Research Council, an anti-abortion lobby.

"Justice Marshall's opinions on the court led to the slaughter of innocent boys and girls," said Randall Terry, founder of Operation Rescue.

One of the harshest judgments came from *Insight*, the magazine supplement of the *Washington Times,* the newspaper financed at the loss of a billion dollars by the Unification Church of the Reverend Sun Myung Moon, who said he had founded the newspaper "to save America."

"For years, observers had viewed Marshall as irritable and cranky, an outdated liberal in conservative judicial times," wrote *Insight's* Charlotte Allen. "And — worse — ," she continued, "as increasingly inattentive to his duties to the court where he has served for 23 years, to the point of watching television in his chambers, some said."

This magazine declared that "after almost a quarter century on the court, . . . Marshall left little to show for his time and effort" except for "a large number of competent majority opinions in routine tax, securities and antitrust cases — the sort of unglamorous bread-and-butter judicial stuff that Marshall got more than his share of, for some reason."

Columnists who were hardly household names except on the conservative fringes, such as Paul Craig Roberts, got their moment in the sun of the nation's op-ed pages by attacking Marshall. Roberts wrote that "it is a sad commentary on the state of American law that a person who helped to destroy equality before the law [by supporting affirmative action programs and contract set-asides] is hailed as a civil rights hero. It is our tragedy that a person who did so much to advance legal equality for all citizens in his early career would wind up laying the foundation for a racially classified society."

Conservatives hated Marshall because they thought he had influenced Blackmun and others on the Court to embrace the doctrine that affirmative action programs were constitutional because in order to get *beyond race,* the curse of *past racism* had to be dealt with frontally by remedying myriad previous injustices.

Marshall had no need to lapse into self-pity over these criticisms, because there was praise aplenty to keep his ego in good health. Harvard professor Alan Dershowitz said: "The Marshall era was characterized by a vindication of the rights of the downtrodden, the underdog, the minority and the unpopular. It was personified by the only justice in American history whose entire distinguished career at the bar was in the service of the poor, the disenfranchised and the victims of discrimination."

John J. Curtin, Jr., president of the American Bar Association, asserted: "His eloquence as a lawyer gave a voice to those who had no voice. His judicial opinions transformed general precepts of the Constitution into specific protections of the rights of all Americans. His dedication to principle has never wavered. He will be missed."

Blacks by the millions expressed their shock and pain over Marshall's retirement, but voices from white America shouted most forcefully and eloquently what he had meant to jurisprudence in this country. The *Washington Post* declared: "His stalwart dissents spoke not only for the accused, the impoverished and the victims of discrimination who were the focus of his life's work but for all who are anxious about the court's drift away from these concerns. In his absence, the court will be more united next term; that is not a pleasing prospect."

"Marshall's presence on the Supreme Court both symbolized and extended the achievement of human rights through law and the Constitution," the *New York Times* said. "His retirement, though richly earned and long expected, is nevertheless a hurtful blow to the causes he personified.

"His . . . work in mustering America's moral force to atone for past racism remains a monument and a model. Meanwhile, it hurts to see him go."

Marshall was not preoccupied with reading his clippings on June 28. He had no power or right to tell President Bush how to fill his seat. But he feared that under the cover of keeping a minority person on the Court, Bush would name a black conservative of the stripe of Scalia — someone who would move without conscience to undo everything that Marshall had done. You didn't have to read much between the lines spoken by Marshall at the press conference on June 29, two days following his letter of retirement, to understand what was on the mind of the old civil rights warhorse:

Q.: Do you think the president has any kind of obligation to name a minority justice in your place . . . ?

MARSHALL: I don't think that should be a ploy, and I don't think it should be an excuse, one way or the other.

Q.: An excuse for what?

MARSHALL: Doing wrong. I mean for picking the wrong Negro and saying I'm picking him because he's a Negro. I'm opposed to that. . . . My dad told me way back . . . that there's no difference between a white snake and a black snake. They'll both bite. . . .

It suddenly was obvious to all but the densest reporters in the room that Marshall feared Bush was going to name a reactionary black, at worst, or a conservative Hispanic, at best, and assume that his or her skin color would provide such a shield that the Senate could not refuse to confirm.

> *Q.*: Mr. Justice, in view of the president's political philosophy, it's
> inevitable that he is going to select a conservative.
> *MARSHALL*: Well, in the first place, I don't know what [Bush's]
> philosophy is.
> *Q.*: Do you think *he* knows what his philosophy is?
> *MARSHALL*: I don't know whether he knows or doesn't know. It's
> none of my business.
> *Q.*: What do you think about the idea of having Clarence Thomas
> as the person to succeed you?
> *MARSHALL*: I think the president knows what he's doing and he's
> going to do it.

Marshall knew in his heart that Bush was going to nominate
Thomas, but he let a reporter speak Thomas's name first. The retiring justice had delivered a not-so-subtle message to Bush, but he
knew the president would ignore it.

Marshall damaged his credibility and his image a bit in that press
conference by denying what his friends and foes knew was the truth.
The following exchange did not serve him well:

> *Q.*: Your retirement has been characterized as leaving in anger and
> frustration, finding yourself on the dissenting side.
> *MARSHALL*: Of course.
> *Q.*: Is that true? Is that an accurate characterization?
> *MARSHALL*: Who said that?
> *Q.*: It's on the front page of the *New York Times* this morning.
> *MARSHALL*: The front page of the *New York Times* said that I was
> frustrated?
> *Q.*: And angry at finding yourself in dissent . . .
> *MARSHALL*: That's a double-barreled lie.

Many of the justice's friends listened to that reply in sadness. No
one could read his final dissents in *Payne* and other cases without
sensing that Marshall was an angry man, bitterly hostile toward some
of the most recent arrivals on the Court, frustrated by his knowledge
that he couldn't change them, worried that his seat probably would
be filled by a black man who would ally himself with the most socially
myopic justices that Marshall had ever confronted in the Court's
conference room.

Only those who had known Marshall over the years could understand that press conference behavior. Marshall had never been will-

ing to admit defeat in anything. As a boy in Baltimore *he* had won the fistfight with the white guy who called him "nigger." When he was in physical peril in the South, he had outwitted would-be lynchers. In the argument with some blacks over the wisdom of going all-out against "separate but equal," his view had prevailed. Against small armies of well-financed lawyers, in dozens of cases, he had prevailed in the courts, especially the Supreme Court. When up for confirmation to a federal judgeship, he had survived a Senate inquisition. There was absolutely no chance that Marshall was going to tell a bunch of reporters, "I'm losing, so I quit."

Marshall had too much pride to concede in any way that after almost twelve years, Reagan and Bush and their attorneys general and solicitors general and appointments to the high tribunal had weakened his spirit. Only Cissy and a few very close friends would hear him voice his disillusionment, his worries about the direction in which America was going.

Even in retirement, Marshall was still one of the brethren, whose bond forbade harsh public criticism of each other. In a withering dissent, he could excoriate those voting in the majority on *Payne,* but he just couldn't say publicly what he thought personally of Scalia or Kennedy. He absolutely could not personally attack Clarence Thomas, the black man who was taking his seat, no matter the depth of his ideological disagreements with Thomas, or of his personal contempt for him. So Marshall would bridle in anger that newsmen would write that he was pointing to Thomas when he said that "a black snake will bite you as quick as a white one."

Marshall knew what the newsmen did not — that he would be going to his Supreme Court office every day, and that he would see his brethren, including Thomas, on many occasions. He was just not going to breach the historic aura of brotherhood that was a vital part of the Court's mystique.

Once during the June 29 press conference, Marshall abandoned his surly "Huhs" and brightened up at a question about whether black Americans are, as Dr. King had once exclaimed, "FREE AT LAST!"

Marshall repeated his old story of the Pullman porter who said he had never been in any city in the United States where "he had to put his hands up in front of his face to find out that he was a Negro."

Marshall was saying a dismaying number of times, "I will not comment on the Court or any justices thereon"; "It was in the conference room, and anything said and done there remains there"; "For the eighty-seventh time, I will not discuss cases or justices"; "How can I comment on that [the future of school integration]?"

My spirits were lifted somewhat when Marshall reverted a bit to his old spirited candor:

> *Q.*: Justice Marshall, would you share with us some of the medical facts?
>
> *MARSHALL*: Some of the *what?*
>
> *Q.*: Some of the medical evidence. What's wrong with you, sir?
>
> *MARSHALL*: What's *wrong* with me? I'm old and coming apart!

Another reporter provoked another outburst of unvarnished truth.

> *Q.*: Do you have any plans for retirement?
>
> *MARSHALL*: Yep.
>
> *Q.*: What are they?
>
> *MARSHALL*: Sit on my rear end.

Marshall was furious in noting that he had *retired*, not resigned. He still had a Supreme Court office, to which he went daily, and in some circumstances, as is the Court's rule, would be called upon to hear an important case.

Even as this book went to the printer, I found that on any day that I called Justice Marshall's private number he was on his rear end — but in his Supreme Court office. He answered the phone himself. It was as though Thurgood was having the last word against the critics and detractors who said he was lazy and didn't keep even banker's hours, and that he spent Court time watching soap operas while his clerks did the work.

Marshall would, at eighty-four, tell me: "I'm still kickin', but not very high."

Yet, he declined to discuss his personal feelings about the Court and the people on it. The bond of "the brethren" still sealed his lips.

Each time I called him I remembered how as a civil rights lawyer, he worked on a shoestring for a chronically impoverished NAACP; how he had gone up against the best constitutional lawyers that money and racist appeals could buy in the Deep South; how he did not have the support of timid or hustling blacks who were inclined to go down like dogs and lap the trickle-down waters of Jim Crow.

Marshall could bask in the knowledge that his peers and most of America had already recorded their judgments that his "best" was great and nation-building.

But there were those in the media, in law schools, who still asked,

"Did having a *black* liberal on the Court really make a difference?"
"Did Marshall in fact change the legal landscape?"

In 1979, writing for the *Black Law Journal* at UCLA (University of California, Los Angeles), Chief Justice Warren Burger said:

"Few judges have influenced the development of Constitutional law in the United States to the extent that Thurgood Marshall has.

"Marshall brought to the Court a breadth of experience equaled by few. To his working knowledge of legal craftsmanship he adds a practical, common sense understanding of the law in relation to its ultimate objectives. He chooses a reasoned approach to Constitutional problem-solving, examining all the issues before him. When confronted with potentially emotional issues, he maintains objectivity in such a way as not to jeopardize either the personal warmth or sense of humor for which he is so well known and admired."

David L. Bazelon, then chief judge of the District of Columbia Court of Appeals, wrote:

"His commitment to protection for the poor and disadvantaged goes beyond his leadership in the area of civil rights and extends to his less heralded concern for assuring the basic fairness of the criminal justice system.

"Before coming to the bench, Justice Marshall's career was that of a lawyer at the cutting edge of a legal revolution which changed the nature of American society."

In his personal reflections, Robert L. Carter, a Marshall protégé at the NAACP who became a federal judge, emphasized Marshall's never-ending defense of the rights of women and the poor:

"When the Court sustained state Medicaid regulations barring use of public funds for nontherapeutic abortions, Justice Marshall wrote a forceful dissent attacking the majority opinion as victimizing the poor:

'The enactments challenged here brutally coerce poor women to bear children whom society will scorn for every day of their lives. Many thousands of unwanted minority and mixed-race children now spend blighted lives in foster homes, orphanages and 'reform' schools. . . . Many children of the poor will sadly attend second-rate segregated schools. . . . And opposition remains strong against increasing AFDC [welfare] benefits for impoverished mothers and children, so that there is little chance for the children to grow up in a decent environment. . . . I am appalled at the ethical bankruptcy of those who preach a 'right to life' that means, under present social policies, a bare existence in utter misery for so many poor women and their children.' "

Probably no one knows a judge better than his law clerks. Four

of them, David A. Barrett, Susan L. Block, David M. Silberman, and Allan B. Taylor wrote a joint article in which they said:
"One of the first things Mr. Justice Marshall tells his law clerks is not to call him Mr. Justice. He rejects this ostentatious title, preferring to be called simply 'Judge,' the title by which he is uniformly and affectionately known to his law clerks. Although he is one of only nine members of the nation's most important court, 'The Judge' is not a man who is comfortable with displays of adulation or self-congratulation. These introductory instructions tell the new law clerk a good deal about the individual for whom he or she will be working for the next year.

"The Judge's directness, lack of pomposity, strength of conviction, and sense of humor combine to make working for him a particularly pleasurable experience. His willingness to share the knowledge, understanding, and wealth of good stories he has accumulated during a unique career of leadership makes that experience extraordinarily educational as well. As in all close and demanding relationships, there are difficult moments, but at bottom, one sees in the Judge a profound humanity. It is a love of people, all people — all races, faiths and nationalities — that graces both his opinions and his personal relationships."

I think something closest to the whole truth came from one of the great judges of American history, Irving R. Kaufman, when he wrote: "Implicit in the very concept of an organic, growing Constitution is the notion that the finest representatives of each successive generation will continue to breathe the vital spirit of the nation into it. Among my contemporaries Thurgood Marshall is the foremost example of this rare and yet indispensable type of man. He achieved national prominence as a staunch advocate of racial equality and social justice at a time when it was essential, but not fashionable, to be one.

"From his youth in Maryland, Thurgood possessed proper dosages of both pugnacity and sagacity — the staple of which great advocates are made."

In 1980, Judge Kaufman recalled:
"My most abiding memory of Thurgood on this court was his ability to infuse his judicial product with the elements of the advocate's craft. As an attorney Thurgood stressed "the human side" of the case. As a judge he wrote for the people. He possessed an instinct for the critical fact, the gut issue, born of his exquisite sense of the practical. This gift was often cloaked in a witty aside: 'There's a very practical way to find out whether a confession has been coerced: ask, how big was the cop?' But behind this jovial veneer is a precise and

brilliant legal tactician who, to quote his 1966 Law Day speech in Miami, was able 'to shake free of the 19th century moorings and view the law not as a set of abstract and socially unrelated commands of the sovereign, but as an effective instrument of social policy.' Thurgood was able to sear the nation's conscience and move hearts formerly strangled by hoary intransigence. And, because of him, we are all more free."

I have written earlier of the official opinions and dissents in which Marshall influenced the Court and widened the parameters of personal liberty. I must not fail to record the fact that Marshall was one of the few members of this secretive, hoary-minded Court who dared to influence America with extra-judicial, often controversial public remarks.

In 1987, when the country was indulging in what some regarded as an ill-informed orgy of celebrations of the Bicentennial of the Constitution, Marshall decided that he would deliver a back-to-sanity speech in Cissy's homeplace, Maui, Hawaii, at the annual seminar of the San Francisco Patent and Trademark Law Association:

> I do not believe that the meaning of the Constitution was forever "fixed" at the Philadelphia Convention. Nor do I find the wisdom, foresight, and sense of justice exhibited by the Framers particularly profound. To the contrary, the government they devised was defective from the start, requiring several amendments, a civil war, and momentous social transformation to attain the system of constitutional government, and its respect for the individual freedoms and human rights, we hold as fundamental today.
>
> For a sense of the evolving nature of the Constitution we need look no further than the first three words of the document's preamble: "We the People." When the Founding Fathers used this phrase in 1787, they did not have in mind the majority of America's citizens. "We the People" included, in the words of the Framers, "the whole Number of free Persons." On a matter so basic as the right to vote, for example, Negro slaves were excluded, although they were counted for representational purposes — at three-fifths each. Women did not gain the right to vote for over a hundred and thirty years.
>
> These omissions were intentional. The record of the Framers' debates on the slave question is especially clear: The Southern States acceded to the demands of the New England States for giving Congress broad power to regulate commerce, in exchange for the right to continue the slave trade. . . .
>
> Nearly seven decades after the Constitutional Convention, the

Supreme Court reaffirmed the prevailing opinion of the Framers regarding the rights of Negroes in America. It took a bloody civil war before the 13th Amendment could be adopted to abolish slavery, though not the consequences slavery would have for future Americans.

And so we must be careful, when focusing on the events which took place in Philadelphia two centuries ago, that we not . . . lose our proper sense of perspective. Otherwise, the odds are that for many Americans the Bicentennial celebration will be little more than a blind pilgrimage to the shrine of the original document now stored in a vault in the National Archives. If we seek, instead, a sensitive understanding of the Constitution's inherent defects, and its promising evolution through 200 years of history, the celebration of the "Miracle at Philadelphia" will, in my view, be a far more meaningful and humbling experience. We will see that the true miracle was not the birth of the Constitution, but its life, a life nurtured through two turbulent centuries of our own making, and a life embodying much good fortune that was not [of our own making].

Thus, in this Bicentennial year, we may not all participate in the festivities with flag-waving fervor. Some may more quietly commemorate the suffering, struggle, and sacrifice that has triumphed over much of what was wrong with the original document, and observe the anniversary with hopes not realized and promises not fulfilled. I plan to celebrate the Bicentennial of the Constitution as a living document, including the Bill of Rights and the other amendments protecting individual freedoms and human rights.

One of Reagan's black stooges, the late Clarence Pendleton, who turned the U.S. Civil Rights Commission into a bad joke, said Marshall was "senile." Another young black Reaganite, Clarence Thomas, then chairman of the Equal Employment Opportunities Commission, attacked Marshall for his Maui speech.

These numerous assaults on Marshall for telling an obvious truth were exacerbated by Pendleton's and Thomas's anger over things Marshall had said to me in a television interview:

ROWAN: I'd be fascinated to have you look back at the presidents who've been in power during these years that you've been in the great struggle for human rights, and just tell me a little bit about how you perceive each of these presidents. We'll start with Roosevelt.

MARSHALL: I don't think Roosevelt did much for the Negro. Truman did everything he could, because the southern bloc controlled Roosevelt, and Truman took over and told the southern bloc where to go. And you bear in mind, Truman's mother was the opposite of being pro-Negro. And yet — Truman loved her very dearly, but he didn't let that persuade him. And Eisenhower, I don't think did anything except to try to undermine the school decision.

ROWAN: Well, let's do Kennedy next.

MARSHALL: Well, Kennedy was held back by the attorney general, his brother. His brother said, "Don't do anything for the Negroes because you won't get reelected. Wait until you're reelected, and then do it," and then he got killed.

He had all the plans, though. But Johnson — if Johnson — his plans were too far out for Negroes and civil rights.

ROWAN: Too far out for them?

MARSHALL: He wasn't thrown out because of Vietnam. They just used that as an excuse to get rid of him.

ROWAN: You think he was the greatest civil rights president we ever had?

MARSHALL: In my book he was. I talked to him a lot, and he was pretty good. He really knew what the score was. I mean, when you talked to him, you got to the nitty gritty.

ROWAN: What about Richard Nixon? There are people who think that the decline of the civil rights movement began in the Nixon years and has been going downhill ever since.

MARSHALL: Well, I have a personal story about Nixon. I had pneumonia back around 'sixty-eight, and I was out at Bethesda [Naval Hospital] for five or six weeks. It was a real bad deal. And when I got through, the commandant at Bethesda said to me, "I've been requested to give a full report of your illness and prognosis, et cetera." And he said, "I won't do it without your permission." I said, "Who wants it?" And he says, "The president wants it."

I said, "Well, Admiral, you have my permission to give it to him only on one condition. That you put at the bottom of it, quote, 'Not yet.' " And he did.

That's what I can remember about Nixon.

ROWAN: So Nixon was eager to name somebody to replace you on the Court?

MARSHALL: Right.

ROWAN: What about Ford?

MARSHALL: Nothing. I don't think he had a chance.

ROWAN: What about Jimmy Carter?

MARSHALL: Generally speaking, I think his heart was in the right place, but that's the best I can do with him.
But I think Truman is going to come out on top.

ROWAN: You do?

MARSHALL: I really do.

ROWAN: What about Ronald Reagan?

MARSHALL: The bottom.

ROWAN: The bottom?

MARSHALL: Honestly. I think he's down with Hoover and that group, and Wilson, when we didn't have a chance.

ROWAN: Yet he's been one of the most popular presidents the country has ever had.

MARSHALL: Is he more popular than the average movie star? Movie stars are just fashionable people. You want a movie star, get one.

ROWAN: So you're saying that historians are going to look past the glitter and glamor of moviedom and put Reagan at the bottom?

MARSHALL: In my book he is.

Probably no one described Marshall's influence on the Court better than Marshall's closest friend on the Court, Justice William Brennan, during an interview with me:

"There isn't any doubt," Brennan said, "that in a period in our history when racial issues have been among the most prominent, he brings from his own personal experience a perception of racism which is invaluable for us who have not had the same experiences. And his stories — he's a great story-teller, perhaps you know — he's constantly breaking up the conferences, in moments of tension, with some story. I've never heard him repeat one, either.

"But he can tell you from personal experience what it was like to ride for miles and miles and miles and not even be able to get a sandwich in a restaurant along the way. He couldn't get a bed to sleep in at night. And when you arrived, particularly in his case, when he was defending both the criminally accused and the other kinds of cases, in so many states, time after time there were not merely protests but dangerous efforts at harming him. And the knowledge of that sort of thing in the cases that we've had to deal with, has been very valuable to all of us on the Court."

"Has he told you stories indicating that there is a lingering bitterness over personal slights and insults?" I asked Justice Brennan.

"I don't think I'd put it quite that way," he replied. "Only because he tells them in a very jocular context, usually. I don't doubt, myself, that there has to be some residue of bitterness about those days. I've heard him be quite resentful that he personally had not been admitted to a white law school, for example. That kind of bitterness, I think, still hangs on, but not any general one.

"I think, though he might not admit it really, that he's disappointed that progress has not been faster and more extensive and worries that there might be some retreat from the gains that have been made. Ordinarily he's a very patient man and he knows that, with a subject like this, one has to be patient and he has been, but on occasions now he manifests an increasing impatience with the failures of those who could be doing more."

I said, "I know he expressed some concern to me about the judicial appointments of President Reagan and his tendency to name mostly white males. Is this the kind of thing that has bothered you, too?"

"Well," Brennan replied, "this isn't limited to this administration, Carl. I have never thought yet we have adopted the principle of proportionality that would reflect representation not only of blacks but of women. And to that extent, yes, I, too, think that we're not making sufficient progress in that direction. It's not only one administration, it's been the case with several."

I noted that Marshall had said to me that the only way to guarantee justice in this country is to have blacks, women, people who represent the population, in the judicial system.

"Do you share that view?" I asked.

"I certainly do," Brennan replied. "I think the only test really ought to be competency to do the job. The day may come, I hope, and I can expect I might see it, Carl, when I can look at you and never see the color of your skin. And that's the sort of thing that Thurgood thinks we're not getting to as fast as he would like."

"Justice Marshall went to Hawaii and gave a speech in which he criticized the original Constitution, and he created quite a furor," I noted. "Then in an interview with me he ranked the presidents and in fact criticized a sitting president. Do you think he went too far?"

"Nothing Thurgood says goes too far as far as I'm concerned."

CHAPTER TWENTY-THREE

THE CLARENCE THOMAS FIASCO

WHILE JUSTICE MARSHALL knew that he could not pass public comment on anyone whom President Bush nominated to succeed him, no one in America watched with greater interest and concern than Marshall, just four days after his retirement, when Bush walked out of his seaside retreat in Kennebunkport, Maine, with Clarence Thomas at his side.

Bush announced that after a private conversation, in which he said he imposed no litmus test about abortion or any other issue before the Court, he had decided to nominate Thomas to become the 106th justice of the nation's highest Court — and the second black person to serve there.

"I believe he'll be a great justice. He's the best person for this position," Bush said. "I have followed this man's career for some time, and he has excelled in everything that he has attempted. He is a delightful and warm, intelligent person, who has great empathy and a wonderful sense of humor. He's also a fiercely independent thinker with an excellent legal mind who believes passionately in equal opportunity for all Americans.

"Judge Thomas is a model for all Americans, and he's earned the right to sit on this nation's highest court."

Thomas fought back tears as he responded: "As a child I could not dare dream that I would ever see the Supreme Court, not to mention be nominated to it. In my view, only in America could this have been possible."

"Only in America . . ." That line, when uttered by a black person, ensures that only the most unpatriotic of whites could possibly rise in opposition. Here was the quintessential George Bush, trying always to be all things to all men, hoping Thomas would get the blessings of independent black Democrats and conservative whites.

But a lot of Americans did protest. Arthur Kropp, president of People for the American Way, said the nomination was troubling. Thomas was anti–affirmative action, hostile in almost all respects to the civil rights movement. John Jacob, president of the National Urban League, offered some mumbo-jumbo doubts that Thomas would ever hear "voices from the walls" of Marshall's office charging him with protecting "minority and disadvantaged people." NAACP leader Hooks had warned Bush that if he nominated someone who was unacceptable to the civil rights community he would face "the mother of all confirmation battles."

Meanwhile, the press was emphasizing Thomas's previous poverty rather than his political and social views. "FROM POVERTY TO U.S. BENCH" was emblazoned on the front page of the *New York Times*. "SELF-MADE CONSERVATIVE," heralded the *Washington Post*.

Marshall, who even in retirement would be asked to participate in some important federal court cases, was muzzled. Thousands of black "leaders" were paralyzed by the dilemma of campaigning against a black right-winger when they assumed that if Thomas were rejected, Bush would choose a white right-winger more hostile to America's minorities.

Marshall saw Thomas in terms of the issues and causes that had dominated his life. Such as affirmative action, which Marshall had fought for as a way of giving long-cheated minorities, women, everyone, a fair grasp at the American dream. Thomas had derided affirmative action as "a narcotic of dependency." Marshall would shake his head in wonderment that a black man who grew up poor in Jim Crow Georgia, and who had benefited from a thousand affirmative actions by nuns and others, and who had attended Yale Law School on a racial quota, could suddenly find affirmative action so destructive of the characters of black people.

Over forty years I had heard Marshall curse, in a hundred ways, "the goddamn black sellouts." I had no doubt what he was saying about Thomas.

Marshall had warned in his retirement press conference that Bush might use race as a cover to "do the wrong thing." He was suggesting that in nominating a black conservative, Thomas, to replace him, Bush was dividing and disarming blacks, liberals, moderates, who would find it difficult to oppose filling the seat with another black person, no matter what his ideology. Marshall knew that it was a deft political move by the president.

But not all black Americans were conned by Thomas's color. Professor Derrick Bell of Harvard said he was "appalled" and "insulted" by the nomination. Other prominent blacks said that Thomas would do more damage to the hopes and dreams of black people than any white conservative that Bush could have named, because Thomas would give "cover" to the Court's white ultraconservatives, who would be able to say, "Me a racist? Clarence Thomas voted with me." On the other hand, one black talk-show host in Washington expressed the view of millions of black people: "Any black person on the Supreme Court is better for us than any white person."

Blacks who opposed Thomas wished fervently that Marshall could thunder, in his inimitable way, "What is this crap about a black sell-out being better for the suffering people of America than an Earl Warren or a Bill Brennan?" But this time they knew that Marshall's "no comment" binge was based on good common sense, not on cantankerousness. Still, Marshall could have given some guts to the National Urban League, which had chickened out into a neutral position. He could have emboldened Benjamin Hooks, the executive director of the NAACP, who waffled and wrung his hands over the fact that some branches had publicly adopted the line that "any black on the Court is better" and had announced support for Thomas. But Marshall couldn't give the backbone speech that black Americans needed — such as his defense of integration in Texas.

So the NAACP floundered in semiparalysis, which was painful to the old NAACP legal warhorse, Thurgood. The Congressional Black Caucus, and some women's groups, came out forcefully against the confirmation of Thomas. But the delegates to the NAACP annual convention in Houston were sent home with only a timid promise that Hooks and others would "talk to Judge Thomas" and see where he really stood. Marshall noted privately the ludicrousness of the NAACP pretending that while no one else in the world could get Thomas to speak out on any issue of importance, it expected him to bare his soul to Hooks. The NAACP was engaging in the kind of cop-out that Marshall had never seen in all his years of fighting within that organization.

On June 2, 1992, the *Baltimore Sun* published an astonishing article about how one of its black reporters, Arch Parsons, had maneuvered to immobilize Hooks and pass word to President Bush that he could nominate Thomas without fear that Hooks would "leap to judgment."

Parsons, at age sixty-six, had left the *Sun* in a retirement agreement. He admitted that he was a friend of Thomas's, that he wanted a black person to replace Marshall, and that he relayed to the White House a Hooks pledge that he and the NAACP would not "be part of a lynch mob." "Lynch" would become the critical word in Thomas's confirmation hearings.

The *Baltimore Sun* said it would have fired Parsons had it known that he was writing its stories about Thomas while secretly plumping for his confirmation. Parsons, in the pathetic midnight of his journalistic career, said he had engaged in an egregious conflict of interest. The about-to-retire Hooks protested furiously that he had done nothing wrong.

Here was one of the most sordid moments in the history of the NAACP. Here was an indelible blot on the record of Hooks. A generation later the black, brown, yellow, aged, poor, of America would ask whether, deliberately or as a dupe, Hooks had become a party to the sabotaging of Thurgood Marshall's dreams.

While Marshall could not speak out against Thomas, some of us knew that we could. I said on television that "if you sprinkled some flour on Thomas's face you might think you were listening to David Duke," the former Ku Klux Klan leader. That brought me a rebuke from Vice President Quayle, who was quickly silenced when Duke declared that on issues such as welfare and affirmative action his views were the same as Thomas's.

I received a barrage of mail from blacks and whites who thought I was myopic not to see that if Thomas were rejected, Bush would nominate someone more distasteful. I replied, "You don't swallow a dose of arsenic because you fear that someone will give you strychnine tomorrow. You fight off the arsenic to live for another day, when you might also reject the strychnine."

Still, Thomas rolled along breezily toward confirmation. The American Bar Association on August 28 rated him "qualified" for the Supreme Court. Most nominees in the past two decades had received "well qualified" ratings, the top endorsement. Two of the fifteen members of the ABA's Standing Committee on the Federal Judiciary found Thomas "not qualified." No nominee receiving "not qualified" votes had been seated on the Supreme Court for at least twenty years, according to the ABA and the Senate Judiciary Committee.

But Thomas's blackness made him different from Haynsworth, Carswell, Bork, and other rejected nominees. Some southern senators, seeing ambivalence in black America, felt that they did not dare to vote against a black man, however obnoxious he seemed to them.

On September 10, confirmation hearings began in the Senate Judiciary Committee. Thomas professed not to have a view on anything of consequence. He could not recall ever in his life expressing a view about *Roe v. Wade,* the historic case that said women have a constitutional right to an abortion! Marshall, like most of America, was incredulous.

The hearings concluded on September 20, with Thomas still an enigma to the committee and the nation, and it seemed to his opponents that there was no way to block his confirmation.

But another scenario was being played out in secret, according to *Congressional Quarterly* magazine. It said that the Alliance for Justice, a liberal group that had led the fight to block Bork from a Supreme Court seat, had received a tip in August that one of Thomas's former employees had alleged that Thomas had harassed her sexually. This tip was passed to Senate staffers, who contacted the alleged victim, University of Oklahoma law professor Anita Hill. James J. Brudney, an aide to Senator Howard Metzenbaum of Ohio, listened to Hill's charges and relayed them to Metzenbaum, who passed them along to the full Judiciary Committee staff, which was controlled by Senator Joseph Biden, a Delaware Democrat.

After an internal Judiciary Committee war in which Republicans Strom Thurmond, Marshall's longtime nemesis; Orrin Hatch, Mr. Unctuous of Utah; and Arlen Specter of Pennsylvania did all they could to protect Thomas, the committee decided to hold hearings into Hill's charges of sexual harassment. This produced startling, galvanizing testimony of a nature never before seen and heard on American television.

Hill said that while in Thomas's office he told her that he had found pubic hairs on his Coke can, and implied that he was an expert at cunnilingus. She said he boasted to her of his sexual prowess and the size of his penis, and suggested she ought to see porno movies, especially one featuring "Long Dong Silver," a male freak who, as legend has it, had a penis so long he could tie it into a knot. Most humiliating, she said, was Thomas's discussing with her "pornography involving these women with large breasts who engaged in a variety of sex with different people or animals."

Hill testified that Thomas liked to discuss with her "specific sex acts and frequency of sex," which she took as an invitation for her to have sex with him.

Senator Specter was the prime inquisitioner, who tried to shake Hill's story. He implied in many ways that there was something irrational, queer, and scheming about the accuser. Anita Hill stood up to him so brilliantly that a nation glued to its TV sets knew that only Thomas could save himself.

The nominee was also brilliant, first in disarming the committee by declaring "unequivocally, uncategorically, that I deny each and all allegations against me today that suggested in any way that I had conversations of a sexual nature or about pornographic material with Anita Hill, that I ever attempted to date her, that I ever had any personal sexual interest in her, or that I in any way ever harassed her."

Thomas then intimidated the committee with a declaration that he would not discuss his personal life. This meant that no senator was to ask him if he ever rented pornographic movies, especially ones featuring Long Dong Silver, or films featuring big-breasted women engaging in sex acts with animals. It was striking that no senator, not even a Democrat, dared to ask Thomas about his movie-watching habits.

That critical evening of October 11 Thomas went on the attack, saying:

> I think that this hearing today is a travesty. I think that it is disgusting. I think that this hearing should never occur in America. This is a case in which this sleaze, this dirt, was searched for by staffers of members of this committee, was then leaked to the media, and this committee and this body validated it and displayed it at prime time over our entire nation.
>
> How would any member on this committee, any person in this room or any person in this country like sleaze said about him or her in this fashion? Or this dirt dredged up and this gossip and these lies displayed in this manner, how would any person like it?
>
> The Supreme Court is not worth it. No job is worth it. I am not here for that. I am here for my name, my family, my life and my integrity. I think something is dreadfully wrong with this country when any person, any person in this free country, would be subjected to this.
>
> And from my standpoint, as a black American, it is a high-tech lynching for uppity blacks who in any way deign to think for themselves, to do for themselves, to have different ideas, and it is a message that unless you kowtow to an old order, this is what will happen to you. You will be lynched, destroyed, caricatured by a committee of the U.S. Senate rather than hung from a tree.

What a bitter twist of fate. This black man who had, in hustling the favors of Bush and the right-wingers who currently controlled

America, and who had disparaged and ridiculed Thurgood Marshall, Walter White, James Weldon Johnson, Roy Wilkins, and others who wiped out lynching, was now crying "lynching" to justify his confirmation. This child of Georgia poverty who had, in modest success, exhorted blacks never to fall back on cries of "racism," was shouting "racist lynching" in the most galling of ways.

Black Americans who considered Thomas a consummate con man knew that they were right.

But the key senators on the Judiciary Committee, Dennis DeConcini and Specter, were loath to risk being called "high-tech lynchers."

On September 27, in a 7 to 7 vote on party lines, except for Democrat DeConcini of Arizona supporting Thomas, the committee failed to recommend the confirmation of Thomas. Normally, this tie vote would have been the end of the line, because no Supreme Court nominee had been seated since the 1950s without a favorable vote in the Judiciary Committee. But Biden allowed the Thomas nomination to go to the full floor. There it would not be a party-line vote. The "support a local boy" syndrome was at work. More powerful was the fact that black votes had given Senate seats to southern Democrats John B. Breaux of Louisiana, Wyche Fowler, Jr., of Georgia, Richard C. Shelby of Alabama, and Bennett Johnston of Louisiana; and that these men believed polls indicating that their black constituents wanted Thomas confirmed. Senator Sam Nunn of Georgia, like Fowler, didn't have the guts to stand against a black Georgian, however obnoxious he might be. Then there was Charles S. Robb of Virginia, who himself was agonizing over charges of sexual misconduct, and who voted for another suffering "soul brother." There is no logic to explain why David Boren of Oklahoma, Jim Exon of Nebraska, and Alan Dixon of Illinois voted for Thomas. It is noteworthy that Illinois voters promptly dumped Dixon.

Only two Republicans dared to cross Bush and vote to reject Thomas — James M. Jeffords of Vermont and Bob Packwood of Oregon. Nancy Kassebaum of Kansas was under great pressure to vote against Thomas; the other female senator, Barbara Mikulski, the Maryland Democrat, did vote against him. Kassebaum put party loyalty first. "Some women suggest that I should judge this nomination not as a senator but as a woman," she said. "I reject that. Throughout my years here I have taken pride in the fact that I am a U.S. senator, not a 'woman senator.' "

These sordid Senate hearings taught Americans a lot. They revealed the confusions in black America that Marshall had spent half a century trying to erase — his rush to Denison, Texas, to stop blacks from swallowing "separate but equal," his constant decrying of black hustlers who were selling out the most basic of black aspirations for jobs of no power and no ultimate consequence in the American social equation.

The hearings enabled women and minorities to see Senator Alan Simpson, the Wyoming Republican, at his eloquent worst — which was incredibly bad. The cameras prodded him into warning Anita Hill that if she detailed charges of sexual harassment against Thomas she would be "caught in the maw," that her career would be ruined, her family disgraced.

Every woman ever harassed sexually, or raped, has known the possible humiliating and costly consequences of making public charges, but to have a senator on the Judiciary Committee lay this reality out as a threat was shocking and dismaying to millions of Americans, female and male.

Then there was the shameful performance of Specter, who faced re-election and clearly was trying to regain the support of Republican right-wingers in Pennsylvania. He showboated, telling Professor Hill that "this is not an adversarial proceeding," and then rushed to call her a "perjurer."

The Hill appearance provoked most members of the Judiciary Committee to behave like sexist asses, who rushed to initiate a stupid, then half-abandoned Senate probe to try to find out who leaked the existence of the Hill charges that turned the Thomas hearings into such an agonizing test of their characters.

On October 15, 1991, after one of the wildest television spectacles, one of the nastiest plunges into sexual prurience in the nation's history — at least up till the William Kennedy Smith Palm Beach rape trial — the Senate voted 52 to 48 to confirm Thomas. This was the closest Supreme Court confirmation in more than a century, and the second closest ever.

The reaction to Thomas's confirmation was divided about as closely as the Senate vote. President Bush said that Thomas demonstrated that "he is a man of honesty, dedication and commitment to the Constitution and the rule of law." Thomas's chief sponsor in the Senate, Senator John Danforth of Missouri, a Republican, predicted, "Clarence Thomas is going to surprise a lot of people. He is going to be the people's justice."

On the other side, Democratic senator Harry Reid of Nevada, who had pledged to vote for Thomas before the hearings but reversed himself in the final showdown, explained, "From a political standpoint I badly wanted to vote for Clarence Thomas. However, my conscience wouldn't let me do it. I thought she [Anita Hill] was telling the truth." Democratic senator Robert C. Byrd of West Virginia said that he had written a speech supporting Thomas, but changed his mind after seeing Hill, "who did not flinch, who showed no nervousness, who spoke calmly throughout."

The gut-wrenching internal tug-of-war that many senators experienced was reflected by Kassebaum. While voting for Thomas, she acknowledged that he would "live under a cloud of suspicion he can never fully escape."

Two of the nation's most influential newspapers responded to the final vote with let's-get-on-with-business editorials. The *Washington Post* said, "[Thomas's] contributions can only be enhanced if it turns out that his reluctance to be specific about his judicial thinking during his confirmation hearings reflects a determination to think through anew the questions that come to him on the court." The *New York Times* expressed hope that "everyone involved in this brutal divisive battle will work toward restoring comity and good will."

Political division was reflected by men and women in the street. *Washington Post* reporters who spoke with local residents after the final Senate vote found "some visibly disgusted and outraged. Others . . . pleased and relieved."

If public and official opinion was split about Thomas himself, there was unanimity on two related issues: women's rights emerged as a winner, the confirmation process a loser.

In an open letter to Anita Hill on its editorial page, the *New York Times* said, "You simply spoke the truth as you saw it, and in so doing, exposed a dark subject whose power all women know and countless men have begun to grasp. For bearing witness to that, what you have earned is their thanks."

No such appreciation was heard from any quarter for the confirmation process. President Bush termed the hearings "a messy situation," adding, "I was troubled thinking of my little grandchildren, hearing some of the specific sexual allegations." Bush only heard testimony about pubic hairs on Coke cans. The issue of justice eluded him. Several senators called the procedure "flawed" and "perverted." Several, along with historians, law professors, and others, urged that the process be changed. There had been too much personal posturing by Biden, Specter, Hatch. A bunch of old white men acted as if they had no idea what sexual harassment was all about.

Knowing Marshall and his wife, Cissy, as well as I did, I could surmise that they found ironic, though unwelcome, satisfaction in the grilling of Thomas on his "nonviews" regarding *Roe,* and his confrontation with Anita Hill. Marshall would surely see that that sordid Senate episode was doing more for women's rights than all the arguments he had made, the tirades he had uttered in the conference room, the dissents that had sometimes become splenetic. The Thomas hearings had awakened the women of America, had made them stand up for the rights that he had defended judicially for a quarter century. Anita Hill had become a catalyst for changing America in areas that were dear to him.

As Thurgood and Cissy watched, with most of America, the lurid, dismaying confirmation hearings, they could not imagine how far their impact would reach. Bush's insistence on putting Thomas in his seat created the political "year of the woman." All of a sudden, ten women Democrats and one female Republican were nominated to run for seats in the U.S. Senate, where only two out of one hundred members were women. One hundred and six women campaigned for election to the House of Representatives. In November 1992 Carol Moseley Braun of Illinois was elected as the first black woman ever in the United States Senate. California made history by electing two women — Dianne Feinstein and Barbara Boxer — to represent that state in the Senate. We now have six women in the Senate, triple the highest number ever. Virginia elected its first woman to the House of Representatives. "Womanpower," thanks to Anita Hill, has become a critical part of a sea change in American politics.

America was wrought up over the issue of abortion in ways that Marshall could not have hoped for before.

I had at first assumed that Marshall would consider the Thomas hearings, the result, the fallout, part of a great American tragedy. He had in one moment of sudden candor said, when the vote confirming Thomas was final, "We've gone from chicken salad to chicken shit." But by the summer of 1992 it was clear that the overall results included some mixed blessings.

No Supreme Court justice had ever taken office under such sordid, humiliating circumstances. Hundreds of cartoonists portrayed Thomas as a sex maniac, a porno plague who would lie on the floor of the Supreme Court conference room and look up the robe of Justice O'Connor. The question arose as to whether a black justice so humiliated could ever have any moral force for liberty and justice on a Court that was sinking into the depths of harshly insensitive conservatism. The answer was clear that this strange black man,

Thomas, had no desire or intention of influencing the Court in the ways of Thurgood Marshall.

Still, millions of Americans, including powerful members of the judiciary, hoped and prayed that once secure in a lifetime post on the Supreme Court, Thomas would remember the racial insults and deprivations of his Georgia beginnings, would understand the sufferings and dreams of his sister and other blacks working at poverty wages, would ask why his young black brothers get arrested and imprisoned in such disproportion in America, and say to the white far right: "Gotcha, didn't I?"

An eminent black federal senior judge, A. Leon Higginbotham, Jr., of the Third Circuit Court of Appeals in Philadelphia, took the extraordinary step of writing Thomas "An Open Letter . . . from a Federal Judicial Colleague," urging him to let his roots temper his rulings.

This letter by Higginbotham, sixty-four, to Thomas, forty-four, is emotional, sometimes angry, often condescending, but it is worth quoting at some length for those who seek to understand the world of Thurgood Marshall. On November 29, 1991, Higginbotham wrote:

Dear Justice Thomas:

At first I thought that I should write you privately — the way one normally corresponds with a colleague or friend. I still feel ambivalent about making this letter public but I do so because your appointment is profoundly important to this country and the world, and because all Americans need to understand the issues you will face. . . .

. . . You can become an exemplar of fairness and the rational interpretation of the Constitution, or you can become an archetype of inequality and the retrogressive evaluation of human rights. The choice as to whether you will build a decisional record of true greatness or of mere mediocrity is yours. . . . You must reflect more deeply on legal history than you ever have before. You are no longer privileged to offer flashy one-liners to delight the conservative establishment. . . .

During the time when civil rights organizations were challenging the Reagan administration, I was frankly dismayed by some of your responses to and denigrations of these organizations. . . . If that is still your assessment of these civil rights organizations or their leaders, I suggest, Justice Thomas, that you should ask yourself every day what would have happened to you if there had never been a Charles Hamilton Houston, a William Henry Hastie, a Thurgood Marshall, and that small cadre of other lawyers associated with them who laid the groundwork for success in the twentieth-century racial civil rights cases? . . . If there had never been an effective NAACP, isn't it highly probable that you might still be in Pin Point, Georgia, working as a laborer as some of your relatives did for decades? . . .

In my lifetime, I have seen African Americans denied the right to vote, the opportunities to a proper education, to work and to live where they choose. I have seen and *known* racial segregation and discrimination. But I have also seen the decision in *Brown* rendered. I have seen the first African American sit on the Supreme Court. And I have seen brave and courageous people, black and white, give their lives for the civil rights cause. . . . I wonder whether their magnificent achievements are in jeopardy. I wonder whether (and how far) the majority of the Supreme Court will continue to retreat from protecting the rights of the poor, women, the disadvantaged, minorities, and the powerless. And if, tragically, a majority of the court continues to retreat, I wonder whether you, Justice Thomas, an African American, will be part of that majority.

No one would be happier than I if the record you will establish on the Supreme Court in years to come demonstrates that my apprehensions were unfounded. You were born into injustice, tempered by the hard reality of what it means to be poor and black in America, and especially to be poor because you are black. You have found a door newly cracked open and you have escaped. I trust that you shall not forget that many who preceded you and many who follow you have found, and will find, the door of equal opportunity slammed in their faces through no fault of their own. And I also know that time and the tides of history often call out of men and women qualities that even they did not know lay within them. And so, with hope to balance my apprehensions, I wish you well as a thoughtful and worthy successor to Justice Marshall in the ever ongoing struggle to assure equal justice under law for all persons.

Sincerely,
A. Leon Higginbotham, Jr.

Thomas telephoned Higginbotham upon receipt of the letter for what each described only as an "amicable" conversation. But black conservatives assailed Higginbotham for "moral conceit" and "a long, ugly, cheap attack." Conservative legal activist Clint Bolick, the Arch Parsons contact who passed word to Bush that Hooks would not "rush to judgment," told the *Washington Post* that he "found the entire [Higginbotham] article extremely patronizing."

At the bottom of the fallout is the fact that Higginbotham's letter had no noticeable influence on Thomas, whose first votes as a justice made it clear that he was everything Marshall, Higginbotham, and millions of other Americans feared he would be — and much worse.

First it became clear that Thomas had lied his way into confirmation.

A crucial issue during confirmation hearings was whether Thomas, who benefited from an affirmative action (in fact, quota) program at Yale Law School would vote to outlaw such programs for minorities and women who now needed them so desperately. Thomas gave the Senate Judiciary Committee a dose of double-talk, leaving every senator in doubt about how he would rule on affirmative action.

Then *Legal Times,* a weekly newspaper in Washington, D.C., published a story asserting that Thomas already had written the majority opinion in a 2 to 1 decision of the Court of Appeals for the District of Columbia declaring that it was unconstitutional for the Federal Communications Commission to give women preferences in the awarding of some broadcast licenses. *Legal Times* suggested that the release of this opinion was being held up to conceal Thomas's real views about affirmative action.

Some disturbed Senate supporters of Thomas asked him pointblank if the *Legal Times* story was true. "No," Thomas replied. The decision, in *Lamprecht v. FCC,* was released after confirmation, showing that Thomas had written exactly what *Legal Times* said.

More nauseating than this was Thomas's deceitful testimony about the rights of the accused and the constitutional protections of criminals. Time and again during the hearings he faked great compassion for young men ensnared in the criminal justice system. He told, with Hollywood emotion, how he had looked out his window at prisoners arriving in vans and said to himself, "There but for the grace of God, go I."

Once seated on the Court, Thomas got a chance to apply a little of the grace of God and the justice of the Eighth Amendment to Louisiana prisoner Keith Hudson, who was shackled and beaten by two guards who split his lip, loosened his teeth, and broke his dental plate. Justice Sandra Day O'Connor and six other justices concluded that this was cruel and unusual punishment, which the Eighth Amendment forbids.

Thomas wrote a dissent suggesting that Hudson's complaint was akin to gripes about prison food, and that the Court majority was stretching the scope of the Bill of Rights. Confirmation "compassion" had turned to cruelty.

A major fear expressed during confirmation hearings was that this momentarily enigmatic black man would help to make the Supreme Court an instrument for wiping out the major civil rights gains Marshall had shepherded to reality during the previous forty years. Sure enough, when some southern whites finagled to strip power away from black elected officials, the Justice Department said the whites had violated the Voting Rights Act. But Thomas and a Court majority ruled that rooking the black officials was constitutional.

A few who voted to confirm Thomas began to see the ever-growing damage that they had done. But they watched knowing that their decisions were, for all practical purposes, irreversible.

Thomas's vote in the case of the beating of prisoner Keith Hudson provoked the *New York Times* to assail him editorially, in a headline, as "THE YOUNGEST, CRUELEST JUSTICE." The *Times* called Thomas's dissent a "crashing disappointment" because "He might well serve until the year 2030 or beyond . . . he could attract enough support from future appointees to move the Court still further to the right."

Perhaps the ten Democrats, Arlen Specter, Nancy Kassebaum, and others who voted for Thomas out of political cowardice, cynicism, or bad judgment are finding that for all Americans the "chicken salad" days of Thurgood Marshall are over, and the chicken shit has come home to roost.

CHAPTER TWENTY-FOUR

MEASURING MARSHALL WITHOUT SENTIMENT

ONE ADMIRER of Thurgood Marshall has written that "he used the Constitution the way Moses used the Ten Commandments." Detractors have called Marshall a "baby killer," a "coddler of criminals" who "almost destroyed the country." Some people may idolize him, while others despise him, but there is no disagreement on the fact that Marshall had a profound effect upon the legal and social freedoms of the people of America and the world.

If you could get dead men to talk, voices from the grave of the University of Maryland's Curley Byrd; of the great constitutional lawyer John W. Davis; of the judges who heard *Briggs v. Elliott* in 1951, Parker, Timmerman, and Waring, would say that Marshall was an unusual lawyer, in style and results, and was an unforgettable force. If those still living would speak the truth — Thurmond and Wallace, Nixon and Agnew, Reagan and Bush — they would acknowledge that Marshall as lawyer, judge, and human being made America infinitely better for everyone. The white soda fountain clerk and the little black girl who wants to drink a Coca-Cola are both liberated by laws saying that people who own that soda fountain may not stigmatize groups of Americans by declaring them unfit to sit and sip a soda pop. Politics is fairer for all Americans when those who already have money and power are forbidden to seize more by making race, a poll tax, the ownership of property, a condition of enfranchisement.

There are thousands of encomiums citing Marshall as the protector of the poor and the other "outcasts" of America of every color and origin. Some are in the earlier pages of this book. But I am compelled to look beyond the praise, past the insults from his foes, and deliver an unsentimental summation regarding his achievements. Most of his great victories seem enduring, many are eroding under the assaults of virulent conservatism, on and off the Supreme Court, and a few of his victories appear to have been Pyrrhic. Let us assess, important issue by issue, the current state of his litigations and his judicial decisions:

POLITICAL POWER FOR NONWHITES

You talk to Marshall and, depending on the day and his mood, he might tell you that the most important thing he did was to break up the white primaries of South Carolina, and to win, in *Smith v. Allwright*, the Texas case that enfranchised black people. He believed fervently in the power of the ballot.

Marshall would watch "militants" such as Stokely Carmichael and Rap Brown crying "BLACK POWER" in the 1960s, but he knew that black votes were more powerful than any hoodlum's ability to torch a business, especially if that business belonged to a black person. In 1969, he told a predominantly black audience at Dillard University in New Orleans, "Anarchy is anarchy, and it makes no difference who practices it. It is bad, it is punishable, and it ought to be punished."

Blacks applauded vigorously when Marshall said, "You can't use color as an excuse for not doing what you should be doing. Race is not an excuse for not keeping up your home properly, nor is race an excuse for not keeping your children in school, even though they may still be segregated."

He went on to assail the black separatists, the advocates of intellectual segregation in which the minds of black children would be focused primarily on "African culture."

"You are not going to compete in the world," he warned, "until you have training exactly like everyone else, and hopefully better. Because when you're a Negro you've got to be better."

Marshall insisted that the ballot would deliver more "black power" than the cries of "Burn, baby, burn."

Marshall stated that he was not opposed to all public protests, but he insisted that the rule of law had to prevail in the end. It rankled him that the demonstrators and rioters always got more press than he and his legal team did.

When JFK and Bobby Kennedy got a lot of election votes — even media credit — for getting Dr. King out of the Albany, Georgia, jail, Marshall said sarcastically: "They [the media] seem to think everybody got him out but the lawyers."

When the media were glorifying the Montgomery bus boycott, Marshall noted to me that it finally took a Supreme Court decision to get blacks to the front of the bus.

"All that walking for nothing," Marshall said to me. "They might as well have waited for the Court decision."

King's sudden super-black-leader status seemed to arouse enough jealousy and resentment in Marshall to blind him to the reality that the sacrificial marching in Montgomery did a lot to turn American public opinion against Jim Crow in transportation, and that the boycott and the press it got probably influenced the Supreme Court to declare Montgomery's segregation laws unconstitutional. Marshall did not seem to accept the likelihood that King's speeches, the sit-ins and boycotts, influenced Congress to pass the 1964 Public Accommodations Act.

But Marshall's litigation clearly opened the door to the political power that Congress secured by passing the Voting Rights Act of 1965. Some eight thousand black elected officials serve as governor of Virginia, mayors of New York, Los Angeles, Detroit, New Orleans, Atlanta, and other great cities of America. Blacks are on school boards, city councils, wearing the badges of sheriffs — all places of power that no black could aspire to before *Smith v. Allwright.*

Yet, Marshall's victory is far from complete. Nixon, Reagan, and Bush rendered "black political power" a bit hollow when they played the "race card" in ways that provoked whites, especially white southern males, to rush to the polls to neutralize the new masses of black voters.

EDUCATION

If you catch Marshall in a different mood, on another day, he might cite *Brown,* the historic public school segregation case, and *Murray, Gaines, Sipuel, McLaurin,* and *Sweatt,* the college cases, including Autherine Lucy's, as the greatest achievements of his life.

Getting Donald Murray into the University of Maryland and Ada Sipuel Fisher into the University of Oklahoma were legal achievements of enduring value. It is impossible to overstate the importance of making college and professional studies available to blacks in their home states. Marshall opened doors here that no bigots have been able to close completely.

Marshall found a powerful ally in this area. President Johnson pushed through Congress the Federal Aid to Higher Education Act of 1965, making college degrees and advanced training available to millions of Americans, black, white, or whatever. Ronald Reagan tried to undercut this act by reducing the money available to poor, though brilliant, youngsters; he and Bush put racism back into the college picture by turning the civil rights laws upside down and declaring that scholarship programs specifically reserved as remedies of injustice for black students are unconstitutional "discrimination against whites."

I have rarely been more disillusioned than to see Secretary of Education Lamar Alexander become putty in the hands of Bush and his political advisers and of Education Department racists whose goals were not to educate all Americans, but to ensure the re-election of Bush.

As for education at elementary and secondary school levels, *Brown II* also has to be a rock in Justice Marshall's craw. "All deliberate speed" turned out to be a snail that sometimes crawled backward. White America adopted Nixon's harsh assaults on "forced busing." White flight to suburban areas made real integration impossible in most metropolitan areas. The high tribunal, to Marshall's dismay, ruled against desegregation of schools across city-suburban boundaries. Federal courts turned blind eyes at the gerrymandering of school districts, devious decisions as to where to build new schools, and other gimmicks designed to keep blacks in predominantly black schools, while whites attended schools with overwhelming white populations. As in the Oklahoma City case, some judges simply gave up on old, unenforced desegregation decrees.

Marshall surely sits in lonely anger now — which he would deny publicly — remembering Kenneth Clark's black and white dolls that were so important to the judges who heard the Topeka case, and so troublesome to the judges in South Carolina who insisted that integration held the greater seed of peril — dolls so dominating in the 1954 *Brown* decision. Marshall reminisces every day he sits in his Supreme Court retirement office about his real-world strategy of trying to convince leaders of our system of jurisprudence and criminal justice that *people, human beings,* are involved. That *little boys and girls* are the victims of racial hatred and political cowardice and indifference. That America as a nation is in decline because white people would not accept fully his demands that educational opportunities be extended without references to race, color, or economic status.

As he remembers, Marshall surely sees how cruelly black school children are still being stigmatized. The injury that Marshall saw as his great foe on that train to Charleston, South Carolina, in 1951 is being inflicted in 1993 in the white flight through which Caucasian parents say, "We don't want our children close to dangerous black youngsters." *Stigmatic injury* is at the heart of resegregation in so many school districts. It is the arouser of the rage among the black youths of America that thrusts them into crime, violent revenge, abandonment of hope for success, and has made so many of them the occupants of bulging prisons — or funeral homes and grave-yards.

Even when it became obvious that America was losing its economic competitiveness with Japan, Germany, Taiwan, because we were not educating properly a third of America's children — the black, the brown, the very poor whites — George Bush refused to give any budget priority to financing and improving the public schools. He became a Johnny-one-note in his crusade for vouchers that would give federal public funds to parents who wanted the "choice" of sending their children to private or parochial schools. Aside from any issues of a constitutional requirement for the separation of church and state, Bush steadfastly refused to face the certain result that federal vouchers would lure the best, least troublesome youngsters away from public schools and virtually destroy public education as we have always known it in America.

Bush's bait of vouchers lit up every greedy eye of almost every "entrepreneur" working the education beat. Tennessean Chris Whittle conjured up an education-for-profit scheme called the Edison Project, which promised that if parents, the federal government, or someone put up $5,500 per pupil it would prove that Whittle's pay-and-learn schools could outperform the public schools. Many people were stunned when Whittle induced Benno C. Schmidt, Jr., to leave the presidency of Yale University to run the Edison Project.

The Whittle-Schmidt scheme is not a lurch into nation-saving educational philanthropy. It is a money-grubbing operation. The tragedy is that in this nation there still are too few strong voices in behalf of the children of America's shamefully large underclass — children who, even with a Bush voucher, will not be able to attend one of the Whittle-Schmidt schools. We remain a society that is caught up wretchedly in race politics and naked profiteering regarding education.

Meanwhile, as this ploy to raid the treasury for private schools was unfolding, a dismaying little news dispatch was being sent from

Topeka. Forty-two years after Oliver Brown sued to get his daughter Linda into the "white" school near their home, blacks had filed another lawsuit asserting that thirty-eight years after the Supreme Court sided with black children in *Brown I*, the city of Topeka still had not desegregated its schools.

The "polite" failures to bend to the law in Topeka and many other cities arose from the knowledge of most of the white power structure that numbers of federal judges had tired of the struggle and decided "To hell with it." Some judges began to lose the faith when Marshall and his colleagues scored some presumably "great" school-busing decrees that turned out to be public opinion disasters. It wasn't just that white parents objected to having their children bused to something other than the neighborhood school; many black parents hated such an inconvenience, especially if busing took their children into the lair of violent white bigots, as in South Boston and Pontiac, Michigan.

The *Brown* decisions and decrees, and the myriad lawsuits that followed, add up to disappointment, perhaps even bitterness, for Marshall, who found that the Constitution could be changed from a Moses-like stone tablet into a marshmallow.

TRANSPORTATION AND PUBLIC ACCOMMODATIONS

This area is one in which Marshall's contribution to justice and tranquility has been most enduring. Efforts have been made to turn the clock back on civil rights gains in most areas, but there has been no meaningful movement to resegregate the trains and buses, or the waiting rooms and their toilets, restaurants, or water fountains.

It would be unthinkable in most communities for someone to advocate a return to Jim Crow in hotels, theaters, and other public facilities. Marshall freed nonwhites from egregious humiliations, and lifted a badge of shame off the hearts of the white majority, in the field of public accommodations.

Americans, black and white, take these changed social circumstances for granted, with most having no understanding whatsoever of the bravery and perseverance Marshall and his friends showed in delivering dignity to nonwhites who had been insulted in public places for generations. Most blacks of this generation also do not know of the courage millions of white Americans and blacks inside the vortex of the racial storms once showed in standing up against axe-handle-wielding Lester Maddox of Georgia, or Orval Faubus,

George Wallace, and the other "official" perpetrators and defenders of Jim Crow in its most egregious forms.

HOUSING

Meanwhile, real progress in teaching America's children to study, to dream, to build with each other, was made virtually impossible by the fact that the nation never accepted the moral imperatives flowing from *Shelley v. Kraemer* and other restrictive-covenant cases, which said agreements between white sellers and buyers that the property would never be sold or transferred to a black person, a Jew, or whomever, could not be enforced by an American court. Marshall now sits in his integrated Virginia community of Lake Barcroft knowing that restrictive housing barriers are alive and virulent in the hearts and minds of millions of Americans who say "they" can never reside in "our" neighborhood. He, as one of the most powerful men in the land, found white eyebrows raised and black separatists complaining when he bought his home in the till-then-all-white Lake Barcroft area. In Bensonhurst and Brahmin Boston, in Iowa and Illinois, barriers to blacks' buying homes in white areas are still as strong as the Berlin Wall ever was.

Fifty years after Marshall investigated the terrible riots in Detroit, today the "Motor City" is still supercharged with racial hostility and, in terms of housing, one of the most segregated metropolitan areas in this nation.

Not all of Marshall's disappointments are the result of white resistance. He *won* the debate in favor of integration at the NAACP state conference in Denison, Texas. Walter White *won* the debate with Du Bois in favor of integration. But that did not stop the eruption of a "black separatism" movement in the 1960s, or attacks on integration in 1991 by some black "new Republicans," such as journalist Tony Brown. Marshall has long had to live with the black schizophrenia that grew out of the same kind of disillusionment that the justice himself manifested when he retired — the realization that millions of whites will *never* accept blacks as neighbors or social equals.

AFFIRMATIVE ACTION

It was always clear that, for Marshall, the school desegregation, college and professional education, and voting rights cases were but means to an end: the promotion of affirmative steps to have black scholars, scientists, teachers, bricklayers, carpenters considered a normal part of American life. But Marshall knew that in police and fire departments, in the labor unions, in faculty councils, in corporate boardrooms, and in almost every school district in the land, racial discrimination was rampant and entrenched. Few whites enjoying power were willing to risk losing any of it by violating South Carolina senator Hammond's "mudsill" judgment that every society had to have people at the bottom, doing the dirty, distasteful, unremunerative work. Marshall didn't know many whites who would echo Hammond by saying *publicly*, "We use them for our purpose and we call them slaves." But he knew they were out there, pulling the levers of power in all its forms.

Much of America was saying of blacks who had gained skills and education, "They are no longer slaves, but we have no purposes that allow *us* to use *them* to their full potential."

The night of June 28, 1991, Marshall would sit watching the fireflies and lightning bugs spark pictures on his Lake Barcroft, and think about how profoundly he had lost the affirmative action issue to Reagan and Bush. Marshall knew that America had become a different place from the days when Dr. King said, "I have a dream," and dream breakers such as Reagan and Bush were saying, "Your dream is based on a quota."

But Marshall could not dwell on the contributions to rising racism in America by Reagan and Bush until he got through anguishing over the "civil rights massacre of 1989" within his own Supreme Court. The Court's decision in *City of Richmond v. J. A. Croson Company* had been a lasting cut, an ideological abrasion that would forever scar his heart.

Richmond had set aside 30 percent in economic terms of city construction contracts for minority firms, this a mere recognition of the truth that a city that was by this time more than 50 percent black had a brazen record of denying public — and private — business to black entrepreneurs. The city finally was trying to remedy an obvious age-old injustice. A white company, J. A. Croson, said the set-asides discriminated unconstitutionally against whites. Marshall had been crestfallen when Justice O'Connor got a majority of the Court to say that the city had not "identified" any specific discrimination against blacks in Richmond's construction industry, and thus the city had failed to demonstrate a "compelling interest" in justifying a drastic race-based remedy.

"While there is no doubt that the sorry history of both private and public discrimination in this country has contributed to a lack of opportunities for black entrepreneurs," O'Connor continued, "this observation, standing alone, cannot justify a rigid racial quota in the awarding of public contracts in Richmond, Virginia."

This outraged Marshall, and warned him of many antiminority legalistic contortions that were to come. The city of Richmond *knew* that it had discriminated against black contractors. It had tried to remedy myriad biases going back to pre–Civil War days. But here was a majority of the Court saying Richmond could not redress its old sins, no matter how much the damage done to black businessmen and children today — not unless Richmond could cite a specific egregious discrimination against a specific black businessman.

Marshall had celebrated earlier affirmative action decisions (*Fullilove,* even *Bakke*). But his victories in this area were being wiped away rapidly.

The Supreme Court decided at least five other cases in 1989 that won it the title of civil rights destroyer.

Marshall refused to think it possible, but 1990 and 1991 became worse in terms of the Court eroding the legal rights and destroying the aspirations of black people. Marshall somehow recovered from his shock over what he considered High Court betrayals, and fought doggedly to stanch the sentiment for "white Americans first" that was rising across the land.

The Court seemed to be the betrayer at first, because Marshall was a part of it, but upon reflection he knew that it was the executive branch that had poisoned the well from which all America drank, spreading racial sickness throughout the legislative and judicial branches.

In the closing days of Congress in 1990, the lawmakers passed a civil rights bill designed to reverse Supreme Court decisions that narrowed absurdly the remedies minorities and women could get when they felt victimized by discrimination. Bush vetoed this measure, calling it a "quota bill." The president had himself followed Agnew and Reagan and made "quota" a dirty word in the minds of white males, and then exploited the term to the delight of the far right of the Republican party.

One of those Bush was trying to please, and rescue politically, was one of the most conscienceless dream breakers in American history, Senator Jesse Helms. This North Carolina Republican was fighting off an incredibly powerful challenge from a black politician from Charlotte, Democrat Harvey Gantt, who was leading in some polls. Inspired by Bush, Helms saturated North Carolina with commercials showing two white hands crumpling a letter of rejection for a job that the announcer said had been given to a less-qualified black person, or some other minority or woman.

Helms's advertising tirades about "reverse discrimination" turned the tide and got him six more years in the U.S. Senate. Bush became more strident in his assaults on the straw man he called "unfair preferences" for minorities. The power of this poison was manifest in newsrooms, on college campuses, in factories — everywhere that a white male thought he could claim that someone else got a scholarship, a job, a promotion that belonged to him.

Marshall saw that Reagan, his Justice Department aides, and Bush had turned the civil rights laws of the 1960s upside down in their opposition to affirmative action. Here were laws that Congress passed to halt, reverse, remedy myriad atrocious discriminations against blacks, Hispanics, Asians, Native Americans, women — and Reagan and Bush had distorted and corrupted the civil rights laws to say that they forbade "discrimination" against long-privileged white people seeking jobs, scholarships, promotions.

Marshall's warning that a black snake will bite you as fast as a white one was given truth by the number of *nouveau noticeable* blacks who were speaking and writing against affirmative action.

Marshall had convinced the Warren Court that the stigmatic injury of state-enforced racial separation wounded black children permanently. But along had come Shelby Steele, a professor of English at San Jose State University in California, writing that "one of the most troubling effects of racial preferences for blacks is a kind of demoralization or . . . an enlargement of self-doubt. Under affirmative action the quality that earns us preferential treatment is implied inferiority."

How galling for Marshall and most of us who had had any role in the civil rights movement to see Steele and others, who would have been semislaves without the NAACP's lawsuits, pretending that they were the first superblacks who had survived on *merit*. Steele and a tiny black army of sycophants of Reagan and Bush wanted the world to believe that they could speak and write good English, eat daily from good jobs, because they were so morally and intellectually strong that they did not need, and could not afford the taint of, the barrier-breaking efforts of Marshall, White, Wilkins, King, Whitney Young, Mary McLeod Bethune — not to mention the victims of lynch mobs, and the Donald Murrays, Autherine Lucys, Ada Sipuels, Harry Briggses, who faced death in order to open up colleges for the Clarence Thomases, the Shelby Steeles and the other I-did-it-on-my-own "superblacks." Selling out by blacks suddenly was selling in white bookstores.

Despite Bush's embrace, the Steeles never got smooth sailing in white America, and surely no respect in that separate American black world. Roger Wilkins, a professor at James Mason University and nephew of Roy Wilkins, took umbrage at Steele's assertion that giving a black person a job under affirmative action is "implied inferiority."

Wilkins insisted that centuries of racism and discrimination, not "preferential treatment," are what had undermined the self-esteem of black Americans. Roger Wilkins had long understood and accepted the talk of Marshall, Kenneth Clark, and hundreds of non-black sociologists, psychologists, and psychiatrists about stigmatic injury. Roger Wilkins — and Marshall — knew that there was not a single black person in America who had not been injured by the stigma of slavery, of state-sanctioned Jim Crow, or by the Nixon-Reagan-Bush versions of racial insult and deprivation.

PRIVACY

Marshall was solicitor general in 1965 when the Supreme Court made a historic ruling in *Griswold v. Connecticut* that the state could not prohibit married couples from using birth control devices. A majority of the Court said that a "right to privacy" was implied in several amendments to the Constitution, and that this shielded citizens from state intrusions into bedrooms.

Marshall, whose father had taught him to be fiercely protective of his privacy rights, thought the Court had gotten its decision just right. It did not disturb Marshall in any way that millions of Americans wanted this right to privacy extended to a woman's right to choose an abortion. Once on the Supreme Court, he was delighted to join Blackmun in arguing that there were zones of privacy protected by the Bill of Rights. He voted with the majority in *Roe v. Wade* in declaring that a woman had a right to abort a pregnancy.

Marshall was soon to learn that privacy rights could vanish in a spasm of homophobia and fear of the spread of AIDS, the deadly disease that was just becoming known to much of the world. In August 1982, a practicing homosexual, Michael Hardwick, was arrested for committing sodomy in the bedroom of his home. Georgia had a law defining sodomy as "any sexual act involving the sex organs of one person and the mouth or anus of another."

Hardwick challenged the law, but a federal judge ruled that it did not violate his privacy. In 1983 the Eleventh Circuit Court of Appeals struck down the Georgia statute, declaring that homosexual activity is a private and intimate affair that is beyond state regulation. After hearing emotional arguments about morals and the threat of AIDS, Justice Byron White spoke for the majority of the Supreme Court in saying that it was "at best, 'facetious' to argue that any kind of private sexual conduct is constitutionally insulated from state proscription." Chief Justice Burger wrote a concurring opinion asserting that "to hold that the act of homosexual sodomy is somehow protected as a fundamental right would be to cast aside millennia of moral teaching." Rehnquist, Powell, and O'Connor made up the majority.

Blackmun was so outraged that he read long portions of his dissent from the bench:

"If [the right to privacy] means anything, it means that, before Georgia can prosecute its citizens for making choices about the most intimate aspects of their lives, it must do more than assert that the choice they have made is an abominable crime not fit to be named among Christians.

"We protect those rights not because they contribute, in some direct or material way, to the general public welfare, but because they form so central a part of an individual's life."

COERCED CONFESSIONS

Marshall had carried a little blot on his memory and a pain in his heart for almost fifty years because of his failure to win freedom for Lyons, the accused triple murderer in Hugo, Oklahoma. Yet, Marshall had won many cases in which the Fourteenth Amendment was declared an unbending barrier to the courtroom use of the forced confessions that were used so wantonly in the 1930s and 1940s to send minorities, poor whites, the uneducated, to prison or to death in the electric chair or a gas chamber.

Marshall began to believe that this was an area in which he could never again lose when, in 1936, in reversing a murder conviction based on the "confession" of a man with a hangman's noose already around his neck, Chief Justice Hughes spoke eloquently against "the chief inequity, the crowning infamy of the Star Chamber, and the Inquisition."

Despite the soul-wounding defeat in the *Lyons* case, Marshall could see that the nation was moving in ways he'd prayed and fought for to protect weak individuals accused of crimes from the anger, the "legal lynchings" perpetrated by the frightened rich, the timid politicians, and those who apparently never would understand the importance of the Bill of Rights, the post–Civil War amendments, and the rest of the Constitution.

In 1963, when he was no longer a civil rights advocate, but a court of appeals judge, Marshall could celebrate privately the Supreme Court's *Gideon v. Wainwright* decision that under the Sixth Amendment, every person accused of a serious crime had to be provided an attorney. He would later complain bitterly that many of the attorneys supplied were incompetent, but he reveled in the High Court's acceptance of the idea that in America people would not be railroaded to prison because they could not afford to defend themselves in trial rooms.

A year after *Gideon*, the Warren Court handed down *Escobedo v. Illinois,* holding that "any admission made by an arrested suspect was inadmissible as evidence if the suspect had been denied the opportunity to see his lawyer."

Then came the landmark decision *Miranda v. Arizona*, in June 1966, with Marshall telling friends joyously how much he agreed with the slim majority. *Miranda* laid down specific guidelines as to what law enforcement authorities could or could not do in trying to gain evidence for conviction. The Court said that once law officers had a suspect in custody and attempted to interrogate him, if the suspect "at any stage [indicates] that he wishes to consult with an attorney before speaking, there can be no questioning. Likewise, if the individual is alone and indicates in any manner that he does not wish to be interrogated, the police may not question him."

Marshall had many reasons to exult over the *Miranda* decision. It took America a quantum social and moral leap away from the Mississippi case where the defendant showed up in court with the marks of a hangman's noose on his neck, or the *Lyons* case in which the bones of murder victims were put in the defendant's lap, and he was taken to see the electric chair — all by way of extorting a "confession."

The *Miranda* decision outraged millions of law enforcement officials, and it became a major issue in every national political campaign thereafter. Nixon assailed the Supreme Court for giving criminals an advantage over law enforcement authorities.

But Nixon never was able to undermine *Miranda*, which lead to a zealous public awareness in all those movies and TV dramas in which cops had to read suspects their "Miranda rights." Reagan's attorney general, Edwin Meese, assailed *Miranda* as "an infamous decision," but he could not undo it.

But that is small consolation to a Thurgood Marshall who now, in lonely retirement, reflects upon the evidence that *Gideon, Escobedo, Miranda,* and all related Supreme Court decisions did not give full protection to those who get arrested just because they are blacks walking in a white neighborhood, the poor-of-dress who are automatically hassled by private security agents in high-falutin' shopping centers, or who cannot afford a first-rate lawyer — or who refuse to be meek young black males when they are hassled by cops, black or white, all carrying fear mixed with the authoritarian complex in a violent time when cops, too, have to worry about survival.

When Marshall sits of an evening at Lake Barcroft, he cannot possibly see triumph in the numbers of young black males who did not get protected by his rulings, and who are today the major residents of jails and prisons that are literally bursting at their seams — so much so that judges are saying, "Let some go before you put any more in."

It has got to wound Marshall when he sees that for all his efforts to protect the poor and the hated among America's accused, the Nixons, John Mitchells, Reagans and Meeses, Bushes and Thornburghs still managed to fill up the jails and prisons with blacks, Hispanics, the poor, the hopeless outcasts of this society.

We Americans hear a lot about how the United States lags behind other nations in health care coverage, infant mortality, industrial production, math and science test scores, and more.

Well, we have the number one spot in one area nailed down — though I doubt you'll hear anyone bragging about it. The U.S. is, far and away, the world's leading jailer. This is not a new title; we led last year, too. But we have increased that lead.

There were more than 1.1 million inmates in U.S. jails and prisons in 1990, according to the Sentencing Project, a private research and advocacy group. That is double the number we had in 1980 and triple the 1970 figure. It figures out to an incarceration rate of 455 people per 100,000 population.

That puts America well ahead of the number two jailer, South Africa, which has 311 inmates per 100,000 population. The U.S. incarceration rate is ten times higher than the rates of Japan, Sweden, Ireland, and the Netherlands, the Sentencing Project reports.

About half a million inmates, almost half the U.S. prison population, are black males. That is nearly five times the rate of black incarceration in South Africa, despite the troubles that arise out of that nation's apartheid policy. On any given day, almost one out of four black Americans aged twenty to twenty-nine is either in prison, on parole, or on probation.

No one, not even criminal justice experts, is certain about the cause of the astronomical incarceration rate in the U.S. One commonly cited factor is the extremely high rate of crime. Some 50,000 murders — 64 percent by guns — were reported over the last two years nationwide, and dozens of cities set homicide records. Another reason for our large prison population is that the American public has grown increasingly fed up with crime and has adopted a tougher attitude. As a result, we're seeing a higher percentage of convictions by prosecutors, tougher sentences imposed by judges and more laws that require mandatory sentences. A black youth is far more likely to be arrested than a white one for the same offense, far more likely to be convicted, given a longer sentence, and denied probation longer than his white counterpart.

Trouble is, this doesn't accomplish the goal that get-tough proponents hope for — a reduction in crime. While prison overcrowding grew last year, violent crime also rose. And so did violent alienation in Los Angeles and other cities.

Bulging jail cells create a financial burden. It costs about $20,000 to maintain a prisoner for a full year — which comes to more than $20 billion annually for the nation as a whole.

Imagine a society driven by anger and fear to spend $20,000 to lock up a stigmatized, neglected, abused member of this society when that society would not dream of spending $20,000 on education, job training, or any other productive program to make that individual a contributor to society!

Marshall had lost the battle in the sense that a public fearing crime beyond reason was tolerating the arrests of people because they "looked different," meaning "guilty of something." Many in the public were saying, "Take prisoners, but don't make me pay to feed them. Execute them!"

THE DEATH PENALTY

If Marshall felt himself betrayed, a loser, as the nation, with Court approval, incarcerated thousands and thousands more poor and minority people, he had to feel doubly wounded by the fact that the United States had embraced the electric chair, the gas chamber, and poison injections as magical cures for their problems of violence, rape, homicide in record-breaking numbers in some cities, and in grotesque serial murders in other places.

Marshall's seemingly flippant assertions that the death penalty was final, and that judges could not later say, "Oops! We made a mistake," were just his ways of delineating this issue before the American people. In truth, Marshall and Brennan held stubbornly to their conviction that "the death penalty is in all circumstances cruel and unusual punishment prohibited by the Eighth and Fourteenth amendments."

So certain was the joint view of Brennan and Marshall, in some minds, that "they don't even purport to judge the cases; they vote against the death penalty no matter what," complained George Smith, litigation director of the Washington Legal Foundation. "They've abdicated their judicial function and reduced it to a rubber stamp in death penalty cases."

Marshall was unperturbed by such criticism. It was in 1986, at the height of such criticism, that Marshall dared to exhort Second Circuit Court of Appeals lawyers and judges to give a fairer shake to those at risk of the death penalty. Marshall rejoiced that he had won a rare one, getting a majority of the Court to agree that an insane person could not be executed in the United States.

Marshall had at one time argued that American public opinion would never support capital punishment. He thought Americans saw the electric chair and the gas chamber as akin to the medieval practices in some countries of chopping off the hand of a pickpocket, or castrating or killing those who engaged in sex before marriage. Marshall knew that colleagues on the Court believed that imposing the death penalty, in whatever dreadful form, only increased the spirit of violence in America. They could cite statistics showing that capital punishment not only did not *deter* crime, but that it intensified the spirit of violence in America.

Yet, the most the Supreme Court would say in 1972, in *Furman v. Georgia,* was that capital punishment as practiced in America was so "arbitrary" and "capricious" in practice that it violated the "cruel and unusual punishment" clause of the Eighth Amendment.

Marshall did not see, or ignored, the fact that American public opinion regarding the death penalty was changing profoundly, and that, as so many times before, the Court would bend to public passions, or "th' illiction returns," and shift its rulings drastically.

Violent crimes in the U.S. had risen 126 percent between 1960 and 1970. Whereas Americans had opposed capital punishment by 47 to 42 percent in 1966, according to the Gallup Poll, they *favored* the death penalty by 65 to 28 percent in 1975.

Marshall railed against the death penalty till the day of his retirement, noticing along the way that two things were happening:

1. The numbers of homicides were still setting abominable records, and other violent crimes were forcing the building of more jails and prisons.

2. The increasing number of executions were thrilling blood-thirsty mobs in some places, but they did not deter people from committing capital crimes. In truth, every application of the death penalty somewhere seemed to encourage some vigilante, some gun for hire, to escalate the level of violence in America.

Surely no one in America read with greater passion than the just-retired Marshall the July 10, 1991, open letter that New Jersey's Democratic senator Bill Bradley wrote to President Bush. "There are still a lot of good white people here," Marshall said again. Bradley insisted that he was writing as a worried citizen, not as a Democrat or political candidate, a pledge he kept in refusing to run against Bush for the presidency in 1992. Now, and forever, the words of Bradley should be of paramount value to all Americans who really want a just and tranquil society.

An open letter to President Bush.

Dear Mr. President, in 1988 you used the Willie Horton ad to divide white and black voters and appeal to fear. Now, based on your remarks about the 1991 Civil Rights Bill, you have begun to do the same thing again. Mr. President, we implore you — don't go down that path again.

. . . When did you realize there was a difference between the lives of black people and the lives of white people in America? Where did you ever experience or see discrimination? How did you feel? What did you do?

. . . Mr. President, you say you're against discrimination. Why not make a morally unambiguous statement and then back it up with action?

. . . Back in 1964 you ran for the Senate and you opposed the Civil Rights Act of that year.

. . . Why did you oppose that bill? Why did you say that the 1964 Civil Rights Act, in your words, "violates the constitutional rights of all people?" Remember how America functioned in many parts of our country before it passed? Separate restrooms and drinking fountains for black and white, blacks turned away from hotels, restaurants, movies. Did you believe that black Americans should eat at the kitchen steps of restaurants, not in the dining room? Whose constitutional rights were being violated there?

Were you just opposing the Civil Rights Bill for political pur-poses? Were you just using race to get votes?

. . . Mr. President, over the last 11 years of Republican rule the poor and the middle class in America have not fared well. The average middle income family earned $31,000 in 1977 and $31,000 in 1990. No improvement. During the same time period, the richest 1% of American families went from earning $280,000 in 1977 to $949,000 in 1990. Now, how could that have happened? How could the majority of voters have supported governments whose primary achievement was to make the rich richer? The answer lies in the strategy and tactics of recent political campaigns.

. . . It is a cynical manipulation to send messages to white working people that they have more in common with the wealthy than with the black worker next to them on the line, taking the same physical risks and struggling to make ends meet with the same pay.

Mr. President, I detest anyone who uses that tactic — whether it is a Democrat like George Wallace or a Republican like David Duke. The irony is that most of the people who voted for George Wallace or David Duke or George Bush because of race haven't benefited economically from the last decade. Many of them are worse off. Many have lost jobs, health insurance, pension benefits. Many more can't buy a house or pay property taxes or hope to send their child to college.

. . . Mr. President, you need to be clearer, so that people of all sides understand where you are, what you believe and how you propose to make your beliefs a reality. Until then, you must understand that an increasing number of Americans will assume your convictions about issues of race and discrimination are no deeper than a water spider's footprint.

. . . Mr. President, as you and your men dawdle in race politics consider these facts: We will never win the global economic race if we have to carry the burden of an increasingly larger unskilled population. . . . Our greatest doubt about you is this: is winning elections more important to you than unifying the country to address the problems of race and poverty that beset us?

Mr. President, this is a cry from my heart, so don't charge me with playing politics. I'm asking you to take the issue of race out of partisan politics and put it on a moral plane where healing can take place.

We shall never know whether Bradley's cry from the heart affected Bush in any way. Bush did back off his shrill cries of "quota bill" and sign the Civil Rights Act of 1991. That brought him grief, because when far-right columnist Pat Buchanan challenged him for the Republican nomination he assailed Bush mercilessly for signing "a quota bill." The Neanderthals in the Republican party screamed so frenetically that it was difficult for Bush to hear Bill Bradley's appeal. In April 1992 Bush took steps to campaign against welfare recipients, especially black ones, giving a fresh face to Willie Horton demagoguery.

By mid-1992 there were growing signs that American public opinion was shifting back toward the views of Marshall on the death penalty. An execution at San Quentin in California aroused widespread protest about the lingering cruelty of death by gas chamber. More and more articles were written about what an eye-for-an-eye policy of vengeance and retribution had done to exacerbate the spirit of violence that had become an American plague. Jeffrey Dahmer, the cannibalistic mass murderer in Milwaukee, surely had not been deterred by a concern for any kind of punishment. In states with and without the death penalty, serial killers, sudden mass murderers who had lost their jobs or gotten a bad grade in college, hired killers resolving love triangles, drive-by killings on streets and freeways had become a chilling part of the American life.

Marshall could hear more Americans deploring the fact that we were almost alone in the Western industrialized world in the business of the state killing people, yet we were at the same time the victims of the violent crimes of homicide, rape, robbery, mugging, and other assaults far in excess of the rates of such crimes in most of the rest of the world.

This issue of the death penalty is only one reason why Marshall need not despair. Some have tried to turn back the clock on all his life achievements, but the clock is still ticking. Marshall was a results-oriented judge, and time is showing that pragmatism, an understanding of human nature, a sense of compassion that guarantees real justice for the poor and the alienated, will deter more crime than state brutality, blind anger, court-endorsed vindictiveness, and official executions to which death voyeurs are invited, much as Sunday School children were taken to view the body of a Maryland lynching victim during Marshall's boyhood.

Marshall should be secure in the belief that while he was untraditional, even unorthodox, folksy and earthy to the point of seeming irreverence, he never lost sight of the reason the framers of the Constitution and *we* call Supreme Court members "Justice." The ultimate purpose of all the stuffed protocol and the joustings in legalisms was and is to do justice. The Scalias and Thomases may reject this as "judicial activism," and they surely will chip away for two generations at the monuments to justice built by Earl Warren, Bill Brennan, Thurgood Marshall, and others; but they will never wipe them away because Marshall, Blackmun, Brandeis, Douglas built the pilings that undergird the bridges of freedom that link the destinies of all of us, no matter on which side of the river of life we live.

I remember Thurgood most for the fact that, whether in the courtroom or in his personal life, Marshall never pretended to be other than what he was: driven, sometimes compassionate, but often ornery; hard-working, hard-cussing and sometimes hard-drinking; hard-to-get-along-with under pressure, self-effacing and graceful in triumph.

No one who knows Marshall and honors the truth would ever say that during his tenure on the Court he was "Mr. Humility." Most of the time he was happy to go along with the secrecy, the aura of almost "divine" guidance of a Court that would reveal little about itself or its members to the people. Marshall cursed pomposity, but he could be as dogmatic as the most regal of his colleagues.

Members of my old prize-winning crew at WUSA-TV in Washington, D.C., still laugh together about the day in 1986 when Marshall lifted his lid of silence and agreed to talk to me on-camera about the Constitution, the Court, and the important legal issues of the time. I wanted "B-roll," or stock footage of certain places and things in the Supreme Court, especially of the conference room in which the justices deliberate before making their historic decisions.

Marshall said in a tone of royalty that the conference room was off limits, that it was a sort of "sanctified" territory, and that he knew that "the Chief" [Burger] did not want us to tape in this room. I suspected that Marshall knew that I was just as arrogant as he was, and that journalistic integrity would rule over friendship. But he must have doubted that I would say to Toni House, the longtime press person at the Supreme Court: "Justice Marshall is in one of his irascible, impossible moods. He says, unreasonably, that I can't shoot footage of the seating arrangement, the nameplates on the backs of the chairs, or other things in the conference room. You tell Chief Burger that I know I have a right to shoot there, and I want to do it immediately."

Within the hour, Ms. House led us into the conference room, where we filmed what we wished.

The next day my crew and I were in Marshall's chambers, conducting a second interview, which went beautifully. But at the end, apropos of nothing, Marshall went into a tirade about the "filming in the conference room against my will, against the policy of the Chief, embarrassing me. . . . Get 'em outa here," he said to a U.S. marshal.

"Cool it, and pack up," I said to my crew. As we were departing,

I said, "Thurgood, I did what any journalist of integrity would have to do. Thanks for the interview."

Two days later Marshall's secretary, Mrs. McHale, called me to say, "Mr. Rowan, Justice Marshall wants to know if you got everything you need for your television special."

"No," I said, "we need more information." She set up times for additional hours of interviews.

Marshall never said another word about the conference room photography. He knew that he had asserted his desires too imperiously and I knew that I had emphasized with some arrogance the rights of a newsman. We got back to the TV show on his life in an honest way.

Last July 4, in Independence Hall, Marshall was given the Philadelphia Liberty Medal and a cash prize of $100,000. He had been chosen by an international selection commission that was charged with honoring "an individual or organization from anywhere in the world who has demonstrated vision and leadership in the pursuit of liberty of conscience, or freedom from oppression, ignorance or deprivation." The *Philadelphia Inquirer* said editorially that "Justice Marshall has fulfilled every aspect of the description many times over."

In citing Marshall, Martin Meyerson, the president emeritus of the University of Pennsylvania, said: "Because of Justice Marshall's efforts for more than half a century, America is a superior land."

The selection commission had been influenced deeply by a tribute to Marshall in the *Stanford Law Review* — written by someone who often had disagreed with him, Justice Sandra Day O'Connor. In recounting the ways in which Marshall had influenced her, she wrote:

> His was the eye of a lawyer who saw the deepest wounds in the social fabric and used law to heal them. His was the ear of a counselor who understood the vulnerabilities of the accused and established safeguards for their protection. His was the mouth of a man who knew the anguish of the silenced and gave them a voice.
>
> At oral arguments and conference meetings, in opinions and dissents, Justice Marshall imparted not only his legal acumen but also his life experiences, pushing and prodding us to respond not only to the persuasiveness of legal argument but also to the power of moral truth.
>
> Although I was continually inspired by his achievements, I have perhaps been most affected by him as raconteur. In my early months as the junior justice, I looked forward to these tales as

diversions from the heavy, often troublesome, task of deciding the complex legal issues before us. But over time, I realized that behind most of the anecdotes was a relevant legal point.

. . . Justice Marshall's experiences are inspiring, not only because of what they reveal about him but also because of what they instill in, and ask of, us. I have experienced discrimination, such as when firms would only hire me, a "lady lawyer," as a legal secretary, to understand how one could seek to minimize interaction with those intolerant of difference. That Justice Marshall never hid from prejudice but thrust himself into its midst has been an encouragement and challenge to me.

His stories reflect a truly expansive personality, the perspective of a man who immerses himself in human suffering and then translates that suffering in a way that others can bear and understand. He is a man who sees the world exactly as it is and pushes on to make it what it can become. No one could avoid being touched by his soul.

Marshall, one day past his eighty-fourth birthday, spoke from a wheelchair on July 3, citing the conditions of America in 1992:

The battle for racial and economic justice is not yet won; indeed, it has barely begun. . . . The most effective context for achieving racial and economic parity lies now in the legislative arena. With the mere passage of corrective legislation, Congress can regain valuable ground in civil rights. With more Afro-American and progressive congresspersons and mayors and city council leaders, and yes, perhaps even a new president, we can pressure governments to fund vital social programs — for job training, affordable housing, child-care, decent education, health care — programs necessary for the attainment of *true* liberty.

Here was an unsubtle declaration that freedom-seekers could no longer rely on the Supreme Court or the White House unless Bush was replaced.

At the July 4 ceremony Marshall issued a challenge:

I wish I could say that racism and prejudice were only distant memories . . . and that liberty and equality were just around the bend. I wish I could say that America has come to appreciate diversity and to see and accept similarity.

But as I look around, I see not a nation of unity but of division — Afro and white, indigenous and immigrant, rich and poor, educated and illiterate. Even many educated whites and successful

Negroes have given up on integration and lost hope in equality. They see nothing in common — except the need to flee as fast as they can from our inner cities.

But there is a price to be paid for division and isolation, as recent events in California indicate. Look around. Can't you see the tension in Watts? Can't you feel the fear in Scarsdale? Can't you sense the alienation in Simi Valley? The despair in the South Bronx? The rage in Brooklyn?

We cannot play ostrich. Democracy cannot flourish amid fear. Liberty cannot bloom amid hate. Justice cannot take root amid rage. . . . We must go against the prevailing wind. We must dissent from the indifference. We must dissent from the apathy. We must dissent from the fear, the hatred and the mistrust. We must dissent from a government that has left its young without jobs, education, or hope. We must dissent from the poverty of vision and the absence of moral leadership. We must dissent because America can do better, because America has no choice but to do better.

The legal system can force open doors, and, sometimes, even knock down walls. But it cannot build bridges. That job belongs to you and me. We can run from each other, but we cannot escape each other. We will only attain freedom if we learn to appreciate what is different and muster the courage to discover what is fundamentally the same. Take a chance, won't you? Knock down the fences that divide. Tear apart the walls that imprison. Reach out; freedom lies just on the other side.

In 1992, the American people got a chance to vote in favor of knocking down our fences that divide, our "Berlin walls'" that have imprisoned so many of us Americans for so long. They voted for the "new president" that Marshall had called for in his Philadelphia speech. They gave power to Bill Clinton of Arkansas, the land of dream breaker Orval Faubus, and to Al Gore, from the state where Thurgood Marshall was almost lynched. What irony that two sons of the once-stigmatized South should now be entrusted with keeping alive the dreams of Thurgood Marshall.

An exultant schoolteacher noted that, at the age of eighty-four, Marshall was still fighting, and she quoted for me Alexander Pope's line, " 'An honest man's the noblest work of God.' "

I look at the majesty of Thurgood Marshall, of what this one common kid from the Jim Crow precincts of Baltimore brought out of adversity to the Supreme Court's hallowed halls and to all America, and I say, "A noble man's the greatest gift of God."

BIBLIOGRAPHY

Adler, Mortimer, gen. ed., Charles Van Doren, and George Ducas, eds. *The Negro in American History: Black Americans 1928–1968*. Chicago: Encyclopedia Britannica Educational Corporation, 1969.

Aldred, Lisa. *Thurgood Marshall*. New York: Chelsea House Publishers, 1990.

Allen, Steven J., and Richard A. Viguerie. *Lip Service: George Bush's 30-Year Battle with Conservatives*. Chantilly, Va.: CP Books, 1992.

Ambrose, Stephen E. *Nixon: The Triumph of a Politician 1962–1972*. New York: Simon and Schuster, 1989.

Berman, Daniel M. *It Is So Ordered: The Supreme Court on School Segregation*. New York: W. W. Norton, 1966.

Bernstein, Richard B., ed. *Defending the Constitution: Selections of Writings by Webster, Jay, Hamilton, Madison, Jefferson*. Mount Vernon, N.Y.: A. Colish, 1990.

"Black and White in America." *U.S. News & World Report*, July 22, 1991, p. 18.

Black Law Journal. UCLA Edition 6, no. 1 (1978).

Burns, James MacGregor. *Roosevelt: The Soldier of Freedom 1940–1945*. New York: Harcourt Brace Jovanovich, 1970.

Califano, Joseph A., Jr. *The Triumph and Tragedy of Lyndon Johnson: The White House Years*. New York: Simon and Schuster, 1991.

Cannon, Lou. *President Reagan: The Role of a Lifetime*. New York: Simon and Schuster, 1991.

Cannon, Poppy. *A Gentle Knight*. New York: Rinehart & Company, 1956.

Carlson, Jody. *George C. Wallace and the Politics of Powerlessness: The Wallace Campaigns for the Presidency, 1964–1976*. New Brunswick, N.J.: Transaction Books, 1981.

Cotman, John Walton. *Birmingham, JFK and the Civil Rights Act of 1963: Implications for Elite Theory*. New York: Peter Lang Publishing, 1989.

Crass, Philip. *The Wallace Factor*. New York: Mason/Charter, 1975.

Dickson, Harris. "The Vardaman Idea: How the Governor of Mississippi Would Solve the Race Question." *Saturday Evening Post*, April 27, 1907.

Dorman, Michael. *The George Wallace Myth.* New York: Bantam Books, 1976.

Dugger, Ronnie. *On Reagan: The Man and His Presidency.* New York: McGraw-Hill Book Company, 1983.

"Supreme Court Justice Thurgood Marshall." *Negro History Bulletin,* October 1967, pp. 4–5.

Frady, Marshall. *Wallace.* New York: World Publishing Company, 1968.

Garraty, John A., ed. *Quarrels That Have Shaped the Constitution.* New York: Harper & Row, 1964.

Gentry, Curt. *J. Edgar Hoover: The Man and the Secrets.* New York: W. W. Norton, 1991.

Greenshaw, Wayne. *Watch Out for George Wallace.* Englewood Cliffs, N.J.: Prentice-Hall, 1976.

Hall, Perry D., and the staff of *Quote,* eds. and comps. *The Quotable Richard M. Nixon.* Anderson, S.C.: Droke House Publishers, 1967; distributed by Grosset & Dunlap, New York.

Johnson, Haynes. *Sleepwalking Through History: America in the Reagan Years.* New York: W. W. Norton, 1991.

Kellogg, Charles Flint. *NAACP: A History of the National Association for the Advancement of Colored People.* Baltimore, M.D.: Johns Hopkins Press, 1967.

Lukas, J. Anthony. *Nightmare: The Underside of the Nixon Years.* New York: Viking Press, 1973, pp. 74, 76.

MacGregor, Morris J., Jr. *Integration of the Armed Forces 1940–1965.* Washington, D.C.: Center of Military History, United States Army, 1981.

Mankiewicz, Frank. *U.S. v. Richard M. Nixon: The Final Crisis.* New York: Quadrangle/New York Times Book Co., 1975.

McBee, Susanna. "Negro Lawyer Thurgood Marshall Now Becomes Advocate for U.S." *Life,* Nov. 12, 1965, p. 57.

Miller, Merle. *Lyndon: An Oral Biography.* New York: G. P. Putnam's Sons, 1980.

Muse, Benjamin. *Ten Years of Prelude: The Story of Integration Since the Supreme Court's 1954 Decision.* New York: Viking Press, 1964.

Nalty, Bernard C. *Strength for the Fight.* New York: Free Press, 1986.

O'Reilly, Kenneth. *"Racial Matters": The FBI's Secret File on Black America, 1960–1972.* New York: Free Press, 1989.

Pierce, Ponchitta. "The Solicitor General." *Ebony,* Nov. 1965, pp. 11–65, 67.

Ploski, Harry A., Ph.D., and Warren Marr II, eds. and comps. *The Negro Almanac: A Reference Work on the Afro-American.* New York: Bellwether Publishing Company, 1976.

Poling, James. "Thurgood Marshall and the 14th Amendment." *Colliers,* Feb. 23, 1952, p. 29.

Powledge, Fred. *Free At Last? The Civil Rights Movement and the People Who Made It.* Boston: Little, Brown, 1979.

Ross, Irwin. "A *Post* Portrait: Thurgood Marshall." *New York Daily Post Magazine,* June 13, 1960, p. 23.

Rowan, Carl T. *Breaking Barriers: A Memoir.* Boston: Little, Brown, 1991.

Rowan, Carl T. *Go South to Sorrow.* New York: Random House, 1957.

Safire, William. *Before the Fall: An Inside View of the Pre-Watergate White House.* New York: Doubleday, 1975.

Smith, Hedrick et al. *Reagan the Man, the President.* New York: Macmillan, 1980.

Bibliography 457

Smythe, Mabel M., ed. *The Black American Reference Book*. Englewood Cliffs, N.J.: Prentice-Hall, 1976.

Sorensen, Theodore C. *The Kennedy Legacy*. New York: Macmillan, 1969.

St. John, Jeffrey. *Constitutional Journal: A Correspondent's Report from the Convention of 1787*. Ottawa, Ill.: Jameson Books, 1987.

Truman, Harry S. *Memoirs by Harry S. Truman. Vol. 2, Years of Trial and Hope*. Garden City, N.Y.: Doubleday, 1956.

Tussman, Joseph, ed. *The Supreme Court on Racial Discrimination*. New York: Oxford University Press, 1963.

United States Commission on Civil Rights. "Desegregation of the Nation's Public Schools: A Status Report." Washington, D.C.: Feb. 1979.

United States Commission on Civil Rights. "Twenty Years After Brown." Washington, D.C.: 1974.

United States Supreme Court Oral Arguments, vols. 1–3, 1953–1955. Washington, D.C.: Ward and Paul.

Wallace, George, Jr., as told to James Gregory. *The Wallaces of Alabama*. Chicago: Follett Publishing Company, 1975.

Warren, Earl. *The Memoirs of Earl Warren*. Garden City, N.Y.: Doubleday, 1977.

White, Theodore H. *Breach of Faith: The Fall of Richard Nixon*. New York: Atheneum Publishers/Reader's Digest Press, 1975.

Wofford, Harris. *Of Kennedys and Kings: Making Sense of the Sixties*. New York: Farrar Straus & Giroux, 1980.

Woodward, Bob, and Scott Armstrong. *The Brethren: Inside the Supreme Court*. New York: Aron Books, 1979.

Woodward, Bob, and Carl Bernstein. *The Final Days*. New York: Simon and Schuster, 1976.

INDEX